S0-BRR-757

"These nineteenth- and early-twentieth-century biographies, now republished by Chelsea House, reveal an unsuspected significance. Not only are a good many of them substantively valuable (and by no means entirely superseded), but they also evoke a sense of the period, an intimacy with the attitudes and assumptions of their times."

      —Professor Daniel Aaron

Last photograph taken, October, 1897.

Other titles in this Chelsea House series:

LOUISA MAY ALCOTT, *Ednah D. Cheney*
AUDUBON AND HIS JOURNALS, *Maria R. Audubon*
HENRY WARD BEECHER, *Lyman Abbott*
WILLIAM CULLEN BRYANT, *John Bigelow*
JAMES FENIMORE COOPER, *Thomas R. Lounsbury*
RICHARD HENRY DANA, *Charles Francis Adams, Jr.*
RALPH WALDO EMERSON, *Oliver Wendell Holmes*
BENJAMIN FRANKLIN, *John Bach McMaster*
HORACE GREELEY, *W. A. Linn*
NATHANIEL HAWTHORNE, *George E. Woodberry*
O. HENRY, *C. Alphonso Smith*
OLIVER WENDELL HOLMES, *John T. Morse, Jr.*
WASHINGTON IRVING, *Charles Dudley Warner*
JAMES RUSSELL LOWELL AND HIS FRIENDS, *Edward Everett Hale*
COTTON MATHER, *Barrett Wendell*
THOMAS NAST, *Albert Bigelow Paine*
MARGARET FULLER OSSOLI, *Thomas Wentworth Higginson*
THOMAS PAINE, *Moncure D. Conway*
EDGAR ALLAN POE, *George E. Woodberry*
HENRY DAVID THOREAU, *Frank B. Sanborn*
MARK TWAIN, *Albert Bigelow Paine*
NOAH WEBSTER, *Horace E. Scudder*
WALT WHITMAN, *Bliss Perry*
JOHN PETER ZENGER, *Livingston Rutherfurd*

HENRY GEORGE

HENRY GEORGE, JR.

INTRODUCTION BY
PAUL M. GASTON

American Men and Women of Letters Series

GENERAL EDITOR
PROFESSOR DANIEL AARON
HARVARD UNIVERSITY

CHELSEA HOUSE
NEW YORK, LONDON

1981

Cover design by Abner Graboff

Copyright © 1981 by Chelsea House Publishers, a division of
Chelsea House Educational Communications, Inc.
All rights reserved
Printed and bound in the United States of America

Library of Congress Cataloging in Publication Data

George, Henry, 1862-1916.
  Henry George.

  (American men and women of letters)
  Originally published in 1900 by Doubleday &
McClure Co., New York under title: The life of
Henry George.
  Includes index.
  1. George, Henry, 1839-1897   2. Economists--
United States--Biography.   3. Social reformers--
United States--Biography.   I. Series.
HB119.G4G4 1981   330'.092'4 [B]   80-27958
ISBN 0-87754-164-7

Chelsea House Publishers
Harold Steinberg, Chairman & Publisher
Andrew E. Norman, President
Susan Lusk, Vice President
A Division of Chelsea House Educational Communications, Inc.
133 Christopher Street, New York 10014

TO ALL WHO STRIVE FOR
THE REIGN OF JUSTICE

For it is not for knowledge to enlighten a soul that is dark of itself ; nor to make a blind man to see. Her business is not to find a man eyes, but to guide, govern and direct his steps, provided he have sound feet, and straight legs to go upon. Knowledge is an excellent drug, but no drug has virtue enough to preserve itself from corruption and decay, if the vessel be tainted and impure wherein it is put to keep.

Montaigne.

First Period.
> FORMATION OF THE CHARACTER.

Second Period.
> FORMULATION OF THE PHILOSOPHY.

Third Period.
> PROPAGATION OF THE PHILOSOPHY.

His form and cause conjoined, preaching to stones,
Would make them capable. — *Hamlet*.

CONTENTS.

CONTENTS

❦

SECOND PERIOD.

CONTENTS

THIRD PERIOD.

CONTENTS

CONTENTS

CHAPTER XI.

Now I saw in my dream that they went on, and Greatheart before them.

Bunyan's " Pilgrim's Progress."

LIST OF ILLUSTRATIONS

General Introduction

THE VISITABLE PAST
Daniel Aaron

THE TWENTY-FIVE BIOGRAPHIES of American worthies reissued in this Chelsea House series restore an all but forgotten chapter in the annals of American literary culture. Some of the authors of these volumes—journalists, scholars, writers, professional men—would be considered amateurs by today's standards, but they enjoyed certain advantages not open to their modern counterparts. In some cases they were blood relations or old friends of the men and women they wrote about, or at least near enough to them in time to catch the contemporary essence often missing in the more carefully researched and authoritative later studies of the same figures. Their leisurely, impressionistic accounts—sometimes as interesting for what is omitted as for what is emphasized—reveal a good deal about late Victorian assumptions, cultural and social, and about the vicissitudes of literary reputation.

Each volume in the series is introduced by a recognized scholar who was encouraged to write an idiosyncratic appraisal of the biographer and his

work. The introductions vary in emphasis and point
of view, for the biographies are not of equal quality, nor are the writers memorialized equally appealing. Yet a kind of consensus is discernible in
these random assessments: surprise at the insights
still to be found in ostensibly unscientific and old-
fashioned works; in some instances admiration for
the solidity and liveliness of the biographer's prose
and quality of mind; respect for the pioneer historians among them who made excellent use of the
limited material at their disposal.

The volumes in this American Men and Women
of Letters series contain none of the startling
"private" and "personal" episodes modern readers
have come to expect in biography, but they illumi-
nate what Henry James called the "visitable past."
As such, they are of particular value to all students
of American cultural and intellectual history.

Cambridge, Massachusetts
Spring, 1980

INTRODUCTION
TO THE
CHELSEA HOUSE EDITION

Paul M. Gaston

In 1909, twelve years after his father had died, Henry George, Jr., made a pilgrimage to Russia to meet Count Leo Tolstoy. On the study wall was a photograph of Henry George. "Your father was my friend," his host explained. The old man wore a skullcap and a long peasant blouse and sat in the wheelchair he had used in recent years. "I am quite old—eighty-one. I do not expect to stay much longer," Tolstoy said. "But I am keeping at my work." What, his visitor wanted to know, was the work; did it deal with political econqmy? "No," Tolstoy replied, "this is not on political economy. It treats of moral questions, which your father put first."

The son would agree. In his father's biography, published in 1900, he had said that "the essence of Henry George's economics is ethical." Now he had special reason to remember that judgment. As the interview drew to a close, Tolstoy looked closely at his visitor. "This is the last time I shall meet you," he said. "I shall see your father soon. Is there any commission you would have me take to him?" Lost for a moment in the meaning of the question, George replied, "Tell my father that I am doing the work."

Henry George, Jr., had been "doing the work" for most of his life; he was not likely to quit. When his father collapsed with a fatal stroke five days before the 1897 New York mayoral election, the son was chosen to stand in for the fallen leader—a symbol for the bereaved electorate. Three years later he finished a long biography, the work reprinted here, and soon after, he saw through to completion a handsome edition of all the published works of his father. Meanwhile, he wrote magazine and newspaper articles (he was, by this time, a successful journalist) and two more books. *The Menace of Privilege* (1905) was a slashing work that caused one reviewer to say, "The son is more than a pupil of his father; he is his father's heir." Next, he turned to fiction with a novel called *The Romance of John Bainbridge* (1906), which borrowed from both his father's life and his doctrines. "Henry George, Jr.," a friendly critic observed, "is carrying forward the work of social justice by use of his strong and vigorous pen, in a way that would give his father the keenest joy were he still with us."

The children had always been a great joy to Henry George, and his way with them inspired their deep devotion. The youngest, Anna, also wrote a biography of her father, published a half-century after her brother's. How many times, one wonders, have two children written biographies to secure their father's place in history? The Georges, apparently, would not have thought that unusual. Agnes de Mille, Anna's daughter, said of her mother that "like all George women she believed her activities valid only in service to others, but above all in service to her father's cause." The children grew up with this attitude. Thus, Henry George, Jr., gave up school as a teenager to become his father's secretary. He helped him while he wrote *Progress and Poverty* and afterwards committed himself to spread its message. He traveled with his father on speaking tours at home and abroad, edited his newspaper, *The Standard*, and helped to manage his political campaigns. More successful politically than his father—he served two terms in the House of Representatives, from 1911 to 1915—he saw his role as public servant as advocate of his father's cause. He died in 1916 at the age of fifty-four.

The man who inspired such family devotion also had a galvanizing effect on his generation of Americans. In an age anguished by new forms of poverty and torn by industrial violence, class conflict, and political turmoil, millions were stirred by Henry George's simple statement that "This association of poverty with progress is the greatest enigma of our times." *Progress and Poverty* declared that vice and misery sprang from the unequal distribution of wealth and privilege. Marveling at the industrial and technological genius of the nation—the invention of laborsaving devices and the creation of spiraling amounts of wealth—he described in explosive detail how this genius had thwarted human needs and aspirations. He employed images and examples resonating with the experience of his readers. He counterpointed his analysis of exploitation with a positive, optimistic faith and a program of reform that promised a better social order. Reading *Progress and Poverty* converted newly hopeful men and women to radicalism and protest. None of his contemporaries—even those who were more charismatic, more learned, or more politically astute—rivaled his influence in this respect.

With an analysis that ramified in many directions, meshing economic reasoning with moral inquiry, George traced the enigma ultimately to the monopoly of natural resources, to the institution of private property in land. "Poverty deepens as wealth increases, and wages are forced down while productive power grows, because land, which is the source of all wealth and the field of all labor, is monopolized," he wrote in *Progress and Poverty*. The solution was simple: *"We must make land common property."* How this was to be done was not made entirely clear, but by 1887 the term "single tax" had come into common usage, to describe the favored method: individual ownership of land might remain, but government—which would abolish all taxes on labor and capital—would derive its revenue from a single tax on land values. George, according to the son's biography, "never regarded the term as describing his philosophy, but rather as indicating the method he would take to apply it." Here George lost many readers: committed to social action, they often tossed aside the "problem solved" section of his work. Everywhere—in America, in Britain, and on the Continent—he made converts, but relatively few of them became single taxers. George Bernard Shaw, for example, said his life was changed by the American crusader, but instead of becoming a single-taxer he was "swept into the great Socialist revival of 1883," where he found that nearly all of those who were "swept in" with him "had been converted by Henry George." And so it went for other causes and revivals as well. That he was a catalyst in the lives of so many, but the founder of a specific reform movement followed by so few, may be taken as a comment on his shortcomings as a social reformer and economic theorist. On the other hand, it is also an indication of his brilliant articulation of the central problems of his age.

A man of rare achievements, Henry George was in many ways the quintessential American. Born in Philadelphia in 1839, he enjoyed a loving and supportive family. When he dropped out of school at sixteen, he had his parents' blessing to sign on as a foremast boy on a sailing ship bound for Australia and India. He loved the sea and did his job well. A restless youth—every account uses this adjective to describe him—he was lured to California in the fifties. In the rawness and flux of that society he grew to maturity. It was back east, on a trip to New York City, that the sight of misery and squalor in the midst of plenty made him vow to discover the reason for such injustice. But it was in the West, out of his California experience, that he came to understand the connection between land speculation and social disorder.

As printer, journalist, lecturer, and sometime political candidate, he wrestled intellectually with theoretical questions and materially with his own straitened circumstances. When at twenty-two he proposed to eighteen-year-old Annie Fox, he had one coin in his pocket. Not long after their marriage, "near to starving to death," as he related it, he demanded five dollars of a man in the street because his wife had nothing to eat. In time he was secure enough to put together eighteen relatively uninterrupted months and write *Progress and Poverty*. The Appleton Company, to whom he sent it, returned the manuscript with the comment that it "has the merit of being written with great clearness and force, but is very aggressive. There is very little to encourage publication of any such work." After a fellow printer offered credit and the use of his shop, Henry George, Henry George, Jr., and their friends set type themselves, the author revising all the while, to produce a handsome limited edition of five hundred copies. Only then did Appleton, coaxed by the offer of the plates thus struck, agree to a New York edition, which was published early in 1880. "It will not be recognized at first," Henry George wrote to his father in Philadelphia, "but it will ultimately be considered a great book, will be published in both hemispheres, and be translated into different languages." George spent the next eighteen years working to make that prediction come true.

A man so finely tuned to the deepest anxieties and most cherished hopes of his age has naturally appealed to biographers, historians, and philosophers. John Dewey ranked George among the world's top ten social philosophers and he has been the subject of much good writing. Albert Jay Nock's brilliant *Henry George, An Essay* (1931) and George R. Geiger's exhaustive *Philosophy of Henry George* (1933) are two early examples. A generation ago Charles A. Barker's magisterial biography, *Henry George* (1955), and Eric F. Goldman's influential history of modern American reform, *Rendezvous with Destiny* (1952), fully established his historical reputation.

What of the son's biography? It would be too much to claim, as one contemporary reviewer did, that "whoever wishes to know what manner of man Henry George was, can by reading this book satisfy his curiosity as well as he could have done by meeting him face to face." But it is a biography rich in personal details. The author draws freely and effectively upon diaries and family letters, contributing his own observations and recollections skillfully and unobtrusively. One scarcely notices how often the intimate portraits of the father are furnished by the son's firsthand observations, yet this quality of the book is perhaps its greatest strength. For example, the account we have of the composition of *Progress and Poverty* owes everything to the son's presence. We learn that "the eldest son had reached the top grade in the grammar school, which was thought to be enough schooling, so that he was taken away and became amanuensis to his father." It is from the secretary's observations that we learn how Henry George worked; that "he read mostly reclining, a pile of books drawn up beside him"; or "as he wrote much by inspiration, especially on the more elevated parts of his book, he could not always work at a set time or continuously. When his mind would not act to his suiting he would lie down and read, or go sailing or visit friends." During these diversions his subconscious was at work, for when he returned to the study "he could write freely on the point that before was confused." There are similarly revealing insights into his lecturing techniques. We learn that he never read a text or spoke from notes, but lay down before speaking to fix the main ideas of the subject in his mind, depending on inspiration from the audience for the development of the details. The book abounds with glimpses of a happy marriage and of family members secure in each other's affections, another debt to the son's personal observations.

The discussion of ideas is restrained, sometimes almost bland, in contrast to the vividness of the personal history. There is neither the exuberance of a proud son nor the pointed comparisons of a loyal disciple. This seems surprising until one remembers that the author wrote of ideas bred in him from childhood, ideas that appeared so natural, understandable, and right as to arouse no special amazement and need no extensive explanation or defense. They are simply presented, clearly, without fanfare. It was part of the author's strategy to keep himself out of the book, for this was to be Henry George's book; the record was enough, the author believed, without any judgments from him. On the other hand, the naturalness with which he accepts his father's ideas, the ease with which he accounts for their spread and development, is a different kind of testament to the father as well as ample evidence that the son, as he told Count Tolstoy, was "doing the work."

Charlottesville, Virginia
December, 1980

FIRST PERIOD

FORMATION OF THE CHARACTER

Out upon nature, in upon himself, back through the mists that shroud the past, forward into the darkness that overhangs the future, turns the restless desire that arises when the animal wants slumber in satisfaction. Beneath things he seeks the law; he would know how the globe was forged and the stars were hung, and trace the steps in the infinite progression. And then arises the desire higher yet — the passion of passions, the hope of hopes — the desire that he, even he, may somehow aid in making life better and brighter, in destroying want and sin, sorrow and shame. He masters and curbs the animal; he turns his back upon the feast and renounces the place of power; he leaves it to others to accumulate wealth, to gratify pleasant tastes, to bask themselves in the warm sunshine of the brief day. He works for those he never saw and never can see; for a fame, or maybe but for a scant justice, that can only come long after the clods have rattled upon his coffin lid. He toils in the advance where it is cold, and there is little cheer from men and the

Reduced facsimile of page of original manuscript of
"Progress and Poverty," Book II, Chap. III.

CHAPTER I.

BIRTH AND EARLY TRAINING.

1839-1855.   To the 16th Year.

HENRY GEORGE was born on September 2, 1839,[1] in a little two story and attic brick house, yet standing in a good state of preservation, in Philadelphia, Pa., on Tenth Street, south of Pine, not half a mile from the old State House where the Declaration of Independence was signed.

His father's blood was English, with a tradition of Welsh; his mother's blood English and Scottish. In the main he came of middle-class stock. The only persons among his ancestors who achieved any distinction were his grandfathers; on his mother's side, John Vallance, a native of Glasgow, Scotland, who became an engraver of repute in this country in the early days of the republic and whose name may be seen on some of the commissions signed by President Washington; and on his father's side, Richard George, born in Yorkshire, England, who was one of the well-known shipmasters of Philadelphia when that city was the commercial metropolis of the new world.

Captain George married Mary Reid, of Philadelphia, and to them were born three children, the youngest of

---

[1] John Stuart Mill was then in his thirty-fourth year and Adam Smith had been forty-nine years dead.

whom, Richard Samuel Henry, in New Brunswick, New
Jersey, in 1798. This Richard Samuel Henry George
became the father of Henry George, the subject of the
present volume. In 1873, on the day preceding his sev-
enty-fifth natal anniversary, he wrote his son Henry a
letter of reminiscences, of which the following serves to
show the man and the early conditions in Philadelphia:

"I have seen all the Presidents, from Washington down
to the present, Grant—that is, I cannot say I saw Washington, who died in December, 1799, but I think, although an infant, that I saw his sham funeral. . . .

"I go back to 1810, during Jefferson's long embargo.
Then Front Street, Philadelphia, was what Chestnut
Street is now—the fashionable thoroughfare of the city.
All the principal merchants lived on Front Street and
on Water Street above South. Below South lived mostly
sea captains, all handy to business.

"Your grandfather had two ships, the *Medora* and
Burdo Packet, and during the embargo and the war with
England they were housed in; and from the navy yard
down to the Point House, now called Greenwich, all the
principal ships in port were housed in and hauled up on
the mud, with noses touching the bank.

"Although times were hard, I did not feel them. I
had a pleasant, happy home, let me tell you. The first
thing to be done was to provide for winter. Wood was
burned for cooking and heating. Your grandfather
would purchase a sloop-load of wood, so that I had a
good time helping to throw it down cellar. We would
have enough to last all winter and late into the spring.
Then there was a supply of beef to corn and two or three
hogs to cut up. That was a grand time! We had a
smokehouse at one corner of the yard, and when father
had cut up the hogs we would have a number of hams to
smoke and cure. I do not taste such now, nor ever will
again. At hog time mother made all sorts of good things
—scrapel, sausage and all that hog could do for man.
And didn't I go in for it all with the rest of the boys,

for father had four 'prenticed boys and two girls in the kitchen, all in good tune and happy. We had all sorts of songs and wonderful stories, both of the sea and of the land.

"It was at this time (I am sorry I have no dates) that my father arrived at Almond Street wharf from France, to which he had gone with a flag of truce, carrying out a lot of passengers and bringing back a lot. Well, it was Sunday morning, about light, when I was waked up by mother. I asked what was the matter. She said that pop had arrived and that he had on board of the ship General Moreau and family from France;[1] and she wanted to get some fresh provisions for their breakfast. So I took on board lots of things—nice fresh milk and cream, butter, nice bread, chickens, etc.—for the general and his family. I tell you it was hard work getting on board, the crowd was so dense. On Almond Street from Second clear down to the wharf was a line of private carriages with invitations of hospitality. The boys crowded me hard, and one or two fellows I had to fight before I could pass.

"Going so often to the ship, I found I was as much noticed as the general himself. It gave me a big lift among the downtown-gang. I was made captain of a company and had to fight the Mead Alley and Catherine Street boys every Saturday afternoon. Many bricks I got on the head while leading my men (or boys) into battle. . . .

"One fight I had built me right up, and afterwards I was A No. 1 among the boys, and cock of the walk. I went on the principle of *do nothing that you are ashamed of and let no living man impose on you.*

"In my youth I could swim like a duck and skate well. And I was considered a good sailor. I could handle a boat equal to anybody. I got a good amount of praise, both on the Delaware and the Mississippi, for my sea-

---

[1] Jean Victor Moreau, the Republican French general, made famous by the extraordinary retreat through the Black Forest and the brilliant Battle of Hohenlinden, and afterwards exiled by Napoleon's jealousy.

manship. I could go aloft as quick and as handy as any seaman. Going to New Orleans, I often lent a hand on topsails, and could do as well as most of them."

R. S. H. George made this trip to New Orleans when a young man, and there engaged in the dry goods business. Returning to Philadelphia, he settled down and married Miss Louisa Lewis, by whom he had two children, one of whom died while an infant, and the other, Richard, while at boarding school in his twelfth year.[1] Within four or five years after marriage this wife died, and several years later R. S. H. George married another Philadelphia lady, Catherine Pratt Vallance. As has been said, her father was John Vallance, the engraver, born in Glasgow, Scotland. Her mother was Margaret Pratt, born in Philadelphia, but of English extraction. John Vallance died in 1823 leaving his widow, seven daughters and one son in modest means, which Henry Pratt, a wealthy merchant of Philadelphia and first cousin of the widow's father, improved by giving to each of the seven girls a small brick house. These girls received a good boarding school education, and Catherine and Mary were conducting a small private school when Catherine was married to R. S. H. George, who then had a book publishing business.

Mr. George had for several years occupied a good clerical position in the Philadelphia Custom House, and left it in 1831 to enter a book publishing partnership with Thomas Latimer, who had married Rebecca, the eldest of the Vallance girls. The business was confined to the publication and sale of Protestant Episcopal Church and Sunday School books, and for a time became the depository of the General Episcopal Sunday School Union, the Bible

---

[1] There was also an adopted child, Harriet, who, growing up, married J. H. Evans.

and Prayer Book Society and the Tract Society. After two and a half years Thomas Latimer withdrew and others were associated successively in the business, which for seventeen years Richard George carried on, the store for a time being at the north-west corner of Chestnut and Fifth Streets. A contemporary in the business was George S. Appleton, who afterwards went to New York and merged with his brother in a general book publishing and book selling business, under the firm name of D. Appleton & Co.—the same D. Appleton & Co. who, several decades later, were to be the first publishers of "Progress and Poverty."[1] By 1848 the business of the general book houses had encroached so much on denominational business that the latter became unprofitable, and Mr. George withdrew and went back to the Custom House, obtaining the position of Ascertaining Clerk, which he thereafter held for nearly fourteen years.

To the union of R. S. H. George and Catharine Pratt Vallance ten children were born, six girls—Caroline, Jane, Catharine, Chloe, Mary and Rebecca, the last two of whom died early—and four boys—Henry, Thomas, John and Morris—the second child and oldest boy being the subject of this work. Like the son by the former marriage, this boy was named after his father; but as the former bore the name of Richard, the first of the father's three Christian names—Richard Samuel Henry—the last of the names was selected for this son; and as the father desired a short name, complaining of the annoyance to himself of a long one, the simple one of Henry George was chosen.

Henry George's father was a strict churchman. He was a vestryman at St. Paul's Episcopal Church, when

---

[1] This circumstance had nothing to do with their decision to publish the book, as its author was unknown to them.

that church, under the earnest preaching of Dr. Richard Newton, was at the height of its prosperity. The congregation was of the extreme "Low Church" division and regarded "High Church" tendencies with the utmost abhorrence. Sunday was a day for austere devotions—church services morning and afternoon, and frequently in the evening. On other days there were morning and evening family prayers. Rt. Rev. Ignatius F. Horstmann, Catholic Bishop of Cleveland, O., who was a boy in the neighbourhood at the time, has said:[1] "I can recall Henry George going to church every Sunday, walking between his two elder sisters, followed by his father and mother —all of them so neat, trim and reserved."

But that there were occasional breaks in the austerity may be certain. Rev. George A. Latimer, Henry George's cousin, has said:

"Henry George was in my Sunday school class. It was the custom of Dr. Newton to have the children of the church in the main lecture room once a month in the afternoon for catechising. One Sunday the subject was that part of the catechism that declares our duty towards our neighbour, and the special topic, 'to keep my hands from picking and stealing.' Our class was on the front row. The Doctor asked the question: 'Boys, why do the grocerymen have that wire netting over the dried peaches in the barrel at the store door?' Henry George at once answered with a loud voice: 'To keep the flies out.' The Doctor's face turned as red as blood, while at the same time he said: 'Yes, to keep the hands from picking and stealing.' "

Rev. William Wilberforce Newton, son of the rector, who was in this school with Henry George, said in an

---

[1] Letter to " National Single Taxer," Aug. 31, 1898.

address after the latter's death that "that school turned
out some remarkable men," naming Bishop Charles R.
Hall of Illinois, Bishop Wm. H. Odenheimer of New
Jersey, Rev. Wm. W. Farr, Henry S. Getz, Rev. Richard
N. Thomas, editor of the "American Church Sunday
School Magazine," George C. Thomas, of Drexel & Co.
bankers, and Treasurer of the Missionary Society of the
Protestant Episcopal Church, and Rev. R. Heber New-
ton, William Wilberforce Newton's brother.　Mr. Newton
told this anecdote:

"Our class was located in that part of the church
known as the basement, and as we looked out at the
window, our view was obstructed by innumerable grave-
stones.

"My people were extremely hospitable to missionaries.
One time Missionary Bishop Payne of Africa came with
his wife to our house and staid six weeks.　They
brought with them a lot of monkeys and other beasts
of the tropical clime.　We used to have great times
among ourselves—the boys of the neighbourhood and
the monkeys and the dumb animals—playing 'firemen.'
One day we were having a parade.　There was no flag.
So I went into the house and got a Sunday school banner with an illustration of Paul preaching at Ephesus.
It was not exactly appropriate, but it answered the purpose.　Henry George insisted upon carrying the banner which all the boys thought a good deal of.

"As our firemen's parade was turning the corner of
the house that day, Henry George heard my father say
to the missionary that if he saw anything about the
house that he thought would be of service to him in
Africa he was welcome to it, and the missionary replied
that he thought the tool chest would come in handy.
George passed the word along the line and very soon
our parade was broken up and we became an army of
warriors for the protection of that tool chest.　But it
went to Africa just the same."

At the time of his son Henry's birth, the book business enabled Mr. George to keep his family in comfort. Giving care to his children's education, he sent them as they grew old enough to Mrs. Graham's private school, on Catharine Street near Third, the family having moved from Tenth Street to the west side of Third Street, three doors north of Queen, where they remained for nearly twenty-five years. After three years at Mrs. Graham's, and when he was in his ninth year, the eldest son, Henry, was sent to a public school, Mount Vernon Grammar, where Ignatius Horstmann attended in a class above him. A year later, in 1849, he was sent to the Episcopal Academy.

This institution, flourishing to-day, was founded in revolutionary times, but seemed to decline until Bishop Alonzo Potter raised it at the end of the forties to first rank as a place of instruction in the city and State. Rev. Dr. Hare was then principal, and the institution was frequently spoken of as Hare's Academy. The Bishop's two sons, Henry C. and E. N. Potter were at the Academy then, and in the years to come were to achieve distinction, the former as the Episcopal Bishop of New York City and the other as president of two colleges successively. R. Heber Newton and William Wilberforce Newton were also fellow students. Dr. Heber Newton remembers the school as being in a most prosperous condition, "the large chapel being quite filled with boys, and the class rooms seemingly well filled, and attendance upon it was esteemed an advantage and a privilege."

But though it was a good school, young George did not stay there long. His father had now ceased to be publisher of Church books, yet he obtained for his son the reduced rate of tuition granted to clergymen's sons. This concession was regarded by the boy as something to

which he was not entitled and he believed that every boy
in the school knew of it; and perhaps it was for this
reason that from the start he did not get along well there.
At any rate, his father, yielding to his entreaties, took
him away and put him in the hands of Henry Y. Lauderbach to be prepared for High school. This short period, Henry George always recognised as the most profitable portion of his little schooling. Mr. Lauderbach had
a way of his own, drawing out and stimulating the individuality of his pupils. Thirty years afterwards he
clearly remembered Henry George as a student remarkable among boys for quickness of thought, originality and
general information. The special training under Lauderbach enabled the youth at little more than thirteen to
enter a class in the High school that was to produce some
notable men in Pennsylvania—Theodore Cramp, ship
builder; Charles W. Alexander, journalist; James Mor-
gan Hart, professor and author; Samuel L. Gracey, Methodist Episcopal clergyman; David H. Lane, a Recorder
of Philadelphia; and William Jenks Fell, Commissioner
of Deeds. This school, like the Episcopal Academy, was
an excellent one, but later in life Henry George said that
while there he was "for the most part idle and wasted
time." Perhaps it was that he had his mind's eye set
on the world outside of school! Perhaps it was that conscious that the growing family was putting a strain on
his father, whose sole income was the $800 salary of a
Custom House clerk, he felt that he should be supporting
himself. It was probably his Uncle Thomas Latimer who
at this time gave him advice of which he spoke in a
speech about thirty years later: "I remember when a boy,
I wanted to go to sea. I talked with a gentleman, who
wanted me to go into business as a boy in a store. I had
nothing, no particular facility, yet I remember his saying

to me: 'If you are honest, if you are steady, if you are industrious, you can certainly look forward to being able to retire at forty with comfort for the rest of your days.' "[1] These words may have had a strong influence on the boy's mind. At any rate, after less than five months in the High School, he induced his father to take him away, to stop his schooling altogether, and put him to work; and he never went to school afterwards. He was then less than fourteen years old.[2] He first obtained employment in the china and glass importing house of Samuel Asbury & Co., at 85 South Front Street, at $2 a week. His duties were to copy, to tie up bundles and to run errands. Afterwards he went into the office of a marine adjuster and did clerical work.

But though he had left school for good, his real education suffered no interruption. In school or out of it, he had acquired a fondness for reading. Or perhaps it was that at his birth, while the Fairies of Gain, Fashion and Pleasure passed him by, one came and sat beside his cradle and softly sang

> "Mine is the world of thought, the world of dream;
> Mine all the past, and all the future mine."

First he had a grounding in the Bible; and the Puritanical familiarity with book, chapter and verse, which in the elders moulded speech, established habit, and guided the steps of life, filled the young mind with a myriad of living pictures. Then, though his father while a pub-

---

[1] Speech, "Crime of Poverty," 1885. After uttering the foregoing passage, Mr. George asked : "Who would dare in New York or in any of our great cities, to say that to a young clerk now ?"

[2] At fourteen Adam Smith was attending the University of Glasgow ; while John Stuart Mill was learning Greek at three, Latin at eight, logic at twelve and political economy at thirteen.

lisher handled only religious books, and those confined to the Episcopal Church, there were the strange tales of missionaries in foreign lands to feed the imagination. Afterwards when the father left the book business there was still an atmosphere of reading about the home, and other books came in the boy's way. He delighted in history, travels and adventure, fiction and poetry. While in his strong democratic principles and practical side, the boy followed his father, it was in a love of poetry that he resembled his mother, who as an elderly woman could quote verse after verse and poem after poem learned in her girlhood. She manifested at all times an intense fondness for Scott, and had a taste for Shakespeare, though owing to her austere principles, she never in her life attended a Shakesperian play.[1] This religious ban extended in the boy's reading to much in the realm of romance and adventure, such works as the "Scottish Chiefs," for instance, having to be read in the seclusion of his attic bedchamber. But in the open or in the smuggled way books were obtained, and the old Quaker Apprentice's Library and the Franklin Institute Library furnished inexhaustible mines of reading matter. Book after book was devoured with a delight that showed that now certainly the youthful mind was not "idle" nor his "time wasted." He

---

[1] In a speech in Liverpool many years later (Nov. 30, 1888) Henry George said : " I was educated in a very strict faith. My people and the people whom I knew in my childhood, the people who went to our church and other churches of the same kind, had a notion that the theatre was a very bad place, and they would not go to one on any account. There was a celebrated fellow-citizen of mine of the name of Barnum. Barnum went to Philadelphia, and he recognised that prejudice, and he saw that, although there were a number of theatres running for the ungodly, a theatre he could get the godly to go to would pay extremely well. But he did not start a theatre. Oh, no ! He started a lecture room, and we had in that lecture room theatrical representations, and it was crowded every night in the week and there were two matinées."

absorbed information as the parched earth a summer shower, and what he thus took in he retained. To this fondness for reading he always ascribed the beginning of his real education and the commencement of his career.

And what came like enchantment to his mind and supplemented his reading were popular scientific lectures at the Franklin Institute. This institution, named after the famous townsman, Benjamin Franklin, and incorporated in 1824 for "the promotion and encouragement of manufactures and the mechanic and useful arts," in the forties and fifties took first rank in scientific learning in the city, which at the same time was without peer in this country for its public libraries, museums and private cabinets. Of the Institute, Henry George's uncle, Thomas Latimer, was a member. To him the boy was indebted for access to the lectures—lectures that revealed the wonders of the physical sciences in simple language and magic lantern pictures. Like a torch they lit up the young understanding and made a fitting attendant to that university of reading to which he was of his own volition applying himself.

This reading fed a desire that his father's stories and the tales and traditions about his grandfather had kindled in him for the sea. "One of our chief play grounds," Rev. W. W. Newton has said, "was about the wharves of the city. He had a friend who was a sea captain and I a cousin, and both of us had our minds set on a sea voyage." Mr. George encouraged in his son an active life, going to see him skate and swim. One day he saved him from drowning by putting down his cane when the boy had dived under a float. Though a strict churchman, the father could not forget his own early warlike days and was not averse to having his boy fight in just quarrels. But it was the shipping that chiefly interested father and son, and as they strolled along the river-piers together, the father talked about hull and rig, wind and weather, and the wonders of sea and foreign lands, so that the wharves had a fascination for the boy, and it was around them that with Willie Newton or Bill Horner, Col and Charley Walton and Will Jones he spent much of his play time, climbing about vessels, going swimming or sailing toy boats. And this was not all idle play, but served its purposes in later life, for the boy's powers of observation and reasoning were in constant exercise.[1]

After a while, when the boy left the crockery house and went into the marine adjuster's office, the desire for the sea increased so much that he went to his cousin, George Latimer, who was ten years older than himself, and asked him to speak in his behalf to an acquaintance of the fam-

---

[1] "When I was a boy I went down to the wharf with another boy to see the first iron steamship which had ever crossed the ocean to our port. Now, hearing of an iron steamship seemed to us then a good deal like hearing of a leaden kite or a wooden cooking stove. But, we had not been long aboard of her, before my companion said in a tone of contemptuous disgust: 'Pooh! I see how it is. She's all lined with wood; that's the reason she floats.' I could not controvert him for the moment, but I was not satisfied, and sitting down on the wharf when he left me, I set to work trying mental experiments. If it was the wood inside of her that made her float, then the more wood the higher she would float; and mentally I loaded her up with wood. But, as I was familiar with the process of making boats out of blocks of wood, I at once saw that, instead of floating higher, she would sink deeper. Then I mentally took all the wood out of her, as we dug out our wooden boats, and saw that thus lightened she would float higher still. Then, in imagination, I jammed a hole in her, and saw that the water would run in and she would sink, as did our wooded boats when ballasted with leaden keels. And thus I saw, as clearly as though I could have actually made these experiments with the steamer, that it was not the wooden lining that made her float, but her hollowness, or as I would now phrase it, her displacement of water."— Lecture on "The Study of Political Economy" at University of California, March 9, 1877.

ily, a young man named Samuel Miller who was mate and whose father was captain of the ship *Hindoo*. No better insight into the habits of the boy and of his constant thought of the sea can be obtained than from extracts from a short journal that he kept at the beginning of 1855, probably at the suggestion of his uncle, Thomas Latimer. Though then scarcely more than fifteen, and although he had spent all his life in a town of brick houses and perhaps had never more than seen the ocean, he noted wind and weather with the care of a veteran sea captain. Incidentally the journal shows the important part the lectures at the Franklin Institute were playing:

"Jan. 7, Mon. Rose at 6. Went to store. Evening went to lecture.

"Jan. 8, Tues. to Fri. Rainy, warm and muddy.

"Jan. 13, Sat. Went to store. Coming home stopped in at library. Saw in 'New York Herald': 'Arrived, Ship *Hindoo*, Miller; Canton, July 22; Angier, Sept. 28; Cape Good Hope, Nov. 6; St. Helena, ——. Was 68 to Angier. In month of August only made 200 miles against S.W. monsoon and strong northerly currents.' I have been expecting her for some time. Stopped at Latimer's. Got Tom [his brother] and came home. Little Augustine, the Chilian boy from the ship *Bowditch*, came. He found his way alone. Only been here once before, on Tuesday night. Went up to Mrs. McDonald's and got my pants. Went with Augustine to buy a collar.

"Jan. 14, Sun. Clear and cold, wind N.W. Went to Sunday school with Charley Walton. Mr. Newton preached good sermon. Was coming home, corner of Third and Catharine met Augustine. After dinner took him up to Uncle Joe's. In evening he came again. Took him to Trinity Church.

"Jan. 15, Mon. Wind S., moderating. Went to store. Evening went to lecture. George Latimer said they had received a letter from Sam Miller saying that he would be home in a few days.

"Jan. 16, Tues. Wind N.E., clear and warm. George told me he had written to Sam Miller and told him about me.

"Jan. 17, Wed. Cloudy. Wind went around to N.W. and blew up clear. Went to lecture, last on electricity. Augustine at home.

"Jan. 18, Tues. Wind N.W., clear and cold. In evening Augustine and Charley Walton came. Went around to library and up to McDonald's for Cad [Caroline, his sister].

"Jan. 19, Fri. Told Sam that I was going to leave. He gave me $12. . . . In morning met Augustine, who said he had got place on steam tug *America*—$2 a week. Evening went to lecture.

"Jan. 20, Sat. Wind N.E. Last day at store. They expect Sam Miller home to-night.

"Jan. 21, Sun. Wind S., warm, cloudy. Sam Miller did not come home last night. They expect him home next Saturday. Went to Sunday school and Church. Augustine sat in our pew. Took him in afternoon to Sunday school. . . . It blew in the evening very strong and about one o'clock increased to perfect hurricane, blowing as I never had heard it before from the South.

"Jan. 22, Mon. Took up a basket to the store for crockery Mr. Young said he would give me. . . . In afternoon went down to Navy Yard with Bill Horner. Evening went to lecture. Brought home a lot of crockery.

"Jan. 23, Tues. Wind N.W., clear and cool. Evening went to Thomas's book sale. Bought a lot of six books for seven cents.

"Jan. 24, Wed. Went to lecture in evening, first on climatology. Liked it very much.

"Jan. 25, Thurs. Went to store in morning. . . .

"Jan. 26, Fri. Snowed all the morning. Aunt Rebecca [Latimer] says that Sam Miller did not get George Latimer's letter. George wrote to him again yesterday. He will be here next Wednesday. . . . Cleared off with N.W. wind. In afternoon snow-balled. Went to lecture in evening, first on organic chemistry. Liked it very much.

"Jan. 27, Sat.   Went skating morning and afternoon.

"Jan. 28, Sun.   Augustine came in the afternoon. He is going to Cuba in Brig *Aucturus* of Union Island.

"Jan. 29, Mon.   Went to navy yard and brig [*Aucturus*] in morning.   Lecture in evening.

"Jan. 31, Wed.   Skating in afternoon.   Sam Miller did not come home.   Will be home on Saturday morning.

"Feb. 1, Thurs.   Skating in afternoon.

"Feb. 2, Fri.   Evening went to see the panorama of Europe.

"Feb. 3, Sat.   Sam Miller came home yesterday afternoon.   Went to George Latimer's office to see him.   He says if he goes as captain he will take me.   The owners of the *Hindoo* have bought the clipper *Whirlwind*.   Both will sail for Melbourne about the middle of March and from there to Calcutta and home.   *Hindoo* probably make it in 11 months.   *Hindoo* is 25 years old, 586 tons register, 1,200 burden; carries 14 able seamen, cook, steward, two mates and captain—in all 19 men.   Sam Miller intends going back to New York on Wednesday.   Went skating in afternoon.

"Feb. 5, Mon.   Afternoon went to Uncle Dunkin George's office.   His boy is sick.   Evening Pop met Sam Miller and George Latimer in Chestnut street.   .   .   . Pop asked Sam Miller to tea on Saturday.   Very cold.

"Feb. 6, Tues.   Very cold; thermometer at Zero.

"Feb. 7, Wed.   River blocked up.   Commenced snowing.   Wind N.E. till night.

"Feb. 8, Thurs.   Snowed again all day.   In afternoon went sleighing with Uncle Joe Van Dusen.

"Feb. 9, Fri.   Clear.   Delaware pretty nearly closed. Skated a little on the ice in the afternoon.   Saw Augustine on the first ice he had ever been on.   Went to Aunt Rebecca Latimer's to tea.

"Feb. 10, Sat.   Sam Miller and George and Kate Latimer came about five o'clock and staid to supper.   .   .   .   Sam said he had received a letter from his father saying he need not come on to New York until he sent for him.

"Feb. 11, Sun.   Clear and cold.   Up at Uncle Dunkin's office all the week.

"Feb. 19, Mon. Came home at night along the wharf. Saw Augustine on the Brig *Globe* of Bangor, about to sail for Cuba. Stopped at Aunt Rebecca's. Sam Miller had heard nothing from his father.

"Feb. 20, Tues. Auntie Ann came to our house to dinner. Said Sam Miller had heard from his father to go on immediately. He went on at two o'clock. . . .

"March 26, Mon. Uncle Dunkin's in the morning. Saw in New York papers at Exchange the *Hindoo* advertised to sail on the 5th of April—a week from next Thursday.

"March 27, Tues. Office in morning. Staid home in afternoon working on my brig [toy boat]. . . . Before supper went to Aunt Rebecca's. George received a letter from Captain Miller [Sam Miller, just made captain]. Said he would sail about Thursday, April 5, and that he would come on to Philadelphia on Saturday and stay till Monday and take me with him. It surprised them all.

"March 28, Wed. Went to Uncle Dunkin's in the morning. Told him I should not come up any more, as I had so little time.

"March 31, Sat. Stayed at home in the morning finishing my brig. Painted her. After dinner, my last dinner at home, went with father and mother to get our daguerreotypes taken. Came home and went to Aunt Rebecca's to supper in company with Cad and Jennie. Went home at eight P.M."

Young Samuel W. Miller, then about twenty-five, had obtained command of the ship *Hindoo*, an old East Indiaman, on which he had formerly sailed as mate under his father, who was now transferred to a new ship. At the suggestion of George Latimer, and after talking with Henry George's father, he had formally invited young Henry to sail with him. For Richard George was a clear-headed, common-sensed man. Much as he disliked to have the boy go to sea, he knew that his son inherited the longing. Moreover, knowing the strong, wilful nature of his son, he feared that if objection was raised the boy might run away, as he had done once before while yet going to school. The lad had made an impertinent reply to his mother, and his father, overhearing it, reproved him with words and a blow. To be struck by his father was so unusual that he was humiliated. He stole away, got his school books and a little cold lunch—all that he could get to eat—and left the house with the resolve never to return again. He remained out until half past nine o'clock that night, when he returned with a tamer spirit and was forgiven. The father had not forgotten this incident, and he was determined that if the boy must go to sea he should go with his parents' consent. So he talked to Captain Miller and suggested to him not to make the boy's berth too comfortable, but to let him see and feel the rigours of a sailor's life, so that by a single voyage the desire for roving should be destroyed. Henry George was then accepted as foremast boy on the *Hindoo*, bound for Melbourne, Australia, and Calcutta, India.

CHAPTER II.

BEFORE THE MAST.

1855-1856.   AGE, 16-17.

AUSTRALIA and India swam in the boy's fancy as in a shining sea of gold. Australia, the island continent nearly as large as the United States, giving promise of a great rival, English-speaking republic in the southern hemisphere, had riveted attention by its gold discoveries in the early fifties and by the enormous treasure since taken out—equal almost to that of wonderful California. It was the new land of wealth, where poor, obscure men in a day rose to riches. India lay like a counterpoise in the mind's picture. With her jungles and monkeys, tigers and elephants; her painted idols, fantastical philosophies and poppy smokers—this land of mysteries, old when the pyramids of Egypt and Syria were young, shone through partings in her gorgeous tropical foliage with the gleam of gold and precious stones, despite the pillage of the ages. Whatever the boy had read, from Bible to "Arabian Nights," in magazine or in newspaper; and all that he had heard, in lecture or sermon, from traveller or sailor, burned in his imagination and made him eager to be gone.

The *Hindoo* was to sail from New York Harbour early in April. On Sunday, April 1, after Sunday school,

Henry George received a Bible and a copy of "James's Anxious Enquirer"; and the next morning, bidding farewell at the wharf to his father, and uncles Thomas Latimer and Joseph Van Dusen, his cousin George Latimer and his friends Col Walton and Joe Roberts, he and Captain Miller went aboard the steamboat, crossed the Delaware, took train, and four hours afterwards were in New York. Two letters from him, written from the ship before she got away, have been preserved. They are in large, clear, firm hand, with some shading, some flourishes and a number of misspelled words. In the first, under date of April 6, he says:

"I signed the shipping articles at $6 a month and two months' advance, which I got in the morning.

"While we were down town we stopped at the Custom House, and Jim [an ordinary seaman] and I got a protection, for which we paid $1 each to a broker.

"The New York Custom House looks like a cooped up affair along side of the Philadelphia one—there are so many people and so much business and bustle.

"The upper part of New York is a beautiful place—the streets wide, clear and regular; the houses all a brown stone and standing ten or twenty feet from the pavement, with gardens in front."

To the foregoing letter was added this:

April 7, 1855.

"I was stopped [writing] suddenly last night by the entrance of the men to haul her [the vessel] to the end of the wharf and was prevented from going on by their laughing and talking. At about twelve o'clock we commenced and by some pretty hard heaving we got her to the end of the wharf. It was then about two o'clock. So we turned in and slept until about half past five. We got our breakfast, and being taken in tow by a steamboat about 7.30 A.M., proceeded down the stream till off the Battery, where we dropped anchor and now lie.

"The view from this spot is beautiful—the North River and New York Bay covered with sailing vessels and steamers of every class and size, while back, the hills, gently sloping, are covered with country seats. . . .

"I ate my first meals sailor style to-day and did not dislike it at all. Working around in the open air gives one such an appetite that he can eat almost anything. We shall go to sea Monday morning early. I should love to see you all again before I go, but that is impossible. I shall write again to-morrow, and if possible get the pilot to take a letter when he leaves, though it is doubtful that I shall be able to write one."

It was in these days preparatory to starting, when there were a lot of odd things to do, that the boatswain, busy with some splicing, sent the boy for some tar; and when the boy stopped to look around for a stick, the sailor in surprise and disgust cried to him to bring the tar in his hand! Another incident of a similar kind appears in his second letter, which is dated April 9 and is addressed to his Aunt Mary, one of his mother's sisters, a most unselfish and lovable maiden lady who helped raise the large brood of George children, and who, until her death in 1875, had never been separated from her sister, Mrs. George. She was loved as a second mother by the children.

"We are not at sea, as we expected to be by this time, but still lying off the Battery. The ship could not sail this morning for want of seamen. They are very scarce in New York now and all sorts of men are shipping as sailors. Two Dutch boys shipped as able seamen and came on board yesterday afternoon. The smallest one had been to sea before, but the largest did not know the difference between a yard and a block.

The second mate told them to go aloft and slush down the masts. This morning the smallest went up, but the other could not go up at all. So I had to go aloft and do it. The work was a good deal easier than I expected. I don't mind handling grease at all now."[1]

Then the letter proceeds:

"Captain Miller has been ashore all day trying to get men. There is to be one sent on board in place of the largest Dutchman. I pity the poor fellow, though to be sure he had no business to ship as seaman. He says he has four trades—baker, shoemaker, etc. Another man came aboard this morning as able seaman who could not get into the foretop. They sent him ashore. The captain shipped to-day as ordinary seamen two lads, one a Spaniard and the other English, I believe. They are fine sailor looking fellows. The cook, steward and two of the men are from the West Indies. All sailed in whalers. There are no cleaner looking men in Parkinson's.

"We have better living than I expected—fresh and salt beef, potatoes and rice—and all cooked in the finest style; but I cannot like the coffee as yet.

"They have just brought two men aboard and taken the Dutchmen off. This is the last letter that I shall have a chance to send till we get to Melbourne, where I hope there will be letters awaiting me."

April 10.

"We have just been heaving the cable short and shall be ready as soon as the tow boat comes. I hope that by this time Morrie [his baby brother] is well. I could

---

[1] When a boy, his mother would frequently buy a piece of sweet suet and melting it down, would mix with its oil or fat a little bergamot, thereby making a pomade for the hair. Henry George never during his life liked fats with his meat at the table, and at times would say in the family that it was because when a boy he had to put it on his head. Notwithstanding the use of the hair preparation, he and all his brothers followed their father and grew bald early.

spin out four or five pages, but I have not time. I would have written a great many more letters, but could not. When you read this letter you must remember where it was written—on the top of my chest in the after house (where I sleep, along with Jim, the carpenter and the cook). I have to dip my pen into the bottle at almost every word. Good-bye father and mother, aunts and uncles, brothers and sisters, cousins and friends. God bless you all and may we all meet again.

"P. S. I have received letters from Martha Curry and George Latimer and shall reply the first chance."

9.30 A. M.

"We are now going down the bay in tow of a steamboat and shall soon be at sea. I shall get the captain to send this ashore by the pilot. God bless you all. It is cloudy and drizzling—blows a stiff breeze from the south.

"Good-bye,

"HENRY GEORGE."

So it was that the *Hindoo*, a full-rigged ship of 586 tons register—a very large ship at that time[1]—with 500,000 feet of lumber aboard and a crew of twenty men, all told, started on her long voyage; and as she glided down the bay and through the "Narrows" on her way to the ocean, on the left bank, eighty feet above the water, stood an old white house that forty years later, when his fame had spread through the world, was to become Henry George's home and witness the end of his career. But the boy, all unconscious of this, had been set to work, as he says in his sea journal, "in company with the other boys to

---

[1] "In the last generation a full-rigged Indiaman would be considered a very large vessel if she registered 500 tons. Now we are building coasting schooners of 1000 tons"—"Social Problems," Chap. V. (Memorial edition, p. 46.)

picking oakum for the carpenter, who was busy fastening
and calking the hatches."

This journal or log, covers most of the voyage, and
with the few letters that still exist, and an account of
the passage written by Captain Miller for his friend,
George Latimer, furnishes pretty full and clear information as to this important formative period. The journal
consists of an original in two parts and three incomplete
fair copies. The original parts are quite rough and show
marks of wear and stains of water. One is of white, the
other of blue, unruled, large sized letter paper, folded so
as to make neat pages of four by six inches, and stitched
together with heavy linen thread, such as might have been
used in sewing sails. The entries are mostly in pencil,
the spelling not of the best, and the writing not uniform
—in some places quite faint—but generally small, condensed, round and clear. The fair copies are in a fine
state of preservation. They are written in large, bold
hand in commercial blank books and the spelling is correct. Two of them may have been copied while at sea,
but the fullest and best looking one was doubtless written in Philadelphia after the voyage.[1]

From Captain Miller's account it appears that when the
Hindoo cast off the tug that was taking her to sea, the
wind was from the south-east and right ahead, and the
pilot advised him to anchor at Sandy Hook; "but," says
the Captain, "we could not wait. We set all sail and
stood E.N.E. until we saw the rocks of Long Island.
We then tacked to the south'd and stood down until we
were abreast the Capes of Delaware. Then a gale of wind

---

[1] In the back pages of this little journal are some historical, scientific
and other notes probably made while reading. These bear date as late as
April, 1859, at which time its owner was in California.

from the north-west commenced, lasting four days; during which time we made good progress off the coast." The boy's log for these four days runs as follows:

"Tues. 10. . . . About 12 A.M. we passed Sandy Hook, and a slight breeze springing up, set all fore and aft sail. About 3 P.M. discharged the tow boat and pilot. Soon after I began to feel sea-sick, and the breeze dying away, the tossing of the vessel very much increased it. . . . After supper all hands were called aft and the watches chosen. I was taken by the mate for the larboard. . . . It being the larboard watch's first watch below, I turned in at 8 P.M.

"Wed. 11. I was roused out of a sound sleep at 12 o'clock to come on deck and keep my watch. On turning out I found a great change in the weather. The wind had shifted to N.W. and came out cold and fierce. The ship was running dead before it in a S.E. direction, making about 8 or 9 knots an hour. After keeping a cold and dreary watch until 4 A.M. we were relieved and I was enabled to turn in again. All this day sea-sick by spells. . . . It will be a long time before we are in this part of the world again, homeward bound. Twelve months seem as if they would never pass. In the afternoon all hands were engaged in getting the anchors on the forecastle and securing them for a long passage. The colour of the sea is green on sounding, the shade varying according to the depth of water, and a beautiful blue outside, and so very clear that objects can be seen at a great depth.

"Thurs. 12. A brisk breeze all day from N.W. with frequent showers of rain. Numbers of Stormy Petrels or Mother Carey's Chickens hovering about the quarter. Weather rather cool.

"Fri. 13. A fine bright day; wind still the same. Hoisting the lower stun'sail in the forenoon, the halyards parted, and the sail was with difficulty secured. The sea-sickness has now entirely left me."

The old ship after twenty-five years of hard service was pretty nearly worn out, and the log reveals a series of breakages, and some consequent accidents.

"Sat. 14. Commenced with fine clear weather and brisk breeze from N.W. About 5.30 A.M., the larboard watch being on deck, the tiller of the rudder suddenly broke in half. All hands were immediately called and everything let go and clewed up. Tackles were got on the rudder and the ship steered by them, while the carpenter immediately set to work on a new one. While furling the main top-gallant sail a man belonging to the larboard watch, John Prentz by name, fell from the yard to the deck. Luckily the main topsail, which was clewed up, broke his fall, or he would certainly have been killed. On taking him forward, his arm was found to have been broken in three places, but otherwise he had sustained no serious injury. His arm was set and bandaged by the mate. The carpenter finished the tiller about 4 P.M., when, everything being replaced, sail was again made on the ship and she continued on her course with a fair, though light wind. The old tiller which had suddenly broken, and which outwardly appeared so firm and sound, was in the centre completely rotted away. . . . The account which the man who fell from aloft gave of his mishap when he had recovered his senses was that he was pulling on the gasket with both hands when it suddenly parted and he was precipitated backwards. He knew no more until he found himself in the forecastle with his arm bandaged up."

The fifteenth of April is noted in the log as the "first Sunday at sea," and that instead of being seated in St. Paul's Church, they were "ploughing the ocean a thousand miles away." Soon the entries take more of the formal aspect of a ship's log and less of a personal journal, though once in a while they relax into general observation

reported to be "very hard ashore, thousands with nothing
to do and nothing to eat." Notwithstanding this, the
crew wished at once to get away.

> "As the captain was getting into a boat to go ashore,
> the men came aft in a body and requested their dis-
> charge, which being refused, they declared their inten-
> tion of doing no more work. After supper the mate
> came forward and ordered the men to pick anchor
> watches, which they agreed to do after some parley.
> The mate told Jim and me to keep watch in the cabin
> until 12 and then call him. This I did until 10, when,
> after having a feast of butter, sugar and bread in the
> pantry, I turned in, leaving Jim to call the mate."

For several days the men refused to work, demanding
to see the American Consul, and on Wednesday, four days
after casting anchor, the captain got the Consul aboard.
The Consul "took his seat on the booby hatch with the
shipping articles before him," and called up the crew one
by one. He finally "told the men that, as the passage
would not be up until the cargo was discharged, he could
do nothing until that time; but that Dutch John (the
man who in the early part of the passage fell from the
main topgallant yard) was entitled to his discharge if he
wished it." The captain then promised that if they would
"remain by the ship until she was discharged, he would
pay them their wages and let them go in peace." They
demanded this in writing, saying that he might change
his mind, "but the captain refused to give them any fur-

---

in his "Diary in America" (First Series), Philadelphia, 1839, says, p. 186:
"It appears, then, that from various causes, our merchant vessels have
lost their sailing properties, whilst the Americans have the fastest sailers
in the world; and it is for that reason, and no other, that, although sailing at a much greater expense, the Americans can afford to outbid us, and
take all our best seamen."

ther guarantee than his word." As they still desisted
from work on the *Hindoo*, they were taken off in a police
boat, and sentenced to one month's hard labour in the
prison ship, at the end of which time, still refusing to
work, they would perhaps have been sentenced to further imprisonment if the captain had not reached court
too late to appear against them. Before he sailed, the
captain had to ship a new crew.

There is nothing in the journal to indicate that the
boy thought Captain Miller unjust, but the incident made
an indelible impression, revealing the tremendous powers
for tyranny the navigation laws put into the hands of a
captain, and this was to inspire a remarkable fight for
sailor's rights in years to come.[1]

The ship lay in Hobson's Bay twenty-nine days discharging chargo and taking in ballast. Captain Miller in
his account says: "Harry went up to Melbourne once, but
did not see much to admire." Perhaps the boy saw more
than the captain realised, for thirty-five years later, in
a speech in Melbourne, he said, that he had a vivid recol-
lection of it—"its busy streets, its seemingly continuous
auctions, its crowds of men with flannel shirts and long
high hoots, its bay crowded with ships." No letters written from there now exist, but it is clear that the Australia
of his dreams did not appear to be such a wonderful place
after all; that there was not much gold in sight and that
in this respect the "Land of Promise" was something of
a disappointment. Land monopolisation and speculation
had set in and cut off the poor man's access to nature's
storehouse.

Other dreams were to be dissipated on reaching India.
The best description of the passage and arrival there is

---

[1] Sunrise Case in San Francisco.

found in a letter to his father and mother, dated Calcutta, December 12, 1855.

"We hove up anchor in Hobson's Bay about 11 o'clock on the 24th of September, made sail, proceeded down the bay under charge of a pilot, and at about 5 P.M. passed the heads and discharged the pilot. After leaving Port Philip and until we had rounded Cape Lewin we had strong winds, mostly head, and cool weather. . . . Then the weather gradually became milder as we got to the northward, with fair, though not very strong winds. Near the line we had light airs, not even sufficient to fill the sails, but under the pressure of which the ship would go two or three miles per hour. We crossed the line November 5, when 42 days out. . . . From this place until we arrived at about 10° north we had the same fair airs as on the other side of the line, with every prospect of a short passage. Then the wind became stronger and more variable, but dead ahead. It would seldom blow from one point of the compass for more than an hour. Indeed, it seemed as if a second Jonah was aboard, for tack as often as we would, the wind was sure to head us off. . . . Progress under the circumstances was impossible. For over a week we did not gain a single inch to the northward. What she would make one hour she would lose the next. During this time the weather was delightful, warm without being uncomfortably so, and so pleasant that sleeping on deck could be practised with impunity.

"At length on the morning of the 29th of November the colour of the water suddenly changed to green, and by noon we were abreast of the lightship, which marks the outer pilot station. The tide was running so strongly that with the light air we could hardly hold our own against it. About 3 P.M., in obedience to a signal from the pilot brig, we cast anchor with 30 fathoms of chain, furled all sail, and cleared up decks for the night. At 8 P.M. set anchor-watch and turned in for *all night*. . . ."

Then came the first impressions of the country—impressions that always afterward remained vivid and helped before long to direct thought to social questions; that changed the fancied India—the place of dreamy luxury, of soft and sensuous life—into the real India, with its extremes of light and shadow, of poverty and riches, of degradation and splendour; where the few have so much, the many so little; where jewels blaze in the trappings of elephants, but where, as he has since said in talking with his son Richard, "the very carrion birds are more sacred than human life!" These impressions are preserved in a description of the trip to Calcutta up the Hooghly branch of the Ganges River scribbled in pencil on the back pages of one of the journal records.

ARRIVAL AT GARDEN REACH AND FIRST IMPRESSIONS OF THE TOWN.

"Mon. Dec. 3. We turned out about 3 A.M. and after some heavy heaving got up anchor. About 5 A.M. we were taken in tow by the steamer and proceeded up the river. The night air was misty and chilly and a monkey jacket proved very comfortable. The day soon began to break, revealing a beautiful scene. The river, at times very broad and again contracting its stream into a channel hardly large enough for a ship of average size to turn in, was bordered by small native villages, surrounded by large fruit trees, through which the little bamboo huts peeped. As we advanced, the mists which had hitherto hung over the river cleared away, affording a more extensive prospect. The water was covered with boats of all sizes, very queer looking to the eye of an American. They were most of them bound to Calcutta with the produce and rude manufactures of the country—bricks, tiles, earths, pots, etc. They had low bows and very high sterns. They were pulled by from four to ten men, and steered by an old fellow wrapped up in a sort of cloth, seated on a high platform at the stern. Some had sails to help them along, in which there were more holes than threads. On the banks the natives began to go to their daily toil, some driving cattle along, others loading boats with grain, while the women seemed busy with their domestic affairs. As we approached the city, the banks on both sides were lined with handsome country residences of the wealthy English. About 10 A.M. we came to Garden Reach, where, as there was no Harbour Master's Assistant ready to take us up, we were obliged to drop both anchors. After getting fairly moored we had a little time to look around us. The river which here takes a sudden bend, was crowded with ships of all nations, and above nothing could be seen but a forest of masts. On the right hand or Calcutta side, are the East India Company's works, for repairing their steamers, numbers of which, principally iron, were undergoing repairs. On the other side was an immense palace-like structure (the residence, I believe, of some wealthy Englishman) surrounded by beautiful lawns and groves. The river was covered with boats and presented a bustling scene. One feature which is peculiar to Calcutta was the number of dead bodies floating down in all stages of decomposition, covered by crows who were actively engaged in picking them to pieces. The first one I saw filled me with horror and disgust, but like the natives, you soon cease to pay any attention to them.

"Tues. Dec. 4. About 4.30 A.M. the Harbour Master came along side and we were roused up to get up anchors. . . . It astonished me to see with what ease the pilot took the vessel up . . . steering her amidst the maze of vessels as easily as if she was at sea. The port seemed crowded with vessels, a large proportion of them American, some of which I recognised as having seen at Philadelphia. At length about 10 A.M. we cast anchor off our intended moorings. About 2 P.M. we hauled in and made fast along side of an English clipper, the *British Lion*. After getting all fast we had dinner and cleared up decks and squared the yards."

While the ship lay at her moorings, visits were made to Barrapore, eighteen miles away, and other places of interest in the vicinity, and the boy saw those things that are observed generally by travellers. But the event of perhaps most interest to him was the receipt on December 10 of letters from home—the first since he had left. His father sent family news and said: "Your little brig is safely moored on the mantelpiece. First thing when we wake, our eyes rest upon her, and she reminds us of our dear sailor boy."

The mother's letter also touched on family matters, but gave chief place to other things engaging her devout mind.

"And now for the news. The best news just now is the religious news—a great work going on in New York and Philadelphia and all the principal cities of the Union; prayer-meetings all over the land; all denominations uniting together in solemn, earnest prayer; Jayne's Hall (you know its size) is crowded to excess, even those large galleries literally packed with men of the highest respectability—merchants, bankers, brokers, all classes. Those who have never entered a church and have hitherto scoffed at religion meet at this prayer-meeting every day to hear the word of God read and solemn prayer offered for their conversion. . . . I might fill many pages to show you that this is truly the work of God—the out-pouring of the Holy Spirit. . . . That same Holy Influence will be given to all that ask for it in simple faith: 'Lord, teach me to pray.'"

The event to the lad next in interest to the receipt of home letters was the acquisition of a pet monkey, of which he wrote in later years:[1]

---

[1] "The Science of Political Economy," p. 30.

"I bought in Calcutta, when a boy, a monkey, which all the long way home would pillow her little head on mine as I slept, and keep off my face the cockroaches that infested the old Indiaman by catching them with her hands and cramming them into her maw. When I got her home, she was so jealous of a little brother that I had to part with her to a lady who had no children."

In his account of the voyage, Captain Miller says that the ship left Calcutta with quite a menagerie of monkeys and birds aboard, but that before long "Harry's was the only survivor." The others died or got away, two of the sailors without intentional cruelty throwing theirs overboard to see "which would swim ashore first," but the animals quickly drowned. The boy cherished his little creature most fondly; though for that matter he always showed a warm love for animals, and this was but one of a great number that he had about him during his life.

On the 15th of January, 1856, the *Hindoo* having completed her loading, consisting of nearly twelve hundred tons of rice, seeds, etc., took a new crew aboard and started down the river, homeward bound. Henry George at the time estimated that he would have when he reached New York and settled his accounts "about fifty dollars to take clear of everything—not much for thirteen or fourteen months." The distance down the Hooghly from Calcutta to the sea is eighty miles, but what with head winds, the scarcity of tow boats and a broken windlass, the vessel was twenty days making the passage, during which time the hot weather played havoc with the fresh provisions, so that the crew was the sooner reduced to "salt horse and biscuit." Light winds blew down the bay of Bengal and the ship crossed the equator on the 23rd of February. On the 27th the cook, Stephen Anderson, fell sick and young

George went into the galley temporarily. The journal says:

"Wed. Feb. 27. Cook laid up. Went into the galley.

"(Not having written down the events of the inter-vening space, I do not remember them fully, being obliged to work pretty hard.)

"Sun. Mar. 2. Fine clear day. Breeze from S.W., course, S.S.E. For several days there have been thou-sands of fish playing around, but, although the men tried hard to catch them, they were unsuccessful until this morning, when an albicore was captured. The mate made sea-pie for all hands for supper. 8 P.M. sail in sight.

"Mon. Mar. 3. Calm all day. The cook so weak that he cannot raise a spoon to his mouth. I think it a chance whether he lives.

"Tues. Mar. 4. Calm, fine day. Cook seems a little stronger, but can scarcely speak.

"Wed. Mar. 5. Commenced with breeze from W.N.W.; course S.S.W. Four sail in sight. Last evening the cook appeared a great deal stronger, getting up and moving about, turning in and out; but still could scarce-ly speak. About 7 A.M. he was taken with a fit, when he was brought on deck and laid by the capstan. About 11.30 A.M. he died. He was sewed up and buried at 5 P.M."

The cook having gone, the boy, to his great satisfac-tion, for he had an extreme distaste for the task, was superseded in the galley by one of the crew, who remained there for the rest of the voyage. The ship passed the Cape of Good Hope on April 13 and within sight of St. Helena on the 27th. On May 12 she crossed the equator for the fourth time during the voyage. Long before that date the journal entries had become short, and after May 6 stopped altogether, possibly because there was a great deal of work to do in handling, cleaning,

repairing and painting the ship.   April opened with this
entry:

"April 1, 1856.   Lat., 31, S.; long., 40, E.   One year
has passed since the Sunday when I took farewell of
my friends—to me an eventful year; one that will
have a great influence in determining my position in
life; perhaps more so than I can at present see.   O that
I had it to go over again!   Homeward bound!   In a
few months I hope to be in Philadelphia once more."

And it was not long before he was home, for on June
14, after an absence of one year and sixty-five days, and
from Calcutta one hundred and fifty days, the *Hindoo*
completed her long journey and dropped anchor in New
York Bay.

CHAPTER III.

LEARNS TO SET TYPE.

1856-1857.   Age, 17-18.

ON getting back, home seemed very sweet to the boy on account of the loved ones and comforts, and the association of his boy friends. A year and a half afterwards, when he had gone to California, Jo Jeffreys, at that time the closest of his friends, wrote:

> "Don't you recollect our Byronic quotations? Amusing weren't they? And yet I dare say we had more pleasure in those long moonlight nights spent in conversation—in counsel and reflection—than we had in a like number of hours at any other time. I remember well, too, how night after night we sat together and alone in your little room, smoking slowly and looking —sometimes at the little bed which was to contain us both and which rested in a corner near the door, at the little case of books on the bureau, at the dim gaslight which could so seldom be induced to burn brightly and which shed its dim light upon all around—and then turning from this picture, so familiar to me now (though I have never been in that room since, though often in the rooms beneath it), and gazing upon each other, would talk of the present and the future."

In this little back-attic bed room all the boys at times gathered and talked about books or public affairs or boyish amusements, and it was Henry George's habit, while engaging in conversation, to throw himself down on his bed, and frequently while the discourse was raging he would sink into placid slumbers. It was common enough for the family to see the boys come down stairs alone and hear the explanation: "Oh, Hen's asleep and we think it is time to go."

Thus the home life had much attractiveness for young George, yet he found it full of restrictions, for with all the heavy toil and hard discipline of sea life, there was during the preceding year and a quarter complete freedom of thought, and of actions, too, in the hours off duty. And now to come back to conditions where the most innocent of card-playing was regarded as an evil and riding in a public conveyance on Sunday as a desecration of the Lord's Day, made the energetic, masterful boy, or rather youth, for he was now in his eighteenth year, see new charms in the sea life; and for a time, all efforts failing in the search for employment ashore, his thoughts reverted to the water. Learning of this inclination, Captain Miller, before sailing on a new voyage in the *Hindoo*, wrote to him:

"I hope you will find some agreeable and profitable employment before long. Take my advice and never go to sea. You know of the troubles of a sailor's life before the mast. It never gets any better. A second mate leads proverbially a dog's life. The mate's and captain's are very little better."[1]

---

[1] This was probably the last letter he received from Captain Miller, and before the *Hindoo* had returned from her voyage and the captain had run on to Philadelphia, Henry George had sailed for California, so that they never again met. The captain died in Brooklyn, in May, 1877, in his forty-eighth year, and his friend, Rev. George A. Latimer, Henry George's cousin, officiating, was buried in Greenwood Cemetery, where Henry George himself, twenty years later, was to rest.

The boy's parents were most anxious not to have him again go to sea, and at last in the fall the father through his former book publishing connections obtained a situation for his son with the printing firm of King & Baird, at that time one of the important printing houses in Philadelphia. The father's idea in putting his son there was threefold: to keep the boy at home, to give him a trade and to teach him to spell. This latter short-coming in the boy was very conspicuous, requiring a second draft or fair copy of letters to insure the correct spelling of many even common words, as drafts of such letters that have survived show.

Learning to set type effected a marked improvement, and the printer's experience later in California perfected it. In after years his letter-writing at times revealed lapses in spelling, but these, as was manifest on the surface, arose from habits of abstraction.

This learning to set type marked another distinct step in the education of Henry George for his life work. Not that it lay so much in type-setting itself, or in correcting his spelling; but rather in bringing him into familiar contact with another field of human activity—among type-setters, who, as a class of men, if they belong to a trade, possess, as a rule, much correct general information and are given to habits of intelligent thought. Edmund Wallazz, who was a type-setter at King and Baird's in 1856, said in after years: "Henry George was a remarkably bright boy, always in discussion with the other boys in the office. He got in the habit of appealing to me (I am seven or eight years older) for support as to his dates and facts, historical and political." Thus through the channel of polemics he was acquiring knowledge of various kinds, and was also learning to observe and to present his thoughts. He had a habit of stowing away things in his memory that would have passed another—things that

in his matured years often found expression in his writings. To this period he assigned the first puzzling question in political economy. An old printer observed to
him one day that while in old countries wages are low, in
new countries they are always high. The boy compared
the United States with Europe, and then California and
Australia with Pennsylvania and New York, and the old
printer's words seemed true enough, though neither the
printer nor he could explain why. The thing stuck in
his mind and kept rising for answer.

This propensity for investigating and arguing showed
itself wherever he happened to be, when with old or with
young, abroad or at home. As his Uncle Joseph Van
Dusen said: "Henry is not tongue-tied."

For years stories of slave auctions in the South, friction over the return of runaway slaves in the North, the
hot agitation of Garrison and Phillips in the East, and
conflicts in "Bleeding Kansas" and through the West kept
public thought seething. In 1850 appeared Mrs. Stowe's
"Uncle Tom's Cabin," and later arose the Republican
party with its anti-slavery proclivities and that in 1856
forced the issue and ran John C. Frémont for President.
Though James Buchanan, the Democratic pro-slavery candidate, was elected, the new party had waged a fierce fight,
and four years later was to elect Abraham Lincoln.

Young George soon after returning from sea showed
a lively interest in the slavery question, and, although his
father was a Democrat and inclined to support Buchanan,
the boy independently took the anti-slavery side, which
he discussed with his mother. In the interest of peace
and of "property rights,"[1] and doubtless supported in

---

[1] " I was born in a Northern State, I have never lived in the South, I
am not yet gray; but I well remember, as every American of middle age must
remember, how over and over again I have heard all questionings of slavery silenced by the declaration that the negroes were the *property* of their

mind by what she regarded as the sanction of the Scriptures, she upheld slavery, not perhaps as a good thing in itself, but because of the great cost of disestablishment. The mother in repeating this conversation in after years to her son's wife said that in arguing she held that the hardships of slavery "were exaggerated," for, "while some of the slave owners might be brutal, the majority were not likely to be so," most of them doubtless being the same kind of "humanely-disposed people" as she herself. The boy stoutly held to his position and answered that her argument rested "on policy, not principle"; that she spoke of what slave owners *"seemed likely* to do," he of what they *"could* do"; "for if slaves were property, their masters, having the right to do what they pleased with their own property, could ill-treat and even kill them if so disposed."

The argument seemed sound enough to the parents, but the boy was still a boy to them. One night soon after returning from sea he came home late and his father reproved him. The boy hotly said that he was a child no longer and then went off to bed. Reflection cooled the father's anger. He realized that his son was, in mind at least, maturing to manhood, and that the reproof was not quite just or wise. He concluded that in the morning he would talk to his son about it. But when morning came the son was first to speak, saying that he had thought upon what had happened, and that while he regarded his conduct in remaining out as in itself innocent enough, he now recognised what he had not before observed—his father's right to object—and that being conscious of having been impudent, he asked his father's pardon. The

---

masters, and that to take away a man's slave without payment was as much a crime as to take away his horse without payment."—"The Land Question," Chap. VII. (Memorial Edition, p. 49).

father strained his son to his bosom and thereafter gave him more domestic freedom.

High strung and impetuous, Henry George was at this period prone to sudden resolves. From September, 1856, to June, 1857, he worked steadily at type-setting at King & Baird's, when one afternoon, having a quarrel with Mr. Scott, foreman of the job-room, he left the house's employ. When he told of what had happened, his father found for him an opening with Stavely & McCalla, printers, who offered $2.25 a week for the first year, and afterwards as much as he could earn, providing he remained until twenty-one. The pay was so small that he hesitated. Just then a boy friend, John Hasson, sent word of a strike in the "Argus" newspaper office. George applied for and obtained employment. To Emma Curry, a girl friend, he wrote (June 29, 1857) explaining some of these matters:

> "I left King and Baird's about two weeks and a half ago. I was learning nothing and making little ($2 a week) when I left. The immediate cause of my leaving was that I would not quietly submit to the impositions and domineering insolence of the foreman of the room in which I then worked. Week before last I worked on the 'Daily Evening Argus.' The foreman of that paper and the members of the Printers' Union (who have full control of the various newspaper offices) quarrelled, and they refused to work unless the foreman was discharged. This the proprietor, Mr. Severns, refused to do, and the consequence was that the Union would not allow any of its members to work on the paper. The foreman had, therefore, to get printers who did not belong to the Union. I applied for a situation as a journeyman compositor and got it; but unluckily for me, at the end of the week the Union had a meeting and wisely supported the foreman by a large majority. This compelled the proprietor to discharge us

who were working there at the time and take on the
Union men, who, having control of the other offices,
could have put him to great inconvenience had he refused to do so.

"During the six days I worked there I made $9.50,
the largest sum of money I have ever made in the same
time. I had also the satisfaction of seeing that I was
but very little inferior to any of the journeymen, my
bill for the week being as large as any of theirs, with
the exception of a couple who had worked in the even-
ings also. I believe that I can set on an average of
5,000 ems of solid matter a day, including distributing
and correcting, which according to the prices you tell
me the printers get in Oregon, would be worth nearly $4."

Emma Curry, her sisters, Martha and Florence, and
their widowed mother, Rebecca D. Curry, had been neighbours of the George family. They had early in the year
gone to Oregon Territory to join the widow's nephew,
George Curry, who had been appointed Governor. Mrs.
Curry was a bright, discerning woman. Her brother, William D. Kelley, from 1846 to 1856 was Judge of the Court
of Common Pleas of Philadelphia and afterwards represented one of the Philadelphia districts in Congress for
almost thirty years and was commonly known as "Pig
Iron" Kelley. Henry George had had many a long, earnest
talk with Mrs. Curry, who took a deep interest in him.
In a letter to her (April 3, 1857) he said:

"I am still at printing and am getting along very
well, considering the time I have been at it. I should
be able to make at least $5 a week were I getting jour-
neyman's prices, but that is impossible here. If you
can find out and will be kind enough to write me the
rates at which printers are paid in Oregon, I shall be
able to tell exactly how much I could make there.

"I commenced last evening to take lessons in penmanship, and if all the old fellow (I mean teacher) says is true, by the time I write my next letter to you my chirography will be so much improved that you will hardly recognise the hand. I have taken your advice and am trying to improve myself all I can. I shall shortly commence to study book-keeping. After I get through that I shall be Jack of three different trades, and, I am afraid, master of none.

"I am still of the same determination in regard to going West. . . . I only wait for your promised account of Oregon, and advice, to determine where and when I shall go."

Before receipt of his letter, Mrs. Curry had already written (April 19):

"We talk and think of you a great deal and I have talked with Mr. Curry [the Governor] about you. He says, 'Do not go to sea, but come here.' He will see what you can make at your business at Salem. He thinks you may do well. He will inquire as soon as possible, and I shall write you. Everything pays well here. He is giving a boy $20 a month for hoeing, chopping wood, washing a little and bringing up the cattle. A man was paid by him in my presence $25 for ploughing from Tuesday noon till Friday noon. Give all attention to your business and you will, I trust, be successful. It is best to have that at your command."

Emma Curry wrote in a similar strain, and to her the boy replied (June 29):

"Give my thanks to the Governor for the trouble he has taken in my behalf and for the information which he has communicated to me through you. Your statement of the prospects that I may anticipate in Oregon has decided me. I *will* go out as soon as possible and in the best manner possible, even if I am obliged to work my way around the Horn—unless by a lucky windfall I shall get into some business."

But the "lucky windfall" in Philadelphia showed no signs of coming. The boy vainly looked for permanent employment. He obtained a position on a weekly paper called "The Merchant," but this proved only temporary, and he became restless and thought the more earnestly of Oregon, and also of California, where he had a cousin, son of his Uncle Dunkin George. But these places seeming remote, again he thought of the sea, if only as a means of livelihood for the time being. He probably was the more restless because of the reaction from the old home rigorous beliefs and restraints. A blank book with some diary entries covering a few days during this period contains this:

"Tues. July 3. Saw Jo Jeffreys in afternoon. In evening Bill Jones and I took Sallie Young and Amelia Reinhart to the Academy of Music. But Sallie Young deserted me there and went with Bill Jones. Curse these girls; they won't fool me so confoundedly again. After taking them home we adjourned to Stead's [cigar store], where Bill Horner was awaiting us. As we came down we stopped at Cook's and Bergner's [taverns]. Coming up again, we serenaded Charlie Walton with the national anthem, after which Bill left us. Horner and I again repaired to Stead's, where after a little while we were joined by Jo and a friend of his, John Owen, by name. They, together with Ebenezer Harrison [a young Sunday School teacher], had been enjoying themselves in Owen's room, drinking punches and making speeches. At the corner of Sixth and Walnut Jo and I commenced to box, when Jo fell down and cut his head awfully. We raised him up, took him to Owen's, washed his wound and then set off to find a doctor. We dragged him around for about two hours before finding any person who could dress the wound. At length we took him to a German physician, who dressed the cut and charged a V for his trouble. We left him at Owen's and returned home about daybreak."

It was at this time that the boys—Jeffreys, Jones, Horner, Walton, Harrison, George and the others—formed "The Lawrence Literary Society" and met in a small building which once had been a church. Two original essays by "Hen" George are still preserved, one on "The Poetry of Life" and the other on "Mormonism," a very hostile view. There also exists a contribution from the pen of Charley Walton treating of the wide-spread industrial depression then prevailing and ascribing its rise to "extravagance and speculation which have since the revolution characterised the American people."[1] But starting with this self-improving literary idea, the "Lawrence" came in the course of things to have other characteristics which Walton later described in a letter to "Hen" (July 29, 1863):

"I have often thought of the time gone by when the 'Lawrence' in Jerusalem Church was in its palmy days. . . . Can you or I forget the gay, refreshing and kindred spirits that formed that association and gave it a character so unenviable and noticeable as eventually to cause it to be ordered out peremptorily; its sympathy with ghost stories, boxing gloves, fencing foils and deviltry; its exercises tending to promote muscular rather than literary abilities; and its test of merit and standard of membership—to drink Red Eye, sing good songs and smoke lots of cigars?"

---

[1] This essay covers four pages of paper, the first page evidently written with great care, and the last with great carelessness, the whole terminating with the ejaculation, "Thank God, I'm done!"

But however innocent all this may have been, the fact of knowing anything whatever about liquor or of card playing was significant of the break-down of the old home influences; and it partly explains, with the loss of employment and the ambition to be independent, the return of a desire for the sea. At any rate, Henry George embarked on a topsail schooner laden with coal and bound from Philadelphia for Boston. Often afterwards, even towards the end of his life, he spoke with pride of the compliments he received on that voyage. For when he applied as ordinary seaman, the captain measured him with something like contempt and asked what he could do.

"I can handle, reef and steer," was the answer.

"You can't steer this schooner," returned its commander, "but nevertheless I'll try you."

Notwithstanding George's short stature and light weight, the captain found him so useful that at the end of the voyage he paid him off at the full rate of an able seaman, saying that he had been of as much use as any man aboard.

The outlook ashore seemed even worse when he got back from this short schooner trip, as may be seen from a letter to one of his young friends (B. F. Ely, September 30):

"The times here are very hard and are getting worse and worse every day, factory after factory suspending and discharging its hands. There are thousands of hard-working mechanics now out of employment in this city; and it is to the fact that among them is your humble servant, that you owe this letter. If you will send on without delay the V. you owe me you will be doing the State a service by lessening the pressure of the hard times upon one of the hard fisted mechanics who form her bone and muscle, and will at the same time be easing your conscience of a burden, which I have little doubt bears heavily upon it.

"   .   .   .   I am pretty hard up at present and haven't as much money as you could shake a stick at. Indeed, I would not have any hesitation in taking a situation on board a good canal boat for a short time, provided that it would pay.

"I have been trying for some time to secure a berth on board the United States Light-house Steamer *Shubrick*, now fitting out at the Navy Yard for California; but she will not sail for two weeks at least, and even then it is very doubtful whether I can succeed and go out in her.

"There is a ship loading here for San Francisco on board of which I have been promised a berth, but in the present stagnation of business it is doubtful whether she will get off before a month or two at least. So that you see I am in a pretty bad fix, having at least two weeks of loafing to look forward to."

Subsequently (October 5) he wrote a letter to Congressman Thomas B. Florence of his district asking his support.

"I have long wished to go to Oregon, where, if I may believe the many assurances I have received, prospects of fortune are open to me which it would be vain to hope for here. But as it is impossible for me to raise means sufficient to defray the expenses of a passage, I must strive to adopt the only plan practicable, and work my way out.

"The Light-House Steamer *Shubrick* will sail in a couple of weeks for California, where she is to be employed. I have been waiting for her for some time, hoping to get a chance to go in her; but I now learn from good authority that in all probability only a few able seamen will be shipped for her, in which case I would be unable to do so, unless I can obtain permission to ship from the Light-House Bureau.

"I have been to sea before, and am competent to ship as ordinary seaman or first class boy.

"If you would be kind enough to write to the proper

authorities at Washington in support of my application, it would be of great assistance to me in obtaining their permission."

Much to his delight, he not only was accepted for the *Shubrick,* but received the appointment of ship's steward, or storekeeper, at forty dollars a month; though like every one else on board, he was compelled to sign the ship's articles for one year's service, and not for the voyage to California alone, which was all that he wished to do. On December 22, 1857, he said farewell to his loved ones, and the little vessel under Commander John DeCamp of the U. S. Navy steamed down the Delaware River and started on her long journey around the southern extremity of South America.

CHAPTER IV.

WORKS HIS PASSAGE TO CALIFORNIA.

1858.   AGE, 19.

AND now the boy having left home to face the world and
seek his fortune in the new country, it may be instructive to get some more definite knowledge of his character. A key to it, or at any rate to his own estimate at
that time of it, exists in a phrenological sketch that he
wrote of himself while still in Philadelphia. It is in his
clear hand-writing and covers two half-sheets of blue, unruled, legal-cap paper, on the back of one of which are the
words, "Phrenological examination of head by self." The
examination is as follows:

"Circumference [of head], 21⅝; ear to ear, 12½.
1. Amativeness .... Large.
2. Philoprogenitiveness .... Moderate.
3. Adhesiveness .... Large.
4. Inhabitativeness .... Large.
5. Concentrativeness .... Small.
6. Combativeness .... Large.
7. Destructiveness .... Large.
8. Alimentiveness .... Full.
9. Acquisitiveness .... Small.
10. Secretiveness .... Large.
11. Caution .... Large.
12. Approbativeness ....
13. Self-esteem .... Large.

14. Firmness .... Large.
15. Conscientiousness .... Large.
16. Hope .... Large.
17. Marvellousness ....
18. Veneration ....
19. Benevolence ....
20. Constructiveness ....
21. Ideality ....
22. Imitation ....
23. Mirthfulness .... Small.
24. Individuality .... Large.
25. Form ....
26. Size .... Large.
27. Weight ....
28. Colour ....
29. Order ....
30. Calculation .... Small.
31. Locality .... Large.
32. Eventuality .... Full.
33. Time .... Large.
34. Tune ....
35. Language .... Moderate.
36. Causality .... Large.
37. Comparison .... Large.

"An ardent, devoted, fervent and constant lover; will defend the object of his love with boldness, protect his or her rights with spirit. Will feel much stronger attachment than he will express.

"Is not very fond of children. May love them as friends, rather than as children.

"Is strong in his attachments; readily takes the part of friends, resents and retaliates their injuries; yet may occasionally fall out with them.

"Chooses as his friends the talented, intellectual and literary, and avoids the ignorant.

"Is extremely fond of travelling. Has an insatiable desire to roam about and see the world and afterwards to settle down.

"Is patriotic and ready to sacrifice all in defence of his country.

"May get angry quickly, but, unless the injury is deep or intended, cannot retain his anger.

"Will be more likely to make a general than a critical scholar. May have bold and original ideas upon a variety of subjects, yet will not without effort or excitement have a train of connected thoughts upon any.

"Is qualified to meet difficulties, overcome obstacles, endure hardships, contend for privileges, maintain opinions, resent insults and defend his rights to the last; generally takes sides on every contested question; naturally hasty in temper.

"Desires money more as a means than as an end, more for its uses than to lay up; and pays too little attention to small sums.

"Generally keeps his thoughts, feelings, plans, etc., to himself. Will effect his purposes indirectly and without detection. May sometimes communicate his feelings to his nearest friends, yet will seldom do this, and will exercise more attachment than he expresses. May restrain for a long time the anger which is burning in his bosom; yet when he does give vent to it, it will blaze forth in good earnest. Is slow in commencing, yet when once interested in any project pushes it with great spirit. May be timid and fearful until his courage is once excited, but will then be bold and fearless. In cases of danger, will be perfectly self-possessed; and yet will have fore-thought enough to do just what the occasion demands. Cannot soon be worked up to the sticking point; but is determined, if not desperate, when once kindled.

"Is inclined to enter largely into business and to push his projects with so much energy and zeal as to appear rash and nearly destitute of caution; yet will come out about right in the end and will seldom fail entirely in his projects, though he may be obliged to retrace his steps."

This "phrenological examination," tested by what others can remember of him at that period and by the traits shown later in life, must be regarded, so far as it goes, as a fairly accurate presentation of the boy's chief characteristics. But this should not be set down to phrenology, for there is nothing to show that he placed particular confidence, or even had more than passing interest, in that teaching.[1] Nor is it to be set down as a lucky kind of guess about himself. It is in truth, more than anything else, the fruit of a habit of introspection which had begun about the time of the return from the first sea voyage and which was afterwards to be shown more and more strongly.

Meanwhile the little *Shubrick* was boldly pushing her way down the coast. This was her first trip in commission, Henry George having seen her building in the Philadelphia Navy Yard that very year. She was named after Rear Admiral William B. Shubrick, of the U. S. Navy, who had been Chairman of the Light-House Board since 1852. She was to become the first vessel on light-house duty on the Pacific coast, to which service she was now proceeding; and the first tender under steam in the light-house department of the United States. She was of 372 tons burden, 140 feet in length, 22 feet in beam and 19 feet in depth of hold; with black hull, red side-wheels, black funnel and two masts, the foremast square rigged. She looked as sharp and trim as a yacht, but, as in addition to her regular duties of supplying light-houses and maintaining the buoyage along the west coast, she was intended to give protection to government property along

---

[1] Thirty years later, when his son, Richard, manifested interest in phrenology, Henry George discouraged him, saying that though indirectly or collaterally there probably was truth in it, the subject was one that, in his opinion, Nature did not intend to have man know much about, since the discovery of constitutional characteristics would with most men seem to indicate foreordination, and checking free and independent action, would tend to produce fatalism. Moreover, he said, phrenology was not needed for man's progress, for *that* did not depend upon a knowledge of the relative development of the faculties, but rather upon the *use* of the faculties, whatever they might be.

the sea shore of Oregon and Washington from the depredations of Indian tribes, she was armed with six brass
guns and a novel contrivance for squirting scalding water
on the redskins when at close quarters.

On Christmas day, while the *Shubrick* was steaming
along over a sun-kissed sea some distance off the Hatteras
coast, the wind, which had been fair, subsided, and then
without warning rose into a white squall, blowing from
the north-east. The boat's head was swung around and
she was brought to under low-steam. At night the wind
blew a hurricane, the sea breaking over her fore and aft
with great violence. The after part of the wheelhouse,
engineer's storeroom and starboard bulwarks were stove
in, and everything movable on deck washed overboard,
including port shutters, harness-casks, deck engine, and
spare spars and lumber. At ten that night, deeming that
she was in danger of foundering, thirty tons of sacked
coal and some other things were thrown overboard.[1]
Many times during his life Henry George spoke of the
terrors of this storm, on one occasion[2] saying:

> "A negro deckhand and I worked together throwing
> over bags of coal to lighten her. The sailing master
> hung on the bridge shouting to us through the speak-
> ing trumpet and barely able to make himself heard,
> as he told us the work we were doing was for life or
> death."

This relieved the vessel and at day-light she was enabled to proceed on her course, nine days after leaving

---

[1] Notes from record of *Shubrick*, by courtesy of the U. S. Light-
House Board at Washington, D. C., and of Captain Geo. W. Coffin,
U. S. N., Inspector 12th Light-House District, San Francisco, Cal.

[2] From shorthand notes by Ralph Meeker of a conversation, New York,
October, 1897.

Philadelphia putting into St. Thomas, West Indies, to
renew her coal supply and make necessary repairs.

To Jo Jeffreys, his young friend in Philadelphia,
Henry George sent from St. Thomas a clear account of
the passage and of the danger the ship had been in; but
to his parents, under same date (January 6, 1858), he
wrote in quite different style to save them from anxiety,
omitting all mention of danger. The letter to his parents
read:

"Here I am this winter's afternoon (while you are
gathering around the parlour stove, perhaps thinking
and talking of me) sitting in the open air in my white
sleeves almost roasted by the heat. I wish you could
view the scene which surrounds me. The noble mountains rising from the water, covered with perpetual vege-
tation of the tropics and varied in colour by the shad-
ows of the clouds which seem to climb their sides; the
little town with its square red-roofed, Dutch houses
and white forts, surrounded by the palm and cocoanut
trees which line the head of the bay; the ships and
steamers which deck the harbour; and the boundless
sea stretching away to the edge of the horizon, glittering in the sunlight—form a picture which I know you
would enjoy.

"Now that I have tried to give you a faint idea of
the scenery that surrounds me, I shall try and give you
an account of our passage.

"We had head winds and a rough sea most of the time;
and as the steamer was very slow, the spray which in-
cessantly flew over her made the deck very wet and, consequently, unpleasant. However, we made the run in
nine days from the time we left the breakwater and
arrived here early on Saturday morning.

"I went ashore last Sunday and attended church, and
then together with Jim Stanley (the young fellow who
I told you was going out as Engineer's Store Keeper)
climbed the mountain to the ruins of the castle of
Blackbeard, a notorious pirate chieftain, who for a

long time made this island his home and stronghold. After coming down, we wandered all over the town and saw all that was to be seen, which I suppose is the same as in the generality of West Indian islands—plenty of darkies—men, women and children—bamboo shanties, soldiers and cocoanut trees. . . .

"I expect our next passage to be much more pleasant than the last, as we shall not be heavily burdened by coal, and important additions have been made in the shape of booby-hatches, etc. . . .

"I know, my dear parents, that you felt deeply the parting with me—far more so than I did. But let the fact that I am satisfied and that my chances are more than fair comfort you. As for me, I, for the first time in my life, left home with scarcely a regret and without a tear. I believed that it was my duty both to myself and to you to go, and this belief assuaged the pain of parting.

"I am now setting out for myself in the world, and though young in years, I have every confidence in my ability to go through whatever may be before me. But of that I shall say nothing. Let the future alone prove."

In reply to the letter he received from St. Thomas, Jo Jeffreys wrote (February 1):

"While such fools and intolerable dolts as James McMullen[1] live, it is almost impossible to expect your family to be kept ignorant of your great danger. I will elucidate the matter. Some few days since a telegraphic despatch (from Boston, I think) appeared in the 'Pub-

---

[1] "Jim" McMullen, as he was commonly called, was regarded by his boy friends as slow of comprehension. One day wishing to go swimming without McMullen, they tried the expedient of telling him one after another that his head was swollen and that he must be sick. This succeeded so well that the boy went home and to bed in a fever of excite. ment, and they had great difficulty in convincing him that they had been deluding him. The experience so frightened Henry George that he never again indulged in that kind of a practical joke.

lic Ledger' setting forth that the U. S. S. *Shubrick* had
put into St. Thomas in great distress, want of coal, etc.,
etc. This I presumed somewhat alarmed your mother;
but she received your letter about the same time, and
you saying nothing of any storm, but merely mentioning
rough weather encountered in the Gulf, she thought no
more of it. But here McMullen steps in on last Saturday night (he called once before since your departure)
and after propounding several knotty interrogatories to
your father, very kindly informed your mother that he
had seen an extract from a private letter written by
one of the *Shubrick's* engineers to a friend in this city
in the 'Evening Journal' (or as Collis says, the 'Evening Disturber') the purport of which was that the
Shubrick had encountered a terrific storm, that they
almost went down, etc., etc.

"I happened to call in a few minutes after and was
subjected to a series of questions which made me wince.
I had received a letter from you? Yes. Well, what
did you say? You said you were well and in good
spirits. Was that all? Yes, about all. I was sorry
to say I had left the letter at the office. (It was in the
breast-pocket of my coat.) Did you say anything about
a storm? (This question was propounded by your
mother, who looked me straight in the eye, while Cad,
Janie and Kate followed her example, and your father,
who was reclining on the sofa, turned round to hear
the answer, which, with this awful battery of unflinch-
ing eyes in front, and the consciousness that your father
might have some information upon the subject which
he designed to level at me in the rear, I was endeavouring to manufacture into as ingenious a shape as possible. They looked at me; I returned the gaze as steadily as an honest fellow who knew he was going to
dissimulate for the sake of an absent friend—but an awful bad fellow—could do. At last I broke silence.) *No.*
You had said, however, that you had encountered rough
weather and had got out of coal. (My hair almost
stood on end, and the perspiration rolled in mad tor-
rents down the exterior covering of my seething brain.)

To this succeeded a number of questions that tortured me almost to martyrdom, for, as you know, my very bowels *yearned* to tell the truth. I, however, satisfied your mother that the 'Evening Disturber' had made false representations, and so ends that difficulty.

" . . . You are right, Hen. 'There never was any affectation of sentiment in speech between us when face to face,' and none shall exist now. How do *you* know that we shall never meet again? I should be obliged to you if you would *not* send such letters to me in the middle of business—letters which are calculated to distract my mind and render me as weak as a child. Your ideas absolutely make me gloomy, truth though they be. You know I love you, Hen, as much *as any-one* in this wide world. . . .

"I have commenced to reform, and Bill Jones and myself have for some time been studying geometry together. I spend but little, 37 cents a week on cigars, and loaf only occasionally. I go to the office sometimes in the evening and study law. Bill and I are to take up natural philosophy and grammar in a few days."

The father's letter soon after the departure of the *Shubrick* shows the man's robust nature.

"My dear boy, we have missed you. I have hardly become reconciled to your absence. It seems that I cannot lock the front door without the thought of your coming in; and when the boys visit us—Jeffreys, Jones and the others—it seems as if it leaves a blank when we find you absent. Don't think I regret the step you have taken. On the contrary, the more I think of it, the more I see the hand of Providence in it. . . .

"Nothing has transpired since you left worthy of note. Things are much as you left them. The times are rather on the mend [industrially]. In political matters things look gloomy. The nigger question, Mor-

monism and General Walker,[1] etc., will, I think, give us
trouble; but notwithstanding all this and as much more,
the Union is and will be safe as long as there is bunt-
ing to make stars and stripes. They may bluster North,
East, South and West as much as they please. Our
nation is in the hands and under the guidance of a
higher Power, who created this republic for a higher and
holier destiny, which is not revealed, and will not be
until I am long gathered to my fathers."

From St. Thomas to Barbadoes and thence to Pernam-
buco and Rio Janeiro the little *Shubrick* proceeded, having fair weather and making fair time. A letter written
at Monte Video to one of the young friends in Philadelphia (Charley Walton, February 18) gives some characteristic notes:

"We arrived here yesterday morning after a passage
of five days from Rio. We lay five days in the latter
port and had very fine weather and a pleasant time
generally, marred only by one or two little accidents.
. . .   The first night we stayed there all hands went
ashore, wandered over the island, and as a matter of
course, got drunk. A couple of the men in trying to
come aboard fell over a precipice about forty feet in
height. One escaped uninjured, but the other was
nearly killed. He is now recovering fast, but it will
be some time before his arm, which was broken, will
be entirely healed.

"I enjoyed myself very well while we were coaling,
wandering along the rocks, catching crabs and toad-

---

[1] Probably a reference to William Walker of Tennessee, who led a filibustering expedition into Lower California and was driven out. Then he
went to Nicaragua, C. A., assumed the title of President of that State,
and re-established chattel slavery, which had been abolished. He was
driven from power in May, 1857, but escaped to New Orleans. In 1860
he led a filibustering expedition against Honduras, but within four
months was captured and shot at Truxillo.

fish and paddling from one island to another in a canoe, the exact model of the famous one constructed by Crusoe, and like his, made of a single piece.

"I was ashore in Rio but once—on Sunday afternoon—and saw but little of the town, as it was too infernally hot to walk the narrow streets."

The chief incident of the voyage—an event of singular nature—occurred at the port of Monte Video. Two letters containing a brief mention of it have been preserved, but a full and graphic account appeared under the title of "Dust to Dust" in a sketch written by Henry George eight years subsequently and when he was less than twenty-seven, at the request of his friend Edmund Wallazz, for publication in the "Philadelphia Saturday Night,"[1] a prosperous weekly paper, of which Wallazz was then foreman and part owner.

The story in substance is this. An hour after leaving Rio, yellow fever had broken out on the *Shubrick* and several were taken down. All recovered except the Second Assistant Engineer, S. W. Martin, a popular young man on board.

"The crisis seemed past, and if his strength would only last until he neared the Cape, all would be well. . . . Only one port remained to be passed before we should hail the rain and fog, and strength-giving winds —Monte Video. But when we entered that great stream, more sea than river, the mighty La Plata, on which the city is situated, young Martin was dying. . . .

"For some time in intervals of consciousness, Martin had been aware of his approaching end, and the only thing that seemed to trouble him was the idea of dying so far from those he loved, and of being buried where

---

[1] This sketch on the following month, July 14, 1866, was republished in the San Francisco "Californian," conducted by some printer friends of Henry George.

affection might never mark his resting place. It was his last and earnest request that his grave might be made on shore, where his body could be recognised by his friends, and not committed to the waves; and though it was very doubtful if the privilege could be granted, yet the captain resolved to take the corpse into the harbour, and try to obtain permission to bury it ashore.

"And when night came, sadly we talked in little groups upon the deck, while the sound of hammer and plane from the gangway, told that the 'last house' of one of us was being built. Though no star shed its light, still it was not all blackness. The 'river of silver' beamed with a lustre of its own. Not alone the furrows our prow threw aside, or the broad wake we left behind, but the whole surface of the water glowed with phosphorescent brightness, and we seemed to force our way through a sheet of molten silver.

"All night long we steamed up the river, and when the sun again arose—it showed us the harbour of Monte Video. Out beyond all the other shipping lay a stately frigate, the Stars and Stripes of the great republic streaming from her peak in the morning breeze—the old *St. Lawrence*, flagship of the squadron. . . . We were bringing them news and letters from home, and every port of the great ship thronged with faces eager to see the comer from the land they loved. Running up under her quarter, we were hailed and answered, and after the usual inquiries, our captain mentioned the death of young Martin, and his wish to have him buried on shore; but was told that it was impossible, that we would infringe the quarantine rules by even entering the port with the corpse; and was directed to steam back some miles and commit the body to the waves, before entering the harbour.

"The shrill whistle of the boatswain sounded; a boat dropped from the frigate's davits, reached our side, took letters and papers, and our little steamer turned slowly round to retrace her path. We had felt sad while coming up, but a darker gloom hung over all while going down the river. It seemed so hard that the last and only request of the poor boy could not be complied with.

"But swiftly down the current in the bright, fresh morning dashed our little boat, and when the lofty frigate was hull-down behind us, we turned and stopped for the last sad rites.

"Upon the quarter-deck, in reverential silence, all hands were gathered. The large box-like coffin, in which we had hoped to commit our dead to mother earth, bored full of holes and filled up with heavy materials, was placed by the side, covered with the flag. The beautiful burial service was commenced, its solemn sentences sounding doubly solemn under such mournful circumstances—there was a pause—then came the words, 'We, therefore, commit his body to the deep!' and with a surge the waves closed above the dead.

"Hardly a word was spoken as the wheels again took up their task, and we began to ascend the river, but every eye was fixed on the spot we were leaving, and at the same instant an exclamation sprang from every lip as the coffin was seen to rise! The engine was quickly stopped, a boat lowered, and taking a small anchor and some heavy chain, they tried to secure and sink the box. But it was no easy task in the fresh breeze and short, chopping sea, and the coffin seemed almost instinct with life and striving to elude their efforts. Again and again they were foiled in their attempt to fasten the weights, but were at last successful, and once more the water closed above the corpse.

"After waiting some time, to make sure that it could not float again, we started once more up the river, and this time awe was mingled with our grief. Most men who follow the sea have a touch of superstition. There is something in the vastness with which Nature presents herself upon the great waters which influences in this direction even minds otherwise sceptical. And as we steamed up the river, it was more than hinted among many of us that the strong desire of the dying man had something to do with the difficulty of sinking his body.

"This time we passed the frigate, saluting, but not stopping, and entered the port. It was war time; on the Pampas some phase of the interminable quarrels of this Southern federation was being fought out, and the harbour was crowded with men-of-war. Nearly all the Brazilian navy was there, watching the progress of events; and besides these, and the numerous merchantmen, the ensign of almost every nation was displayed above some armed vessel. By direction of the officer who boarded us, we proceeded past them all, to the farther side of the harbour, where we were ordered to lie in quarantine seven days before being allowed to coal.

"The new scene, the various objects of interest around and the duties of clearing up, conspired to make us forget the events of the morning, but the sun was yet some distance above the western horizon when a startling circumstance occurred to recall them to our minds.

"Nearly all hands were busily engaged below, only two or three loitering around the deck, when the quartermaster, sweeping the harbour with his glass, noticed something floating in, which riveted his attention. Again and again he looked at it; then, with surprise and dismay in his face, called the officer of the deck. The whisper spread through the ship, and in a few minutes all were watching in silence the object that seemed drifting towards us. Onward it came, through all the vessels that lay beyond us—now lost to our view, now coming in sight again—turning and tacking as though piloted by life, and steadily holding its course for our steamer. It passed the last ship, and came straight for us. It came closer, and every doubt was dispelled—it was, indeed, the coffin! A thrill of awe passed through every heart as the fact became assured.

"Right under our bows came the box; it touched our side; halted a moment, as if claiming recognition, and then drifted slowly past us towards the shore.

"There was an excited murmur forward, a whispered consultation in the knot of officers aft; then one advanced—'Man the quarter boat, boys; take pick and spades; tow the coffin ashore, and bury the body!'

"It was the work of a moment—the boat shot like an arrow from our side, the ashen oars bending with the energy of the stroke. Reverently and gently they secured the box, and with slow, solemn strokes, towed it to the foot of the desolate looking hill that skirts the bay. There, breaking it open, they bore the corpse, covered with the flag, a little distance up the hillside, and making in the twilight a grave among the chaparral, laid it to rest, marking the spot with a rude cross, which, concealed from observation by the bushes, would yet serve as a mark of recognition, and secure the grave, should it be noticed, from the intrusion of vandal hands. "And so, spite of all, that dying wish was gratified, and the body which the waters refused to receive was laid to rest in its mother earth."[1]

From Monte Video the *Shubrick* proceeded to the Strait of Magellan, arriving at Cape Virgin on March 6; for instead of taking the long route followed by sailing vessels around Cape Horn, she was to steam by the short route through the strait. The heavy westerly winds and strong currents peculiar to that region made such boisterous weather that progress was greatly retarded and nearly all the coal consumed, so that the crew had to go ashore and cut fire-wood with which to make the next port.[2] To his family Henry George has described the scenery in the western part of the strait as perhaps the most magnificent and impressive he ever beheld.

"The water was clear and green with depth even up to the banks, which in places were sheer walls of rock running up perhaps three thousand feet and mantled at their summits with dazzling snow. In the valleys between these and the mountains beyond were glacial formations, white and green and iridescent; and at the bases where the land flattened out, were heavy growths of evergreens.

---

[1] If Mr. George had any superstitious feeling at the time regarding the matter — and there is nothing to indicate that he had — he certainly did not continue to entertain it in after years, but believed the movements of the coffin due to the accidental loosening of weights, peculiarities of currents and other natural causes.

[2] '*Shubrick's* log.

"Being short of fuel, we brought the little steamer against a bank, and tieing her there, went ashore and cut wood. This consumed a number of days. We ran into a little harbour in the strait and came upon a schooner which belonged to English missionaries with whom we exchanged letters. The missionaries were praying and working with the native Terra del Fuegians. We saw a number of these natives, and they were not at all attractive. I heard afterwards that the Patagonians killed and ate these missionaries."

On the passage up the Pacific coast the *Shubrick* touched at Valdivia, Valparaiso, Panama, and San Diego, and on the 27th of May, 1858, after a voyage of one hundred and fifty-five days from Philadelphia, arrived at San Francisco.

CHAPTER V.

AT THE FRAZER RIVER GOLD FIELDS.

1858.   AGE, 19

WHEN the *Shubrick* glided through the Golden Gate and cast anchor, it was with mixed emotions that Henry George gazed about him. California, bursting on the world ten years before with her astonishing gold discoveries, had now begun to reveal to the prospectors who found that the mineral regions had meanwhile been occupied, a new wealth of soil in her amazing agricultural fecundity. She had now been for eight years a State in the Union, and had a population of about three hundred and fifty thousand, of which her chief city, San Francisco, claimed some fifty thousand.

Like a new Eternal City, San Francisco nestled upon a cluster of hills. These hills rose on a narrow spur or peninsula, washed on the west by the ocean and on the east by the bay; and on the north formed one portal of the Golden Gate. The bell in the little pioneer adobe church of the missionary Franciscan monks still tinkled at the "Mission Dolores," and though many substantial buildings had arisen since the entrance on Statehood, the city for the most part still consisted of "cloth and paper shanties." The whole world was sending the flower of youth and energy into the new city; and to the young and bold and adventurous of spirit, San Francisco, for all her newness and roughness, wore a charm, and even fascination, that only they could understand. Should Oregon fail, this, to Henry George, seemed the place to seek his fortune.

He had expected on reaching San Francisco to find a letter from Mrs. Curry telling him of the Oregon prospects, and perhaps inviting him to come up. When a letter came to hand, several days after his arrival, it contained no information on this subject and gave no counsel, and to it he replied (May 29, 1858):

"About an hour after we dropped anchor my cousin, Jim George, came on board. I went ashore with him and spent the day. He has his family here and is doing well. Although we have been here but a short time, yet I have already seen a good deal of the city and agree with Emma that 'it is a dashing place,' rather faster than Philadelphia.

"My mind is not fully made up as to what I shall do. I should feel grateful for your advice. Please write to me as soon as possible. If you still think I can do well in Oregon I will go up as soon as I can procure my discharge from the ship, which I hope to do in two or three weeks. I do not think I shall remain where I am at present, as I wish to settle down as soon as possible; and the old Oregon fever has not entirely died, as you may judge from the fact that I write from San Francisco. I have worked hard and long to get here and have at last succeeded, and I feel convinced that the same spirit will carry me through."

The "Cousin Jim George" referred to was son of Henry's Uncle Dunkin, his father's only brother. James George was book-keeper for the retail clothing firm of J. M. Strowbridge & Co., doing business at Commercial and Sansome streets, and composed of Jerome and W. C.

Strowbridge and E. F. Childs. Childs had a young brother-in-law there named George B. Wilbur, a Rhode Island
Yankee, who had gone to California with the hope shared
by almost everyone going there—of finding a fortune.
Wilbur and Henry George became acquainted, and Wilbur showed the newcomer around town; thereby beginning
a friendship that was to be of mutual use in the near
years, and though their aptitude and careers became distinct, was to last to the end of life.

And now since the prizes ashore seemed large and many
for him who was free and could move quickly, young
George had resolved not only not to remain at sea, but
not even to embrace the prospect of a place in the Navy
Yard at the head of the bay, which Commander DeCamp,
who expected to be stationed there, had talked of helping
him to get. Though he had no fixed plans, yet it was
the boy's wish to be free, and free at once. The obstacle
was the *Shubrick's* shipping articles, which he, like everyone else on board, had been compelled to sign at Philadelphia for one year's service, and which would hold him
until November 11, 1858. He talked the thing over with
Ellen George, James George's wife, a warm-hearted, sympathetic woman, who showed a lively interest in the youth's
affairs. It was agreed that he should go into retirement
for awhile, seeking the seclusion of a bed at her house,
while she should confer with Commander De Camp, which
she did. The Commander, as a consequence, failed to
notice the absence of the boy, who, after a short season
of this retirement, regarded himself as free of the
Shubrick[1] and at liberty to go where he would. But as yet

---

[1] Though the *Shubrick's* record shows that later on there were a
number of desertions among the officers and crew of the vessel, there is
no indication whatever as to when Henry George left, or that he did not
remain until the expiration of his term of service — Nov. 11, 1858.

no word of encouragement came from Oregon; nor in San Francisco, though he looked about him, did any inviting opening appear, so that he was left in idleness, consuming his little store of money consisting of wages earned on the *Shubrick*. All the while letters were coming from home which yet had a strong influence over him. From his mother (April 3, 1858):

"There is nothing stirring or startling in this great city. Religion seems to be the all-engrossing subject. Christians are looking for great results from this outpouring of the Spirit. Look to Jesus, my dear child."

From his mother (May 3):

"O my dear boy: how much you occupy my thoughts. Sleeping and waking your whereabouts, your doings, your comfort, your conduct, your prospects and a thousand other things fill my mind. Away from all you love and those who love you and would counsel you, O seek, my child, that wisdom that cometh from above. Then you will need no other counsellor."

From his father (May 18):

"We have accounts to-day that Brigham Young, the Mormon scamp, has submitted to the United States authority and that forces are entering Salt Lake City. I hope it may be true. I should like to see him punished for his rebellion."

From his Sister Jennie (June 3):

"I dreamed of you, Henry, not long ago for three nights in succession, and I thought each night that you had returned home. I thought I came home from school and saw you sitting in the rocking chair in the front parlour. I ran to you and just as you kissed me I woke up. I was glad that I was in time for the kiss anyhow."

The same intense affection that Henry George kindled in the friends of his manhood was shown for him by the friends of his youth. The evidence of this on the part of Jeffreys we have already seen.[1] A letter from Jennie George (July 2) tells about Charlie Walton:

"Charlie Walton came around the other evening. . . . He said that you had written four or five letters to Jo Jeffreys and but one to him. I never saw him in such a rage. He really almost cried. I pacified him as much as I could and he went away a little cooler than he came. I really believe he thinks more of you than any of the other boys."

This from Edmund Wallazz who had been a printer in King and Baird's and who was now a man of about twenty-seven (July 15):

"Your letters dated the 15 and 19 ult., received this morning. . . .
"To understand my feeling of a peculiar relation existing between us I will mention the feelings which I experienced when we first heard of the yellow fever on board the *Shubrick*. Jeffreys told me of the report and of your father's fears near midnight of a day, I think, in the latter part of February or the early part of March. I was at first stunned; a cold, chilly sensation overpowered me for a few minutes; but after awhile I said, with an earnestness which made Jeffreys look surprised: 'Harry is not dead. If he were I should know it.' He asked if I believed in ghosts. Of course not, in the vulgar idea of ghosts. And yet I felt certain

[1] Page 61.

that if you were dead I should be informed of it. Nay, more. So strong was this feeling that for several days I sat alone in the dark at midnight waiting for you. And in those hours of terrible suspense how cften did I think of your probable death, and picture your poor body tossed about by the billows of the Southern Atlantic, far, far from all who loved you! Firmly, I believe, if you had been dead, and if you had come to me, I would not have been frightened at all, only awe-struck, and it may be heart-wrung, by the thought that my advice had much to do with your going. But let this rest forever now. You cannot doubt my love; I cannot doubt yours."

But now Henry George was ready to act. For in June had come the thrilling news of large gold discoveries just over the American line, in the British possessions, on the Frazer River, not far from its mouth. There was much excitement in San Francisco, especially among that multitude of prospectors and adventurers, who, finding all the then known placer lands in California worked out or appropriated, and not willing to turn to the slow pursuits of agriculture, had gathered in the city with nothing to do. A mad scramble for the new fields ensued, and so great was the rush from this and other parts that fifty thousand persons are said to have poured into the Frazer River region within the space of a few weeks. Indeed, all who did not have profitable or promising employment tried to get away, and the *Shubrick's* log shows that most of her officers and crew deserted for the gold fields.[1]

---

[1] "There is no mystery as to the cause which so suddenly and so largely raised wages in California in 1849, and in Australia in 1852. It was the discovery of placer mines in unappropriated land to which labour was free that raised the wages of cooks in San Francisco restaurants to $500 a month, and left ships to rot in the harbour without officers or crew until their owners would consent to pay rates that in any other part of the

James George was doing well with the San Francisco clothing house, but caught in the gold excitement, he thought he saw a chance for a fortune in the sale of miner's supplies; and he formed a co-partnership with O. F. Giffin, of San Francisco, a dealer in nuts, dried fruits, etc., doing business on Front Street, between Sacramento and Clay. The agreement was that James was to go to Victoria, on Vancouver's Island, just off the mouth of the Frazer, and open a miner's supply store.

This project of James George's had much attractiveness for Henry George, but he resolved to be cautious and not venture on reports that might prove to be false. To Martha Curry, who now had become Mrs. Malthrop, he wrote (June 29) :

"I have left the steamer I came out in and am now staying at the same house as my cousin. In all probability I will be able to get employment of some kind in a few days. I think I shall stay here until next spring, and then, if the diggings on Frazer River turn out to be as good as reported, I shall go up there. . . .

"Messrs. Byron and Pipe are both well, though rather the worse for their long journey and long handling."

A few days following this came a letter from Mrs. Curry (July 9) that ended all present thought of Oregon and increased that of the Frazer River. "As for this place," wrote she, "business is dull. The mines seem to be the all-absorbing theme." So with hope of Oregon closed and with no chance of work offering in San Francisco, the

---

globe seemed fabulous. Had these mines been on appropriated land, or had they been immediately monopolised so that rent could have arisen, it would have been land values that would have leaped upward, not wages." — "Progress and Poverty," Book V. chap. ii (Memorial Edition, p. 290).

young man found himself urged along the line of his inclinations—toward the Frazer; and with the promise from his cousin James of employment as clerk in the store, should he fail at the diggings, Henry George's hopes burned high and he wrote home of golden expectations. But the news of his starting for Victoria carried something like dismay to the quiet home in Philadelphia. His mother wrote (August 15):

"I think this money-getting is attended with too many sacrifices. I wished it all in the bottom of the sea when I heard of your going to Victoria, but since it has been explained to me I feel better. . . . I shall never feel comfortable until you are settled down quietly at some permanent business. This making haste to grow rich is attended with snares and temptations and a great weariness of the flesh. It is not the whole of life, this getting of gold. When you write explain about the place and how you are situated. Then we will look on the bright side."

A month later (September 18) she wrote:

"We all feel happy and thankful that you have arrived safely at Victoria and that your prospects appear bright. Don't be too anxious or too sanguine. This making haste to be rich I am afraid of. Remember you are but young. We do not expect great things as yet. You have just passed your nineteenth birthday. Did you think of it, or were you too busy? If you had been home we would have had a jollification. What a kissing time there would have been, playing Copenhagen and so forth. Hen, kissing is quite out of the fashion since you left; no kissing parties at all, I believe."

His father in the same letter wrote:

"Your letter from Victoria came safe to hand and you may be sure we were glad to receive it. I had become quite anxious about you, inasmuch that your last letter gave us the information that you were off on a trading expedition. I did not know how you would be situated, but now I feel more reconciled and think that your chances are fair. But I hope you will not build your castle in the air. Fortunes are not to be made in a hurry; it takes time and application. However, I say again, your prospects are fair. Nurse your means and use all the economy you can and I think in the end a fortune will be sure. Still, my dear son, consider; contentment is better than both hands full with labour and travel."

Henry George, working his way as seaman on a top-sail schooner, reached Victoria when the excitement was at the flood. That place, established in 1843 as a trading-fort of the Hudson Bay Company—those pioneers of commerce through the north-western part of the continent—and beautifully situated on Vancouver's Island in the majestic Puget Sound, had, with the gold discoveries, suddenly swelled in population, until it was estimated that at times ten thousand miners, in sheds and tents, gathered about the more substantial structures.

Henry George arrived at Victoria when the river, still at the season that rains and melting snows on its great mountain water-sheds swelled high its volume, came tearing down its long, twisting course and rushed through its rocky gorges like a roaring flood of destruction, earning the name sometimes given it—"The Terrible Frazer." The gold had been found at Yale and Fort Hope, a hundred miles up stream, in the exposed bars and the bed of the river when the water was low, so that with the water in flood, all gold-seeking operations had to come to a stand-still and there was nothing to do but to wait until the water had subsided. The young fortune hunter, therefore, went into James George's store.

The store was in a rough wooden structure of one story and an attic, or rather loft. It stood on Wharf Street, beside the Victoria hotel, facing the harbour. Henry George worked very hard there. Part of the time he slept in the loft, reaching it by a ladder. He fastened a note outside the street door inviting customers who came out of the regular hours to "Please give this door a kick." In a letter to his Sister Jennie subsequently from San Francisco (December 6, 1858) he said:

"You innocently ask whether I made my own bed at Victoria. Why, bless you, my dear little sister! I had none to make. Part of the time I slept rolled up in my blanket on the counter, or on a pile of flour, and afterwards I had a straw mattress on some boards. The only difference between my sleeping and waking costumes was that during the day I wore both boots and cap, and at night dispensed with them."

But the full picture of his condition was not at once revealed to the folks at home. He had on starting for Victoria written of such large expectations that pride now prevented him from saying more than he could help about the poor results. Jo Jeffreys wrote (October 3):

"There is one remarkable thing in your letters, or rather *not* in your letters, which is this, that you fail to say whether you are prospering *at all* in your present business, or even if it supports you, and which I certainly should be glad to hear."

From his Sister Carrie (October 4):

"How I should like to see you in your new situation. Your account of your cooking is quite laughable. I should just like to look in upon you while you were thus engaged and see what kind of a cook you make."

His father wrote him a letter containing worldly wisdom (October 4):

"We have all sorts of things going on here in Philadelphia. On the first of September we had the grand Ocean Telegraph celebration, though the cable has never spoken since, and I have great doubts that it ever will. Yet a great thing has been accomplished; or at any rate, if the practicability of a lightning rod through the ocean be not accomplished in my day, it will be in yours.

"Uncle Joseph Van Dusen took dinner with us yesterday. He seems much pleased with your present prospects and bade me when I wrote to say that if this thing should be successful their house would be glad to send you a load of goods direct which would cost much less than at San Francisco. About that I do not know—I mean as regards cheapness. You know Uncle Joseph and his partners. Show them where they can invest safely and profitably and they have the means and the nerve. This information may in the future, if this thing succeeds, be of great advantage to James and yourself. Recollect old John Sharp's advice: 'When thee makes a friend use him and keep him.'

"We are all well. Tom [one of Henry's brothers] is just promoted in school and is making very good progress. He is sharp, and will, if spared, make a smart and active man. I don't think I told you of his Fourth of July speech at dinner. When we were about half through Tom rose and said: 'Ladies and Gentlemen: This is the first time in my life that I have sat down to a Fourth of July dinner without ice-cream. I will, therefore, put the question. All who are in favour of ice-cream will please say, aye.' Of course it was unanimously carried, to the joy of all present. After he found it so, he very gracefully turned to me, saying: 'It is carried unanimously, Mr. Chairman. Will you please advance the money?' I could not get out of this, and put up fifty cents, which proved to be satisfactory."

Ferdinand Formhals, now a well-known citizen of San Francisco, who had charge of a stove and tinware store beside James George's store on Wharf Street, Victoria, says that he knew Henry George there, and that "George had nothing to say about the single tax or political economy then." Yet that the youth's mind was even then quietly at work is proved by a speech he made in San Francisco thirty-two years later:[1]

> "Let me, since I am in San Francisco, speak of the genesis of my own thought. I came out here at an early age, and knew nothing whatever of political economy. I had never intently thought upon any social problem. One of the first times I recollect talking on such a subject was one day, when I was about eighteen, after I had come to this country, while sitting on the deck of a topsail schooner with a lot of miners on the way to the Frazer River. We got talking about the Chinese, and I ventured to ask what harm they were doing here, if, as these miners said, they were only working the cheap diggings? 'No harm now,' said an old miner, 'but wages will not always be as high as they are to-day in California. As the country grows, as people come in, wages will go down, and some day or other white men will be glad to get those diggings that the Chinamen are now working.' And I well remember how it impressed me, the idea that as the country grew in all that we are hoping that it might grow, the condition of those who had to work for their living must become, not better, but worse."

But now something caused a falling out between the cousins. What the trouble was does not appear, though in after years Henry George said that he had "behaved badly towards Jim George." The offence could not have been grave, as they were on the old friendly terms soon again in San Francisco. But however this may be, Henry

---

[1] Metropolitan Hall, Feb. 4, 1890.

left James' employ and went to live in a tent with George Wilbur, who had come up from San Francisco to dig gold. Wilbur had since his arrival made an unsuccessful trip up the river, but was determined to try again. Meanwhile he was driving a water cart for a living. Henry George proposed to go up the river with Wilbur, but before they could set off they were daunted by the stories of failure that returning miners were bringing down. While in this wavering state of mind, Ferdinand Formhals gave Henry George information that caused him to abandon the project. Formhals was something of a chemist and had from curiosity been analysing some of the samples of "pure gold from the river" that were being handed about, and found them to be a mixture of tin, lead and other metals. He believed that there was some gold at the diggings, but only a little—not enough to be worth searching for. Time has confirmed Formhals' judgment, comparatively little gold having at any time been taken out of this part of the Frazer River, the really rich deposits being found in the Cariboo region, several hundred miles farther up; but these places were not discovered for a number of years afterwards.

Hope of finding a fortune at the diggings thus closing before him, and having no other employment, and for that matter without prospect of any at Victoria, Henry George decided to return at once to San Francisco, and when there, should no opening offer, to take again to the sea, and keep to it as a calling. With this determination, he borrowed enough money from George Wilbur and others to buy steerage passage down to San Francisco. George Wilbur says of the setting off:

"He had no coat; so I gave him mine. An old fellow named Wolff peddled pies among the tents, and

thinking that Harry would enjoy these more than the
food he would get aboard the ship, we bought six of
them, and as he had no trunk, we put them in his bunk,
and drew the blanket over them so that nobody would
see them and steal them.   He wrote me from San Francisco when he got down that the first night out he was
so tired that he threw himself down on his bunk without undressing, and that he did not think of the pies
until the morning, when he found that he had been
lying on top of them all night."

CHAPTER VI.

TOSSED ABOUT BY FORTUNE.

1858-1859.   AGE, 19-20.

TOWARDS the end of November, 1858, Henry George arrived at San Francisco from Victoria "dead broke." And now commenced a stretch of years notable for a restless pitching about, with shifting scenes of prosperity and adversity—years, though, that showed progress, if irregular and jolting.

This period opened with soft sunshine, for as the impecunious youth walked the streets, meeting only strange faces and getting only rebuffs when he applied for work, and when his mind had again turned to the sea as a means of livelihood, he came face to face with David Bond, a compositor whom he had known at King & Baird's printing house in Philadelphia. Learning of his plight, Bond took him to Frank Eastman's printing office and got him employment to set type. The next letter home breathed of prosperity. To his Sister Jennie (December 6) he said:

> "I am at present working in a printing office and am, therefore, busy all day, and the evenings I spend in reading, unless (as is often the case) I go to see Ellie George.
>
> "After being deprived of reading for such a time,

83

it is quite delightful to be able to read as much as I wish. In the house in which I am stopping there is a good library, which to me is one of its prominent attractions.

"I am glad that you are so nearly through school. How would you like to come out here and teach? Teachers here get very good pay, the lowest—the A, B, C, teachers—getting $50 per month; the principals, $200. Ellie George gets $100 a month. Lady's board costs from $25 to $30 per month.

"Women are sadly wanted here. In Victoria there are hardly any, and you can plainly see the effects of the absence of women on society at large.

"I have few acquaintances either here or in Victoria —I mean boys or men. Don't on any consideration think I have thought of girls, for I haven't seen one to speak to, save those I told you about, since I left Philadelphia. But I suppose in some respects it is much better, as I spend less money.

"I am boarding now, and have been for these past two weeks in the 'What Cheer House,' the largest, if not the finest, hotel in the place. I pay $9 per week and have a beautiful little room and first rate living.

"I get $16 per week the way I am working now, but will soon strike into something that will pay me better. . . .

"I suppose you have all grown somewhat since I left. I have not changed much, except that I am even uglier and rougher looking. You thought I looked hard when I came home from Calcutta, but you should have seen me in Victoria!

"How I should like to be home to-night, if only for an hour or two.

"Give my love and respects to *all*. I would write to them if I wasn't so lazy. (You see I call things by their right names once in a while.)

"So good-bye my *dear* sister. I will write you a longer letter when I feel more like it.

"Your affectionate brother,
"H. GEORGE."

"P. S. Wouldn't that signature look nice at the bottom of a check for $1,000—that is, if I had the money in the bank."

Four years before young George wrote this letter a young man of thirty-two named Ulysses S. Grant had for a short time slept in an attic room in this same hotel, the "What Cheer House." He had come down from Ft. Vancouver, Columbia River, where, utterly disgusted with himself and the life he was leading, he had resigned from a captaincy in the United States Army, and was, when in San Francisco, trying to make his way eastward with a view to going into business or farming. Fame was to claim him in the rapidly approaching events.

The "What Cheer House" still stands and is doing business, though in a humble way. In the fifties it was the best house of its kind in the city. A temperance hotel, and a model of propriety and cleanliness, it was for the accommodation of men entirely. No women were ever received and not one was engaged on the premises. It was established by R. B. Woodward, a New Englander, who from its proceeds founded Woodward's Gardens, famous all over the Pacific Coast for more than two decades as a beautiful pleasure resort, containing a menagerie, a museum, a theatre, an art gallery, an aquarium and a variety of other attractions. One of the distinguishing features of this house was a little library, numbering several hundred volumes, well selected, and among them some economic works. Hon. James V. Coffey, who twelve or fourteen years later became an intimate friend of Henry George's, questioning him as to where he had during his busy life found time and books to read, was told that his solid reading was begun in this little library, while staying at the "What Cheer House" and at intervals following:

"Mr. George told me that he spent much of his time when out of work in that little room and that he had read most of the books. That, he said, was the first place he saw Adam Smith's 'Wealth of Nations,' though I cannot remember that he said he read it then. Indeed, in his last writings, he has said that he did not read a line of Adam Smith until long after this period."

This new state of things gave Richard George, the father, undisguised satisfaction. He wrote (January 19, 1859):

"I rejoice to find that you are doing so well. You now see the propriety of a young man just starting in life having some trade to fall back on in time of need, and you will say, 'Pop was right, not only in this, but in many other things in which I dissented.'

"However, so far God has ordered all things well, and my earnest and sincere prayer is that he may still watch over you until he brings *all* at last to his eternal Kingdom. . . .

"My dear boy, let me say again to you: Be careful and nurse your means; lay up all you can and *owe no man anything* and you will be safe. Do not let others entice you. Act on your own judgment, and I hope and trust before I am called hence, to see you return prosperous and happy, which may God grant."

His mother took up another matter (February 2):

"I am very glad you have left Victoria and have some of the comforts of life, and sorry to hear that Ellen is going there. I should not think that Jim would want her until he could make things more comfortable, and the people were more civilised—better society, a few of her own sex, at least. But this, you say, is what they want—women. Ellen will be a star of the first magnitude. Then I hope she will persuade others to go with her—some that have husbands there. Then there will soon be a better state of things. A writer of great celebrity has said: 'All men that avoid female society have dull perceptions and are stupid, or have gross tastes and revolt against what is pure.' One of the great benefits a man may derive from women's society is that he is bound to be respectful to them. The habit is of great good to your moral man. There is somebody to whom he is bound to be constantly attentive and respectful. Moreover, this elevates and refines him.

"What will you do without Ellen and the children? . . . Have you made no other acquaintances? Is there no other place you visit?"

Jo Jeffreys had a word of advice (February 3):

"After having talked with Ned Wallazz and Billy Jones for some three hours, I turn with great pleasure to the consideration of you, my very respectable and respected friend.

"It was not my purpose to induce you to follow the legal profession, though I think you in every way capable to discharge its responsibilities with honour. I meant by what I said in a former letter to induce you to adopt *some one particular employment* to the exclusion of *every other*. *If you mine,* do so *until* you have succeeded in your object. If you enter a house as clerk, stay at it in God's·name. If you should unfortunately resolve to follow printing, follow it with all your abilities and energy until there shall no longer be any necessity for it. You will allow me to say that your great fault (and I think it is your worst one) is that of half-doing things, *in this sense,* that you vacillate about the execution of that which alone secures permanent success and lasting fame. Few men are competent in *one* lifetime to win honour by more than *one* employment, and these few you would perhaps find were—unlike you —favoured by circumstances.

"Now you are competent for any labour to which your inclinations may direct you. You are not competent to succeed at a dozen employments, nor can you hope to amass a fortune by labouring at them alternately. If you live on as you are doing now, why, *you will live on;* you will earn sufficient to maintain you in comfort, *but that is all.* You can hardly hope by mining one month, by printing the next, and by serving in a clerkship a third, ever to arrive at a competence.

"Why you do this is evident. You are dissatisfied, either because you are not advancing or for trivial reasons, and then you undertake something different. Now you cannot expect to avoid unpleasant things, and you cannot expect to jump on a fortune, like a waif thrown away by a thief in his flight. Success is the reward of long exertion, not the triumph of a momentary energy. It is the crown for which, like Cromwell, you must struggle long and well. It is like happiness hereafter, only to be obtained by patient and continued servitude. . . .

"I wish I could make you feel as I do. You wouldn't then complain in after life (as you *will* do without you adopt my opinions) of the caprice and the wanton vacillation of Fortune's Goddess. . . .

"I recognise the difficulties of your position and how you are situated, and am aware that you are not at liberty to strike out into anything, as you were here. But do the best you can. Take my advice wherever it's possible to do it; I mean that which respects your employment and notwithstanding other embarrassing difficulties."

But notwithstanding Jo Jeffreys' counsel, a change quickly came, for business becoming slack at Eastman's and the other printing houses, George was unable to follow his trade. But refusing to remain idle, he obtained a position of weigher in the rice mill of Waite & Battles, on Fremont Street, near Mission. He wrote home (February 16, 1859):

"I am still in the rice mill and like it very well. I

shall stay, of course, until I am sure I can make a change for the better. I have to get up pretty early though, and consequently retire early. Indeed, you would be pleased to see what regular hours I keep. For months past 10 o'clock has invariably seen me in bed, for I have no friends here, and neither the disposition nor the money to go to the theatre or other places of amusement.

"Everything is still very dull, but the late rains, by increasing the gold yield, will tend to make times better."

Soon after this George Wilbur came down from Victoria and Henry George and he went to room together. First they lived in Natoma Street, then one of the quiet residence portions of the city. Afterwards they roomed on Pine Street, Henry George taking his meals at the "What Cheer House." Mr. Wilbur says of his companion at this period:

"Very soon after our acquaintance I discovered that he was studious and eager to acquire knowledge, and when we came to room together I frequently woke up at night to find him reading or writing. If I said: 'Good heavens, Harry, what's the matter? Are you sick?' he'd tell me to go to sleep or invite me to get dressed and go out for a walk with him. A spin around for a few blocks would do and then we'd get to bed again. I never saw such a restless human being."

That Henry George was in other ways restless was clear enough. His active, energetic nature would doubtless have made him restless anywhere, but in California the conditions were peculiarly conducive to it, for it was a country where thousands of active, independent young men like himself were opening up the richest mineral region in the world; a country which, within twenty years from the first gold discovery in 1848, was to yield $800,-000,000 of the precious metal.[1] "California," he wrote to his Sister Caroline in January, "is sadly in want of missionaries and I think it would be a good notion for the Sunday school to send a few out, provided they be gold-fever proof." As shown by his Frazer River adventure, Henry George himself was not "gold-fever proof"; and now he kept thinking of the stories of fortune that were coming in from the California mines, and he talked with a young Philadelphian, Freeman A. Camp, who came to see him at the "What Cheer House," as to the chances they would have there. His mother, doubtless perceiving what was floating through his mind, wrote (March 3):

"Are you getting lazy? You do not write as long letters as you used to, nor tell us much when you do write. You change your business so often I should think you would have a great deal to tell. Remember, everything that concerns you will interest us. . . . I suppose the old proverb does not apply in California: 'A rolling stone,' etc. Be that as it may, we will rejoice when you are settled."

Two weeks later (March 17) his mother again wrote:

"I am sorry Ellie has left you, though it is all right; she certainly should be with her husband. I hope you have found some acquaintances among her friends, where you can go and spend a social evening. I don't believe in living without society, and least of all female society. And here I know you will have to be careful, for if the women are not of the right stamp, instead of elevating and refining you, they may prove your ruin. I like your early hours, but not your lonely ones. You should have a few good friends. Here, as in all other anxieties concerning you, I can only breathe the prayer: 'My Father, be thou the guide of his youth.'"

---

[1] Hittell's "History of California," Vol. III. p. 160.

But even if her son had the disposition to keep steadily
at work, the rice mill gave indications of temporarily closing down.   In April he wrote to his Sister Caroline:

> "We have not been very busy at the mill lately, ex-
> cept for a day or two at a time; but this does not make
> much difference to me, as I have to stay there whether
> busy or not.   I generally get up about 6 A.M., go to the
> hotel and take breakfast, and from there to the mill.   I
> come up again at about half past six in the evening,
> eat supper, go into the library and read until about 9
> P.M., when I come up to the room and write or think
> for an hour or two and then turn in.   A pretty quiet
> way of living; but there is no telling what will turn
> up next."

And what did "turn up next" was anything but quiet,
for the rice mill closing down, he was thrown out of work,
and he started off into the interior of the State for the
mines.

The day had passed when more than the occasional man
could find some overlooked and unappropriated spot on
river bed or bar, where, with no more equipment than
shovel, pick and pan, he could draw forth any considerable amount of the precious metal.   Though the gold-
bearing region of California, including the northern mines
and the southern mines, extended from Mt. Shasta to Mt.
Whitney and embraced an area approximately as great as
England's territory, every river bank, bar or bed giving
the slightest indication of gold had been worked over and
over.   The nature of mining then became different.
From "wet diggings" in the river channels, operations
had turned to "dry diggings" in arid ravines, hill slopes
and elevated flats; which led to "coyote-hole" mining (bur-
rowing into the side of hills or boring wells); to "hydrau-
lic mining" (the concentration of a powerful column of

water against a hill or mountain side so as to wash the gravel or "pay dirt" down through the sluice box or strainer) ; and lastly to "quartz mining," with its shafts and tunnels, stamp mills and heavy machinery. Gold mining, therefore, had changed its aspect, so that the average, common man could no longer expect to find, except occasionally, places unappropriated, where, with no special knowledge, or special appliances or other capital, he could find any considerable amount of the precious metal or where he could "dig" and "wash out" even ordinary "wages."

What drew most gold seekers, and what drew Henry George, into the mining regions was not so much the hope of mining in itself as of "prospecting" or "locating a claim"—finding on the unworked and unappropriated lands places that would yield to the newer processes the precious metal in quantities sufficient to pay for the working. Such a claim might be sold to or worked on shares by others who had the skill and capital, so that as soon as the rumour of a rich discovery had spread, multitudes of "prospectors" came rushing to the locality, eager to "stake off claims." The prospector was, therefore, essentially one who roamed from place to place at the beck of the Golden Goddess; and since she was whimsical and beckoned hither and thither, the prospector was always on the move.

There are no clear evidences as to what locality Henry George had set his hopes on, though the probabilities are that hearing in San Francisco confusing reports from a hundred different points, he concluded to strike off for some nearer and more advantageous centre, there to determine to which particular mining spot to go; and it seems likely that his first objective point was Placerville, formerly known as "Hangtown," and before that as "Dry

Diggings." For Placerville had not only developed rich finds in its immediate vicinity, but in some instances large treasure was found by digging into the very ground on which its cabins and houses stood. Moreover, it was on the old emigrant route from the East and the road from the Carson River to the Sacramento valley; and with its stores, hotels and saloons, was a place of recreation and supply for all that region of the Sierras.

To purpose to go to the mines was one thing; to get there was another, but young George was determined. "Having no other way of reaching them," he said subsequently,[1] "I started out to walk. I was, in fact, what would now be called a tramp. I had a little money, but I slept in barns to save it and had a rough time generally." But soon he had to spend his money, and then though slight in build and never what would be called muscular, he was forced to do farm work and other manual labour to keep himself alive. He had got some distance towards the mines, but for sheer want of living necessaries, could go no farther; and with great toil, and some real suffering, he worked his way back to San Francisco.

This covered a period of nearly two months—for physical labour the hardest two months in all his life—during which time he seems not to have written a single letter home. While he was in the mountains, the Currys had written of an opportunity to set type on the "Statesman," in Portland, with pay according to competency; but when he had got back to San Francisco the time to accept had passed. Then it was that he learned of the death at Victoria of his sincere friend, Ellen George, and this news, taken with the experience just closed and a poor out-look for work in San Francisco, depressed his spirits, though

---

[1] Meeker notes, October, 1897.

he tried to write cheerfully home to his Aunt Mary (June 17):

"Jim George has gone up to Victoria again, but will be down as soon as he can settle up his business, which will probably be in two or three weeks. The children are here going to school; they are in the best health and spirits.

"We are enjoying splendid weather, just warm enough, though for the last few days it has been quite hot, reminding one of the summers at home. For some time past we have had plenty of green peas, strawberries and all the early summer vegetables and fruits. In ten or fifteen years this will be one of the greatest fruit countries in the world, for fruit trees are yearly being set out by the thousand and grape vines by the million.

"I am doing nothing just now, but expect to go to work next week. I have given up all idea of going to the mines.

"Frazer River seems to have given out at last, and every steamer that comes down is filled with miners. The rich deposits of a month or two ago appear to have been without foundation.

"I must bring my letter to a sudden close, for the clock has struck eleven, and I will just have time to get down to the post office to mail this. I intended to write a longer letter, but coming up here I stopped to look at the operation of moving a house, which must have consumed more time than I was aware of. The way they raise, lower, and pull big houses around the city here is astonishing."

He had, indeed, given up all hope of going to the mines and also pretty much all hope of remaining ashore, where there seemed to be no work for him and no future. Thoughts of the sea came back in a flood tide. They ranged along the line of ocean heroes, and he asked himself why he should not follow that calling and rise to

fame? He was thinking earnestly of this, and stood at
the parting of the ways, when his career was decided as
if by accident. For the second time David Bond, through
a chance meeting, offered a kindly service and obtained
for his young friend a position as compositor—this time
on the weekly "Home Journal" owned by Joseph C. Duncan. Thought of a career at sea never returned.

Printer's wages in California were at that time still
high, the union rate for piece work being seventy-five cents
a thousand ems and for time work to the average man,
thirty dollars a week. But as George was still a minor,
he got only a boy's pay for work in the regular hours—
twelve dollars a week. He resolved now to keep, if he
possibly could, to type-setting until he should come of age
and be qualified as a journeyman. When somewhat settled he wrote to his Sister Jennie (August 2):

"You ask me about my studies. I am afraid I do
not study much. I have not time and opportunity (or
nearer the truth, perhaps, will enough) to push through
a regular course. But I try to pick up everything I
can, both by reading and observation, and flatter myself
that I learn at least something every day. My principal object now is to learn my trade well, and I am
pitching in with all my strength. So anxious am I
now to get ahead and make up for lost time that I never
feel happier than when at work, and that, so far from
being irksome, is a pleasure. My heart just now is
really in my work. In another year I'll be twenty-one
and I must be up and doing. I have a pretty good
prospect ahead and think that before many months I
shall get into something better where I can make good
wages. . . .

"My time is now pretty well taken up. As soon as I
rise in the morning I go to breakfast and then immediately to work, which I seldom leave until nearly seven
o'clock and once in a while not until one or two in the

morning. There are only three others in the office—
nice social fellows—which makes it pleasant for me.
I do not make much, but I am learning a good deal
and think I have a pretty good prospect, so that I am
quite satisfied."

This contentment of mind was broken by news of the
death of the dearest friend of his boyhood, Jo Jeffreys.
Mrs. George revealed her sympathetic heart (August 18):

"I feel as though I must say something to you, but
my heart is full of the one theme, poor Jeffreys, poor
Jo. O I cannot tell you of the anguish I feel when I
think of him, and I can think of nothing else. . . .
The agonising thought with me is the uncertainty of
his state. O had he time to call upon his Saviour; to
say: 'God, be merciful to me, a sinner.' . . .
"O his youth, his bright mind, his sensitiveness, his
love for you made me feel an interest in him of no common kind. I do mourn for him sincerely. I know
your heart too well to doubt your grief.
"Pop thought you would like to have a lock of his
hair."

By the same mail Will Jones wrote:

"Poor Jeffreys has paid the debt of nature, unan-
ticipated and mourned by all. Brilliant in life, flashing upon our vision as a meteor, and as a meteor so soon
to be lost in the impenetrable gloom of night. . . .
"We buried him at the Odd Fellows' Cemetery, in our
lot there, the last tribute of regard I could offer. None
of his family was there save his two brothers, who came
on from New York to the funeral."

Jo Jeffreys' death was a bitter and heavy loss. It
snapped the tie of boyhood. Henry George's life from
that time forward was the life of the man. In November
(20) he wrote to his mother:

"For the past week we have had beautiful weather, and I have employed every possible opportunity to sun myself. The shortness of the days makes this almost impracticable, except on Sundays, when I generally take a long walk outside of the city.

"There is nothing of any interest going on here now. Even the news of the 'bloody Harper's Ferry rebellion,' couldn't get up the smallest kind of an excitement, except among the political papers. General Scott has returned from San Juan, and therefore, all danger from that quarter has ceased for the present. Even the interior towns have for the time stopped burning down; so that, excepting the non-arrival of the mail steamer, we are left without even a decent topic of conversation.

"Letters from the Currys are getting more and more like angel's visits.

"I am still pursuing the even tenor of my way—working, walking, reading and sleeping.

"Thursday is Thanksgiving day for us Californians, as I suppose it is with you at home. I shall try and observe the day with the usual ceremonies, and will think of home even more than usual. I hope you will have a pleasant time, and oh! how I wish I could share it with you."

He wrote in this slighting manner of public matters in California doubtless to calm his mother's mind should she hear rumours from the West; for as a matter of fact most sensational events growing out of the slavery struggle there were crowding into this period. Only the year before the Supreme Court of the State had delivered a decision in the case of a negro named Archy which was described as "giving the law to the North and the nigger to the South." And now, on the just past 7th of September (1859), after the most bitter and tumultuous political campaign ever held in California, the Lecompton, or proslavery, party swept the State. Bad blood raised during the canvass left many scores to be settled after election, the most conspicuous resulting in a duel between David S. Terry, Chief Justice of the California Supreme Court, a pronounced pro-slavery supporter, and U. S. Senator David C. Broderick, the foremost anti-slavery man west of the Rocky mountains. Eighty persons were present to witness Broderick get a death-wound and Terry go unscathed. Broderick was carried to San Francisco and half-hourly bulletins were posted before a surging and excited multitude. He was accorded a public funeral and his name became a rally-word in the anti-slavery cause on the Pacific Coast.[1]

Henry George was not unconscious of such events; on the contrary he took a burning and apprehensive interest in them. His father's mind, also, was filled with apprehension arising from similar events in the East, for he wrote (December 3):

"We have had a high old time with the Harper Ferry 'rebellion,' (as it is called) and John Brown. The abolitionists are making all the capital they can out of this poor fanatic. He is magnified and glorified beyond anything human, and dies a martyr, according to their belief. It is having a great effect upon business, and has thrown trade into something of a panic. Our iron men suffer, I am told, on account of the Southern merchants everywhere refusing to have anything to do with Northern men. What the result will be none can tell. I have always been of the opinion that this Union could never be dissolved, but if the present feeling is kept up and we do not get another Andrew Jackson for our next President, I fear I shall be mistaken in my opinion.

"Brown was hanged yesterday at 15 minutes past 11 without any disturbance. But the end is not yet."

---

[1] "Broderick and Gwin," by James O'Meara, pp. 225-254. Terry was shot and killed by a Deputy U. S. Marshal in 1889, when committing an assault upon U. S. Supreme Court Justice Field, growing out of a case in which Terry had been committed to jail by Judge Field for contempt of court.

CHAPTER VII.

SIX PRINTERS AND A NEWSPAPER.

1860-61.   AGE, 21-22.

THE year 1860 opened auspiciously for the young printer. He was earning steady if small wages at his trade, and purposed not to be diverted, but to keep at it until he came of age in the following September, when he would qualify as a journeyman, and could then demand a man's full pay. To his father he wrote (January 4):

"Christmas and New Year's days were passed by me as pleasantly as could have been expected. The weather, however, on both days was bad, although fine both before and after. On New Year's day I took supper with two of the *Shubrick's* boys, and a friend of mine who likewise hails from Philadelphia. We had a very social, pleasant time, talking over our old adventures; and in the evening we went to the theatre to see Richard III. I have been to a play but three or four times since I have been in the country. I haven't much taste that way, and unless the performance is very good, I would rather be reading or talking. . . .

"I intend to stay where I am until my next birthday —if the paper lasts that long—when I will be admitted to the Union, and to all the rights and privileges of a journeyman printer; and then to work as hard and save as much money as I can, and in a year or two to come

99

home, for a visit, at any rate. A couple of hundred (at the present rates of fare) would enable me to come home, stay a little while, and then come back, if it were best; and it does not take long to raise that if a person can get work."

It may have been to this performance of Richard III. that Henry George referred more than thirty years later in life (February 4, 1890) in a speech in San Francisco, when, tracing the genesis of his thought on social questions, he said:

"I remember, after coming down from the Frazer River country, sitting one New Year's night in the gallery of the old American theatre—among the gods—when a new drop curtain fell, and we all sprang to our feet, for on that curtain was painted what was then a dream of the far future—the overland train coming into San Francisco; and after we had shouted ourselves hoarse, I began to think what good is it going to be to men like me—to those who have nothing but their labour? I saw that thought grow and grow. We were all—all of us, rich and poor—hoping for the development of California, proud of her future greatness, looking forward to the time when San Francisco would be one of the great capitals of the world; looking forward to the time when this great empire of the west would count her population by millions. And underneath it all came to me what that miner on the topsail schooner going up to Frazer River had said: 'As the country grows, as people come in, wages will go down.' "

Many times such thought was to recur and, as he said, "to grow and grow"; but just now a matter of very different nature was to attract his attention. In a letter to his Sister Jennie (February 4) he referred to the newly discovered gold and silver mines in the Washoe mountains in Nevada Territory, just over the California line, perhaps a hundred miles beyond Placerville and not far from Carson. The stories coming in seemed incredible, yet this region was in the next ten years to yield $80,000,-000 worth of bullion, mostly silver; to make celebrated the "Comstock Lode"; and to raise to world renown the names of the "Bonanza Kings," Mackay, Flood, O'Brien and Fair. The letter ran:

"Our library is closed for the present, as they are removing to a new building, put up expressly for the purpose, where there will be ample room. However, I have out a bulky folio—'Constitutional History of the United States'—so that I am well supplied with reading matter. Do you read much? What books do you read, tell me? How I would like to read with you. We can hardly enjoy alone, and my list of acquaintances contains hardly one who reads more than the newspapers. . . .

"We have reports of several rich discoveries of the precious metals, but I hardly think much faith can be placed in them. From present indications there will be a great rush to Washoe in the spring. There is silver there in plenty—of that there can be little doubt—but still there will be many disappointments. One thing is certain—you don't catch me running off anywhere until pretty certain that there is something to be made. I have given up the notion of mining—at least for the present."

Other letters to and from home throw light upon events. From his mother (February 3):

"I really think you are not doing anything more there than you would do at home, at least it amounts to the same thing after expenses are deducted. I hope when you are of age you will see it so, and conclude that *fortunes* can be made at home as well as abroad. We all say, as with one voice, when we get you home we will keep you. No more roving."

From his father (April 16):

"Mr. Brown has a letter of introduction to you. He spent last evening with us. I found him to be a great egotist, but he is an Englishman, and that accounts for it. Treat him politely."

From Henry George to his Sister Jennie (April 18):

"Washoe is walled up by snow at present, preventing both shipping of the ore and prospecting. In another month when it begins to thaw up in the mountains we will have some definite news from that locality. . . .

"I am still on the 'Home Journal.' On the 2d of September next I will be twenty-one years old, and then, if nothing happens, I will have a pretty good thing (comparatively) and be able to make better pay. It is only four months off, and they will fly pretty quickly. . . . I don't expect to work at printing very long after I am of age. I will then have a chance to look around and get into something that will pay better. If Washoe only equals the expectations entertained of it by sober, sensible men, times will be brisk here this summer, and everyone will have a chance for 'a gold ring or a broken leg.'

"Duncan the proprietor of the 'Home Journal,' bought an interest in a silver lead a short time since for a paltry sum which he could sell to-day for $15,000, and which, if it holds out as rich as the assay shows, will be an independent fortune.

"I don't read much now except the newspapers and you are getting far ahead of me in that line. It takes pretty much all my spare time to keep posted on the current topics of the day. What a time we live in, when great events follow one another so quickly that we have not space for wonder. We are driving at a killing pace somewhere—Emerson says to heaven, and Carlyle says to the other place; but however much they differ, go we surely do.

"I am invited out to-morrow evening to join a reading circle, and if it don't rain will make my *début* in polite society on the Coast. Would you like to see me make my bow, or hear me break down when I come to some hard word? But I will do no such thing. I am not as bashful as I used to be. . . .

"You 'do' some pretty heavy reading for a young girl. I wouldn't be so afraid of novels. A good one is always instructive, and your taste is sufficiently cultivated to allow you to like no other. I never read them, but then it is solely because I have not time and am obliged to take my mental food in as condensed a form as possible.

"I have changed my quarters again, and am now rooming in the northern part of the town. I have a long walk to breakfast, but it gives me a good appetite.

"I am sorry anything was wrong about X——'s marriage. However, the more I see of men and things, and the more I examine the workings of my own heart, the less inclined am I to judge anybody else."

It was at this period, that, urged on by his mother's strong counsel, Henry George pushed out to make social acquaintances. He won the friendship of two young men named Coddington and Hoppel, and through them became acquainted with some young ladies. Both of these young men were ardent Methodists—Hoppel an enthusiast, almost a fanatic, and he urged George to attend his church. The young printer had for several years inwardly shrunk from a literal acceptance of the scriptures, such as he had been taught at old St. Paul's and in the family circle. Roving had bred, or at any rate quickened a revolt, so that, though he said little to hurt the feelings of others, and especially of the dear ones at home, he had come to reject almost completely the forms of religion, and with the forms had cast out belief in a life hereafter. He inclined towards materialism. But the burning enthusiasm of Hoppel, even if it expressed in the main only personal magnetism, was contagious to a sensitive, sympathetic nature; and George began to have new thoughts about religion. Drawn by this, and the desire to make acquaintances, he accepted Hoppel's offer, and went with him to the Methodist place of worship, where an upright, earnest, broad-minded man, Rev. S. D. Simonds, preached. Then the young printer wrote home that he had joined a church. Understanding this to mean more than he intended to convey, the quiet circle at Philadelphia received the news with a delight that was only little lessened when they afterwards learned that it was the Methodist and not the Episcopal Church to which he had attached himself. His mother wrote to him (July 2):

"With what thrilling joy did we read your last letter. Good news! Good news! Indeed, so unexpected, so intensely joyful that copious tears streamed from my eyes; but they were tears of joy and gratitude.

"Oh, how much better the Lord has been to us than we have deserved. How weak our faith, that God's rich blessings and overflowing goodness and sure promise should take us by surprise. I now desire to say, 'Bless the Lord, O my soul and all that is within me, bless His holy name. For Thou hast delivered the soul of my child from death, and his feet from falling. I will offer to Thee the sacrifice of thanksgiving and call upon the name of the Lord.'

"Your father will tell you, too, the heartfelt joy with which he received the news. Not all the wealth of California would have caused a tithe of it. We feel now that our boy is safe; his feet are upon the rock. Let the waters lash and surge, the trials and troubles of life come, he is safe as long as he clings to the Cross of Christ in humble, trusting faith. You know our beautiful hymn, 'Rock of Ages.' Turn to it if you have forgotten it. How soothing and comforting its language! With God for your guide, my dear child, you will be safe and happy everywhere.

" 'He that dwelleth in the secret places of the Most High shall abide under the shadow of the Almighty. I will say to the Lord, He is my refuge, and my fortress; my God, in Him will I trust.' "

On September 2, 1860, Henry George came of age. He immediately joined the Eureka Typographical Union, and leaving his old boy's position, obtained work as substitute type-setter on the daily papers at journeyman's wages. This irregular work lasted but a short time. He soon returned to the "Home Journal" as foreman at thirty dollars a week, and allowed the use of his name as publisher. But shortly afterwards he wrote home that, the paper being weak, he did not know how long the position might last.

Up to this time frequent reference was made to a desire to visit home, but on the 12th of October, while he was yet foreman on the "Home Journal," Henry George for the first time met, through the offices of his friend, George Wilbur, a girl who was to affect the whole course of his career—Miss Annie Corsina Fox—the occasion being the quiet celebration of her seventeenth birthday.

Miss Fox was an orphan who had just returned from a convent school at Los Angeles, California, which was then a pretty Spanish town. She was of Catholic faith, and of mingled English and Irish blood. Her father, John Fox, an officer in the British army, was of English parentage and Protestant faith. He was thirty-six years old when he married, in Australia, Elizabeth A. McCloskey, a strict Catholic and scarcely out of her sixteenth year. Miss McCloskey was one of the four children, two sons and two daughters, of Henry McCloskey, who was born in Limerick, Ireland. His wife, Mary Ann Wall, born in Ennis, County Clare, came of an educated family, having three brothers graduated from Trinity College, Dublin, two of whom had become clergymen in the English Established

Church. She herself was a woman of refined and intellectual mind, and strong, commanding nature. Henry McCloskey inherited an established business and was himself a successful man. He had the roving spirit and took his family to Australia and thence to California, stopping for a period in the Hawaiian, or as they were then more commonly called, Sandwich Islands. In Sydney and in Honolulu the family lived in ample means, Henry McCloskey carrying on an important iron-mongering business, and deriving large profits from government contracts which were invested in real estate. He settled his family in California in 1851, and two years later returned to build a railroad in South Australia, where he contracted a fever and died. He was then fifty-four years old and on his way to a big fortune.

But before the family left Australia Major Fox had come to a disagreement with his wife's mother. She had urged the marriage, and when asked subsequently how it was that though staunch Catholic and intense Irish patriot, she had consented to her daughter's marrying a man who was a Protestant and wore a red coat, the reply was that she had been "a mother first and a Catholic afterwards," and had given her sweet, gentle daughter to a soldier and gentleman who could protect her in the new, rough country that Australia then was. Discord between the gentleman and his wife's mother at length ran so high that he requested his wife to choose between them. Elizabeth Fox, feeling a stronger sense of duty towards her mother than towards her husband, chose to stay with the former. The Major then took his last farewell and they never met again. The young wife realising her attachment for him after he had irrevocably gone, fell to grieving, which brought on consumption, of which she died in San Francisco at the age of twenty-nine.

Teresa and Annie were the two daughters of this marriage. Teresa had early shown a serious bent of mind, and at the age of eleven, while reading at her dying mother's bedside, had formed the desire to become a religious. Hope of some day meeting and comforting her father confirmed her in this desire, so that at seventeen she became a member of the Order of the Daughters of St. Vincent de Paul, better known as Sisters of Charity, retaining her name and being subsequently known as Sister Teresa Fox. Many times in after years the sisters tried to get some word of their father, but in vain. He had left the army in Australia, and all trace of him was lost. Sister Teresa died of influenza in St. Louis, Missouri, on January 6, 1899, after a service in the order of forty years to the day.

On leaving school, Annie Fox made her home with her grandmother, who was now broken in health, and her aunt, Mrs. Flintoff, of San Francisco. The keen eyes of the grandmother apparently saw the trend of affairs between Annie and Mr. George, and though she was the kind of woman who could recognise and admire the quality of mind the young man exhibited, she regarded him as physically weak and endeavoured to divert the girl's attention, saying: "Annie, that Mr. George is a nice young man, but I fear he is delicate and will die of consumption." But the girl kept her own counsel. She was at that time engaged to a gifted and handsome young man, who had promise of a competency; but, under the ardent wooing of Henry George, a change of feeling came over her.

Meanwhile the calendar of outside events was being rapidly filled. The remarkable campaign of 1860 ended in the victory of the new Republican party. Henry George, now of age, cast his first vote for Abraham Lincoln. A few weeks later, December 20, the State of South Carolina

formally seceded from the Union. R. S. H. George about
the same time (December 19) wrote to his son:

> "Things look dark and gloomy; men seem dismayed
> at the prospect before them; they confess that they
> cannot see through the gloom. . . . Can it be that
> these United States, formed for the refuge of the down-
> trodden and oppressed of the earth, shall be destroyed,
> and that that glorious flag which is their protection
> throughout the world shall be trodden under foot? I
> can't think so; no, never!"

The minds of most men were charged with apprehension as the year 1861 was ushered in. The States of
Mississippi, Alabama, Georgia, Florida and Louisiana followed South Carolina's example and passed ordinances of
secession. On March 4 the passive Buchanan went out
of office and Abraham Lincoln was inaugurated President
of the United States.

At this time Henry George was adrift again. Duncan
had sold the "Home Journal" and George turned to "subbing" on the daily papers. For a time he considered a
mining project of which he speaks in a letter to his Sister
Caroline a year later (July 5, 1862):

> "A large amount of silver is coming out of Nevada
> near Virginia City and the amount of goods going up
> there is astonishing. One of the companies lately de-
> clared a dividend of $1,400 per share. Their claim,
> however, is situated on the famous Ophir lead, probably
> the richest in the world. A company in which Charlie
> Coddington held some stock struck the same lead a cou-
> ple of weeks ago, raising the value of shares to a price
> which will give him quite a nice little start, and which
> will make his partner rich, if he has not sold out. Hop-
> pel and I and Charlie were going to buy twenty feet

together, when I went into the 'Evening Journal,'
which knocked it in the head—I choosing, as I thought,
a certainty for an uncertainty. At present prices that
is worth $10,000 ($500 a foot) and if it proves as rich
as Ophir, will be worth much more."

The "Evening Journal" with which Henry George now
became connected, grew out of a campaign newspaper
called the "Constitution," which had been run in support of the Union party presidential condidates in the
1860 campaign—Bell and Everett. Five printers—James
J. Knowlton, Abel Gee, son of the Major Gee who was
to keep the Andersonville prison during the war; John
G. Smith, afterwards an Episcopal clergyman in Missouri;
Anson C. Benham, and Freeman A. Camp—entered upon
a partnership to revive the paper under the name of the
"Evening Journal." They all were poor, but they agreed
in addition to gathering most of the news themselves to
put in what at that time in California constituted the
chief item of expense in newspaper making—their printer's services—each man to give his entire time and labour.

For telegraphic news, up to the time the "Journal" was
started, did not occupy much space in West Coast papers.
There was no wire connection with the East, and telegrams had to travel a long part of the distance on the
"Overland Stage." But now a quicker means of transmission was established in what was known as the "Pony
Express." Two relays a week of fast pony riders ran
over the fifteen hundred miles of prairie and desert separating St. Joseph, Missouri, and Carson City, Nevada,
to connect the Eastern and Western telegraph systems.
But this was very expensive, and besides its infrequency
or intermittent nature, almost nine days were required
for so-called telegraphic transmission from New York or
Washington to San Francisco.[1] Under such circumstances

Pacific Coast newspapers did not carry much telegraphic matter, the columns being almost entirely filled with local news and comment[2] and when intelligence of secession and hostilities began to come in from the East the general feeling was that these were only temporary things—mere ebullitions, or "flashes in the pan!" And its promoters believed that if the "Journal" could live the short time until peace and quiet should be restored it could then fall back on the local news and be on equal terms with its contemporaries.

Regarding the new daily as a good venture, Henry George bought an equal share with the others for something over a hundred dollars—money he had saved while foreman

---

[1] The chief business of the Pony Express was to carry mail between St. Joseph, Missouri, and Sacramento, California; St. Joseph being the western limit of the Eastern railroads, and Sacramento being connected with San Francisco by river steamers. The distance to be ridden was 1900 miles, going by way of South Pass, Salt Lake, Humboldt River and Carson Valley. There were 190 stations at intervals of about 25 miles; and 200 station keepers, 80 riders and nearly 500 western native ponies. Postage was $5 for each half ounce. Carson City was on the way, and there telegrams were picked up or dropped. Hittell's "History of California," Vol. IV, pp. 266–268.

[2] For a time the editorial writer on the "Evening Journal" was John R. Ridge, a strikingly handsome man, whose mother was a cultured Connecticut woman, and whose father, educated in Connecticut, was a full-blooded Cherokee Indian, a member of one of what were known as the Civilised Tribes. In later years Henry George wrote of him in "Progress and Poverty," Bk. X, Chap. ii ("Memorial Edition," pages 490–491). "I once knew a man in whose veins ran the blood of Indian chiefs. He used to tell me traditions learned from his grandfather which illustrated what is difficult for a white man to comprehend — the Indian habit of thought, the intense but patient blood thirst of the trail, and the fortitude of the stake. From the way in which he dwelt on these, I have no doubt that under certain circumstances, highly educated, civilised man that he was, he would have shown traits that would have been looked on as due to his Indian blood; but which in reality would have been sufficiently explained by the broodings of his imagination upon the deeds of his ancestors."

on Duncan's paper—and agreed with the others to give his whole time to the enterprise. He wrote to his Sister Jennie (April 10, 1861):

"For the past week I have been working very hard. I have bought an interest in a little paper, copies of which I send you by this mail. We are pushing in—bound to make it a paying concern or perish in the attempt (that is, the paper, not your respected brother). I think we have a good prospect and in a little while will have a good property, which will be an independence for a life-time. Then, and not till then you may begin to fret about a sister-in-law!

"Since I came in the paper has been enlarged and considerably improved, and probably the next copies I send you will present a much better appearance, as we are yet hardly in the working trim. . . .

"I am very tired to-night. This working on a daily paper the hours that we do is harder than digging sand or wielding a sledge."

On April 12 the astounding news spread over the North that the South had fired upon the United States flag at Fort Sumter. Owing to the slow means of communication, this information did not reach California until some days later; but when it did come it produced an extraordinary sensation.

Henry George had invited Miss Fox out to walk that evening, and he was so absorbed that she asked the cause; and when he said, "The terrible news," and told what had happened, she exclaimed: "Is that all? Why, I thought your dear old father was dead." He turned in astonishment: "All!" he said in some excitement; "why, what could be a greater calamity to this country?"

It was not to be wondered at that a young girl born in another country, and just fresh from a convent school, should, in San Francisco, far removed from the seat of the struggle, not at once grasp the significance of events; but the family in Philadelphia thoroughly understood, Mrs. George writing to her son (May 20) a few days after the President had called out seventy-five thousand volunteers for a three months' service:

"We are now, as it were, holding our breath; waiting for the news of the first battle. It is thought by all that it will take place in a few days at Harper's Ferry. O this horrible, calamitous and most sorrowful of all wars; when and what will be the end? I firmly believe the Lord of hosts is with us, and the God of Jacob will be our defence. Though we have sinned against Him, He will not give us to anarchy and confusion, but will right our wrongs and make us again a happy, united people. O pray for this, my dear boy."

His Sister Jennie (by same mail) wrote:

"Mrs. Browning moves two nations with one song. Have you seen her last poem, written at Turin, I think, termed 'Mother and Poet'? It is magnificent. It commences:

" 'Dead! One of them shot by the sea in the east,
   And one of them shot in the west by the sea.
Dead! both my boys! When you sit at the feast,
   And are wanting a great song for Italy free,
   Let none look at *me*.'

"It is all we women can do—give up our husbands and brothers cheerfully. A great many we know are going, some your old friends."

Later (June 10) his father wrote:

"You cannot feel it as we do. All around is warlike, and young men are crowding into the ranks of the forces being raised. Nothing now but the sound of the drum and the march of troops South. . . .

"But, my dear boy, this is what I think I predicted

to you long ago. We are now approaching times and scenes such as never have been seen in these United States; and we old men have come to the conclusion that it is best that it should now be declared whether we are a National Government or not, that our children may know the truth, and what they are to depend upon.

"The new Collector has taken his seat and is cutting right and left. I feel that my time at the Custom House is short, and what to do I know not. Commerce is suspended, and I do not know to-night but that I shall be a pauper to-morrow. . . . If I am discharged I know not what will become of us. And yet all I know are in the same boat—all on a par, like a ship at sea without rudder or compass. But blessed be God. We can and do look up to Him for guidance and deliverance. I feel satisfied that He will not leave or forsake us in this our time of need."

The dismissal from the Custom House which R. S. H. George feared came soon after this. At sixty-four years of age, and when business was demoralised, he was forced to seek means of livelihood. His son Henry, in his prosperous periods had been accustomed to send money home, and even during the hard struggling months on the "Evening Journal" had sent a few remittances. When he heard of his father's threatened plight he at once offered to sell out his interest in the paper for whatever it would bring and send the money on. But the old gentleman would not listen to this. He replied (August 3):

"Your kind letter was to me worth more than silver and gold. It showed me that my dear son far away from us was willing to make any sacrifice to help his parents in distress. And so with all my dear children. Surely my grey hairs will not go down in sorrow to the grave on account of the want of love and affection on the part of my dear children."

He told his son that he had hopes of success in a ship-brokerage business which he and a Custom House associate, who also had been displaced, intended to enter upon.

A never failing complaint in the communications from home at this period was that there were so few and such meagre letters from California. There was ground enough for these complaints, for all connected with the "Evening Journal" had to work long and hard. In a letter to his Sister Caroline (August 19) Henry George shows this:

> "I am still on the paper—working hard to make it go, and as yet without any decided success. We are making now about $6 apiece per week—rather small wages you will justly think for California. But then they are slowly but surely getting larger, and I think the prospect ahead is worth some industry and self-denial."

The little band of poverty-stricken printers pressed resolutely on, with the earnest hopes of Henry George's folks at home. Indeed, the latter took so much interest in the enterprise that when her brother had written that he would sell out at any price to send his father some money, his Sister Jennie had replied (August 29) : "I hope you won't sell your share in the paper. It seems hard to think of your commencing all over again. We all cried when we got your letter; it seemed so hard on you."

The bond between this brother and sister, always close by reason of congenial tastes, seemed now to grow more tender. By his encouragement, she wrote several long news letters from Philadelphia for his paper, and in her personal letters she constantly referred, with something like wistfulness, to the days that seemed long gone when they were happy children together:

> "Uncle Thomas took us all on an excursion Tuesday. . . . He told us that a number of years ago he went

on a similar excursion to Pennsgrove and took you with him. He was very much amused with you. While you were eating your breakfast they gave you some very strong coffee. (I suppose you were not used to it.) All of a sudden you laid down your knife and fork with a very grave face, and they asked you what was the matter. You said quite soberly: 'Why, I do believe the coffee has flew to my head.' "

A long letter to his Sister Jennie at this time (September 15) shows with some clearness the state of the young printer's mind:

"I have been very dilatory about writing and more especially about answering the long letters received from you about two weeks ago, but now I will try to make amends for it, if I can. In the first place, I have been working quite hard, from morning to night, without any intermission, and it is quite a strain. In fact, to sit down and write after the day is over, is but a continuation of the use of the same faculties, which in my trade have been so heavily drawn upon during the day, and though I might at one time send you a few lines, yet I wanted to write you a good long letter, such a one as I used to write, and such as you sent me. Again, I have felt unsettled and worried about business, hoping that each day would make some change that I might tell you of; in fact, until a few days past, hardly knowing whether our paper would get through the next day, as I feared something would occur to bring it to a close, and in truth, feeling something like the sailor in a calm wishing for even—

"　'Storm or hurricane,
　　Anything, to put a close
　To this most dread, monotonous repose!'

"But the days have followed each other, and pretty much like each other, too, and nothing has happened— no prospect of war with European powers, no uprising of Secessionists, no appearance of the Sheriff's officers, nor even of that individual with more money than brains, and an exceedingly strong desire to go into the newspaper business in a small way, whom I have been hoping would come along and buy me out. So we go. What a constant reaching this life is, a constant stretching forth and longing after something. But you know what Emerson in the 'Sphinx' makes his 'Œdipus' say:

" 'The fiend that man harries
        Is love of the Best;
    Yawns the pit of the Dragon
        Lit by the rays from the Blest.'

And so it is—and so it will be until we reach the perfect, and that you and I and every son of Adam and every daughter of Eve, each for himself, knows we are very far from.

" 'For the longing I feel is a part
        Of the hunger and thirst of the heart—
    The frenzy and fire of the brain—
    That yearns for the fruitage forbidden,
    The golden pomegranates of Eden,
        To ease off its hunger and pain.'

"Truly it seems that we have fallen upon evil days. A little while ago all was fair and bright, and now the storm howls around us with a strength and fury that almost unnerves one. Our country is being torn to pieces, and ourselves, our homes, filled with distress. As to the ultimate end, I have no doubt. If civil war should pass over the whole country, leaving nothing but devastation behind it, I think my faith in the ultimate good would remain unchanged; but it is hard to feel so of our individual cases. On great events and movements we can philosophise, but when it comes down to ourselves, to our homes, to those *we love*, then we can only feel; our philosophy goes to the dogs. . . .

"In the meantime we eagerly wait the arrival of each pony. Twice a week it arrives, and from the outer telegraph station in Nevada Territory the news is flashed to us in San Francisco. The last two or three times the news has seemed to me rather more encouraging, not so much by reason of anything that has been done, as by the evident determination of the loyal North to see the thing through.

"I do not get much time to read now. In fact, I have read very little for eighteen months—hardly more than the newspapers; certainly not enough to keep me posted on the current literature of the day. How I long for the Golden Age—for the promised Millenium, when each one will be free to follow his best and noblest impulses, unfettered by the restrictions and necessities which our present state of society imposes upon him—when the poorest and the meanest will have a chance to use all his God-given faculties, and not be forced to drudge away the best part of his time in order to supply wants but little above those of the animal.

". . . . I had a dream last night—such a pleasant, vivid dream, that I must tell you of it. I thought I was scooping treasure out of the earth by handfuls, almost delirious with the thoughts of what I would now be able to do, and how happy we would all be—and so clear and distinct that I involuntarily examined my pockets when I got up in the morning, but alas! with the usual result. Is it an indication of future luck? or do dreams always go by contraries, and instead of finding, am I to lose? But the latter supposition will not worry me, for 'he who lies on the ground cannot fall far.' No, I suppose I dreamed as starving men are said to of splendid feasts, or thirsty desert wanderers of shady brooks and spray-flinging fountains. 'Lust for Gold!' Is it any wonder that men lust for gold, and are willing to give almost anything for it, when it covers everything—the purest and holiest desires of their hearts, the exercise of their noblest powers! What a pity we can't be contented! Is it? Who knows? Sometimes I feel sick of the fierce struggle of our high civilised life, and think I would like to get away from cities and business, with their jostlings and strainings and cares altogether, and find some place on one of the hillsides, which look so dim and blue in the distance where I could gather those I love, and live content with what Nature and our own resources would furnish; but, alas, money, money, is wanted even for that. It is our fate—we must struggle, and so here's for the strife! . . .

"The days and weeks and months never flew so fast with me as they do now. Time we measure by sensations, and working so steadily, there is not room for many. I do not like my trade when forced to work at it so steadily—there is not action enough in it, hardly a chance for the movements of the mind. But it will not always be so. 'It is a long lane that knows no turning,' they say, and I hope the turn will come soon, for I really feel tired.

"It is harder for me to write to you than to anyone else. When I have business to write about I can sit down and spin it right off, but when it comes to writing home, I scrawl a few words and find myself lost in reverie, when I sit and think, and bite my pen, while Memory is busy till the hours fly away unnoticed.

"I am glad Bill Horner and Jim Stanley have gone to the wars. I should like to see them. If I were home, and situated as they are, I would go, too. Not that I like the idea of fighting my countrymen—not that I think it is the best or pleasantest avocation, or that the fun of soldiering is anything to speak of; but in this life or death struggle I should like to have a hand. If they die, they will die in a good cause; and if they live, they will always feel prouder and better when this time is mentioned than if they had remained safely at home while others faced the danger and did the work. I have felt a great deal like enlisting, even here, and probably would have done so, had I not felt that my duty to you all required me to remain, though I did not, and do not, think our volunteers are really needed or will do any fighting that will amount to anything; but I should like to place my willingness on record, and show that one of our family was willing to serve his country. We cannot tell. It may be my duty yet, though I sincerely hope not.

"I never hear from the Currys now, except through

the medium of your letters, and at present there is no probability of my going up there. . . .

"We have been having our usual fine summer, but the rainy season will soon set in and then we will make up for it. Rain is a very nice thing once in a while, but when it gets into the habit of coming down for a month at a time, you almost cease to appreciate it, and would be willing to have it change to snow. It is very little colder, however, in winter than in summer, and I wear precisely the same clothing the year round. . . .

"I have been some time writing this much, but I think we will be able to make arrangements that will place us in a better position. As soon as they are completed I will write, probably in a day or two."

The "arrangements" that the young printer spoke of which should place those on the "Evening Journal" in a better position could not have been completed, or being completed, could not have been of more than temporary duration, for in a short time all connected with the paper were hard-driven again. "I worked," said he afterwards,[1] "until my clothes were in rags and the toes of my shoes were out. I slept in the office and did the best I could to economise, but finally I ran in debt thirty dollars for my board bill."

Miss Fox called at the "Journal" office with some friends one day at this period, after the paper had gone to press. Mr. George was the only person there. He was standing at a case in his shirt sleeves distributing type. On seeing the visitors, he hurried to wash his hands, brush and put on his coat and make himself presentable. He showed Miss Fox about the little office and presently pointed to a kind of folding cot, with mattress, grey blankets and a pillow, that were under one of the imposing-tables. When he told her that that was his bed, the young girl exclaimed,

---

[1] Meeker notes, October, 1897.

"Oh, I hope your mother does not know of this." "Why," he replied, "this is nothing after a life at sea."

What brought the crisis on the "Journal" was the completion of the trans-continental telegraph in October. With the wire joining them to New York, Washington and all the East, the papers that were in the press association monopoly had so much advantage that Henry George concluded that for him to stay longer and fight at such odds would be worse than foolish. He expressed his desire to withdraw. Some friction had grown up between the other owners of the paper and so it was concluded towards the middle of November, 1861, to dissolve partnership. Of this Mr. Knowlton, one of the partners, has since said:

"It was agreed on Mr. Gee's proposal that each of the six partners should make a bid for the 'Evening Journal,' and to write his bid, without showing it to the others, on a slip of paper, which was to be folded and dropped into a hat. Then all the slips were to be taken out and opened. The makers of the three highest bids were to stay in, and of the three lowest bids to go out. George, Camp and Smith were lowest, their bids together making, I believe, $800, or averaging something over $266 apiece."

Even this sum—small, indeed, for the months of strain and privation—would have enabled Henry George to square his debts and have a little remaining with which to make a fresh start, but the instaying partners could not at once pay. In June he had written home that he had been "given a one-third interest in a gold lead in Butte County," but this too, had failed; so that when he went out of the "Journal" to look elsewhere for work his prospects were desperate. At this critical point in his affairs he was called upon to face one of the most important crises of his life.

CHAPTER VIII.

COURTSHIP AND RUNAWAY MARRIAGE.

1861.   Age, 22.

MISS FOX'S family must have marked a change in the appearance of young Mr. George, who at first had dressed well, but whose clothes now, though neat, showed wear. The grandmother had died after displaying every sign of tender care and affection for her daughter Elizabeth's children, orphaned as she felt by her unwise, though most loving interference. Matthew McCloskey, Miss Fox's uncle, had now become virtually the young girl's guardian, and careful man that he was, he wrote privately to Philadelphia to learn something of the young suitor's antecedents, which he found to be satisfactory.

Matthew McCloskey shared his mother's force of character. He was one of those strong, commanding men seen at greatest advantage in pioneer conditions. In "Happy Valley," the section of the city in which he lived and owned considerable real estate, his word was his bond, and his conclusions in ticklish land-title disputes, which his neighbours brought to him to settle rather than go to law, had the respect accorded to decisions of court. And while a just man, he had the generosity of a courageous man, one night during the campaign of '60 going home in a passion because he had been unable to prevent a mob of Douglass Democrats stopping a Breckinridge Democrat from making a public speech; for though a strong Douglass Democrat himself, he wanted all men to have a fair chance to be heard. Thus no man in his neighbourhood was better known or more highly respected. His house, a frame building, like many others at that time, made in Australia and brought to California in sections, was when erected one of the best in that part of the city.

Matthew McCloskey took no exception to the character or possible abilities of young George, but his own nature was too masterful long to brook the same trait in the young man who came courting his niece. For the time he said nothing; while all unconscious, or careless, of smiles or frowns from such a quarter, the young printer was showing in his wooing the strength of his nature and bent of his mind. He brought Miss Fox books, mostly of verse, and they had reading tasks together. One work used in this way was Charles A. Dana's "Household Book of Poetry," a large volume just published containing an admirable collection from the writings of the great poets of the language. The lovers read, memorised and discussed.

One day Henry George said he had just heard his rival's love story, and that he thought the other man ought to have the right to press his suit, and that he himself ought to withdraw. The lady intimated that the other gentleman had few friends at court, whereas Mr. George was well represented. The young printer needed no further word of encouragement, and at all hours, early in the morning, at midday or late at night—for one hour was as pleasant to him as another—he came dropping in at the Flintoff's on Twelfth Street, near Folsom, until unexpectedly the storm broke and Matthew McCloskey, who came out that night to his brother-in-law's, told Mr. George that until he could show more evidence of prosperity—for he was now out of the "Evening Journal," and indeed, of all regular employment—he should make his visits less frequent. The young fellow replied with spirit, and the two quick, hot tempered men would have come to blows had not Miss Fox, who had been the terrified spectator of the quarrel, rushed between them. Her uncle, forgetting that his brother-in-law and not he was master there, ordered the young man from the house and forbade him ever again to enter it.

Much of that night Miss Fox spent praying and next morning, December 3, 1861—a stormy, rainy morning— when Henry George came out, she said that she would no longer remain under the roof of either of her uncles, and had resolved to go to Los Angeles and accept a position as teacher in the school of the Sisters of Charity.

The young man said: "If you go I'll not see you," to which the girl replied that since she could not stay with her relatives in San Francisco, she saw nothing else to do. The young man drew from his pocket a single coin. "Annie," said he solemnly, "that is all the money I have in the world. Will you marry me?"

She gravely answered: "If you are willing to undertake the responsibilities of marriage, I will marry you."

He told her when he came again later in the day that at nightfall he would send a carriage for her to the door inquiring for "Mrs. Brown" and that she should be ready at once to leave. All day long she sat in the parlour of Joseph Flintoff's house waiting for night and the carriage, while Henry George was off telling some of his friends of the matter, getting credit for two weeks' board for two persons, borrowing a little money and some better-appearing clothes than his own, and hiring a carriage. There was some difficulty about the carriage, for when the driver grasped the fact that he was about to take part in a runaway marriage, and that he was to get into the very thick of it by inquiring at the door for "Mrs. Brown," he declined, saying that he already had "a bullet in one leg" for participating in another just such affair. But he agreed to hold his conveyance in readiness at a discreet distance from the residence. Isaac Trump, one of George's *Shubrick* friends, with coat collar turned up and soft felt hat drawn down, went to Mr. Flintoff's residence and asked for "Mrs. Brown." Miss Fox was ready, and followed him out, handing him a heavy cloth-covered package, which from its form and feeling he afterwards said he thought must be boxes of jewels, but which to his astonishment turned out to be the "Household Book of Poetry," and all the other volumes that Henry George had given the young lady, she preferring to take these to any other of her personal possessions. Presently Mr. George joined them and they proceeded to the carriage where the lady that Isaac Trump was engaged to marry was awaiting them. Rev. S. D. Simonds, the Methodist clergyman whom Henry George had been going to hear the year before, was to perform the ceremony. But he was out of town at that hour and would not be back until nine that night. The party, therefore, went to a restaurant to supper. After the repast they walked to Mr. Simond's little Methodist church called the Bethel. The night was bright with moonlight, but wet under foot from the day's storm and when they came to a pool, Henry George lifted his bride-elect over it—a habit which the young man continued, at night at least, for many years.

Charles Coddington and Mrs. Simonds, the wife of the clergyman, were waiting at the church. James George could not get there, but his newly wedded wife, Sophia George, came and brought his hearty good wishes.

Miss Fox, a Catholic in good standing, would have pre-

ferred her own church for the place of the marriage, but
fearing the delay that that seemed to present, was willing
to have Mr. George's Methodist friend, Rev. Mr. Simonds,
perform the ceremony, though soon afterwards in Sacramento she had Rev. Nathaniel Gallagher of St. Rose's
Church give the Catholic sanction.   Broad-minded man
that the Rev. Mr. Simonds was, he voluntarily read
the service of the Episcopal Church in which the bride-
groom had been bred, and which, as he said, "more nearly
approached the Catholic" than his own short Methodist
service.   And in this way Henry George and Annie Fox
—the one twenty-two, the other eighteen—became husband and wife, the ring being the one used at the wedding
of Miss Fox's grandmother.

When the ceremony was over Mr. George wrote out and
sent advertisements to all the newspapers; and the clergyman took down Charles Coddington's name as one of the
witnesses.   He then turned to Mr. Trump, who was to be
second witness, but whom he did not know.   "I. Trump,"
the witness responded.   "I perceive that you do," said the
clergyman, "but what is your name?" and it was several
minutes before the reverend gentleman could be made to
believe that the witness was not joking, and that "I" stood
for "Isaac."[1]

There was no honeymoon trip for this bridal pair; in-

---

[1] Six months later, (July 5, 1862) writing from Sacramento to his Sister
Caroline, Henry George said : "Both friends who were at our marriage
are now in the same fix — Ike Trump and Charlie Coddington (of whom
I have spoken in connection with Hoppel).   Charlie ran away with his
girl, or rather Hoppel did it for him, and they had a queer old time.   When
I was in San Francisco I met Hoppel with a big revolver buckled around
him and he told me the whole story.   Ike's girl went up to Marysville
last week to be married to him, he writing to me to hurry her along ; for
if she lost a day the new licence law would go into effect and he would
have to pay $3 for the privilege."

deed, the young groom arose at five o'clock next morning
to go out and look for work. This he found as a "sub"
type-setter, and worked all day; and in the evening getting
another chance, he worked that night until the small hours
next morning. By irregular "subbing" of this kind he was
able to earn enough to pay their board bills. After a few
days, learning of an opening in Sacramento, the Capital
of the State, he went up and got "subbing" work on the
"Union," a morning daily, and earned good wages. He
at once sent for his wife and for a time at least felt some
sense of security, though adversity was soon again upon
him.

All this while the George family was without knowledge
of what had happened, nor did any but his Sister Jennie
even so much as know of the existence of Miss Fox. Before the crisis came in the love affair, and before he had
drawn out of the "Evening Journal," he had written in
confidence to his sister to tell her of his affection, with-
holding the intelligence from the others because he would
not have his father and mother think that he would so
much as contemplate the taking on of new responsibilities at a time when they were down in their fortunes, and
when he could do so little to help them—a time, indeed,
when, under the circumstances, he could only with difficulty support himself. His sister's reply, without date,
bears evidence of great haste, and runs:

"I felt a sudden choking, a sudden loneliness and
jealousy, when I first read your letter. I have got over
that now; and first of all, no matter what else I say,
my advice to you is: If you *really love Annie, you marry
her as soon as you are able to support her.* I have no
doubt you are sure of loving her . . . though you
cannot be too sure.

"I am sorry she is a Catholic, very sorry. Be care-

ful about that. You say you often talk on religious
subjects; let them not be doctrinal points. The ground
is dangerous to you, no matter how well balanced your
mind may be. I know that our family will object to
that, Ma especially; but still I do not think she will
withhold her consent on that account. The great objection is that you should be married away from home.
Do not, I beg of you. Come home and bring her with
you. I will love her; so will they all, I know.

"I love her already—at least I feel as if I had found
a new friend somewhere by the name of Annie. I call
her Annie to myself; her name is familiar to me now.
. . . Marry her if you love her, for love is too precious a thing to be thrown away. 'For beauty is easy
enough to win, but one isn't loved every day.' . . .

"In the meantime do not forget me; do not cease to
love me as much as ever, will you? There can be two
places in your heart—one for Annie and one for me."

When he wrote in November that he was out of the
"Evening Journal" his mother answered (December 11):

"I see, my son, that you get the blues sometimes as
well as other folks, and I don't wonder. I think you
have had a hard time of it, but don't, I beseech you,
ever allow that to prevent you from writing home. Remember, a whole household is made blue in that case,
though they say they are not, to keep up the mother's
spirits. Keep up your spirits, my dear boy. All will
yet be well. I feel persuaded you will yet come out
right. You know the darkest hour is just before day.
I have always boasted of your happy, cheerful, encouraging tone. Never till late have I detected a shadow of
gloom. Put your trust in God, my dear child."

Then, owing to the disturbed condition of the country,
mails accumulated, and there was a three months' silence
from California. When the mails resumed, a bunch of
letters arrived together, among them one from the son tell-

ing of his marriage and one from his wife, for both of them wrote just after the wedding. Perhaps the folks were too happy on hearing from their son once more in those troublous times and too much astonished at the news that the letters brought, to think of deprecating his marriage. At any rate, the whole family united in a warm and earnest welcome to the new daughter and sister, and nearly all of them wrote messages of love by the next mail. His Sister Kate wrote (March 4):

"My new relationship never struck me so forcibly as it did last night at family prayers, when father prayed for his beloved son and daughter. Before we used only to pray for our dear absent one; now it is for our dear absent ones."

The young couple had on their side waited with something like trepidation through the long months for word of recognition from home, and though neither spoke of it, both had almost settled down into despair when the bundle of letters came to hand, telling of the warm taking into the heart, and then the time slipped merrily along. But his mother and his Sister Jennie pleaded with them in every letter to come home. To her brother, Jennie wrote with a tender love (April 20):

"There are a great many more things here to remind us of you than there are out there to remind you of us. . . . Here everything is associated with you. We live the same as we did when you went away; in the same house, doing the same things over and over again, only each time we do them less light-heartedly, feeling that we are gradually growing older, that things will not always be so.

"We had pretty nice times when we were children, didn't we? Yesterday I was forcibly reminded that

every one of us is growing older. You know it was
Easter Saturday. Don't you remember Ma always dyed
us two or three eggs apiece? Well, yesterday she did
not dye one. She never thought of it and none of the
children asked for it.

"What nice times we used to have Christmas, too.
How sleepless we used to be all night. You used to
be up about 4 o'clock in the morning.

"Hen, in the Spring we used to have such a time
planting seed in our garden. What a handsome garden! Time has not improved it. It is the same little
'snub' it used to be. We thought it was nice though,
didn't we? Don't you remember Tom and Val used
to plant things and pull them up about a week after to
see if they were growing?

"Tell Annie about Tom sitting in the air. I tell him
that that one act is enough to immortalise and hand
his name down to posterity."[1]

The bond between brother and sister was never closer
than now, as shown by his letter a couple of months later:

Sacramento, June 5, '62.

"MY DEAR JENNIE: We are having Summer at last;
and hot enough it certainly is. I feel it more, perhaps,
than I would otherwise from the fact that since leaving Panama I have experienced no really warm weather,
the winds which draw in through the Golden Gate,
making San Francisco almost as cool in summer as in
winter. But we are now living in one of the pleasantest parts of the town—a square from the State Capitol
—and surrounded by trees of all kinds and the largest
growth, and roses in greater profusion than I ever saw

---

[1] Tom George, the brother next in age to Henry, had been told that sitting in the air was possible. So following directions, he procured one of
the household wash tubs, filled it with water, placed a board across it,
stood on the board and then told a younger brother and sister to draw the
board away when he leaped up into the air. He leaped and they pulled
— and then, of course, down he came and took an unpremeditated bath.

before.   Aunt Mary would be delighted with this country, barring the floods.

"A short distance from the house is the slough—
formed by the back water of the American River, which
unites with the Sacramento at this point—a beautiful
sheet of water on which we have a boat, and over which
we frequently sail.   In a word, we are as pleasantly
situated as we could desire, but Annie will tell you all
about how we are fixed.   She will write to-night, being
at the present moment 'amusing' herself by nursing
a baby, the property of one of the ladies in the house,
and of which I must in justice say that I have not yet
heard it cry.   She is a regular woman, and has all the
notions and fancies that seem so strange to a man.

"But while we are so pleasantly situated, 'Old Adversity' walks as close behind as ever.   The Legislature
has adjourned, as I told you before, and though the
weather and roads have much improved, the Overland
Mail stage has not yet commenced running.   We were
under the impression that it had started from the other
side and the first budget of news would be here in a
few days, but on Sunday a telegraphic despatch was
received from New York dated May 26 stating that
operations would probably be resumed in about fifteen
days.   This is disheartening, for to its regular arrivals
we are looking for the revival of our business, which just
now is unprecedentedly dull.   The proprietors of the
'Union' state their determination to commence to run
two double sheets a week as soon as the Overland Mail
resumes, which will give me all the work I care to do.
But we have been expecting and looking for it so long
that it seems that it never would come.   I am not one
of those who love work for its own sake, but feeling
what it brings, I love it and am happiest when hard at
it.   It is no wonder that wealth is sought by all means,
good or bad, for it expresses almost everything.   With
it, it seems to me, I should be supremely happy (perhaps that is the reason I have it not).   It is but the
want of a few dollars that keeps us separate, that forces
us to struggle on so painfully, that crushes down all
the noblest yearnings of the heart and mind.   I do not

complain that no special miracle is worked in my behalf, that by none of those lucky windfalls which sometimes come to fools, I am enriched; but it really seems that strive as hard in whatever direction I may, the current still turns against me. But I will not believe that it will be so always. At any rate I will do the best I can, make the most of my opportunities, and for the rest trust to God.

"Though I have a great deal of time on my hands, I do not think it is wholly lost. I employ it in the development of either body or mind, in rowing or swimming or in reading. Marriage has certainly benefitted me by giving a more contented and earnest frame of mind and will help me to do my best in 'whatever station it pleases God to call me.' This is the only difference I can perceive. Annie and I are so well matched in years and temperament that there was no violent change in either. I feel no older, and my dear sister, I love you as much as ever, and I believe, long to see you more. But I am afraid it will be some time before we can get home, and in the meantime we want to try and get one of you out here. The fare will be reduced in some way or other before long, and when I once get *on the train,* it will not take long to find the means. I wish you were all here, I think you would like the country, or that we were all home, which would be better still. However, we must hope on.

"Every day the telegraph is in working order it brings us the news of the success of the armies of the Republic. I cannot help feeling regret that the contest will be over and the victories won without my having taken the slightest part in it. If I am East after the war is ended I will feel abashed among its heroes. If I had been home I would have gone if I possibly could, but here there was no chance unless one could pay his passage to New York, for those who were raised here were merely to garrison posts and fight Indians, though now a column is being pushed across the deserts to Arizona, though it is very doubtful if they will see any fighting.

"What has become of Will Jones and Charley Walton? You have not told me of them, but I suppose they are in the army.

"Times must be improving now at home. The worst of the war will soon be over and then I think there will be a great revival. Considering the effects of the floods and the northern gold fevers, everything is becoming quite brisk here.

"In future direct to the 'Union' office at Sacramento, and if I am not here my letters will be forwarded immediately. I think, however, that I will stay here for some time, and if I get a situation within a short time, I will be sure to do so.

"For the present I must say good-bye. Give my love to all.

"Your affectionate brother,

"HENRY GEORGE."

"P. S. I have just received a call to go to work, so excuse my abruptness."

And so the current of affectionate communion passed between brother and sister, when one afternoon, returning from an outing for his early evening dinner, the young wife noticed that her husband was depressed and preoccupied, that he ate little, and that when he spoke it was as with an effort to be cheerful. He went off to his printer's work as usual, but when he came home in the early morning she asked his trouble. He said that letters from home bore heavy news which he had withheld as she was to be alone during the long night hours. Now he was ready to tell her—his Sister Jennie was dead! He handed her a letter from his mother, and unable longer to control himself, broke into a flood of passionate tears. The letter, which was unsigned, ran:

Philadelphia, August 7, 1862.

"MY DEAR SON: Uncle Thomas has imparted to you by this mail the dreadful, heart-crushing news. God, I hope, has given you strength to bear it. After my

first gush of agony, and I could think at all, my cry
went up for my boy, Lord, sustain him in this great
trouble. Oh, if he were here to witness the dying scene
and weep with us it would not seem so hard. And then,
dear Annie, your image came up with inexpressible comfort—a dear wife to sympathise with him, on whose
breast he can pour out his agonising cry, tears to mingle with his tears. O I blessed God that he had a wife.

"It is nearly two weeks since we laid our darling
Jennie in the grave, and we miss her more and feel more
desolate than we did at first. O every article, and every
spot, and everything in the house reminds us of her.
O how we mourn our precious child. . . . My
heart would burst without tears.

"I suppose Uncle Thomas gave you particulars of her
death and the impression with her from the first that
she would die. In her first conversation with me (she
had been in bed several days and seemed to be easier
and more quiet, her sickness at first being characterised
by great restlessness and excessive debility by turns)
she said: 'Ma, I want to see Uncle Thomas, and Dr.
Goddard and Dr. Reed.'[1] She had just been telling Pop
before I came in the room the same thing, mourning
over her coldness and hardness of heart, and saying that
she had not lived as she ought and that she was afraid
to die, that her Saviour would not receive her and that
she would not go to heaven. All day when I thought
her easy and quiet she had been struggling and praying. 'O Ma,' said she, 'how everything earthly sinks
into utter nothingness at the prospect of death!' I
tried to comfort her (Pop could not command his voice),
told her neither we nor the doctor had a thought of
her dying, she would get well; but I said, 'Dear, Uncle
Thomas cannot help your peace of mind; no earthly arm
can give you peace.' 'I know it,' she answered quickly,
'but I would love to have him talk and pray with me.'
'Jesus alone,' I again said, 'is all you want. Simply
look to Him; cast yourself upon Him, in all your sin-
fulness and weakness, as you did, my child, when you

---

[1] Drs. Goddard and Reed were clergymen.

first came to Him years ago. He is the same precious Saviour.' I repeated the hymn 'Rock of Ages,' slowly and with emphasis—

> " 'In my hand no price I bring,
>   Simply to thy cross I cling.'

'Yes, yes,' she whispered. . . .

"O then the cruel, crushing blow came. I would not listen to any of them, not until dinner time would I believe my child was going to die. No, no, no; not my Jennie. Others might lose their children, but O no, this could not be. This rebellious spirit lasted some time after she breathed her last, though after the first outburst I was enabled to choke down the agony and appear calm until it all was over. She died peacefully and gently, as an infant just sleeping away. . . .

"Henry, how her mind developed! It was too much for her frail body. She read too much—nearly every day at the library, besides bringing home books.

"A piece of hair for Annie."

After his wife had read the letter the young man, springing to his feet and pacing the floor, as was his habit when mentally roused, protested that he could not bring himself to believe that his dear sister was dead; and with the manner of sudden conviction, said that there *must* be, there *is*, another life—that the soul *is* immortal. But his words expressed his longing, rather than his conviction. Immortality he now earnestly wished to believe in. But the theology of his youth did not persuade him, and it was not until many years afterwards when pursuing the great inquiry that produced "Progress and Poverty" that he perceived the "grand simplicity and unspeakable harmony of universal law," that beneficence and intelligence govern social laws, instead of blind, clashing forces; and then faith from reason came and immortality became a fixed belief.

CHAPTER IX.

SUFFERS EXTREME PRIVATION.

1861-1865.   AGE, 22-26.

THE city of Sacramento, built on the sloping east bank of the Sacramento River, at the junction with the American River, is protected from overflows by a levee. For several weeks at the close of 1861 heavy rains had fallen throughout the State, so that the great Sacramento and San Joaquin river systems had over-flowed their natural banks, and in January, when Mrs. George was sent for by her husband to come to Sacramento, the rainfall amounted to twenty-four and one half inches, the heaviest monthly fall recorded in California. Under the stress of water, the levee broke and the low part of the city was submerged, most of the one-story buildings being entirely covered. Outside the city the entire country as far as the eye could reach, north and south, and as far west as the Coast Range of mountains was a sheet of water, the river course being told only by the tops of trees that grew along the banks.[1]

The Georges at first lived in the old City Hotel on K Street, just around the corner from the "Union" office where the husband worked. One morning Mr. George sent a hurried message to his wife to get her lunch, that

---

[1] Hittell's " History of California," Vol. IV., pp. 294–295.

he would join her at once, for the water was coming. The hotel dining-room was on the ground floor, and out in the street had accumulated a small pool, and so rapidly did the water rise that before the hasty repast was over all in the dining-room were standing on their chairs and left the room on a bridge or pathway of them.

But everybody was showing what is said to be an American characteristic—good humour in face of the inevitable. People abandoned first stories and lived and did business above. Printers in the "Union" office came to the City Hotel over roof tops. The members of the legislature moved about in boats, as did everyone else who could get them; and failing boats, used wash tubs, bath tubs and rafts. All things seemed to pass the hotel, and among them came a section of sidewalk bearing a man and his dog, the man on a stool, calmly contemplating the watery aspect of city and country. Bakers' ovens were early submerged, so that for a time fruit cake in stock became a substitute for bread. Spirituous liquors were, also, for a time exceedingly scarce—a serious deprivation in a community, where, as in every new country, custom had made drinking of some sort one of the common marks of cordiality in daily social life. This afforded Henry George special opportunity for amusement. While on the "Evening Journal" he had obtained from a druggist, who had no other way of settling an advertising bill, some toilet articles, and among them twelve bottles of "New England Rum," all of which he had given to Miss Fox, and which were sent to her with her personal effects by her relatives after her marriage. Mr. George now took the "New England Rum" to his thirsty printer friends, and to his intense amusement, they emptied the bottles in a twinkle. When Mrs. George heard of this she was in consternation. "It was not for the stomach, but for the head—a hair tonic," she said. One of the printers ventured to explain that what was good for the hair must be good for the stomach, and that at any rate the liquid had tasted well and had produced no ill effects.

After perhaps four months' residence at the City Hotel, the Georges went to boarding and then to housekeeping, taking one house after another. They were so restless that in answer to an acquaintance's question afterwards as to what time of year they cleaned house, Mr. George jokingly said: "We didn't clean house; we moved, instead!" In October of 1862 he wrote home to his sisters:

"I have not written for some time—much longer than I should have neglected it; but I have been very busy all this time—busier than I have ever been before. I have been working steadily and literally working all the time. Up to a couple of months ago I could not get enough to do, but since then the Overland Mail has been arriving with great regularity, and I have not missed a day, except when I took a run down to San Francisco for a couple of days on business, trying to get the balance of the pittance for which I sold my share in the 'Evening Journal.' Had not my necessities been so great I would not have worked as I have during that time, for no one can do so for any time and retain good health. But I wanted so much that I could not idle away a day on which I had a chance to work. But we are getting along very well and I will not do so in future. I have been making from $36 to $40 every week, and to do that I have had to be at work constantly, for the work on the 'Union' is what the printers call 'lean,' and every cent made is fully earned. I have not even read the papers; barely glanced over the outlined news each day, and on the one day of the week when I had any time to spare it has been so filled up with things that should have been attended to during the week and I have been so tired out that I have hardly had time to write."

On November 3 (1862) the first child was born, a boy, who was named after his father. Added responsibilities made the young printer ready to turn his hand to whatever would bring him a living. And it happened that a young newspaper man named Samuel L. Clemens, who, under the *nom de plume* of "Mark Twain," had won a reputation on the Coast as a humourist of a dry and original quality, came to Sacramento to lecture. Another newspaper man, Denis E. McCarthy, acting as manager, hired Henry George to take tickets at the door.

Close, hard work had enabled Mr. George to pay up pretty much all that he owed in San Francisco at the time of his marriage. Then getting some money ahead, he had, following the old infatuation, invested it in mining stocks. But these stocks, instead of yielding dividends or even advancing in value, brought constant assessments, which meant privation or more indebtedness, and frequently both. He had in these mining ventures gone in with Isaac Trump, who was deeply interested in what was known as the Gettysburg and Swansea Mining Company, working a copper claim. The situation is explained in letters to and from Trump.

Sacramento, October 12, 1863.

"DEAR IKE: As you cannot come down and I cannot go up, I will write you as much as possible of my views and wishes about our investments. I don't want to bother you and will be as brief as possible.

"It is now eight months since we determined to make our fortunes, and I am afraid, in spite of our sanguine hopes, we have failed. 'Hope deferred maketh the heart sick,' and that is my case, if not yours. From the hopes of making a big raise, I have come down to think if I can get my money back I will be in luck. I need it badly and want to get it as soon as possible. . .

"I asked you the actual, cash value of my stock, and as you say nothing in answer, I suppose you consider the question already answered in your previous letter. In that you set down Swansea at $3 per foot and everything else, exclusive of Banner and Gray Eagle, at $1. That would make the account about this:

100	feet	Swansea	$300.00
100	"	Pine Bark...............	100.00
37½	"	Red Rock................	37.50
25	"	Yorkville	25.00
			$462.50

The others, I don't suppose you count at anything. If this money could be got, however, I would be very well satisfied, you may be sure. I would be willing to take almost half that amount for everything.

"You tell me to sell down here, but that is a sheer impossibility. The claims are not known here. If they were Sacramento companies it might be different. As it is, I could only sell to one who would take my word for their value, which no one but a very intimate friend would do, and to such I would not sell in that way. I suppose it would be a like impossibility with you to get in cash anything like the figures you have named, but I suppose something could be got.

"Outside of the Swansea I should like to sell everything for whatever it would bring. I can't pay any more assessments without getting something back—with my liabilities it is impossible. Twenty-five or fifty feet of the Swansea I would like to hold. The remainder I want to sell.

"The year is fast closing and prices are not likely to improve before another season. I am deeply in debt and I want to make another effort by Spring at farthest and think the sooner we realize what we can the better it will be for us.

"I write you as well as I can what I think and want,

and leave you to act. If you don't want to sell, but can sell for me, without injuring yourself, do so.

"Yours sincerely,

"HENRY GEORGE."

Marysville, Nov. 8, 1863.

"DEAR HARRY: I received your note a few days ago. I do not think I will be able to come down for a month yet. I cannot raise the money. Unless something turns up before Christmas I am gone in. I have gone everything on copper and now I see no way of extricating myself, unless I give up near all my 'feet.' Plenty have Swansea who will not sell at any price, and others again can hardly give it away. We are about giving a contract to sink a shaft 35 feet deeper. The majority of the company think it will pay its own way after we get down 10 feet farther. An assessment on the Swansea is levied—ten cents a foot, payable before the 20th of this month.

"It is very uncertain about my stopping here any length of time, for I am very much discouraged and feel like starting out on the hills to prospect. I want excitement and think I could get plenty of it on a prospecting tour. I have a good locality in view where they have struck the richest kind of copper (so it is said). If I could only hold onto my stock a few months longer I feel confident I *must* come out all right.

"Harry, the Swansea is actually worth $6.00 per foot, but people here have paid out considerable this summer, and likewise the market is over-stocked with 'feet,' and folks have been 'stuck' so often that it is almost impossible to get men to purchase in any claim no matter how cheap it is offered. If one offers to sell low they come to the conclusion it is a *sell*, no matter how good your prospect is. And so it is, and so it will be, so long as men will be found who are ever willing to swindle their fellow men for the sake of a few paltry dollars. If I had been mean enough to take advantage of parties who had placed confidence in me since I have been on the 'copper lay,' I could have come out considerably ahead by this time. I do not regret acting honourably to them, but I do think there is a mighty slim chance for 'the poor whites' ever making anything by acting on the square.

"I feel quite depressed in spirits, but nevertheless, I am determined to persevere and try it again. As Mc-Fadden said: 'It is a gold ring or a wooden leg.'

"I have had sad news from home—a death in the family and my mother in poor circumstances. And to think I cannot send her one dollar at present! 'It is hard, but I suppose fair.' If I live, by the help of God, *I will* come out all right yet.

"My love to all,

"ISAAC TRUMP."

In the end—and the end was soon after the interchange of these letters—the mining ventures involved the two speculators in the loss of nearly all that they had invested. In his efforts to "get his nose out of the space box," George had been trying about this time to promote a project for a newspaper in the mining region of Reese River, but this, too, had failed, and the year was closing with him in what to a man in his circumstances were embarrassing debts.

It had been a year of hard work and considerable worry with the young printer, affording little time for attention to occurrences beyond his own small sphere; yet two events of first magnitude engaged his earnest thought. On January 1, 1863, President Lincoln issued his Emancipation Proclamation, which forever killed chattel bondage in the United States, and in the eyes of the world changing the issue from secession to slavery, gave the North new vigour for the conflict and cut off the South's hope of foreign aid.

The other event that intensely interested George was close at hand. Leland Stanford, a grocery and provision dealer in Sacramento, had been elected to the office of

Governor of California on the new Republican party tidal wave. He was also president of the Central Pacific Railroad Company and on the 8th of January, 1863, amid a crowd of people at the corner of Front and K Streets, Sacramento, he turned the first shovelful of earth in the construction of a railroad system which at that time looked puny enough, but which, under the extraordinarily energetic, able and unscrupulous management of Stanford, Charles Crocker, a Sacramento dry goods merchant, and Collis P. Huntington and Mark Hopkins, Sacramento hardware dealers, was within the next half dozen years to cross the State, climb over the mountains, span the Nevada desert, and meeting the line coming from the Missouri River, join with unbroken track, the West with the East. The young hard-working printer took an intense interest in what nearly everyone in the State at the time seemed to hail with applause. He may, indeed, have been one of the unnoticed men in the crowd at the initial ceremonies; but his mind beginning to open, questions were beginning to creep in, and he was before long to see that the enterprise—and likewise every such enterprise—in private hands, must involve gigantic public evils. And taking a clear mental stand against this, thought was to expand to other and deeper problems, and at length bring the obscure type-setter into the world's gaze as a new champion of equal rights. But no outward sign of such thought was to appear for years yet.

The first break in Mr. George's affairs at Sacramento was on the 26th of January, 1864, after he had been working on the "Union" for more than a year. That evening, after the midnight lunch, he got into an altercation with the foreman, John Timmins, about some matter that does not now appear clear, and was discharged. He was too proud to linger around or try to get back, and two days later left by steamer for San Francisco to look for work there.[1] The day after his arrival in San Francisco he wrote to his wife:

> "Times seem pretty dull here, but I think I can get along. Anyhow we will try. I staid at the 'What Cheer House' last night. My darling, I don't know how much I love you until I am separated from you. I don't believe I could live without you. And the dear little fellow—how I love him!"

The young wife, with the baby, at once followed her husband to San Francisco where they went for a few days to the old Oriental Hotel, then very much run down, and afterwards took private rooms. The husband was on the alert for work from the moment he had arrived. Nothing whatever presented itself until Knowlton of the "Evening Journal" suggested that he canvass for subscribers for that paper on a commission basis. Isaac Trump, pursued by hard luck, had meanwhile come down from the mountains and was trying to see what he could do at selling clothes wringers, and he suggested that George should sell some wringers at the same time that he canvassed for the newspaper. George started out vigorously on the plan, but after five days of hard walking and talking through the suburban parts of Alameda County, just across San Francisco Bay, he returned without having sold a single wringer and with scarcely more than half a dozen subscribers. Then he went to setting type on the "Evening Journal," though the paper was in an obviously shaky

---

[1] A few years later, when Charles De Young was about to start the "Daily Chronicle," with Henry George as managing editor, the latter recommended Timmins for the position of foreman, saying that though he and Timmins had parted in ill-feeling, Timmins was an excellent workman and worthy of the post. Timmins obtained the place.

condition, and he had difficulty in getting his wages. Indeed, the money due for his share in the paper sold more than two years before had not yet been fully paid him. But for a time no other position opened to him. He was now nearly two hundred dollars in debt, with no prospect of steady employment. However, one of the regular typesetters on the "Evening Bulletin" being taken down with a serious illness, George received a call to the place as substitute and made good wages while the position lasted.

In April he left the "Bulletin" and went on the "American Flag." A little later, having got somewhat out of debt, he and his wife took a little house on Russ Street, or rather the upper flat of a two-story wooden house, and paid eighteen dollars rent. A change came in the "Flag" office on October 18, when the foreman, Mr. Bradford, discharged Mr. George for "claiming an advertisement." Next day the young man asked for a meeting of the "chapel" (the body of journeyman printers in the office), and after a hearing, was justified and under the typographical union rules was entitled to go back to work, but feeling that the foreman had taken a dislike to him, he concluded to resign. This threw him back upon "subbing" and he worked around odd days and nights wherever a friend laid off and gave him a call. All during the year he had at various times been talking with first one and then another about newspaper schemes that would give him better wages, in the future if not at once, and a chance to do something more than set type. He talked of the Sonora "Eagle," and of starting papers at Silver Mountain, Susanville, and La Paz, but none of these schemes took form, and when Isaac Trump suggested going into a partnership with him and a skilled job type setter named Peter Daley in a job-printing office, he decided that that was the thing to do.

Isaac Trump was a square, generous-minded man, of restless nature, sanguine temperament and great energy. With small schooling, he had a shrewdness and quickness of mind that adapted him to circumstances, and a love of mechanical contrivances that made him ready to turn his hand to anything. The ways that Trump had tried during the past few years to make a living were legion. He had learned the trade of gas fitter in his native city of Philadelphia, had shipped on the *Shubrick* for California as coal passer, had attempted farming on landing,[1] had lived for a while by mending pumps and when that failed took to mending watches, though he knew little about either; had "gone broke" at mining, and when he had done a job of wall papering and the complaint was made that the figure in the paper was up-side-down, he admitted that that was so, but that he had supposed the job was to be done in "first-class Eastern style" where it had become the fashion to invert the paper! He had got a delivery route on the "Flag," but sold it and now panted for a job-printing office, suggesting that he should solicit business while Daley and George should set type and do the mechancial work. The "Evening Journal" had at last died in June and its plant of type was lying idle. In December, 1864, George purchased some of this plant for the new business, agreeing to pay $400 and give $100

---

[1] In "The Science of Political Economy," Henry George makes reference to Trump's farming (p. 500). "On going ashore in San Francisco, a ship-mate of mine, who could not tell a scythe from a marlinspike, hired out to a farmer in haying-time for $5 a day. At his first stroke with the scythe he ran it so deep in the ground that he nearly broke it in getting it out. Though he indignantly denounced such antiquated tools as out of fashion, declaring that he was used to " the patent scythes that turn up at the end," he did not really feel wronged that the farmer would not pay him a cent, as he knew that the agreement for day's labour was really an agreement for so much mowing."

worth of work, making money payment in what cash he could borrow and giving notes for the remainder.

Thus heavily weighted at the outset, the three men opened their office. But hard times had come. A drought had shortened the grain crop, killed great numbers of cattle and lessened the gold supply, and the losses that the farming, ranching and mineral regions suffered affected all the commercial and industrial activities of the State, so that there was a general depression. Business not coming into their office, the three partners went out to hunt for it; and yet it was elusive, so that they had very little to do and soon were in extremities for living necessities. even for wood for the kitchen fire. Henry George had fitfully kept a pocket diary during 1864, and a few entries at this job-printing period tell of the pass of affairs.

"December 25. Determined to keep a regular journal, and to cultivate habits of determination, energy and industry. Feel that I am in a bad situation, and must use my utmost effort to keep afloat and go ahead. Will try to follow the following general rules for one week:

"1st. In every case to determine rationally what is best to be done.

"2nd. To do everything determined upon immediately, or as soon as an opportunity presents.

"3rd. To write down what I shall determine upon doing for the succeeding day.

"Saw landlady and told her I was not able to pay rent.

"December 26. 7A.M.:

"1st. Propose to-day in addition to work in office, to write to Boyne.

"2nd. To get wood in trade.

"3rd. · To talk with Dr. Eaton, and perhaps, Dr. Morse.

"Rose at quarter to seven. Stopped at six wood yards trying to get wood in exchange for printing, but failed. Did very little in office. Walked and talked with Ike. Felt very blue and thought of drawing out. Saw Dr. Eaton, but failed to make a trade. In evening saw Dr. Morse. Have not done all, nor as well as I could wish. Also wrote to Boyne, but did not mail letter.

"January 1. (Sunday) Annie not very well. Got down town about 11 o'clock. Went with Ike to Chinaman's to see about paper bags. Returned to office and worked off a lot.

"January 2. Got down town about 8 o'clock. Worked some labels. Not much doing.

"January 3. Working in office all day. DeLong called to talk about getting out a journal. Did our best day's work."

From time to time they got a little business, enough at any rate to encourage Trump and George to continue with the office, though Daley dropped out; and each day that the money was there the two partners took out of the business twenty-five cents apiece, which they together spent for food, Trump's wife being with her relatives and he taking his dinner with the Georges. They lived chiefly on corn meal and milk, potatoes, bread and sturgeon, for meat they could not afford and sturgeon was the cheapest fish they could find.[1] Mr. George generally went to the office early without breakfast, saying that he would get it down town; but knowing that he had no money, his wife more than suspected that many a morning passed without his getting a mouthful. Nor could he borrow money

---

[1] Unlike that fish on the Atlantic Coast, sturgeon on the Pacific Coast, or at any rate in California waters, is of fine quality and could easily be substituted on the table for halibut.

except occasionally, for the drought that had made general business so bad had hurt all his friends, and indeed, many of them had already borrowed from him while he had anything to lend; and he was too proud to complain now to them. Nor did his wife complain, though what deepened their anxieties was that they looked for the coming of a second child. Mrs. George would not run up bills that she did not have money to meet. She parted with her little pieces of jewellery and smaller trinkets one by one, until only her wedding ring had not been pawned. And then she told the milkman that she could no longer afford to take milk, but he offered to continue to supply it for printed cards, which she accepted. Mr. George's diary is blank just here, but at another time he said:[1]

"I came near starving to death, and at one time I was so close to it that I think I should have done so but for the job of printing a few cards which enabled us to buy a little corn meal. In this darkest time in my life my second child was born."

The baby came at seven o'clock in the morning of January 27, 1865. When it was born the wife heard the doctor say: "Don't stop to wash the child; he is starving. Feed him!" After the doctor had gone and mother and baby had fallen asleep, the husband left them alone in the house, and taking the elder child to a neighbour's, himself went to his business in a desperate state of mind, for his wife's condition made money—some money—an absolute and immediate necessity. But nothing came into the office and he did not know where to borrow. What then happened he told sixteen years subsequently.

---

[1] Meeker notes, October, 1897.

"I walked along the street and made up my mind to get money from the first man whose appearance might indicate that he had it to give. I stopped a man—a stranger—and told him I wanted $5. He asked what I wanted it for. I told him that my wife was confined and that I had nothing to give her to eat. He gave me the money. If he had not, I think I was desperate enough to have killed him." [1]

The diary notes commence again twenty days after the new baby's birth and show that the struggle for subsistence was still continuing, that Henry George abandoned the job-printing office and that he and his wife and babies had moved into a smaller house where he had to pay a rent of only nine dollars a month—just half of his former rent. This diary consists simply of two half sheets of white note paper, folded twice and pinned in the middle, forming two small neat books of eight pages each of about the size of a visiting card. The writing is very small, but clear.

"Feb. 17, 1865. (Friday) 10:40 P.M. Gave I. Trump this day bill of sale for my interest in office, with the understanding that if he got any money by selling, I am to get some. I am now afloat again, with the world before me. I have commenced this little book as an experiment—to aid me in acquiring habits of regu-

---

[1] Henry George related this incident to Dr. James E. Kelly in a conversation in Dublin during the winter of 1881–82, in proof that environment has more to do with human actions, and especially with so-called criminal actions, than we generally concede ; and to show how acute poverty may drive sound-minded moral men to the commission of deeds that are supposed to belong entirely to hardened evil natures. Out of long philosophical and physiological talks together at that time the two men formed a warm friendship, and subsequently, when he came to the United States and established himself in New York, Dr. Kelly became Henry George's family physician and attended him at his death-bed.

larity, punctuality and purpose. I will enter in it each evening the principal events of the day, with notes, if they occur, errors committed or the reverse, and plans for the morrow and future. I will make a practice of looking at it on rising in the morning.

"I am starting out afresh, very much crippled and embarrassed, owing over $200. I have been unsuccessful in everything. I wish to profit by my experience and to cultivate those qualities necessary to success in which I have been lacking. I have not saved as much as I ought and am resolved to practice a rigid economy until I have something ahead.

"1st. To make every cent I can.
"2nd. To spend nothing unnecessarily.
"3rd. To put something by each week, if it is only a five cent piece borrowed for the purpose.
"4th. Not to run in debt if it can be avoided.

"1st. To endeavour to make an acquaintance and friend of every one with whom I am brought in contact.
"2nd. To stay at home less, and be more social.
"3rd. To strive to think consecutively and decide quickly.

"Feb. 18. Rose at 6 o'clock. Took cards to woodman. Went to post office and got two letters, one from Wallazz and another from mother. Heard that Smith was up and would probably not go down. Tried to hunt him up. Ran around after him a great deal. Saw him; made an appointment, but he did not come. Finally met him about 4. He said that he had written up for a man, who had first choice; but he would do all he could. I was much disappointed. Went back to office; then after Knowlton, but got no money. Then went to 'Alta' office. Smith there. Stood talking till they went to work. Then to job office. Ike had got four bits [50 cents] from Dr. Josselyn. Went home, and he came out to supper.

"Got up in good season.

"Tried to be energetic about seeing Smith. Have not done with that matter yet, but will try every means.

"To-morrow will write to Cousin Sophia,[1] and perhaps to Wallazz and mother, and will try to make acquaintances. Am in very desperate plight. Courage!"

"Feb. 19. (Sunday) Rose about 9. Ran a small bill with Wessling for flour, coffee and butter. After breakfast took Harry around to Wilbur's. Talked awhile. Went down town. Could not get in office. Went into 'Alta' office several times. Then walked around, hoping to strike Smith. Ike to dinner. Afterwards walked with him, looking for house. Was at 'Alta' office at 6, but no work. Went with Ike to Stickney's and together went to 'Californian' office. Came home and summed up assets and liabilities. At 10 went to bed, with determination of getting up at 6 and going to 'Bulletin' office.

"Have wasted a great deal of time in looking for Smith. Think it would have been better to have hunted him at once or else trusted to luck. There seems to be very little show for me down there. Don't know what to do.

"Feb. 20. Got up too late to go to the 'Bulletin' office. Got $1 from woodman. Got my pants from the tailor. Saw Smith and had a long talk with him. He seemed sorry that he had not thought of me, but said another man had been spoken to and was anxious to go. Went to 'Alta' office several times. Came home early and went to 'Alta' office at 6 and to 'Call' at 7, but got no work. Went to Ike Trump's room, and then came home.

---

[1] She was now a widow, James George having died in the preceding August.

"Was not prompt enough in rising. Have been walking around a good part of the day without definite purpose, thereby losing time.

"Feb. 21. Worked for Ike. Did two cards for $1. Saw about books, and thought some of travelling with them. Went to 'Alta' before coming home. In evening had row with Chinaman. Foolish.

"Feb. 22. Hand very sore. Did not go down till late. Went to work in 'Bulletin' at 12. Got $3. Saw Boyne. Went to library in evening. Thinking of economy.

"Feb. 26. Went to 'Bulletin'; no work. Went with Ike Trump to look at house on hill; came home to breakfast. Decided to take house on Perry Street with Mrs. Stone; took it. Came home and moved. Paid $5 of rent. About 6 o'clock went down town. Saw Ike; got 50 cents. Walked around and went to Typographical Union meeting. Then saw Ike again. Found Knowlton had paid him for printing plant, and demanded some of the money. He gave me $5 with very bad humour.

"Feb. 27. Saw Ike in afternoon and had further talk. In evening went to work for Col. Strong on 'Alta.' Smith lent me $3.

"Feb. 28. Worked again for Strong. Got $5 from John McComb.

"Feb. 29. Got $5 from Barstow, and paid Charlie Coddington the $10 I had borrowed from him on Friday last. On Monday left at Mrs. Lauders [the Russ Street landlady] $1.25 for extra rent and $1.50 for milkman.

"March 1. Rose early, went to 'Bulletin'; but got no work. Looked in at Valentine's and saw George

Foster, who told me to go to Frank Eastman's [print-
ing office]. Did so and was told to call again. Came
home; had breakfast. Went to 'Alta' in evening, but
no work. Went to Germania Lodge and then to Stickney's.

"March 2. Went to Eastman's about 11 o'clock and
was put to work.

"March 3. At work.

"March 4. At work. Got $5 in evening."

The strength of the storm had now passed. The young
printer began to get some work at "subbing," though it
was scant and irregular. His wife, who paid the second
month's rent of the Perry Street house by sewing for her
landlady, remarked to her husband how contentedly they
should be able to live if he could be sure of making regularly twenty dollars a week.

CHAPTER X.

BEGINS WRITING AND TALKING.

1865-1866.   AGE, 26-27.

HENRY GEORGE'S career as a writer should be dated from the commencement of 1865, when he was an irregular, substitute printer at Eastman's and on the daily newspapers, just after his severe job-office experience. He now deliberately set himself to self-improvement. These few diary notes for the end of March and beginning of April are found in a small blank book that in 1878, while working on "Progress and Poverty," he also used as a diary.

"Saturday, March 25, 1865. As I knew we would have no letter this morning, I did not hurry down to the office. After getting breakfast, took the wringing machine which I had been using as a sample back to Faulkner's; then went to Eastman's and saw to bill; loafed around until about 2 P.M. Concluded that the best thing I could do would be to go home and write a little. Came home and wrote for the sake of practice an essay on the 'Use of Time,' which occupied me until Annie prepared dinner. Went to Eastman's by six, got money. Went to Union meeting.

"Sunday, March 26. Did not get out until 11 o'clock. Took Harry down town and then to Wilbur's. Proposed to have Dick [the new baby] baptised in afternoon; got Mrs. Casey to come to the house for that purpose, but concluded to wait.   Went to see Dull, who took me to his shop and showed me the model of his wagon brake.

"Monday, March 27.   Got down to office about one o'clock; but no proofs yet.   Strolled around a little. Went home and wrote communication for Aleck Kenneday's new paper, 'Journal of the Trades and Workingmen.'   Took it down to him.   In the evening called on Rev. Mr. Simonds.

"Tuesday, 28.   Got down late.   No work.   In afternoon wrote article about laws relating to sailors.   In evening went down to Dull's shop while he was engaged on model.

"Wednesday, 29.   Went to work about 10.30.   In evening corrected proof for 'Journal of the Trades and Workingmen.'

"Thursday, 30.   At work.

"Tuesday, April 4.   Despatch received stating that Richmond and Petersburgh are both in our possession.

"Wednesday, 5.   Took model of wagon brake to several carriage shops; also to 'Alta' office.   In evening signed agreement with Dull.

"Saturday, 8.   Not working; bill for week, $23. Paid Frank Mahon the $5 I have been owing for some time.   Met Harrison who has just come down from up the country.   He has a good thing up there.   Talked with Dull and drew up advertisement. In evening, nothing."

Thus while he was doing hap-hazard type-setting, and trying to interest carriage builders in a new wagon brake, he was also beginning to write.   The first and most important of these pieces of writing mentioned in the diary notes—on "the use of time"—was sent by Mr. George to his mother, as an indication of his intention to improve himself.   Commencing with boyhood, Henry George, as has been seen, had the power of simple and clear statement, and if this essay served no other purpose than to show the development of that natural power, it would be of value. But as a matter of fact, it has a far greater value; for while repeating his purpose to practise writing—"to acquire facility and elegance in the expression" of his thought—it gives an introspective glimpse into the naturally secretive mind, revealing an intense desire, if not for the "flesh pots of Egypt," at least for such creature and intellectual comforts as would enable him and those close to him "to bask themselves in the warm sunshine of the brief day." This paper is presented in full:

Essay, Saturday Afternoon, March 25, 1865.

"ON THE PROFITABLE EMPLOYMENT OF TIME."

"Most of us have some principal object of desire at any given time of our lives; something which we wish more than anything else, either because its want is more felt, or that it includes other desirable things, and we are conscious that in gaining it we obtain the means of gratifying other of our wishes.

"With most of us, this power, in one shape or the other—is money, or that which is its equivalent or will bring it.

"For this end we subject ourselves to many sacrifices; for its gain we are willing to confine ourselves and employ our minds and bodies in duties which, for their own sakes are irksome; and if we do not throw the whole force of our natures into the effort to gain this, it is that we do not possess the requisite patience, self-command, and penetration where we may direct our efforts.

"I am constantly longing for wealth; the wide difference between my wishes and the means of gratifying them at my command keeps me in perpetual disquiet. It would bring me comfort and luxury which I cannot now obtain; it would give me more congenial employment and associates; it would enable me to cultivate my mind and exert to a fuller extent my powers; it would give me the ability to minister to the comfort and enjoyment of those whom I love most, and therefore, it is my principal object in life to obtain wealth, or at least, more of it than I have at present.

"Whether this is right or wrong, I do not now consider; but that it is so I am conscious.   When I look behind at my past life I see that I have made little or no progress, and am disquieted; when I consider my present, it is difficult to see that I am moving towards it at all; and all my comfort in this respect is in the hope of what the future may bring forth.

"And yet my hopes are very vague and indistinct, and my efforts in any direction, save the beaten track in which I have been used to earn my bread, are, when perceptible, jerky, irregular and without intelligent, continuous direction.

"When I succeed in obtaining employment, I am industrious and work faithfully, though it does not satisfy my wishes.   When I have nothing to do, I am anxious to be in some way labouring towards the end I wish, and yet from hour to hour I cannot tell at what to employ myself.

"To secure any given result it is only necessary to rightly supply sufficient force.   Some men possess a greater amount of natural power than others and produce quicker and more striking results; yet it is apparent that the abilities of the majority, if properly and continuously applied, are sufficient to accomplish much more than they generally do.

"The hours which I have idled away, though made miserable by the consciousness of accomplishing nothing, had been sufficient to make me master of almost any common branch of study.   If, for instance, I had applied myself to the practice of bookkeeping and arithmetic I might now have been an expert in those things; or I might have had the dictionary at my fingers' ends; been a practised, and perhaps an able writer; a much better printer; or been able to read and write French, Spanish or any other modern or ancient language to which I might have directed my attention; and the

mastery of any of these things now would give me an
additional, appreciable power, and means by which to
work to my end, not to speak of that which would have
been gained by exercise and good mental habits.

"These truths are not sudden discoveries; but have
been as apparent for years as at this present time; but
always wishing for some chance to make a sudden leap
forward, I have never been able to direct my mind and
concentrate my attention upon those slow processes by
which everything mental (and in most cases, material)
is acquired.

"Constantly the mind works, and if but a tithe of
its attention was directed to some end, how many matters might it have taken up in succession, increasing its
own stores and power while mastering them?

"To sum up for the present, though this essay has
hardly taken the direction and shape which at the outset
I intended, it is evident to me that I have not employed
the time and means at my command faithfully and ad-
vantageously as I might have done, and consequently,
that I have myself to blame for at least a part of my
non-success. And this being true of the past, in the
future like results will flow from like causes. I will,
therefore, try (though, as I know from experience, it is
much easier to form good resolutions than to faithfully
carry them out) to employ my mind in acquiring useful information or practice, when I have nothing leading more directly to my end claiming my attention.
When practicable, or when I cannot decide upon anything else, I will endeavour to acquire facility and elegance in the expression of my thought by writing essays
or other matters which I will preserve for future comparison. And in this practice it will be well to aim at
mechanical neatness and grace, as well as at proper and
polished language."

Of the two other pieces of writing spoken of in the
diary notes, the "article about laws relating to sailors,"
has left no trace, but a copy of the one for the "Journal
of the Trades and Workingmen," has been preserved. It

was a long letter to the editor, signed "H. G." urging
working men to think about political and social questions,
and find if it be possible to "check the tendency of society
to resolve itself into classes who have too much or too
little." In closing, its author said:

> "And so, Mr. Editor, I hail with joy your establish-
> ment of a paper which shall speak for the working
> classes, and through which their most enlightened views
> may be diffused, which may lead them to think upon
> problems for which it is to their best interests to find
> a solution. At a time when most of our public prints
> pander to wealth and power and would crush the poor
> man beneath the wheel of the capitalist's carriage; when
> one begins to talk of the 'work people' and 'farm ser-
> vants' of this coast, and another to deplore the high
> rate of wages, and each and all to have quick reproba-
> tion for any effort of mechanics or labourers to obtain
> their dues, but nothing to say against combinations to
> deprive them of their rights, I, for one, feel that your
> enterprise is one which we all should feel the necessity
> of, and to which we should lend our cordial support.
> In the columns of your paper I hope to see fearless
> opinions of men and measures ably maintained, and
> the intelligence of our class brought to the solution of
> questions of political and social economy which deeply
> affect us; that we may bring our united efforts to the
> advancement of those great principles upon which our
> republican institutions rest, and upon which we must
> depend to secure for us and our children our proper
> place and rights, and for our country her proud and
> foremost rank among the nations."

It was about this time that in addition to the writings
mentioned in the diary, Henry George wrote a fanciful
sketch entitled "A Plea for the Supernatural," which was
published in the "Californian" and soon afterwards republished by the Boston Saturday "Evening Gazette."

The "Californian" was a San Francisco weekly literary paper founded in 1864, and which, under the editorship of Charles Henry Webb and the contributing pens of Mark Twain, Bret Harte and a lot of other bright writers, had a brilliant, if short, career—being spoken of as having "lived to be three years old and never died." A. A. Stickney, a printer friend, who, while they were in Sacramento working on the "Union" together, induced George to join the Odd Fellows' Order, had bought into the "Californian," and it may have been through his influence that the young printer's sketch was published. But however published is not important, nor is the sketch itself, further than to furnish cumulative evidence of the feverish energy the young man was evincing in pursuit of his purpose to practise writing—a spirit forming one of his most marked characteristics when acting upon an important resolve. He had proved to himself that he could write, and the use to which he put his power came suddenly, unexpectedly and in a way to affect his whole after life.

The Civil War was now about over. On April 9, 1865, Lee's army surrendered. The South, worn out by the terrific struggle and by starvation, lay prostrate, and the whole North and West indulged in demonstrative rejoicings over the prospect of peace and harmony throughout a reunited country—when, on the night of April 14, flashed the appalling news that President Lincoln had been shot. Never before was seen such excitement in excitable San Francisco. This deed seemed like the last desperate act of the slave-power, and all manner of rumours of a vast Southern conspiracy of assassination were afloat. The next day general business was suspended. It was now known definitely that the President, while sitting in a proscenium box at Ford's Theatre, Washington, witnessing the comedy, "Our American Cousin," was shot in the back

of the head by John Wilkes Booth, an actor, who had
stealthily approached from behind, and brandishing a
knife, had leaped from the box to the stage, crying out in
the hearing of the dumb-stricken audience, "*Sic semper
tyrannis:* the South is avenged!"

When news came that Lincoln had died of his wound
excitement in San Francisco ran mad. To many the
first impulse was to destroy the newspapers which had
fostered secession; and the "Democratic Press" edited by
Beriah Brown, the "Occidental" edited by Zachariah
Montgomery, the "Monitor," a Catholic weekly, edited by
Thomas A. Brady, and the "News Letter" edited by Frederick Marriot had their plants demolished and cast into
the street. Mr. George had been terribly wrought up
over the news of the assassination, and talking about the
"copperhead" newspapers with Ike Trump and others, had
determined to lead an assault upon the "News Letter";
but when he reached the spot he found Trump gallantly
leading a party that were hurling type, furniture and
machinery into the street with such a spirited and liberal hand that little remained to be done to complete
the job.

After this physical venting of feeling, higher sentiments
took possession of the young printer, for next day he sat
down in his little Perry Street home and wrote out new
thoughts that were surging through him. He put them
in the form of a newspaper communication, which he addressed to the editor of the "Alta California," the paper
on which he had been setting type when opportunity
afforded. When the communication was finished he took
it to the office and slipped it into the editor's box. Next
day it appeared with an editorial note preceding it, for the
editor had learned who the writer was. Communication
and note appeared as follows:

[The following stirring article on the great patricide of the age was written by a printer in the office of the "Alta California"]:

Sic Semper Tyrannis!

" A man rushed to the front of the President's box, waving a long dagger in his right hand, exclaiming, '*Sic semper tyrannis!*' "
                                          "Alta" despatches, April 15.

"What a scene these few words bring—vivid as the lightning flash that bore them! The glitter and glare, curving circle and crowded pit, flash of jewels and glinting of silks—and the blanched sea of up-turned faces, the fixed and staring eyes, the awful hush—silence of death!

"And there, before all—before all mankind forevermore—stands, for an instant, the assassin, poised for the leap, the gleaming steel in his right hand, and his cry of triumph, of defiance, ringing throughout the house, '*Sic semper tyrannis!*'

"Is it a wonder they are spellbound! They came to laugh at a comedy—and a tragedy is before them which will make a nation weep—and whose mighty import centuries may not guess! Their frightened eyes look on a scene in the grand drama whose first act was the creation and whose last will be the procession of the white-robed and the shouts of the redeemed. Well may they gaze, awe-stricken, speechless, for the spirits of the mighty dead, and generation after generation that shall be, look with them, and the past that has gone, and the future that is to come, join their voices in the shout, '*Sic semper tyrannis!*'

"Poised there for an instant, that black, daring heart—that spirit incarnate of tyranny and wrong—feels the import of the act, and with voice of inspiration, shouts its own doom—'*Sic semper tyrannis!*'

"Amen! and thus it will be. They have struck down the just because of his justice, and the fate they have fixed upon him shall be theirs!

"What fitting time! Good Friday! At this very moment, before bare and black-draped altars, sounds the solemn wail of the Tenebræ, and mournful music bears the sorrow which shall burst into the joy of the resurrection—for, on a day of which this is the anniversary, One died that there might be life, and Death and Hell heard their doom. And now (as close as human type may approach the divine) again has Evil triumphed, and the blood of its victim sealed its fate.

"While the world lasts will this scene be remembered. As a martyr of Freedom—as the representative of the justice of a great nation, the name of the victim will live forever; and the Proclamation of Emancipation, signed with the name and sealed with the blood of *Abraham Lincoln* will remain a landmark in the progress of the race.

"In the hearts of a people whose number shall be as the sands of the sea, his memory will be cherished with that of Washington. And to the ends of the earth—from the frozen sea of the North to the ice fields of the South, in every land on which the sun in his circuit shall look down, whenever the standard shall be raised against a hoary wrong, his name shall be a watch-word and an inspiration.

"And when, on plains and uplands where now the elephant and spring-bok roam, farms shall be tilled and homes arise; and on great lakes and rivers, now the haunts of the hippopotamus—a thousand paddles shall beat, the mothers of nations yet unborn shall teach their children to call him blessed!

"*Sic semper tyrannis!* Blazoned on the shield of a noble State by the giants of the young republic, their degenerate sons shall learn its meaning! The murderer's shout as Lincoln fell, it will be taken up by a million voices. *Thus shall* perish all who wickedly raise their hands to shed the blood of the defenders of the oppressed, and who strive, by wickedness and cruelty, to preserve and perpetuate wrong. Their names shall become a hissing and a reproach among men as long as the past shall be remembered; and the great sin in whose support they spared no crime is numbered henceforth with the things that were. *Sic semper tyrannis!* Amen.

"H. G."

"San Francisco, April 16, 1865."[1]

A few days later the editor of the "Alta" engaged the printer as a special reporter to write in conjunction with others a description of the Lincoln mourning decorations throughout the city, and this was the first newspaper writing for which Henry George received pay. But he had more than a reporter's thoughts in him; and again he sat down in the parlour of his little Perry Street home and wrote a communication to the editor and signed it with his initials. It was on the character of Lincoln. This, like the former one, he put in the editor's box. Next morning he looked to see if it had been printed, and lo! like Ben Adhem's name, "it led all the rest." It did not bear his signature, nor was it printed as a letter to the editor, for it had been made the chief editorial of the paper. A few short extracts will suffice:

"No common man, yet the qualities which made him great and loved were eminently common. . . .

"He was not of those whom God lifts to the mountain tops, and who tell of His truth to ears that will not hear, and show His light to eyes that cannot see—whom their own generation stone, and future ones worship; but he was of the leaders who march close before the advancing ranks of the people, who direct their steps and speak with their voice.

" . . . No other system would have produced

---

[1] This article is copied from a printed proof pasted in a scrapbook kept by Mr. George and containing his early published writings. But since the file of the regular issue of the "Alta California" fails to reveal it, the conclusion is drawn that the communication must have appeared in a special edition of that newspaper.

him; through no crowd of courtiers could such a man have forced his way; his feet would have slipped on the carpets of palace stairs, and Grand Chamberlains ordered him back! And, as in our time of need, the man that was needed came forth, let us know that it will always be so, and that under our institutions, when the rights of the people are endangered, from their ranks will spring the men for the times."[1]

This experience led to the "Alta's" agreement to take from Mr. George some news letters relative to a Mexican liberating expedition in which he was about to embark. While the United States were engaged in their civil war Napoleon III. had sent an army into Mexico to establish an imperial government and place Austrian Arch-duke Maximilian on the throne. The resistance of the Mexican patriots under Juarez excited strong sympathy through all that part of the United States adjacent to Mexico; and ardently desirous of striking a blow for that republic, especially as circumstances had prevented him from engaging in the war in the United States against slavery, Henry George joined an expedition that was being organised to help the Juarez party. He talked it over with his wife, with whom now, after three and a half years of wedded life and extreme trials of poverty, he was sealed in the closest possible relations of confidence and affection. Though the prospect of parting and the danger he would run were sore to bear, and though the peril of being left destitute with two babies was imminent, she would not withhold him, but on the contrary did what she always afterwards did—encouraged him to follow the promptings of what he conceived to be his duty.

He, therefore, arranged with the "Alta California" peo-

---

[1] "Alta California," April 23, 1865.

ple to send his wife whatever money should come from the news letters that he should write, which he thought would be sufficient to maintain her; and then with his wife, took the new baby to St. Patrick's Catholic church, in deference to her, and had him baptised Richard Fox, the first name after his father and the second in honour of his wife's family. Then the couple went back to their home, and kneeling down beside their babies prayed together; after which, kissing his darling ones good-bye, the young man set off for the meeting place. He has described this:[1]

"I was to be first lieutenant in a company commanded by an Indian fighter named Burn; with an acquaintance of mine, Barry, as major; and Hungerford, afterwards father-in-law of Mackay, the millionaire, as colonel. We swore in a good many men, and went down to Platt's Hall to prepare to make a start in a vessel which should be secretly provided. We gathered there in the early evening, but hour after hour passed without receiving the order to start. Finally, at daylight next day we were told where the vessel was, but it was well on in the morning before we made for her.

"When we got down we found an old bark, the *Brontes*, to be the one selected for us. She was short of provisions and equipment for such a company. She had aboard 10,000 American condemned rifles, half a dozen saddles and a few casks of water. We had hardly got aboard before a revenue cutter dropped anchor in front of her and blocked the way. This ended our expedition. The Federal authorities had shut their eyes as long as they could to what was going on, but now could do so no longer.

"Among those who were going with us, and who would have been little less than a crowd of pirates if we had got down, were some who got up a scheme to seize a French transport, and I believe, to capture one of the

---

[1] Meeker notes, October, 1897.

mail steamers which then left for Panama twice a month
with shipments of gold from California to New York.
This got wind and some half dozen or so were arrested
and put on trial for intended piracy.

"This was the *Brontes* expedition, which led to the
charge in some San Francisco papers when I ran for
Mayor in New York years afterwards, that I had been
engaged in a piratical expedition. This is the nearest
I ever came to engaging in war, and I will never forget
the willingness with which my wife, with her two little
children, agreed to my leaving her to go on an expedition that I now know could have had no possible
good end."

A little later Henry George helped in the establishment
of the Monroe League, which was to send an expedition to
the Mexican patriots, a newspaper man named Linthicum
to head it. They swore men in on a bare sword and the
republican flag of Mexico, and Mrs. George was sworn as
the only woman member. Nothing came of the League,
though its failure is not explained.[1] By this time Mr.
George saw a good opening in Sacramento to set type on a

---

[1] Nearly two years subsequently (July 3, 1867) when managing editor
on the San Francisco "Times," Mr. George wrote in an editorial relative to
the downfall of the Mexican tyranny and the execution of Maximilian:
"We should not allow either his position or his private character to blind
our eyes to his public crimes. The men who have inflicted the greatest
evils upon their kind, have not been always the worst men in their personal relations. Charles I. was a good husband and kind father, but he
was not less the enemy of liberty, and his death was not less a salutary
example. . . . . That the execution of Maximilian will excite a deep
sensation in Europe cannot be doubted, but its effects will not be entirely
without benefit. It is a protest against the right of kings to cause suffering and shed blood for their own selfish ends. It is a vindication of justice
upon an offender of a class whose rank has hitherto sheltered them from
the punishment due to their crimes. It will teach princes and princelings
to be more cautious how they endeavour to subvert the liberties of a free
people."

contract for State official work, and so he went there, taking his family with him and settling down at housekeeping. Touching his personal matters he wrote to his Sister Caroline (December 3):

"I am, for the present, only ambitious of working, and will look neither to the right nor left, until I have 'put money in my purse'—something it has never yet contained. I have abandoned, I hope, the hand to mouth style of living, and will endeavour, if not absolutely forced to do so, to draw no drafts on the future. By next year we hope to have enough money saved to return home, and will do so, unless it should seem very inadvisable. I will come, anyhow, as soon as I can, for I have made up my mind it is my duty to do so. I am going to work on the State work as soon as it commences (this week I think) and expect to have steady work for the best part of a year and perhaps more. Since we came up here I have done pretty well—have made a living, paid expenses of coming up, got what was necessary, and owe nothing at all here, and feel more comfortable and hopeful than ever since we have been married."

For nearly a year Henry George, following his trade of type-setting, continued at State work. He lived quietly, and since his wife and he had modest habits, very comfortably. He had joined the Odd Fellows' Order during his former residence in Sacramento, through the advice of his printer friend, A. A. Stickney; and now in 1866 he joined the National Guard, though he soon dropped out of it; and a literary organisation, in which for a while he engaged in discussions on public questions. One of these discussions was of great importance in his life, since it marks another stepping-stone in his thought—his conversion from a belief in the protective principle to the opposite principle of the entire freedom of trade. In "Protection

or Free Trade?" Mr. George has spoken of his strong protection views at this time.[1]

"I was for a number of years after I had come of age
a protectionist, or rather, I supposed I was, for, without
real examination, I had accepted the belief, as in the
first place we all accept our beliefs, on the authority of
others.   So far, however, as I thought at all on the subject, I was logical, and I well remember how when the
Florida and *Alabama* were sinking American ships at
sea, I thought their depredations, after all, a good thing
for the State in which I lived—California—since the
increased risk and cost of ocean carriage in American
ships (then the only way of bringing goods from the
Eastern States to California) would give to her infant
industries something of that needed protection against
the lower wages and better established industries of the
Eastern States which the Federal Constitution prevented
her from securing by a State tariff."

The way in which this belief was changed is more fully
explained in another place:[1]

"One night in Sacramento I went with a friend to a
debating society and there heard a young fellow of great
ability, William H. Mills, the present Land Agent of the
Central Pacific Railroad, deliver a speech in favour of
protection.   I was a protectionist when he began, but
when he got through I was a free trader.   When they
asked me what I thought of it I told them that if what
he said was true, it seemed to me that the country that
was hardest to get at must be the best country to live in;
and that, instead of merely putting duties on things
brought from abroad, we ought to put them on things
brought from anywhere, and that fires and wars and
impediments to trade and navigation were the very best
things to levy on commerce."

---

[1] Chapter IV (Memorial edition, p. 29).
[2] Meeker notes, October, 1897.

Mr. Mills says that he remembers "with reasonable distinctness the incident referred to by Henry George":

"The debating society was known as the 'Sacramento Lyceum.' The subject for the evening was a general consideration of a national tariff, whether for revenue or for protection. I was the leading speaker for the evening and took a position in favour of a protective policy as that best calculated to produce the broadest industrial skill of our people, develop the natural resources of the country, give the largest diversity of employment, confer the highest intelligence, employ a greater proportion of our people in skilled labour which always receives the highest reward and generally confer industrial and commercial independence upon the nation.

"As one of the speakers of the evening, Henry George controverted the doctrine that nationalism was the goal of civilisation, pleading for a broad cosmopolitanism. He contended that national policies should interpose no barrier to harmonious relations between nations of the earth; that if the doctrine enunciated to sustain a policy of high protection were true, absolute national isolation would be the condition best calculated to promote national development; that as relative evolutionary forces, the policy of protection created antagonism between the nations, isolated them, augmented their selfishness, intensified the military spirit, and made standing armies and vast navies necessary to the peace of the world; while free trade, as an evolutionary force, made nations dependent, promoted peace among them and urged humanity on toward a higher plane of universal fraternity.

"In conversation with Mr. George since then, he said to me that while he went to the Lyceum meeting a protectionist, he left a free trader, because protection was defensible only upon the theory that the separation of mankind into nations implied their industrial and commercial antagonism."

But while this period marked what he considered a great step in right thinking, Henry George did not neglect writing. It was now that he wrote for Edmund Wallazz's paper, the "Philadelphia Saturday Night," the account of the *Shubrick* burial[1] under the title of "Dust to Dust." The sketch was republished by the "Californian." For the latter publication he also wrote a fanciful sketch entitled "The Prayer of Kohonah—a tradition of the northwest coast." Both of these, like the Lincoln article, gave proofs of a vivid imagination and a high order of descriptive power, and it is certain from casual notes in his pocket diaries during the next two or three years that he was thinking of writing a novel; so that perhaps it wanted but the accident to have turned his abilities and energy into the realm of fiction instead of to a search for the eternal verities underlying social order.

But public affairs attracted and absorbed more and more of his attention, and he gave vent to his sentiments in the "Daily Union" through the medium of letters to the editor, which he signed with the *nom de plume* of "Proletarian"; and in September, 1866, when printing became slack, he wrote for San Francisco newspapers a number of letters relative to the State fair then being held in Sacramento. Then his newspaper ambition took a leap forward. A daily paper to be named the "Times" was to be started in San Francisco, and he made application for a writing position upon it. A letter to his father (August 8) told about it:

"When you next write direct to San Francisco, for I expect to go down there in about two weeks. The paper that I wrote you of is to start there in about that time. I do not know whether I will get the situation I asked for as reporter or assistant editor, but I can have a position in the composing room, at any rate, with a chance to go in the editorial department in a little while. I

---

[1] Pages 63-67.

can have steady work here if I stay, but have concluded to go down, as I will have a better chance down there. The foreman has given me a case, which is in itself desirable, as it will be a good paper to work on, and will be a steady thing. But even if I do not get a better position than that at the start, I am promised one shortly afterward. And if things go as I wish them to, I may by the first of the year make $50 or $60 a week. I don't say that I will, or even that I expect to, but I see where there is a chance. However, I won't say anything about it until I see more clearly.

"This I hope, is our last move until we step on board the steamer. Our desire to return home increases daily, and all my plans tend to that object. I do not think, though, that we can come till spring, but I hope that this delay will be of benefit, in better enabling me to come home and to do better when I do come. I want, if possible, to secure some little practice and reputation as a writer here before going, which will not only give me introduction and employment there, but help me in going and enable me to make something by corresponding with papers here. If I do not overrate my abilities I may yet make position and money."

He was not destined to go to Philadelphia in the following spring, for fortune threw upon him larger responsibilities than he had dreamed of.

CHAPTER XI.

MANAGING EDITOR AND CORRESPONDENT.

THE San Francisco "Times" was started on November 5, 1866, with Henry George in the composing room setting type. James McClatchy, who, as editor of the "Sacramento Bee," had won a reputation as a forcible writer, became editor of the new paper, and it was mainly through him that George's hope of advancement lay, having won McClatchy's friendship while in Sacramento. McClatchy, having a clear, sound mind himself, was liberal enough to recognise and encourage merit in others. He may be said to have seen signs of promise in the young printer. At any rate, three editorial articles from George were accepted and published in quick succession. The first, for which he received $5, was entitled "To Constantinople," and was published eleven days after the paper was started. It treated of the destiny of Russia to carry the cross to the Bosphorus, and there, overruling the Turk, to make its seat of empire in the city founded by the great Constantine to be the new capital of the Roman world. But after only three weeks' career as editor of the "Times," James McClatchy disagreed with the paper's owners, and stepping out, returned to the "Sacramento Bee."

Noah Brooks, who in later years has become best known

173

in the East as the author of "Washington in Lincoln's Time," tales of the early California days, and juvenile stories, had been chief editorial writer. He now became editor, with William Bausman and N. S. Treadwell as editorial writers. O. B. Turrell was foreman of the composing room and was very friendly to George. Indeed, he next to McClatchy had encouraged the young printer to think of advancement, and now suggested that he submit an article to the new editor. Noah Brooks tells of his side of this transaction:

"Mr. Turrell, the foreman, had come repeatedly to me to recommend a young printer as a writer, and I said that I would look at some of his work. Turrell brought an article that was in editorial form and written in neat, regular and rather small hand, with the lines far apart, on buff sheets of paper such as was used for wrapping and sending the newspaper through the mails. I glanced at the article and then read it somewhat carefully, for it showed a style and largeness of thought that made me suspect that the young man had been borrowing. So I laid the matter aside for a day or two and meanwhile took a glance over the current magazines and other periodicals, but could find no signs of appropriation. I spoke to the foreman and he said that I need have no thought of irregularity—that the young man was bright and original, and that he was entirely honest and would not think of offering another's thoughts. So I put the article in the paper.

"Turrell told me where I should find the printer who had written the editorial. That day I passed through the composing room and saw a slight young man at work at the case Turrell had named. He was rather under size, and stood on a board to raise him to the proper height to work at his case. I was not prepossessed with him and little dreamed that there was a man who would one day win great fame—as little dreamed of it, as no doubt, he did.

"I invited him to write at our regular editorial column rates, which he did for a while, continuing at the same time at his printer's case. Afterwards I called him into the reportorial department, and then, on the death of Mr. Treadwell, invited him to become a regular editorial writer. Soon after this I fell out with the president of the board of trustees of the paper, Mr. Annis Merrill, and resigned, taking Mr. Bausman with me. My quarrel was not Mr. George's quarrel, and he remained, and took charge of the paper."

As reporter of the "Times," Henry George earned $30 a week; later, as editorial writer, $35 a week; and as managing editor, from the beginning of June, 1867, $50 a week. An incident about this time showed his great tenderness for his wife. One evening word was brought that his wife, who was expecting her third child, had fallen down-stairs. The husband ran most of the way home. The doctor feared consequences. But the medicine he gave was effective, for the patient by midnight grew quiet and fell asleep. Her husband, half leaning on one elbow, half bending over her, reclined beside her intently watching, all his clothes on and with hat in hand, ready at the first unfavourable symptom to spring up and run for the physician. When the grey streaks of dawn came, four hours afterwards, the wife awoke, greatly refreshed, to find her husband with unchanged position and tense eyes regarding her. When she spoke of this he simply said that all had depended on her sleeping. The wife fully recovered from the shock, and the child, born three months later, came into the world strong and sound of body and mind, and named Jennie Teresa, after its father's dead sister and its mother's living sister, grew up into beautiful womanhood.

Henry George became managing editor of the "Times"

in the beginning of June, 1867, under the chief-editorship of Dr. Gunn, well known in San Francisco political affairs in that day, and who had bought into the paper. George retained the position of managing editor until he left the paper on August 12, 1868. During the interval, besides the regular office work, he was conducting occasional correspondence with the Hawaiian "Gazette" and other newspapers, so that his income was much larger than ever before in his life. Moreover, his work was telling, making him friends and extending his influence.

But more important than anything else during the "Times" period was the preparation he was going through for his life work. This related to style in writing and development in thinking. While his style always had been free and natural, he had from the beginning aimed at compactness, and it was to the necessity of re-writing news articles and compressing them into condensed items while he was sub-editor on the "Times," that, when reviewing his life, he said he had obtained valuable practice in terse statement. The development in thought was manifested in editorials on the larger questions of the day, such as free trade, government paper money and interconvertible bonds in place of national bank notes; personal or proportional representation; public obligations attached to public franchises; and the abolition of privilege in the army.

But perhaps the most important advance in thought appeared in an article entitled "What the Railroad Will Bring Us" in the "Overland Monthly" in October, 1868, just after Mr. George left the "Times." That San Francisco periodical was then in its fourth number, having started in July of that year, and was edited by Bret Harte, who, with two of its contributors, Mark Twain and Joaquin Miller, constituted "The Incomparable Three" of lighter literature in California. Noah Brooks was one of the assistant editors and numbered in the long list of bright, original writers who made the pages of the magazine, like those of the "Californian" which had preceded it, of exceptional brilliance—the more undoubted since most of the writers were new, and all wrote anonymously. The "Overland" as originally cast did not last very long, but long enough to call the world's attention to Bret Harte's "Heathen Chinee," and other productions.

"What the Railroad Will Bring Us" was a forecast of the era of California which the operation of the then almost completed trans-continental railroad would usher in —adding enormous artificial advantages to the already great natural advantages that San Francisco possessed, and laying foundations for her rapid rise to a commercial and intellectual greatness that should not only make her mistress of all the coasts washed by the vast Pacific, but, indeed, as to population, wealth and power, cause her eventually to overtake and surpass New York and London, and make her the greatest city in the world. But, as if reverting to the question that had arisen in his mind years before when, sitting in the theatre gallery, he saw the advent of the railroad pictured on the new drop curtain[1]—the author asked, would California, with her great population and wealth, and culture, and power, have so even a distribution of wealth as in her earlier, pioneer days? Would she show so much general comfort and so little squalor and misery? Would there then be so large a proportion of full, true men?

"Amid all our rejoicing and all our gratulation let us see clearly whither we are tending. Increase in population and wealth past a certain point means simply an approximation to the condition of older countries—

---

[1] Page 100.

the Eastern States and Europe. Would the average Californian prefer to 'take his chances' in New York or Massachusetts, or in California as it is and has been? Is England, with her population of twenty millions to an area of not more than one-third that of our State, and a wealth which per inhabitant is six or seven times that of California, a better country than California to live in? Probably, if one were born a duke or factory lord, or to any place among the upper ten thousand; but if one were born among the lower millions—how then?

"For years the high rate of interest and the high rate of wages prevailing in California have been special subjects for the lamentations of a certain school of local political economists, who could not see that high wages and high interest were indications that the natural wealth of the country was not yet monopolised, that great opportunities were open to all—who did not know that these were evidences of social health, and that it were as wise to lament them as for the maiden to wish to exchange the natural bloom on her cheek for the interesting pallor of the invalid.

"But however this be, it is certain that the tendency of the new era—of the more dense population and more thorough development of the wealth of the State—will be to a reduction both of the rate of interest and the rate of wages, particularly the latter. This tendency may not, probably will not, be shown immediately; but it will be before long, and that powerfully, unless balanced and counteracted by other influences which we are not now considering, which do not yet appear, and which it is probable will not appear for some time yet.

"The truth is, that the completion of the railroad and the consequent great increase of business and population, will not be a benefit to all of us, but only to a portion. As a general rule (liable of course to exceptions) those who have, it will make wealthier; for those who *have not,* it will make it more difficult to get. These who have lands, mines, established businesses, special abilities of certain kinds, will become richer for it and find increased opportunities; those who have only their own

labour will become poorer, and find it harder to get
ahead—first because it will take more capital to buy
land or to get into business; and second, because as competition reduces the wages of labour, this capital will be
harder for them to obtain. . . .

"And as California becomes populous and rich, let us
not forget that the character of a people counts for more
than their numbers; that the distribution of wealth is
even a more important matter than its production. Let
us not imagine ourselves in a fool's paradise, where the
golden apples will drop into our mouths; let us not think
that after the stormy seas and head gales of all the ages,
our ship has at last struck the trade winds of time. The
future of our State, of our nation, of our race, looks fair
and bright; perhaps the future looked so to the philoso-
ophers who once sat in the porches of Athens—to the
unremembered men who raised the cities whose ruins
lie south of us. Our modern civilisation strikes broad
and deep and looks high. So did the tower which men
once built almost unto heaven."

For this "Overland" article, seven thousand words in
length, Henry George received $40. To many who have
knowledge of California's progress during the past three
decades a remarkable feature about the article is the prophecy of hard social conditions which have since enveloped
the masses and checked—and almost stopped—the State's
growth. But to others its political economy is a still more
remarkable feature. For though there is in the article
what he subsequently may have called a confusion of
what is rent with what is interest, there is in the tracing of
high wages and high interest in California to the fact that
the "natural wealth of the country was not yet monopolised—that great opportunities were open to all"—a distinct foreshadowing of that formulation of the laws of
wages and interest which ten years later, in "Progress and
Poverty," he put in these terms—that "wages depend upon

the margin of production, or upon the produce which labour can obtain at the highest point of natural productiveness open to it without the payment of rent"; and that "the relation between wages and interest is determined by the average power of increase which attaches to capital from its use in reproductive modes—as rent rises, interest will fall as wages fall, or will be determined by the margin of cultivation."

In August, 1868, Henry George left the "Times." He had asked for an increase in salary. This not being granted, he withdrew, though on good terms with and at the convenience of the management. While continuing to send remittances home, he had been able by economy during the stretch of prosperity to save a little money and to open a bank account. He now resolved to carry out the long-cherished plan of going to Philadelphia, and he sent his family East under escort of his brother, John Vallance George, who had come to California three months before— Henry George intending himself to follow as soon as opportunity permitted.

Just then Mr. George was invited by Charles DeYoung to help him develop a morning newspaper from the "Dramatic Chronicle." He was engaged to be managing editor, and at his suggestion, DeYoung made John Timmins foreman—the same John Timmins who was foreman in the Sacramento "Union" office in 1864 and had discharged George. But Mr. George's connection with the "Chronicle" lasted only a few weeks, as he disliked DeYoung's policy.

The success of the San Francisco "Times" in breaking into the press telegraph monopoly had encouraged the starting of other papers, of which the "Chronicle" was one and the San Francisco "Herald" another. There were not many important Democratic papers in the State and

John Nugent's idea was to establish a good one by reviving the San Francisco "Herald," and he engaged Henry George to go to New York and try to get the paper admitted to the Associated Press, or if that should be refused, to establish there a special news service for the paper. Charged with this commission, the young man about the beginning of December started East on the overland and stage route.

> "It was just before the completion of the transcontinental railroad, and I crossed the plains in a four-horse 'mud wagon.' I spent many nights sitting at the driver's side, and I was all the more impressed, therefore, when we reached the railroad and got a sleeping-car. We had to sleep two in a berth, however."[1]

He went first to his old home in Philadelphia where he found father and mother, sisters and brothers, as well as wife and children eager to welcome him. After a short season there, he engaged John Hasson, one of his boyhood friends, to go in with him, and then went to New York and made formal application for access of the San Francisco "Herald" to the Associated Press news service. Writing early in January (1869) to Charles A. Sumner, managing editor of the paper, he said:

> "Nobody received me with open arms, unless I except the Peter Funks. I have made no acquaintances beyond those necessary for my purpose and not yet delivered any letters except business ones. The newspaper offices here are like big manufactories and they don't seem to be in the habit of asking strangers to take seats and look over the exchanges. The bosses come down for a few hours occasionally; the managing editors get down about twelve and leave about four or five in the after-

---

[1] Meeker notes, October, 1897.

noon; and I don't think the smaller guns begin to work
as hard as those on the Pacific Coast."

Before the "Herald" business had advanced far, the active and courageous spirit of the young man manifested
itself by a signed letter in the "New York Tribune" (March
5) attacking two of the great corporations in California—
the Central Pacific Railroad and the Wells, Fargo Express,
the former for its excessive charges; the latter for reckless
treatment of the newspaper mails in the stage-coach intervals on the plains between the yet incompleted Union
Pacific and Central Pacific lines. As to the Central
Pacific Railroad he said:

"So far as cheapening the cost of transportation is
concerned, the Pacific Railroad has, as yet, been of no
advantage to the people of the Pacific Coast, who have to
pay just as much as, and in some cases more than, when
they relied on horse or ox flesh. There would be some
excuse for this, if the road had been constructed by private means; but it has been, and is being, built literally
and absolutely by the money of the people, receiving
liberal aid from cities, counties and State of California,
as well as the immense gratuity of the general government. . . .

"But minor grievances sink into insignificance when
the enormous political power which these great Pacific
Railroad corporations can wield is considered. The
Central Pacific can dictate to California, Nevada and
Utah, and the Union Pacific to the States and Territories through which it passes more completely than the
Camden and Amboy dictated to New Jersey, and each or
both will be able to exert an almost irresistible pressure
upon Congress in any manner in which their interests
are involved. I don't know about the Union Pacific,
but the Central already influences conventions, manages
Legislatures, and has its representatives in both Houses at
Washington. And it is already buying up other corpor-

ations, and bids fair to own the whole railroad system of
the Pacific. . . ."

But returning to the San Francisco "Herald," the Board
of Directors of the Associated Press, after many vexatious
delays, refused its service to that paper, and an independent service had to be made up. Concluding that Philadelphia would suit their purpose better than New York,
Henry George and John Hasson opened their press bureau
in a little coal office occupied at the time by Henry George's
father, on Third Street, almost opposite St. Paul's church
Here they collected by wire from various sources their
news, and dressing it to fit their California requirements,
putting as much as possible in a prearranged cipher, to
save expense, telegraphed it by the Western Union Company, which controlled the only route to San Francisco, at
a rate fixed by a clear agreement and based upon a schedule
adopted before any news war was in sight. In exchange
for the full credit, access was given to the "New York Herald's" special despatches, and in this and other ways a good
news service was supplied; so much better, indeed, than
that which the Associated Press papers in California received that they made a great commotion inside the association, and that body urged the Western Union Telegraph
Company to interfere. The latter hesitated to do so directly, but on the ground of interference with the rules,
refused to allow the use of the cipher code or to receive the
service from Philadelphia; and then finding that the agent
of the California paper at once moved to New York and
continued the service, the company took summary action
by giving short notice of a new schedule of rates, which
in effect increased the San Francisco "Herald's" charges,
while it reduced those of the Association. The "Herald's"
agent vigorously protested and was invited to call upon

Vice-President McAlpine of the Western Union. In a letter of April 21, to John Nugent, the San Francisco "Herald's" owner, Henry George recounts what occurred:

"I saw him accordingly, but was informed by him that the contract had already been signed by at least the San Francisco papers [in the Associated Press] and that the thing was past remedy. I nevertheless protested with all my force, minced no words, but denounced the whole thing as a most outrageous breach of faith which had been procured by the underhand workings of a ring. I told him in very plain terms what I thought of his company and how this operation would appear to the public; that it was meant to crush the 'Herald' and would crush the 'Herald'; was meant to prevent any future opposition to the Associated Press and would do so until a new line was built; that they had virtually agreed to give a monopoly of the news business to the Association for $40,000 a year—less than they were now getting; that I could not say what you would do, but that if it was my paper I would issue my last number on the 1st of May, declare that it was killed by the Western Union Telegraph Company, who had sold a monopoly to the other papers, fill it with the history of the whole transaction and print an immense edition, which I would circulate all over the Union.

"He appeared much moved by what I said, declared that there was great force in it, but that he did not see what could be done; that he had opposed this thing from the beginning; that he had been overruled; and that though he was sorry for it, there was no use of protesting or appealing.

"Afterwards I made a written request to be heard before a full executive board. Pondering over the matter, I came to the conclusion that the case was very desperate, that the only hope of inducing them to go back was by appealing to their sense of shame and dislike of being stigmatised as a monopoly; that nothing could be hoped from their favour; and that it was useless to mince words. I, therefore, abandoned my purpose of making a verbal protest, and during that night wrote out a lengthy protest with the idea of printing it if my other efforts seemed ineffectual; and that if the instructions I expected immediately from you did not direct another course.

"By one next day (Wednesday) I got several copies and sent them in, calling upon Mr. McAlpine about 2.30 P.M. . . . He was anxious for me to see President Orton. . . . I got an interview with Mr. Orton this morning, who read the protest in my presence and seemed unable to say anything in justification. . . . He did not seem disposed to defend it, but said that he was sick of the whole matter; that the Associated Press had been urging this for a long time, and had been growing ugly, threatening to stop their arrangement."

But John Nugent at this crisis was as silent as the grave and gave no instructions. Indeed, he cannot be said to have given any instructions at any time since his paper started, except to get the news as cheaply as possible. The New York agent was left to act entirely upon his own responsibility. And it might have been supposed that having done all that was possible for his paper, he would consult self-interest and avoid aggressiveness, for otherwise he ran the risk of embittering all the papers in the California Associated Press against him and of winning the active and lasting hostility of the great telegraph company. But what he had in mind could be realised only by aggressive action. He wished to make the subject of telegraph service a political question. In other words, this unknown newspaper correspondent from the far Pacific Coast, unbacked by even his own struggling little newspaper, had chosen, like David, to go out and contend with the gigantic telegraph Goliath. What added to the daring of the performance was that the Associated Press people were circulating the report that the San Francisco "Herald" was on its last legs, which the silence to his private despatches seemed to confirm. But counting costs no more now than when two months before he had in the "New York Tribune" openly attacked the California railroad and express corporations, he held to his resolution to strike publicly at the Western Union. He sent his printed protest out to such of the newspapers in New York and other cities in the East as he thought would notice it, and also to Senator Sprague of Rhode Island with a letter, because of his anti-monopoly views; and to the California representatives in Congress—at the same time writing to his friend Sumner, the managing editor of the San Francisco "Herald": "You will hear thunder all around the sky notwithstanding the influence of the Western Union and the Associated Press."

The "New York Herald" was about the only newspaper of influence that published the protest, and whether or not the Western Union directors cared about it, the axe fell, and the San Francisco "Herald's" telegraph news service, so long as that paper could continue to struggle on, had to be reduced to a mere skeleton.

Almost from the beginning John Nugent had been slow to make remittances, and now nearly a thousand dollars was due in New York on salaries and rent and other bills. Confident that he could be of no further use to the paper there, and leaving John Hasson as New York agent, Henry George went to Philadelphia, took leave of his family and relatives, and on May 20 started west over the Erie railroad for California. Under a contract through John Russell Young, its managing editor, he wrote several letters for the "New York Tribune," descriptive of the new transcontinental railroad, and the country through which the road passed. But though paid for, none of these articles were published, for John Russell Young left the paper soon after Mr. George had left New York, and Whitelaw Reid, succeeding as managing editor, not only withheld them, but annulled the contract, to which Mr. George, not wishing to put Mr. Young at the slightest disadvantage for his act of friendship, made no further objection than a mild and formal dissent.

SECOND PERIOD

FORMULATION OF THE PHILOSOPHY

One sole God ;
One sole ruler—his Law ;
One sole interpreter of that law—Humanity.

—Mazzini

CHAPTER I.

COMMENCES THE GREAT INQUIRY.

1869.   Age, 30.

IT is said that what put the iron into Abraham Lincoln's soul against chattel slavery was an auction sale of negroes—men, women and children, husbands and wives, parents and infants—which he witnessed while a young man at New Orleans, to which place he had gone down the Mississippi on a flat boat.

Likewise, what put the iron into Henry George's soul against industrial slavery was the contrast of poverty with wealth that he witnessed in the greatest city in the new world, when on the visit to New York in the winter of 1868-69. Apparently fully occupied with the difficulties of establishing a telegraphic news service for the western newspaper, there were in reality pauses when the mind, swinging clear of all personal affairs, leaped into the realm of problems that beset mankind. For in the idle hours, when another might have sought amusement, this young man, as by a kind of fascination, walked the streets of the great city, thinking how here, at the centre of civilisation, should be realised the dream of the pioneer—the hard conditions of life softened, and society, preserving the general relations of equality, raised as a mass from the bottom into a state of peace and plenty. How different the view

191

that met his gaze! On every hand he beheld evidences of advanced and advancing civilisation, but of a civilisation that was one-sided; that piled up riches for the few and huddled the many in filth and poverty. And just as in assailing the great telegraph and press monopolies he did not wait to be supported, but boldly and alone stepped forth to the contest, so now this unknown man, not yet quite thirty, of small schooling and scarcely tried abilities, whose past had led through poverty and adversity, and whose future was shrouded in uncertainty, audaciously refused to accept the edict of the House of Have—the edict sanctioned by the teachers of learning and preachers of religion, that all this want and suffering was in the nature of things and unalterable. His heart and mind denied it. Everywhere else in creation was order, design. Could they fail on reaching man, "the roof and crown of things?" He could not believe it. Silently, without telling any man of what he did, he set himself the task of finding the natural order. In his speech of acceptance of the first New York mayoralty nomination seventeen years afterwards he said:

"Years ago I came to this city from the West, unknown, knowing nobody, and I saw and recognised for the first time the shocking contrast between monstrous wealth and debasing want. And here I made a vow from which I have never faltered, to seek out, and remedy, if I could, the cause that condemned little children to lead such a life as you know them to lead in the squalid districts."[1]

This was not a vague resolution without backing of thought. It was rather a sudden crystallisation of pro-

---

[1] Also see "Progress and Poverty," Conclusion; and "The Science of Political Economy," Book II, Chap. viii, p. 201.

tracted meditations; a flashing conviction and passionate resolve. For him all at once the bush burned, and the voice spake: "The people suffer; who will lead them forth?" In a letter to Rev. Thomas Dawson of Glencree, Ireland (February 1, 1883), he wrote:

"Because you are not only my friend, but a priest and a religious, I shall say something that I don't like to speak of—that I never before have told any one. Once, in daylight, and in a city street, there came to me a thought, a vision, a call—give it what name you please. But every nerve quivered. And there and then I made a vow. Through evil and through good, whatever I have done and whatever I have left undone, to that I have been true."

Now while the young philosopher's mind was to work gradually towards the solution of the problem of deepening poverty in the midst of advancing wealth, he did something in the East in the early part of 1869 that attracted more attention than anything he had before accomplished. As he has said in "The Science of Political Economy," [1] "John Russell Young was at that time managing editor of the 'New York Tribune,' and I wrote for him an article on 'The Chinese on the Pacific Coast,' a question that had begun to arouse attention there; taking the side popular among the working classes of the Coast, in opposition to the unrestricted immigration of that people." The article appeared on May 1, filled several columns of the "Tribune," and was signed.[2]

The immigration of the Chinese in considerable numbers

---

[1] Book II, Chap. viii, p. 200.

[2] Horace Greeley was the editor-in-chief of the "Tribune," and in the same issue with Henry George's Chinese article appeared the first instalment of Greeley's essays on political economy.

commenced soon after the discovery of gold in California.
They spread over the Pacific Coast and crept into many of
the more common fields of labour, soon incurring general
and active opposition, being regarded as an alien and non-
assimilable race.   In this "Tribune" article, Mr. George
explained and justified this hostile feeling—the first time,
probably, that such views were published on the Atlantic
Coast.   The kernel of his presentation was this:

"The population of our country has been drawn from
many different sources; but hitherto, with but one exception, these accessions have been of the same race, and
though widely differing in language, customs and national characteristics, have been capable of being welded
into a homogeneous people.   The mongolians, who are
now coming among us on the other side of the continent, differ from our race by as strongly marked characteristics as do the negroes, while they will not as
readily fall into our ways as the negroes.   The difference between the two races in this respect is as the
difference between an ignorant but docile child, and a
grown man, sharp but narrow minded, opinionated and
set in character.   The negro when brought to this country was a simple barbarian with nothing to unlearn;
the Chinese have a civilisation and history of their own,
a vanity which causes them to look down on all other
races, habits of thought rendered permanent by being
stamped upon countless generations.   From present ap-
pearances we shall have a permanent Chinese population;
but a population whose individual components will be
constantly changing, at least for a long time to come—a
population born in China, reared in China, expecting to
return to China, living while here in a little China of its
own, and without the slightest attachment to the country—utter heathens, treacherous, sensual, cowardly and
cruel.   They bring no women with them (and probably
will not for a little while yet).   .   .   .
"Their moral standard is as low as their standard of
comfort, and though honest in the payment of debts

to each other, lying, stealing and false swearing are with the Chinamen venial sins—if sins at all. They practise all the unnamable vices of the East, and are as cruel as they are cowardly. Infanticide is common among them; so is abduction and assassination. Their bravos may be hired to take life for a sum proportionate to the risk, to be paid to their relatives in case of death. In person the Chinese are generally apparently cleanly, but filthy in their habits. Their quarters reek with noisesome odours, and are fit breeding-places for pestilence. They have a great capacity for secret organisations, forming a State within a State, governed by their own laws; and there is little doubt that our courts are frequently used by them to punish their own countrymen, though more summary methods are oftentimes resorted to. The administration of justice among them is attended with great difficulty. No plan for making them tell the truth seems to be effective. That of compelling them to behead a cock and burn yellow paper is generally resorted to in the courts. . . .

"The Chinese seem to be incapable of understanding our religion; but still less are they capable of understanding our political institutions. To confer the franchise upon them would be to put the balance of power on the Pacific in the hands of a people who have no conception of the trust involved, and who would have no wish to use it rightly, if they had—would be to give so many additional votes to employers of Chinese, or put them up for sale by the Chinese head centres in San Francisco."

Almost twenty-five years later (November 30, 1893), in a letter to William Lloyd Garrison, the younger, Henry George spoke of the "Tribune" article as "crude," insomuch as he "had not then come to clear economic views." He referred to his exposition of the wages question, which he was led to discuss by the contention of the great California railroad corporation and other large employers of Chinese labour that such employment inured to the benefit of other labourers by liberating the latter for engagement in other fields of industry, at the same time cheapening the cost of production in the primary fields that they had left and thereby cheapening all those primary commodities that all must buy. "Wishing to know what political economy had to say about the causes of wages," he wrote in "The Science of Political Economy" [1] relative to this point: "I went to the Philadelphia Library, looked over John Stuart Mill's 'Political Economy,' and accepting his views without question, based my article upon it." In a conversation at another time he said,[2] "It was the first time I had made any investigation of what political economy had to say on the subject of wages, and I adopted unquestioningly the doctrine of the relation between wages and capital laid down by Mill."

That is to say, doing now as he once had done in embracing the protective principle, and "accepting the belief on the authority of others," he abandoned the suggestion of his own spontaneous thought when writing the article "What the Railroad Will Bring Us," namely, that wages in California had a relation to "the natural wealth of the country. . . . not yet monopolised"—and "adopted unquestioningly" the explanation made by the man famous as the great master of political economy, that wages depend upon the ratio of labourers to the so-called wages fund—to the capital devoted to the payment of wages. How completely this was so is shown by a passage in the "Tribune" article.

"There is a tendency of wages in different industries to an equilibrium, and of wages in general to a level which is determined by the relative proportions of capi-

---

[1] Book II, Chap. viii, pp. 200, 201.
[2] Meeker notes, October, 1897.

tal and labour. . . . Plainly when we speak of a
reduction of wages in any general and permanent sense,
we mean this, if we mean anything—that in the division of the joint production of labour and capital, the
share of labour is to be smaller, that of capital larger.
This is precisely what the reduction of wages consequent
upon the introduction of Chinese labour means."

"This article attracted attention especially in California," Mr. George wrote in his last book.   While just beginning to rise to attention on the Atlantic side of the
country, the Chinese question was a burning one on the
Pacific side.   Some of the California newspapers reprinted
parts of the "Tribune" article and commended it.   The
workingmen's organisations hailed it with particular satisfaction, in the early part of 1871 it being reprinted in full
and circulated by the Mechanics' State Council of California.   This organisation, though intended primarily
for the protection of workingmen's interests, at that time
had considerable influence in California politics.

But long before this action of the Mechanics' State
Council the chief San Francisco newspapers were drawn
into a renewed discussion of the "Tribune" article by a
letter from a high outside source.   Mr. George says in
"The Science of Political Economy" that a copy of the
"Tribune" article he sent from California to John Stuart
Mill brought a letter of commendation.   The letter was
received in November, 1869, at Oakland, an over-bay suburb of San Francisco, where George had just begun the
editing of a little daily called the "Transcript," of which
more will be learned later.   On Saturday, November 20,
he published a long editorial and in it printed the Mill
letter in full, saying by way of explanation:

"It is frequently asserted here that the opposition
upon the part of the labouring classes to the immigra-

tion of Chinese arises from ignorance of the laws of
political economy, and that so far from having a tendency to reduce them to a lower condition, the effect of
Chinese labour will be to elevate them. Conceiving that
the views of so distinguished an authority would be of
much value, the gentleman to whom this letter is addressed wrote to Mr. Mill, requesting an opinion upon
this point, as well as upon the general subject."

Then came the Mill letter:

Avignon, France, Oct. 23, 1869.

"DEAR SIR: The subject on which you have asked my
opinion involves two of the most difficult and embarrassing questions of political morality—the extent and limits of the right of those who have first taken possession
of the unoccupied portion of the earth's surface to
exclude the remainder of mankind from inhabiting it,
and the means which can be legitimately used by the
more improved branches of the human species to protect
themselves from being hurtfully encroached upon by
those of a lower grade in civilisation. The Chinese
immigration into America raises both of these questions.
To furnish a general answer to either of them would be
a most arduous undertaking.

"Concerning the purely economic view of the subject,
I entirely agree with you; and it could be hardly better
stated and argued than it is in your article in the 'New
York Tribune.' That the Chinese immigration, if it
attains great dimensions, must be economically injurious to the mass of the present population; that it
must diminish their wages, and reduce them to a lower
stage of physical comfort and well-being, I have no
manner of doubt. Nothing can be more fallacious than
the attempts to make out that thus to lower wages is
the way to raise them, or that there is any compensation,
in an economical point of view, to those whose labour is
displaced, or who are obliged to work for a greatly reduced remuneration. On general principles this state
of things, were it sure to continue, would justify the

exclusion of the immigrants, on the ground that, with
their habits in respect to population, only a temporary
good is done to the Chinese people by admitting part of
their surplus numbers, while a permanent harm is done
to a more civilised and improved portion of mankind.

"But there is much also to be said on the other side.
Is it justifiable to assume that the character and habits
of the Chinese are insusceptible of improvement? The
institutions of the United States are the most potent
means that have yet existed for spreading the most important elements of civilisation down to the poorest and
most ignorant of the labouring masses. If every Chinese child were compulsorily brought under your school
system, or under a still more effective one if possible,
and kept under it for a sufficient number of years, would
not the Chinese population be in time raised to the level
of the American? I believe, indeed, that hitherto the
number of Chinese born in America has not been very
great; but so long as this is the case—so long (that is)
as the Chinese do not come in families and settle, but
those who come are mostly men, and return to their
native country, the evil can hardly reach so great a
magnitude as to require that it should be put a stop
to by force.

"One kind of restrictive measure seems to me not
only desirable, but absolutely called for; the most strin-
gent laws against introducing Chinese immigrants as
coolies, *i. e.*, under contract binding them to the service
of particular persons. All such obligations are a form
of compulsory labour, that is, of slavery; and though
I know the legal invalidity of such contracts does not
prevent them being made, I cannot but think that if
pains were taken to make it known to the immigrants
that such engagements are not legally binding, and especially if it were made a penal offence to enter into them,
that mode at least of immigration would receive a considerable check; and it does not seem probable that any
mode, among so poor a population as the Chinese, can
attain such dimensions as to compete very injuriously
with American labour. Short of that point, the oppor-

tunity given to numerous Chinese of becoming familiar with better and more civilised habits of life, is one of the best chances that can be opened up for the improvement of the Chinese in their own country, and one which it does not seem to me that it would be right to withhold from them. I am, dear sir,

"Yours very sincerely,

"J. S. MILL."

"Henry George, Esq.,

"San Francisco, Cal."

Commenting on this, the "Transcript" editorial said: "With all its qualifications, Mr. Mill's opinion entirely justifies the position of those who take ground in favour of restrictions upon the immigration of these people," for "Chinese labour has already begun to compete injuriously with white labour, and that it will soon be competing *very* injuriously, no one who has noticed how rapidly these people are entering and monopolising one branch of business after another, can have any doubt." Moreover, nine-tenths of the Chinese immigrants are contract labourers and it would be useless to pass laws against such contracts; while as for slavery, "Chinese women are sold and staked at the gambling table in San Francisco every day of the week." The editorial concluded with this tribute to the eminent English economist:

"Yet, whether we agree or disagree with his opinions; whether we adopt or dissent from his conclusions, no American can fail to have for this great Englishman the profoundest respect. It is not merely the rank he has won in the republic of letters; not merely the service he has rendered to one of the most beneficial, if not the noblest, of sciences; not merely the courage and devotion with which he has laboured for the cause of popular rights in his own country; not merely his high private character and pure life, which set off his great talents and public virtues, that entitle John Stuart Mill to the respect of Americans. Beyond all this, they can never forget that he stood the true friend to their country in its darkest day; devoting his great talents and lending his great reputation to the support of the Republic when she had closed in what seemed there her death grapple; that it was he more than any other man who turned the tide of English opinion and sympathy in our favour, and by exhibiting the true character of the struggle, gave us the moral support of the middle class of Great Britain. Services such as these entitle John Stuart Mill to something more from us than even the respect which is due him as a writer, statesman or philosopher—to our affection as well as our admiration."

The "Transcript" editorial with the Mill letter made something like a sensation throughout California. Some of the pro-Chinese papers republished both in garbled form, and in such form the letter may have got back to Mill. At any rate, an editorial on the subject in the Chicago "Tribune" drew from Mill a communication to Horace White of that paper, saying that judging from the comments, the published copy of his letter must have been a mutilated one. White published this. Mr. George had meanwhile become editor of the "Sacramento Reporter." Seeing the Mill letter to White, he promptly republished it and also the earlier Mill letter to himself, putting both in a signed editorial explaining that there had been no garbling at any time on his part. This article he sent to Mill, who made reply that he was "perfectly satisfied."

Some of the pro-Chinese papers in California, while not attempting to garble the original Mill letter, took to abusing Henry George; one of them, the San Francisco "Bulletin," saying that Mill had been misled by George in the "New York Tribune" article, as that was "written from the exaggerated standpoint of a certain class of political alarmists who either have not carefully studied the facts or who use the question as a good demagogue card to win ignorant votes." But notwithstanding such utterances, George's "New York Tribune" article expressed a strong and strengthening sentiment that soon dominated State politics, inspired a long series of legislative acts, and eventuated in 1892, twenty-three years afterwards, in the passage by Congress of the Geary law, prohibiting "the coming of Chinese persons into the United States" and providing for deportation under certain conditions.

To the end of his life Mr. George held to the views against free entrance of the Chinese set forth in his "Tribune" article in 1869. They appear in many of his subsequent California speeches and writings, and in 1881 were set out fully in a signed article published in Lalor's "Cyclopedia of Political Science, Political Economy and of the Political History of the United States."

And when in the fall of 1893, William Lloyd Garrison of Boston addressed a letter to James G. Maguire, who represented the Fourth California District in Congress, upbraiding the congressman with being false to his single tax principles of equal rights, in supporting and voting for an amendment extending the Geary Chinese Exclusion Act, Mr. George replied (New York November 30), a copy of the letter to Maguire having been sent to him by Garrison:

"To your proposition that the right to the use of the earth is not confined to the inhabitants of the United States, I most cordially assent. But what you seem to think follows from that, 'The humblest Chinaman has as much natural right to use the earth of California as yourself, and it is your inalienable right to change your residence to any land under the sun,' I most emphatically deny. Are men merely individuals? Is

there no such thing as family, nation, race? Is there
not the right of association, and the correlative right
of exclusion? . . .

"Your parallel between those who supported slavery
and those who oppose Chinese immigration is not a
true one. The first of the evils wrought by African
slavery in the United States was the bringing hither of
large numbers of the blacks, an evil which still remains
a source of weakness and danger, though slavery is
gone. Let me ask you: If to-day there was the same
possibility of a great coming of African negroes to this
country as there would be of Chinamen if all restric-
tion were removed, would you consider it a wise thing
to permit it under present conditions? And would you
consider it at all inconsistent with your anti-slavery
principles or with your recognition of human equality
to try to prevent it? I certainly would not. . . .

"I have written to you frankly, but I trust not un-
kindly. I have for you too much respect and affection
to wantonly accentuate any difference there may be in
our ways of looking at things."

But while approving of Chinese exclusion "under present conditions," Henry George could conceive of a state of
things under which such a policy would not be necessary.
In a lecture in San Francisco [1] while writing "Progress
and Poverty," he said: "Ladies and gentlemen, it is not
only more important to abolish land monopoly than to get
rid of the Chinese; but to abolish land monopoly will be
to make short work of the Chinese question. Clear out
the land-grabber and the Chinaman must go. Root the
white race in the soil, and all the millions of Asia cannot
dispossess it."

---

[1] " Why Work is Scarce, Wages Low, and Labour Restless," Metropolitan Temple, March 26, 1878.

CHAPTER II.

STRIFE AND THE NATURAL ORDER.

1869-1871.   AGE, 30-32.

WHEN Œdipus, in Greek mythology, travelled towards the city of Thebes he found widespread distress from deaths wrought by the monster Sphinx, who had
the body of a lion, and the head, breast and arms of a
woman, and who put a riddle to all approaching, which
not to answer meant to be hurled headlong from the rock
where she abode. Many had tried, but all had failed; and
through the country as Œdipus moved on came constant
lamentation and constant warning.

Henry George walking through the streets of New York,
had seen the want and misery wrought by the Sphinx of
modern civilisation, and as if to keep him strung to nervous tension and ever mindful of his vow to charge the
monster and solve the problem, Adversity kept close to his
heels. For when he got back to San Francisco, the pressing personal question was, what was he to do?

But he was not one to wait for something to come to
him. He at once got an anti-telegraph monopoly resolution introduced into the legislature, and this being popular,
was easily passed. Next he sketched out several magazine articles on the Chinese question, (though none of
these were ever finished); and wrote several editorials

for the "Evening Bulletin," for which he was twice urged
to go East as special correspondent, but refused. For
awhile, hard pressed for money, he went into the composing room of the "Herald" and set type. Something over
$700 was still owing from that paper on his back salary
and various accounts in New York. Nugent getting into
a rage when the money was demanded, George retaliated by
wiring Hasson to stop the news service. Small though that
service then was, its absence was a great loss to the paper,
and Nugent came partially to terms, yet did not settle entirely until George sued out an attachment. In the middle
of August (19) George wrote to Philadelphia:

> "As for me, I am doing various miscellaneous work;
> just now for a few days editing an Irish Catholic paper
> for a friend.[1]
>
> "I go around very little—not as much as would be
> wise, I presume, and pass most of my evenings in read-
> ing, something I have not done much of for some years
> —not a tenth part as much as I would like to."

One of the books he read, and was "much impressed"
with, was "Lord Chesterfield's Letters," entering in his
pocket diary: *"Suaviter in modo; fortiter in re."* The
diary also announces that on July 30 after dinner, he
went to his room to read, "fell asleep, and was nearly suf-
focated by gas"; for the supply, cut off at the meter during the day, was turned on as night approached, and the
cock in the room having by some chance been left open,
allowed free escape. This was in the old Federal building
on Washington Street, where Mr. George at the time was
rooming. His wife heard nothing of the matter until
long afterwards. But she did hear something from him
that gave her deep pleasure.

---

[1] The paper was the "Monitor," and the friend, its editor, John Barry.

Acting upon an idea thrown out in a letter from New York to Sumner, Mr. George had got his friends to work for his nomination on the Democratic ticket for the Assembly. Presently he wrote to his wife that her uncle, Matthew McCloskey, who had not exchanged a word with them since the runaway marriage, was showing active hostility by working against the nomination. Next day the husband wrote that he had been misinformed; that Mr. McCloskey was working for him, not against him, and singing his praises for character and ability; and that they had become reconciled. The friendship thus renewed was of the strongest kind, Matthew McCloskey on his death-bed six or eight years later commending his family to Henry George for counsel.

Mr. George's desire for election to the legislature was more than a vague ambition to get forward in the world. For the young man, though he had not yet come to clear ideas on the social problem, had in his mind's eye, as may be judged from his editorial and correspondence experience, a mass of matters to press for legislative attention; and as for big things, there were the anti-telegraph, anti-express company and anti-railroad fights to make, and it was also quite evident that something should be done to discourage the massing of land in California into great estates. But disappointment was in store. He failed to get nominated, or rather, he could have been nominated but refused to pay the assessment asked by the party managers, and that ended his hope for the candidature.

The disappointment was all the harder to bear because it came at the end of a line of failures since his return from the East. He had succeeded neither in making any permanent newspaper connection, nor in getting started in a higher literary field. He had not even contrived to make a good living, getting a mere hand-to-mouth subsistence.

And now the political view had been cut off. The future looked dark, indeed. The one chance seemed to be in the East, where a place on John Russell Young's proposed paper was held out, Mrs. George, who was beginning to develop a lively interest in public questions and to enter understandingly into her husband's ambitions, having written in August (15):

"Mr. Hasson spent two or three hours with us this afternoon. He is a firm friend and ardent admirer of yours. . . . He says that John Russell Young is going to start a hundred thousand dollar paper in the fall, and will want your services, as he thinks there is no one like you. Hasson says that Young told Greeley that when he let you go he let go the very man he had been looking for for two years."

This newspaper project of Young's seemed the only but yet very slender hope, for New York was very far away and the plan a thing nebulous and uncertain. He was greatly dejected. His plight, as he said afterwards, was like that of a traveller on the plains, a mountain range in front. The mountains rose wall-like against the distant sky—unbroken and too high to scale. But as he advanced, a cleft appeared and then deepened and widened into a pass. For in the midst of his depression came a call to him from an unthought of quarter.

Through the organisation in San Francisco of a branch of the American Free Trade League, whose headquarters were in New York, Mr. George came into touch with the Governor of California, Henry H. Haight, regarded by many as the ablest executive the State has ever had. During the war Haight had been a strong Republican, but he revolted against the policy of centralisation and special legislation that followed. He espoused the principles of

Thomas Jefferson and became an avowed Democrat and an out-spoken free trader. Henry George had gone through precisely the same kind of political change. While on the "Times" he wrote many editorials supporting principles and measures leading away from the Republican strict party policy, and as a consequence even then was "rapidly becoming disgusted" with that party. He voted for Grant for the Presidency in the fall of 1868, only to see the soldier, as he expressed it, give himself up to his political friends, so that Mr. George concluded that "the Republican party had served its purpose," that it had become chiefly a party for special interests.

Now, across San Francisco Bay at Oakland was a little Democratic paper called the "Transcript," owned by two men, Hiram Tubbs, proprietor of the leading hotel and much real estate there, and John Scott, a prosperous carpenter and builder and prominent as a politician. Scott was a colonel on the staff of the governor, who thereby was indirectly interested in the paper. Indeed, he and Scott had looked about for a good Democratic editor, and judging of George's principles and abilities by his Chinese article and his editorials in the "Times," and coming in contact with him through the organisation of the Free Trade League, concluded that he was the man they sought, and the position was offered him. He accepted and his name appeared at the head of its editorial columns.

Henry George's connection with the "Transcript" was short, but was marked by three important events. It was then that the John Stuart Mill letter came. Mill was at the zenith of his reputation, so that it was with keen pride that this young country editor published in the columns of his paper a letter that set all the papers of the State to buzzing.

It was also at this time that Mr. George made the acquaintance of William Swinton, brother of John Swinton, the well-known radical of New York. William Swinton was born in Scotland in 1833, was well educated, finishing at Amherst College, Mass.; at twenty wrote a large part of a book, "Rambles Among Words"; later held a professorship of ancient and modern languages; during the war made a brilliant field correspondent for the "New York Times"; afterwards wrote two authoritative works, "Campaigns of the Army of the Potomac" and "The Twelve Decisive Battles of the War"; and in 1869 had come to California to accept the chair of English language and literature, rhetoric, logic and history in the University of California, then just being founded at Oakland. He was a man of wide reading in the field of *belles-lettres*, of quick mind, fine taste and copious suggestiveness; and though sprung from, and following the schools, formed a close affinity with this young editor, who could not boast of ever having had any college connections. Then and in the years following Swinton drew George out and encouraged him to aim at the higher domain of literature.

But more important for the young editor than anything else that occurred during the "Transcript" period was the solution of the Sphinx's question, the discovery of the natural order; the answer to the quest he had set himself in the streets of New York—why poverty accompanies wealth in advancing civilisation. It came about through a trifling incident. Mr. George had now commenced the habit of horseback riding—a habit that continued intermittently for nearly ten years. At any hour that he was free and had the inclination he would hire a horse and find mental change in a lope into the open country of the foothills. But wherever he rode, one thing faced him. The trans-continental railroad system had been completed, only a few months before the last spike, made of gold, having been driven. The California terminal was at Sacramento, and there was a ferment over the proposal to extend the line to Oakland. A very general belief was that the advantages from the railroad would be so important as rapidly to attract population and form a great city in and about Oakland to compete with San Francisco. Land at even far-removed points therefore rose to extravagant figures. Men made themselves "land poor" in order to get and to hold as many feet or acres as possible in anticipation of the rise in value that a swelling population would make. Speculation in land ran far in advance of its use.

Amid these circumstances Henry George went for a ride one afternoon. Of this he has said.[1]

"Absorbed in my own thoughts, I had driven the horse into the hills until he panted. Stopping for breath, I asked a passing teamster, for want of something better to say, what land was worth there. He pointed to some cows grazing off so far that they looked like mice and said: 'I don't know exactly, but there is a man over there who will sell some land for a thousand dollars an acre.' Like a flash it came upon me that there was the reason of advancing poverty with advancing wealth. With the growth of population, land grows in value, and the men who work it must pay more for the privilege. I turned back, amidst quiet thought, to the perception that then came to me and has been with me ever since."

This truth was to dwell in his thoughts and slowly develop for a year and a half, when it should burst into expression. Meanwhile Governor Haight's political plans matured. He determined to broaden out his fight against the Central Pacific Railroad which now, like a monster of fairy lore, had swallowed, or was about to swallow,

[1] Meeker notes, October, 1897. Also see "The Science of Political Economy," Book II, Chap. v, p. 163.

great and small competitors, and all things else that could
be useful or that got in its way. Public feeling expressive
of resentment at the encroachment on popular rights began to appear, and Haight, sharing this feeling, gave
definite form and direction to it by attacking the railroad's subsidy policy. The railroad was gulping down
lands, bonds and money showered upon it, all the while
like a weakling pleading for more. The plain and palpable fact was that leaving out of consideration the imperial
endowment in lands, it had already received several times
more money, or what could immediately be turned into
money, than was necessary to build the system, and that
contemporary with the work of railroad construction had
arisen the private fortunes of the big four manipulating
the corporation—Stanford, Crocker, Huntington and
Hopkins, who, from comparative poverty, had quickly
risen to the class of multi-millionaires.

Aside from the principle of subsidies, these private
fortunes were a proof to such men as Haight that the
policy was wrong for California as a State to pursue, or
to authorise its municipalities to pursue. He, therefore,
prepared for war on the "Great Absorber," and invited
Mr. George to take the management of the chief party
paper at the capital, the "Sacramento Reporter," which,
under the name of the "State Capital Reporter," had been
edited by Ex-Governor Bigler, who now retired. The
State Publishing Company was organised to publish the
paper, and besides a fair salary, Mr. George was offered a
fourth of the stock. The rest was to be held by some of
the Governor's political friends. Mr. George was ready
to leave the "Transcript," as his relations with Colonel
Scott were no longer pleasant. He accepted the "Reporter" offer and in February, 1870, moved to Sacramento
and commenced work in his new field.

Soon after Mr. George took charge of the Sacramento paper a press war opened and he got into the middle of it. It was nothing less than a resumption of the fight against the Western Union Telegraph Company and the Associated Press. A new telegraph system, the Atlantic and Pacific, had entered the field against the Western Union Company. Discontent among the old newspapers and needs of the new ones seized this channel for news competition by the organisation of the American Press Association as a rival to the Associated Press. It was made up of a lot of strong journals in the East and started off under favourable auspices, with John Russell Young, who had just started his New York "Standard," as president, and John Hasson, as general agent. Indeed, Hasson had largely, if not chiefly, to do with the organisation of the association, and in turn acknowledged that he had got much of his experience and preparation under George, when they were warring with the Associated Press and the Western Union Telegraph Company for the San Francisco "Herald." Young and Hasson at once chose George for their California agent.

Mr. George drew a number of papers into the new association, starting with his own, the "Reporter," and including Charles DeYoung's paper, the "San Francisco Chronicle." The Franco-Prussian war being on, foreign news was heavy; accordingly, the expense high. The price of the service for the California papers was advanced and the agent put the increase upon the "Chronicle," the paper which could best bear it and which got most advantage from it. But DeYoung made such an ado that George called a meeting of the papers' representatives. In one of his books, "The Land Question," to illustrate another matter, he in a veiled way told of what occurred at this meeting:

"Once upon a time I was a Pacific Coast agent of an Eastern news association, which took advantage of an opposition telegraph company to run against the Associated Press monopoly. The Association in California consisted of one strong San Francisco paper, to which telegraphic news was of much importance, and a number of interior papers, to which it was of minor importance, if of any importance at all. It became necessary to raise more money for the expenses of collecting and transmitting these despatches, and thinking it only fair, I assessed the increased cost to the strong metropolitan paper. The proprietor of this paper was very indignant. He appealed to the proprietors of all the other papers and they all joined in his protest. I replied by calling a meeting. At this meeting the proprietor of the San Francisco paper led off with an indignant speech. He was seconded by several others, and evidently had the sympathy of the whole crowd. Then came my turn. I said, in effect: 'Gentlemen, you can do what you please about this matter. Whatever satisfies you satisfies me. The only thing fixed is that more money has to be raised. As this San Francisco paper pays now a much lower relative rate than you do, I thought it only fair that it should pay the increased cost. But, if you think otherwise, there is no reason in the world why you should not pay it yourselves.' The debate immediately took another turn, and in a few minutes my action was indorsed by a unanimous vote, for the San Francisco man was so disgusted by the way his supporters left him that he would not vote at all."[1]

This fight on the Associated Press and the Western Union Telegraph Company was kept up, so far as Mr. George was concerned, until the following spring, when he was out of the "Sacramento Reporter" and back in San Francisco.

---

[1] "The Land Question," Chap. XI; (Memorial Edition, pp. 69–70).

Meanwhile he had brought his family to Sacramento from the East, and with them his brother Vallence, and settled down at housekeeping. But now he narrowly escaped losing his life, for one day just as he was about to mount a horse for a ride, the animal jumped, and throwing him, dragged him for some distance before he could free his foot from the stirrup. He received a slight blow on the head and other injuries that were only temporary. That accident made him realise how uncertain life is, so that at once he got out an insurance, a thing that before this he had thought of but lightly. All through this period he was in regular and loving communication with his folks at Philadelphia, his father for instance writing June 2: "Your papers, after I have read them, I give to some good old Jackson Democrats, and many warm congratulations I have received that I have a son so bold and firm and consistent for the old Democratic principles."

The father truly characterised his son's paper. While it vigorously denounced "carpet-bag" rule in the so-called "reconstructed" South, it took high Jeffersonian ground on questions raising local issues. Of necessity the young editor was brought into close touch with Governor Haight, and through this intercourse became acquainted with Haight's private secretary, a young man named Edward R. Taylor, with whom he afterwards grew intimate, until, when "Progress and Poverty" was being written, Taylor was chief friend, critic and adviser.

First of all matters of interest at this period was the anti-railroad war. The Central Pacific had set its heart on a further era of subsidies. Haight set himself to kill the scheme, and with the scheme to destroy the principle in public estimation; for it was a generally approved principle prior to this, the Governor himself, having given his sanction to several subsidy bills in behalf of other corpor-

ations. Under his direction public thought became roused,
the question entered politics and the railroad was suddenly
conscious of formidable opposition—an opposition which
had been awakened, aside from the Governor's official and
personal efforts, largely through the columns of the"Sacramento Reporter."

The Central Pacific had become the overshadowing influence in California. It owned or controlled most of the
press, swayed the legislature, bent the courts, governed
banks and moved as a mighty force in politics. It was
quick to recognise talent and as quick to engage or reward
it.[1] Out of imperial coffers it had fortunes to bestow.
With a word it could make men, and so far as the masses
were concerned, could as easily break men. Of those who
could not, or would not serve, it asked only silence, merely
immunity from attack. Henry George had now come to
have a recognised influence with his pen. What more easy

---

[1] "Among the most prominent figures in the Republican national convention (1888) was Creed Haymond, chairman of the California delegation,
and foremost among the 'boomers' of 'Blaine and Protection.' To those
who knew him years ago it seemed a queer place for him to be. Creed Haymond is a Virginian by birth, and a Democrat by instinct and tradition.
During the War. he was in California, a strong secessionist and afterwards
was prominent and useful as an anti-monopoly, free-trade Democrat.
He is a fine lawyer, a man of exceedingly quick and nimble mind, and
like most Southern men of his class, a born politician. He rendered very
efficient aid to Governor Haight in his struggle with the Pacific Railroad
monopoly, and no one in the country could have better startled the Chicago
convention with a Jeffersonian speech. But like many other men in California, Creed Haymond at length grew tired of what seemed an utterly
hopeless fight, and the railroad octopus, true to its policy of taking into
its service men of ability who might be dangerous to it outside, made
him head of its law bureau with a salary of $25,000 a year. Thus it
comes that Creed Haymond makes his appearance in a national Republican convention at the head of a delegation representing the Central
Pacific railroad ring."— Signed editorial by Henry George, "The Standard,"
New York, June 30, 1888.

than for him to be at peace with the great corporation, and obtaining some dignified place within its giving, as some of his acquaintances had already done, enjoy tranquil days, during which to develop his philosophy of the natural order to a readiness for launching when the favourable moment should come! But the young man was not to be tempted. The one course, then open for the railroad people was to buy control of the "Reporter," which they quietly did. George thereupon found himself to be editor of a newspaper whose policy he could no longer direct—a paper which by reason of its new ownership must favour the very interest which he had been so vigourously opposing. He at once resigned, sold out his fourth interest,[1] moved with his family to San Francisco, and took a little house on Stevenson Street, on the site since occupied by the Odd Fellows' building. This was in the beginning of October, 1870, nine months after going on the paper.

But if the railroad management expected in this way to silence the trenchant pen they made a mistake, for it was Haight's plan, as well as George's desire, to make the subsidy question the chief issue at the State election in the fall. Mr. George therefore wrote a sixteen paged, closely printed pamphlet under the title of "The Subsidy Question and the Democratic Party." The nature and tone of the pamphlet may be judged by the concluding paragraphs:

"Let us recapitulate:

"Railroad subsidies, like protective duties, are condemned by the economic principle that the development of industry should be left free to take its natural direction.

"They are condemned by the political principle that government should be reduced to its minimum—that it

---

[1] The "Reporter" not long afterwards was merged in the "Sacramento Record Union," a strong railroad paper.

becomes more corrupt and more tyrannical, and less under the control of the people, with every extension of its powers and duties.

"They are condemned by the Democratic principle which forbids the enrichment of one citizen at the expense of another; and the giving to one citizen of advantages denied to another.

"They are condemned by the experience of the whole country which shows that they have invariably led to waste, extravagance and rascality; that they inevitably become a source of corruption and a means of plundering the people.

"The only method of preventing the abuse of subsidies is by prohibiting them altogether. This is absolutely required by the lengths to which the subsidy system in its various shapes has been carried—by the effects which it is producing in lessening the comforts of the masses, stifling industry with taxation, monopolising land and corrupting the public service in all its branches. . . .

"But it will be said that the Democratic party is opposed to the building of railroads? On the contrary, should the Democratic party carry out its programme of free trade and no subsidies, it will stimulate the building of railroads more than could be done by all the subsidies it is possible to vote. It will at once reduce the cost of building railroads many thousand dollars per mile, by taking off the protective duty now imposed on the iron used; and the stimulus which the reduction of taxation will give to the industry of the whole country will create a new demand for railroads and vastly increase the amount of their business."

Haight so thoroughly appreciated the value of this pamphlet that he had a large edition circulated throughout the State as a campaign document. Bearing Henry George's name, it did much to extend and strengthen the reputation the young man had already won as newspaper editor and author of the Chinese article.

In June, 1871, the Democratic State convention met in San Francisco, and installing Henry George as secretary. nominated Haight for re-election as governor. There was some friction among Democrats over the radical issue, but the party generally being lined up squarely for a big fight on a straight principle, and he himself beginning to think clearly on the great social as well as the great political questions, Mr. George was even more desirous than he had been two years before to run for the legislature. On August 10 he secured a nomination for the Assembly in a San Francisco district and he made several speeches there and elsewhere. Again his hopes were to be dashed. At dinner time on election day he announced to his wife that the indications were that the Democrats were carrying everything, but late that evening he came home again in laughing humour. "Why," he almost shouted, "we haven't elected a constable!"

Haight had opened and pressed the fight—and George had taken an important part in it—that had stamped out the policy of subsidies in California; but the great railroad corporation had in turn thrown its gigantic power into the election and had cast Haight and his entire party into the dust of defeat. Henry George, whose pen had been so active, was a shining mark for the powerful company, and his vote did not rise to the average of the party Assembly candidates in San Francisco. His one personal satisfaction in that hour of defeat was that he had fought and lost on a principle.

CHAPTER III.

ANSWERS THE RIDDLE OF THE SPHINX.

1871.   Age, 32.

"I CANNOT play upon any stringed instrument, but I can tell you how of a little village to make a great and glorious city." Thus spake Themistocles, the Athenian, when asked if he could play the lyre. It was a reply seemingly arrogant enough; for was this not beyond the powers of any mortal man? Do not communities have their birth, their thriving to maturity, their decline and death, as regularly and immutably as the individual man himself?

Yet there have arisen those in the history of the world who have dreamed of a reign of justice and of the prolonged, if not indeed continuous life of the community. Such a dreamer was this Californian—this small, erect young man; with full, sandy beard; fresh, alert face; shining blue eyes; who, careless of dress, and wrapped in thought, rode a mustang pony about San Francisco. In the streets of the great Eastern city he had seen the want and suffering that accompany civilisation. It had made him who came "from the open West sick at heart." He knew nothing of the schools, but this that he saw he could not believe was the natural order. What was that order?

219

He vowed that he would find it.   And afterwards as he
rode in the Oakland foothills came the flash-like revelation
—the monopoly of the land, the locking up of the storehouse of nature!   There was the seat of the evil.   He
asked no one if he was right: he *knew* he was right.   Had
he not come into the new country and grown up with the
phases of change?   Had he not seen this young community develop the ills from which the older communities
suffered?   He did not need to go to books or to consult
the sages.   There the thing lay plainly to view for any
who would see.

On Sunday night, March 26, in his work-room in the
second story of the Stevenson Street house, Henry George
sat down to write out the simple answer to the riddle of
the Sphinx.   When ultimately finished it made a pamphlet
of forty-eight closely printed pages, equivalent to one hundred and fifty pages of an ordinary book.   To it he gave
the title, "Our Land and Land Policy, National and
State."   He divided his subject into five parts, which we
shall briefly review, following the author's language wherever possible.

I.

THE LANDS OF THE UNITED STATES.

The secret of the confidence of Americans in their own
destiny and the reason of their cheerful welcome to the
down-trodden of every nation, lay in the knowledge of the
"practically inexhaustible" public domain spreading over
the great Western country that would provide farms and
homes for all.   But beginning with the Civil War period,
a policy of dissipation of the public lands commenced, and

so great have been the various kinds of grants, especially
to the railroads, up to 1870, that continuing at the same
rate, all the available arable land will be given away by
1890.[1] To a single railroad—the Northern Pacific—
25,600 acres have been given for the building of each mile
of road[2]—land enough to make 256 good sized American
farms or 4,400 such as in Belgium support families in
independence and comfort. Nor was this given to the
corporation for building a railroad for the government or
for the people, but for building it for itself.

II.

THE LANDS OF CALIFORNIA.

In California, twenty-four times as large as Massachusetts and with but 600,000 inhabitants, free land should
be plentiful; yet the notorious fact is that so reckless has
been the land policy that the immigrant in 1871, has, as a
general thing, to pay a charge to middlemen before he
can begin to cultivate the soil. Already individuals hold
thousands and hundred of thousands of acres apiece.
Across many of these vast estates a strong horse cannot
gallop in a day, and one might travel for miles and miles
over fertile ground where no plow has ever struck, but
which is all owned, and on which no settler can come to
make himself a home, unless he pay such a tribute as the
lord of the domain may choose to exact.

---

[1] This was verified, resort being made at about 1890 to lands (since
Oklahoma Territory) which in Indian Territory had been set apart for the
Indian tribes.

[2] Twenty sections in the States and forty sections in the Territories.

III.

LAND AND LABOUR.

Land, that part of the globe's surface habitable by man, is the storehouse from which he must draw the material to which his labour must be applied for the satisfaction of his desires. It is not wealth, since wealth is the product of human labour. It is valuable only as it is scarce. Its value differs from that of, say a keg of nails, for the nails are the result of labour, and when labour is given in return for them the transaction is an exchange; whereas, land is not the result of labour, but the creation of God, and when labour must be given for it, the result is an appropriation.

The value of land is not an element in the wealth of a community. It indicates the distribution of wealth. The value of land and the value of labour must bear to each other an inverse ratio. These two are the "terms" of production, and while production remains the same, to give more to the one is to give less to the other. The wealth of a community depends upon the product of the community. But the productive powers of land are precisely the same whether its price is low or high. In other words, the price of land indicates the distribution of wealth, not the production. The value of land is the power which its ownership gives to appropriate the product of labour, and as a sequence, where rents (the share of the land-owner) are high, wages (the share of the labourer) are low. And thus we see it all over the world: in the countries where land is high, wages are low, and where land is low, wages are high. In a new country the value of labour is at its maximum, the value

of land at its minimum.   As population grows and land
becomes monopolised and increases in value, the value of
labour steadily decreases.   And the higher land and the
lower wages, the stronger the tendency towards still lower
wages, until this tendency is met by the very necessities
of existence.   For the higher land and the lower wages,
the more difficult is it for the man who starts with nothing
but his labour to become his own employer, and the more
he is at the mercy of the land-owner and the capitalist.

According to the doctrine of rent advanced by Ricardo
and Malthus, the value of land should be determined by
the advantage which it possesses over the least advantageous land in use.   Where use determines occupancy, this
may be called the *necessary* or real value of land, in con-
tradistinction to the *unnecessary* or fictitious value which
results from speculation in land.

The difference between the *necessary* value of the land
of the United States and the aggregate value at which it
is held is enormous and represents the unnecessary tax
which land monopolisation levies upon labour.

Now the right of every human being to himself is the
foundation of the right of property.   That which a man
produces is rightfully his own, to keep, to sell, to give or to
bequeath, and upon this sure title alone can ownership of
anything rightfully rest.   But man has also another right,
declared by the fact of his existence—the right to the use
of so much of the free gifts of nature as may be necessary to supply all the wants of that existence, and which he
may use without interfering with the equal rights of any-
one else; and to this he has a title as against all the
world.

To permit one man to monopolise the land from which
the support of others is to be drawn, is to permit him
to appropriate their labour.

IV.

The Tendency of Our Present Land Policy.

The same causes which have reduced 374,000 land-holders of England in the middle of the last century to 30,000 now are working in this country. Not only are large bodies of new lands being put in the hands of the few, but a policy is pursued causing the absorption of the small farms into large estates.

The whole present system, National and State, tends to the concentration of wealth and the monopolisation of land. A hundred thousand dollars in the hands of one man pays but a slight proportion of the taxes that are paid by the same sum distributed among fifty; a hundred thousand acres held by a single landholder is assessed for but a fraction of the amount assessed upon the hundred thousand acres of six hundred farms.

Concentration is the law of the time. The great city is swallowing up the little towns; the great merchant is driving his poorer rivals out of business; a thousand little dealers become the clerks and shopmen of the proprietor of the marble fronted palace; a thousand master workmen, the employees of one rich manufacturer; and the gigantic corporations, the alarming product of the new social forces which Watt and Stephenson introduced to the world, are themselves being welded into still more titanic corporations.

In the new condition of things what chance will there be for a poor man if the land also is monopolised? To say that the land of a country shall be owned by a small class, is to say that that class shall rule it; to say that the people of a country shall consist of the very rich and the very poor, is to say that republicanism is impossible.

V.

WHAT OUR LAND POLICY SHOULD BE.

When we consider what land is; the relations between it and labour; that to own the land upon which a man *must* gain his subsistence is practically to own the man himself, we cannot remain in doubt as to what should be our policy in disposing of our public lands.

They should be given to actual settlers, in small quantities without charge.

But this policy would affect only the land that is left. It would still leave the great belts granted to railroads, the vast estates—the large bodies of land everywhere the subject of speculation. Still would continue the tendency that is concentrating ownership in the older settled States.

When our 40,000,000 of people have to raise $800,000,000 per year for public purposes [1] we cannot have any difficulty in discovering the remedy in the adjustment of taxation.

The feudal system annexed duties to privileges. One portion of the land defrayed the expenses of the State; another portion, those of the army; a third, those of the Church, and also relieved the sick, the indigent and the wayworn; while a fourth portion, the commons, was free to all the people. The great debts, the grinding taxation, are results of a departure from this system. A recent English writer [2] has estimated that had the feudal tenures been continued, England would now have had at her command a completely appointed army of six hundred thousand men, without the cost of a penny to the public treasury.

---

[1] Estimate of Commissioner David A. Wells.
[2] "The Strength of Nations," by Andrew Bisset.

Why should *we* not go back to the old system, and charge the expense of government upon our lands?

Land taxation does not bear at all upon production; it adds nothing to prices, and does not affect the cost of living. As it does not add to prices, it costs the people nothing in addition to what it yields the Government; while as land cannot be hid or moved, this tax can be collected with more ease and certainty, and with less expense than any other tax; and the land-owner cannot shift it to any one else.

A tax upon the value of land is the most equal of all taxes, because the value of land is something that belongs to all, and in taxing land values we are merely taking for the use of the community something which belongs to the community. By the value of land is meant the value of the land itself, not the value of any improvement which has been made upon it—what is sometimes called in England the *unearned* value.

The mere holder would be called on to pay just as much taxes as the user of land. The owner of a vacant lot would have to pay as much as his neighbour who is using his. The monopoliser of agricultural land would be taxed as much as though his land were covered with improvements, with crops and with stock.

Land prices would fall; land speculation would receive its death-blow; land monopolisation would no longer pay. Millions and millions of acres from which settlers are now shut out, would be abandoned by their present owners, or sold to settlers on nominal terms.

The whole weight of taxation would be lifted from productive industry. The million dollar manufactory and needle of the seamstress, the mechanic's cottage and the grand hotel, the farmer's plow and the ocean steamship, would be alike untaxed. All would be free to buy or sell, to make or save, unannoyed by the tax-gatherer.

Imagine this country with all taxes removed from production and exchange! How demand would spring up; how trade would increase; what a powerful stimulus would be applied to every branch of industry; what an enormous development of wealth would take place. Imagine this country free of taxation, with its unused land free to those who would use it! Would there be many industrious men walking the streets, or tramping over our roads in the vain search for employment? Would there be in such a city as New York a hundred thousand men looking for work; such festering poverty and breeding vice as make the man from the open West sick at heart?

This was the nature of the little book to the writing of which this Californian, not yet thirty-two, devoted himself during the four months and three days between March 26 and July 29, 1871, though in the meantime came the Haight convention and other interruptions. He printed it in small type and in pamphlet form, for he had no money to present it in a better way. At first it made only thirty-one pages and in that form was printed; but when only a few copies were off, he stopped the press and expanded the last part, so that as published the pamphlet made forty-eight pages and had attached to it a folding map of California showing the extent of the railroad land grants.

Perhaps the first question to arise is, how much was Henry George indebted to others for the comprehensive views of political economy as set down in his little book? He answered this himself in later years:[1]

"When I first came to see what is the root of our social difficulties, and how this fundamental wrong might be cured in the easiest way, by concentrating taxes

---

[1] "The Standard," New York, October 19, 1889.

on land values, I had worked out the whole thing for myself without conscious aid that I can remember, unless it might have been the light I got from Bisset's 'Strength of Nations' as to the economic character of the feudal system. When I published 'Our Land and Land Policy,' I had not even heard of the Physiocrats and the *impot unique*. But I knew that if it was really a star I had seen, others must have seen it too."

While Ricardo and Malthus are credited with the formulation of the law of rent; while John Stuart Mill's proposal to compensate land-owners is deprecated, and his phrase "unearned increment," is spoken of as "the unearned value of land," it is not necessary to assume that Henry George was indebted to others further than this, even at points where there chanced to be a similarity of thought. In his last book,[1] discussing the concurrent writings of Adam Smith and the French Physiocrats and the probably independent thought of Smith, where his utterances closely resembled that of the latter, Mr. George has drawn the instance of his own case.

"It is a mistake to which the critics who are themselves mere compilers are liable, to think that men must draw from one another to see the same truths or to fall into the same errors. Truth is, in fact, a relation of things, which is to be seen independently because it exists independently. Error is perhaps more likely to indicate transmission from mind to mind; yet even that usually gains its strength and permanence from misapprehensions that in themselves have independent plausibility. Such relations of the stars as that appearance in the North which we call the Dipper or Great Bear, or as that in the South which we call the Southern Cross, are seen by all who scan the starry

---

[1] "The Science of Political Economy." Book II, Chap. v., pp. 162-164.

heavens, though the names by which men know them are various. And to think that the sun revolves around the earth is an error into which the testimony of their senses must cause all men independently to fall, until the first testimony of the senses is corrected by reason applied to wider observations.

"In what is most important, I have come closer to the views of Quesnay and his followers than did Adam Smith, who knew the men personally. But in my case there was certainly no derivation from them. I well recall the day when, checking my horse on a rise that overlooks San Francisco Bay, the commonplace reply of a passing teamster to a commonplace question, crystallised, as by lightning-flash, my brooding thoughts into coherency, and I there and then recognised the natural order—one of those experiences that make those who have had them feel thereafter that they can vaguely appreciate what mystics and poets have called the 'ecstatic vision.' Yet at that time I had never heard of the Physiocrats, or even read a line of Adam Smith.

"Afterwards, with the great idea of the natural order in my head, I printed a little book, 'Our Land and Land Policy,' in which I urged that all taxes should be laid on the value of land, irrespective of improvements. Casually meeting on a San Francisco street a scholarly lawyer, A. B. Douthitt, we stopped to chat, and he told me that what I had in my little book proposed was what the French 'Economists' a hundred years before had proposed.

"I forget many things, but the place where I heard this, and the tones and attitude of the man who told me of it, are photographed on my memory. For, when you have seen a truth that those around you do not see, it is one of the deepest of pleasures to hear of others who have seen it. This is true, even though these others were dead years before you were born. For the stars that we of to-day see when we look were here to be seen hundreds and thousands of years ago. They shine on. Men come and go, in their generations, like the generations of the ants."

Ex-State Senator John M. Days of California became acquainted with Mr. George soon after the pamphlet was written and bears testimony on the subject:

"In 1871 I was elected a member of the Legislature and introduced a set of resolutions in favour of the land of the United States being held for the people thereof. In preparing my speech I came across Henry George's pamphlet 'Our Land and Land Policy' and I quoted two whole pages. I first met Henry George personally in the month of May, 1872, and I loaned him all the writings of Bronterre O'Brien, together with Gamage's history of chartism. He returned them within so short a time that he could not have had time to read them carefully, let alone study them. He told me that when he wrote the pamphlet he had never read or seen any work on the land question."

But without direct or indirect statements from Mr. George or any one else as to the independence of his thought, a striking proof of it might be found in his writings themselves. He has frankly stated [1] that in the spring of 1869, when writing the Chinese article, "wishing to know what political economy had to say about the causes of wages," he "went to the Philadelphia Library, looked over John Stuart Mill's 'Political Economy,' and accepting Mill's view without question," based his article upon it. Yet in "Our Land and Land Policy," in dealing with the cause of wages, he rejected Mill's view and gave a different explanation to the one assumed in the Chinese article. He, in fact, took up and developed something he had perceived months before the Chinese article was thought of and which he had set forth in his "Overland Monthly" article, "What the Railroad Will Bring Us," in the fall of

---

[1] "The Science of Political Economy." Book II, Chap. viii, pp. 200, 201.

1868. Passages from his former and his later work set side by side, show the development of his thought:

"Overland" Article, 1868.	"Land Policy," 1871.
"For years the high rate of interest and the high rate of wages prevailing in California have been special subjects for the lamentation of a certain school of political economists, who could not see that high wages and high interest were indications that the natural wealth of the country was not yet monopolised, that great opportunities were open to all."	"The value of land and of labour must bear to each other an inverse ratio. These two are the 'terms' of production, and while production remains the same, to give more to the one, is to give less to the other. The value of land is the power which its ownership gives to appropriate the product of labour, and, as a sequence, where rents (the share of the landowner) are high, wages (the share of the labourer) are low. And thus we see it all over the world, in the countries where land is high, wages are low, and where land is low, wages are high. In a new country the value of labour is at first at its maximum, the value of land at its minimum. As population grows and land becomes monopolised and increases in value, the value of labour steadily decreases."

The truth is that primitive conditions were all about Henry George. The miners throughout the early California placers commonly spoke of washing their "wages" out of the soil, and there was a universal if unwritten law among them that "claims" should be limited in size and that ownership should be conditioned upon use. In the agricultural regions, and even in some of the towns, "squatters" had constantly asserted the principle commonly recognised through the whole frontier country that any man was free to use land that was not already actually in use. The passage of statutes permitting the adding of mining claim to claim and promoting monopolisation in the agricultural regions, accompanied by enormous grants to comparatively few individuals, brought a keen sense of scarcity of land to a people who had been accustomed to think of practically "all out-doors" as being free.

With a fresh young people, full of self-confidence and free from restraints and traditions, here were all the conditions needed to quicken original thought—thought that should go back to first principles. Henry George did not therefore have to go to books for his political economy. His keen perception, and active, analytical mind found what he hailed as the fundamental and eternal truths of social order written so that all might read them in the primary conditions of the new country. His political economy he got from nature herself.

But there was one small passage in the pamphlet which should not be overlooked. Of this Ex-Senator Days has since said:

"In 'Our Land and Land Policy' Henry George made a plea for private property in land. In August, 1872, I became president of a Lyceum in San Francisco which discussed various questions every Sunday afternoon. I invited him to open on the land question. In his speech he still favoured private property in land. In closing the meeting I made a few remarks in which I observed that Mr. George said that he favoured private property in land, but that he made a mistake in so saying, for every argument he made on the question showed that he was opposed to it. From that day to the day of his death Mr. George openly opposed by word as well as argument private property in land."

The passage of the pamphlet to which the Senator refers runs:

"It by no means follows that there should be no such thing as property in land, but merely that there should be no monopolisation—no standing between the man who is willing to work and the field which nature offers for his labour. For while it is true that the land of a country is the free gift of the Creator to all the people of that country, to the enjoyment of which each has an equal natural right, it is also true that the recognition of private ownership in land is necessary to its proper use—is, in fact, a condition of civilisation. When the millennium comes, and the old savage, selfish instincts have died out of men, land may perhaps be held in common; but not till then."

The idea that Mr. George wished to convey was the necessity of securing improvements, which could not be the case if titles were to be confiscated and the State were to resume actual possession of all the land. But seeing in the instance of Senator Days the wrong idea his language expressed, when writing "Progress and Poverty" he changed it materially, to wit:

"What is necessary for the use of land is not its private ownership, but the security of improvements. . . . The complete recognition of common rights to land need in no way interfere with the complete recognition of individual right to improvements or produce. . . . I do not propose either to purchase or to confiscate private property in land. The first would be unjust; the second, needless. Let the individuals who now hold it still retain, if they want to, possession of what they are pleased to call *their* land. Let them continue to call it *their* land. Let them buy and sell, and bequeath and devise it. We may safely leave them the shell, if we take the kernel. *It is not necessary to confiscate land; it is only necessary to confiscate rent.*"[1]

This Days incident and others like it bringing to Mr. George a realisation of obscurities of his language in some instances and of his thoughts in others, made him henceforward most patient with those who, sincerely striving to comprehend his ideas, floundered around in self-made confusions; for with all his powers, no one more fully appreciated the difficulty of clear expression, and before that, of clear thinking, than Mr. George himself.

If "Our Land and Land Policy" was sent to John Stuart Mill, the acknowledged master political economist of the day, there is nothing to show it. But E. T. Peters, of the Bureau of Statistics at Washington, whom George had quoted and to whom he presented a copy, wrote strongly commending it; Horace White of the "Chicago Tribune" wrote that George was "entitled to be ranked as an economist"; while David A. Wells, New York Commissioner for the Revision of the Revenue Laws, whose report had been cited, said, "I see you have enunciated a principle relative to value of land and pauperism which strikes me as original and well put." But beyond a few such letters as these, the pamphlet got little attention. Nor even in California did it awaken the public recognition for which he may have looked. "Something like a thousand

---

[1] "Progress and Poverty." Book VIII, Chaps. i and ii, (Memorial Edition, pp. 396, 397 and 403).

copies were sold," he said towards the end of his life,[1] "but I saw that to command attention the work must be done more thoroughly." The work was done more thoroughly eight years later when "Progress and Poverty" was written.

Two articles by Henry George appeared in the "Overland Monthly" during this year of 1871, one in February entitled, "How Jack Breeze Missed Being a Pasha," and the other in December entitled, "Bribery in Elections," in which, pointing at the shameless corruption at the polls in the fall election when Haight was overwhelmed by railroad money, George advocated the adoption in California of the Australian ballot system. But these efforts were trifling compared with the pamphlet, "Our Land and Land Policy." This latter was set aside for a time in a new era of newspaper activity.

---

[1] "The Science of Political Economy." Book II, Chap. viii, p. 201.

CHAPTER IV.

THE "SAN FRANCISCO EVENING POST."

1871-1875.　　　　Age, 32-36.

IT was in 1859, before he came of age and while setting type on the "Home Journal," that, on an alarm of fire one day which brought most of the people of the neighbourhood into the street, Henry George found himself wedged in a doorway with a strange printer from another part of the building, both trying to pass through at the same moment. Seven years later on meeting him again, George learned that this man was William M. Hinton. George was then about to set off on the Mexican filibustering expedition and Hinton deprecated his going, because George would imperil his life and most likely cut off the means of his family's support. That commenced the friendship, and when "Our Land and Land Policy" had been published, Hinton was one of those to whom the author gave a copy. Born in England, in 1830, nearly ten years before George's birth, he was brought to the United States as a child, his father, I. T. Hinton, coming to Philadelphia in 1832 to sell a history of the United States written by himself and his brother, John Howard Hinton. George wavered during the summer of 1871 between remaining in California and going to New York or Philadelphia to establish himself, when he chanced one day to talk with Hinton, of which conversation the latter says:

"Mr. George was talking of going East to settle. I had read his pamphlet, 'Our Land and Land Policy,' and was taken with it, believing its author showed marked ability. In talking with him about it and other things, I asked him why he did not start a newspaper. He replied that he had no money; to which I said that anybody could start one with money, but that the difficult and commendable achievement was to start one without it. I had no thought about entering upon such an enterprise myself, as I was getting a good living out of the job-printing establishment of Mahan & Co., of which firm I was a partner. I made the suggestion to Mr. George simply because at the time he had no employment. Yet as a result of this casual conversation, the idea catching fire in his mind, I found myself before long getting into the thing, though even then I purposed to stay only until it should be set on its feet, planning then to withdraw. Three of us entered into an equal partnership—George, who was to be editor; myself, who was to superintend the printing; and A. H. Rapp, a member of my job-printing firm, who was to be business manager. We got together about $1,800 and this and some more that we got in by the sale in advance of delivery routes, constituted all the capital we had with which to start a daily newspaper. We lost no time, and on Monday, December 4, 1871, the first copy of the 'Daily Evening Post' appeared, with Hinton, Rapp & Co. as publishers, and Henry George as editor. Our office was at 605 Montgomery Street, west side, a few doors north of Clay."

Following the example of very successful newspapers in the East, the price was set at one cent a copy, it being the first penny paper west of the Rocky Mountains. Indeed, the cent piece was not in commercial use on the Pacific Coast, so that it had to be introduced specially;

which was accomplished by inducing the largest financial institution in the Western country—the Bank of California—to import a thousand dollars' worth of pennies on the presumption of their usefulness in a multitude of minor commercial transactions. Then San Francisco was astonished by the spectacle of newsboys crying the new paper on the streets for a cent a copy, and ready with a large supply of pennies to make change. The novelty of the thing caused people to buy the little "Post." For the paper, consisting of four pages, was only eleven by fourteen inches, and the type very small. The early numbers contained little advertising and telegraphic, the space being filled with local news and editorials, written in short, sharp, direct style. In its salutatory it said: "In the higher, wider sense the 'Post' will be Democratic; that is, it will oppose centralisation and monopolies of all kinds. But it will be the organ of no faction, clique or party. It will endeavour to deal with all questions without cowardly reserve, but with firmness and candour; and whether it praises or censures, it will be without reference to party lines or party affiliations."

Towards the end of his life Henry George told of the early history of the "Post."[1]

"The vigour of the little paper attracted attention and it began to run to as large a circulation as could be obtained with our press facilities. We could get only one double flat-bed press. An offer soon came from another newspaper man, H. W. Thomson, now dead, to buy at a good price a fourth interest. The third partner, Rapp, wanted to sell his share, and he did sell it for about $2,500. Mr. Hinton and I concluded that we had better withdraw, and we sold our interests, each getting $2,700. All three of the original

---

[1] Meeker notes, October, 1897.

partners had thus sold to Thomson. This happened
within four months and a half after the first issue appeared. But no sooner was the policy changed than the
circulation of the 'Post' dropped, and in less than
sixty days Thomson offered the paper to us for a merely
nominal sum. This Mr. Hinton and I accepted, and
Frank Mahan, another printer, was given a small interest. I went along editing the paper, which immediately started to grow."

A feature that was quickly recognised by the public
as indicating the independence of the new journal was its
treatment of the land and taxation questions. Frequently
quotations were made from "Our Land and Land Policy"
and more frequently there were editorials favouring the
taxation of land values to the exclusion of all other things.
These editorials were always short and direct. This feature grew strong enough to become the objective point
with the opposition press, which ridiculed "George's fad."
But fad or no fad, the editor kept persistently talking
of it and snapped up every challenge to discuss it with
other papers. When in May, 1873, John Stuart Mill died
at Avignon, France, the "Post" paid a fine editorial tribute
to the passing of this "greatest living master of political
economy," making commendation of the decision of those
having the matter in hand that instead of raising a statue
to him in America, they should publish a memorial edition of his writings—"his best monument."

In national politics the paper was strongly opposed to
Grant, "carpet-bag reconstruction" and centralisation, and
warmly advocated the nomination for the Presidency of
Horace Greeley, editor of the "New York Tribune," who,
although formerly a zealous supporter of war measures,
now wished to ignore sectionalism and bind up the nation's wounds. Mr. George was elected a delegate to the

Democratic National Convention to meet in Baltimore,
Maryland, early in July, 1872. He went East by way
of Philadelphia, where he had sent his family just before starting the "Post," on account of his wife's ill
health. Thence, accompanied by his wife, he went to
Baltimore, where he was elected secretary of the California delegation, Ex-Governor Downey being chairman. On July 10, 1872, Greeley was nominated unanimously and a few days later the California delegation
visited the candidate on his estate at Chappaqua, Westchester County, N. Y., George writing to his paper a long
signed description of the occasion, closing with the words:
"We all felt . . . that in this sturdy, benignant old
man we had a candidate round whom we could all rally,
and who fittingly represented the grandest idea of the
time—the idea of reconciliation."

Then Mr. George hastened back to San Francisco to
plunge editorially into the campaign. In this, as in all
his fights, he grew more and more hopeful as his blood
warmed in the conflict; but his wife, who now was growing to understand public affairs and therefore becoming
more his counsellor in such matters, was not so sure, writing October 8, on the day of the Pennsylvania State election: "This is the day that in a measure determines Greeley's fate. I am not at all sanguine, but I won't give up
even if the Republicans win this contest." Greeley was
badly beaten; and George was sorely disappointed. But
he was not the man to repine. At once he was up and
doing on another line.

Meanwhile in August, when less than eight and a half
months old, the "Post" had been increased in size and
its price advanced to two cents; and a month and a half
later, enlarged to the size of the ordinary newspaper and
the charge for single copies made five cents, "to accommo-

date the price to the currency," the attempt to introduce the one cent piece proving after a long trial
a failure.

As might be imagined, a newspaper that saw evils to
oppose and did not hesitate to oppose them, could find
plenty of work to do. As a matter of fact, the "Post"
was kept busy with fights of one kind or another. One of
these attracted wide attention. It was the case of the
ship *Sunrise*, which sailing from New York harbour in
May, 1873, had a passage to San Francisco marked by
such cruelty towards the crew by the captain and first mate
that three of the men jumped overboard and were drowned.
Attempts were made to hush up the matter when the ship
reached the Golden Gate, but Mr. George learned of it
and at once demanded a prosecution. The captain and
first mate fled, but upon the "Post's" offering a reward,
were apprehended and brought to trial, the newspaper
engaging special counsel. The officers were convicted to
long terms of imprisonment. The "Post" subsequently
took up some less flagrant cases of maritime brutality and
established itself as a champion of sailor's rights.

That personal danger attended the editing of an aggressive Western newspaper has been often attested, and
Mr. George had his share. Ex-Judge Robert Ferral, then
one of the editorial writers on the "Post," says of one of
these cases:

"I went with Henry George to attend an investigation
of the House of Correction, or Industrial School, which
was in charge of a brute named George F. Harris. At
the gate stood the redoubtable Harris, with his hand
on his pistol, looking more like a pirate than the superintendent of a public institution. Without the least
hesitation Mr. George walked right up to him, looked
the burly ruffian straight in the eyes, and passed into

the yard without a word. All through that investigation Harris avoided the steady, indignant gaze of the brave little man who, pressed his charges of brutality and drove him from his position and out of the city."

Another instance of personal danger arose out of the Tarpey case in the beginning of 1873. Matthew Tarpey, a brutal but affluent land-owner in Monterey County, quarrelled with an unoffending woman named Nicholson about a tract of land. He dug a pit, lay in it for hours waiting for her, and shot her in the back and killed her when she took alarm and tried to run away. The country around became fiercely excited, and more so when it was rumoured that Tarpey's wealth would clear him as others had been cleared of late, and that the first step would be to move him to another locality for trial. Word went out at once that the citizens would stop that and take the matter in hand themselves, and despatches came to San Francisco that Tarpey would be lynched. John V. George, Henry's brother, was engaged in the business office of the "Post" and was a witness of what followed.

"Tarpey money and political influence were strong enough to hush the matter up in the other newspapers, but the 'Post' published the news of the intended lynching, and an editorial saying that there would be no regrets if the people should deal out to him the same measure he had meted out to others, and hang him to the nearest tree, as a 'ghastly evidence' that there was 'still a sense of justice in California.' Tarpey's relatives in San Francisco and others of influence came to the office to implore the editor to say no more, and several anonymous letters were received threatening violence if he did not stop, but he would not change his course, and next day, following news of Tarpey's death, he published as a leader an editorial a column and a quarter long de-

nouncing Tarpey's deed and justifying the lynching.[1]
The effect of this was lost by the buying up of a large
part of the edition of the paper by the Tarpey partisans.

"Next day a man, I think named Donally, came to
the office inquiring for the editor. My brother was out
and Donally hung around on the sidewalk. When my
brother returned Donally approached and asked him if
the article of the day represented his sentiments. My
brother answered that it not only represented his sentiments, but that he himself wrote it, whereupon Donally
impeached the article and called its author a liar. My
brother struck him in the face, though Donally was a
much larger and heavier man. The bystanders interfered and Donally left. Nothing came of this, although
there was talk for a time of violence to the editor of the
'Post.' But the paper did not change its front and
short editorials on the Tarpey matter kept appearing."

John V. George tells of another occurrence that almost
resulted in the shooting of the aggressive editor. It grew

---

[1] Touching this method of effecting justice, the editorial said : " Lynch
law is a fearful thing. It is only better than the crime it is invoked to
repress in that the impulses of the many are generally truer and purer
than the passions of the individual. It is liable to terrible mistakes, and
it strikes at the very foundations upon which society is organised. To
say that even in a case like this Lynch law is justified is to admit that
the regular and legal methods by which society protects itself have failed,
that our laws in their practical workings are but a snare and a delusion,
and that justice in our courts is but a matter of chance. . . . The people
of Monterey hung Tarpey themselves because they could not trust the
law to do it. But it will not do to dismiss the case with the simple reflection that justice has been done. There is a deep moral in it, which
we must heed, unless we are willing to drift back to a condition little
short of anarchy. And there is a moral in it, too, for law breakers as
well as law makers — not for murderers alone, but for thieving officials,
corrupt representatives, and the robbers of all grades who make of law a
protection and means of escape. Our society is not too highly organised
to revert upon great provocation to first principles, and to do for itself,
what its ministers and administrators refuse to do."— "Evening Post,"
March 18, 1873.

out of the paper's arraignment of city Chief of Police Crowley, whom it had helped to office, but now hotly denounced for not closing the gambling hells and clearing out the crime-infested Chinese quarter, as commanded by city ordinances.

"It was in May, 1873, two months after the Tarpey case. Accompanied by Mr. Hinton, his partner, and by City Supervisor Stuart Menzies, Port Warden Joseph Austin, and Daniel O'Connell of the 'Post' staff, my brother, one afternoon after the paper had gone to press went to the Mint saloon and restaurant, on Commercial Street, a resort for lawyers and politicians. As they entered, James Gannon, an ex-detective and supporter of Crowley, tapped my brother on the shoulder, saying that he wanted to speak with him privately. My brother stepped aside with him, when Gannon said, 'Let up on Crowley or there will be trouble,' and when asked what he meant, the ex-detective seized my brother by the neck with one hand and struck him in the face with the other. My brother tried to strike back, when Gannon reached down and drew a revolver. But before he could fire, Menzies, a very strong man, caught his wrist and held the weapon down, while he and Supervisor McCarthy, who was in the place at the time, pulled Gannon away. It was proposed at first to bring Gannon to trial, but the matter was dropped and he afterwards became very sorry for his part in it."

William A. Plunkitt, a school director in the early seventies and supported by the "Post" in an investigation into a big scandal in the purchasing of school supplies, has since said:

"Under Henry George's management the 'Post' was a bold, fearless, reform paper. The standard of political morality or public morals in San Francisco at that time was very low. While many good men held public official positions, quite a number of important places in the municipal government were filled by characterless and unscrupulous demagogues. Mr. George neither respected nor feared that kind of public functionary. He lashed them as with 'a whip of scorpions.' The 'Post' and its editor thus became a power, esteemed and respected by all thoughtful and worthy citizens in San Francisco, and feared by all public malefactors."

A yet fuller picture of the editor is presented by another contemporary, Mrs. C. F. McLean, who was then Miss Sallie Hart, and who says that "while writing his editorials or correcting proof, Mr. George received any and all who, with or without excuse, 'dropped in to see the editor.' " [1]

"I was a teacher in the public schools of San Francisco when there arose a question of the reduction of the salaries of the teachers in the lower grades. Picking up the 'Evening Post,' I noticed an editorial protest, which inspired me to write a communication to the editor, which I signed with an assumed name. When the article appeared it was with an editorial request that 'Susan' call at the office. Saturday came and with it the first visit of my life to a newspaper office. The place was up two flights of stairs. . . . To my knock there came a cheery 'Come in,' and on opening the door I came face to face with Henry George. He was seated at a common table piled high with papers, while all about on the small floor space were other newspapers, all, to my unsophisticated eyes, piled in mournful confusion. . . . I was embarrassed, almost frightened, but in an instant my breath was fairly taken

[1] "Henry George : A Study from Life," "The Arena," September, 1898. Mrs. McLean subsequently became an occasional writer for the "Post." She is alluded to in "The Science of Political Economy" (pp. 282, 283) as "the wife of the superintendent of a Western zoological garden, who, coming to New York with her husband on the annual trip he makes to buy wild animals, jokingly speaks of 'shopping for menagerie goods.' "

away, for the man in front of me said: 'Come in, my little girl.' However, I gasped out that I had sent the article signed 'Susan.' . . . 'Now, come sit down,' he said. 'You must excuse me, but you are so small, and you look so young; do sit down.'

"I sat down, and before I knew what I was saying I had told the editor before me all about myself. Even then I noticed his large head and bright eyes, and at once compared them with a picture of Henry Clay that had been familiar to me from childhood, and thought the head before me was the finer of the two. I remember now that my first interview with Henry George was brought to a close by a boy who, I thought, rather imperatively demanded 'copy'; therefore I hastily rose to go, but not before I had promised to call again soon."

Arthur McEwen was a brilliant young contemporary newspaper worker on the Pacific Coast with Henry George and testifies that it was the "editorial policy that marked the 'Post' off from the usual."

"It was as foreign to George to be either a demagogue or a follower in politics as it was for the 'Post' to keep subscribers and advertisers by thrifty silence. Women were appearing at local option elections soliciting votes and receiving disrespectful treatment. Instantly the 'Post' charged upon the ungallant blackguards, and in a day had every saloon in California for its enemy. Subscribers withdrew by the thousand and advertisements were withdrawn by the column, but that made no difference to George."

James V. Coffey, editorial writer on the "Examiner" at this time, and since Judge of the Superior Court of San Francisco, says that Mr. George "had apparently an unsystematic method of work, jotting down a paragraph here and a paragraph there; yet in the end the writing was smooth and connected." This apparently "unsys-

tematic method of work" doubtless came from dictating
to a stenographer. Having a habit of procrastination,
he put off his daily writing until he was cramped for time
and had to work under great pressure. To relieve this
stress he engaged a stenographer, Edward Lande, the first
secretary he ever had. Lande was soon succeeded by
Stephen Potter who remained until George left the "Post"
and who says that his chief had an original way of working.

> "He would dictate for a few minutes, and then leav-
> ing me to transcribe, would continue the thread of his
> thoughts with his own pen. In this way he would dic-
> tate and write, and get through an immense amount of
> work. I ought to say that at this time he had curious
> habits of abstraction, often even on the street he would
> stop, walk to the curb and stand there apparently deep
> in thought and oblivious to the stir about him. I have
> had to speak several times on such occasions to rouse
> him."

Henry George's career on the "Evening Post" termi-
nated November 27, 1875. Starting the paper with
scarcely any capital, it had from the business point of
view a hand to mouth struggle until the close of 1873,
when a comparatively large sum of money was obtained
for it. We have Mr. George's own story for this.[1]

> "John P. Jones, then elected United States Senator
> from Nevada, sought an interview with me and de-
> clared himself interested in such a paper, offering to
> furnish us on our own notes, money enough to buy the
> best press that could be obtained.[2] I had seen in the

---

[1] Meeker notes, October, 1897.

[2] Mr. Hinton, in conversation with Henry George, Jr., in April, 1898,
said that Jones put in two sums of money — $30,000, for which he re-
ceived 30 of the 100 shares of the stock of the paper, and $18,000 for which
he received notes. Jones professed to do this solely from motives of friend-

'Sun' office when in New York in 1869, the first perfecting press, the Bullock, and concluding to accept this offer of Jones, Mr. Hinton went East and made an arrangement with the Bullock Company for a press. It was brought out and set up, the first perfecting press on the Pacific Coast.[1]

"Feeling that we now had facilities for larger circulation and that we should be making a mistake not to improve it, we concluded to establish a morning paper, 'The Ledger,' which we did in August, 1875. This was done on an extensive scale. It was a small daily paper, and for the first time in journalism, an illustrated Sunday paper. We disdained asking for advertisements and designed to fill up the whole with reading matter until advertisements should seek us.

"But a few days after it started there was a great fire in Virginia City, Nevada, in which many San Franciscans were interested; a heavy decline in some of the greatest of the mining stocks and the suspension of payment by the Bank of California. Then came an intense local money panic, during which it became impossible to collect money[2] and we had to suspend the 'Ledger.' While we were thus embarrassed John P. Jones demanded the return of the money he had loaned us or that the paper that we had made should be surrendered to him. I felt like fighting, and a short article in the 'Post' would have ended all hopes of his getting anything from it, but my partner, Mr. Hinton, pleaded the duty of our providing for the employees who were friends, and tired out with the fight, I finally suc-

liness, but if his real motive was the hope of influencing the paper to change its policy of hostility to President Grant, whom he warmly supported, he was disappointed, as his loan and purchase of stock did not affect the editorial columns.

[1] The paper also moved to new and larger quarters, 504 Montgomery Street, corner of Sacramento, and was supplied with a new dress of type and office fittings.

[2] Mr. Hinton says that he saw a man bring an ingot of gold worth $9,000 into the office of Hickox & Spier, money-brokers, and get only $1,500 on it.

cumbed, and without a cent of compensation, on November 27, almost four years to a day after we started it, gave over the paper to the representative of Jones.

"I thus went out with a dependent family to make a living and not caring to ask or to receive any offer of employment from other papers, I wrote to Governor Irwin, whom I had been instrumental in electing a few months before, and asked him to give me a place where there was little to do and something to get, so that I might devote myself to some important writing. He gave me the office of State Inspector of Gas-Meters, which yielded, though intermittently, a sufficient revenue to live on and which required very little work."

But though Mr. George thus obtained a public office that would afford him a living, and though he had the purpose before him of engaging in more permanent writing, the loss of the "Post" seemed to him at the time a great misfortune, for not only was he at a stroke shorn of the fruits of years of labour, but was bereft of his weapon as an active factor in the affairs of the City and State—the keenest of losses to an energetic public man. But this in fact proved another and a momentous turning point in his career.

CHAPTER V.

DOMESTIC LIFE.

1873-1876.   Age, 34-37.

WE break in on the narrative at this point for a glimpse of the home life.

In the fall of 1873 the wife and children had returned from the East and the family settled down in a cozy two-story house at the Mission—on Valencia Street. There was a small garden, and a climbing rose covered the front of the house with a mass of white blossoms in the early summer. It was there that the editor had what was described as a "tan-coloured mustang," riding down to the "Evening Post" office in the morning and back in the afternoon, and at night putting him up at a near-by stable. The horse was one of the small, wiry, native animals, its shaggy hair at most times looking frowsy and "a lick and a promise" generally doing for grooming. The saddle was of the Mexican pattern commonly used in California at the time, covered with embossed leather, and having big horn pommel and ponderous, leather-enveloped stirrups. Horse and rider had a careless, though not ungraceful appearance, Mr. George with his trim figure, square shoulders, and easy posture moving with a swing as the animal quickened into its natural lope. Sometimes he took up behind him one or the other of his two

250

boys, now getting to be ten and twelve; sometimes he rode in company with friends; but for the most part he took solitary "thinking" rides, the free motion of the body in the open air seeming to exhilarate the action of the mind.

It was on a Sunday afternoon in the spring of 1874 while on one of these solitary rides on the ocean road that his horse shied, threw him from the saddle and dragged him by one stirrup. Fortunately the animal at once slowed down from a gallop or his master must have been dragged to death. But Mr. George disengaged his foot, when the horse ran away and was not recovered until several days afterwards. This was the second accident of the kind. Besides having his right hand badly lacerated, Mr. George's wrist was broken. Holding his injured arm against his body, he made the long walk of five or six miles at nightfall back over the lonely roads to the city. Even when he found a doctor his chief thought was of his wife, and before anything was done he sent a message to her not to hold supper as he had been detained. When he got home he said to her, "That mustang has hurt my wrist, and now you must be doubly my right hand to me."

His great energy and restlessness made him the most impatient of patients. Because he could not go to the office, he insisted on having a stenographer to whom to dictate editorials. But by April he had recovered the full use of his injured member and in May the family moved to a house on Rincon Hill, more convenient to the office.

Domestic life was very dear to the energetic public man. Perhaps the necessities of his exacting vocation made him delight the more to be with his family. While the wife sat beside with her work-basket, he would lie on a lounge in the library and read poetry to the two boys and the girl, or have them in turn read or recite before him or such

strangers as he chanced to bring home. Or perhaps, he
went swimming with the boys in a bath-house off Long
Bridge, or took the family for a row or for a sail in a
"plunger." It frequently happened in these trips that
they found lying at anchor the little *Shubrick* in which
the father had come to California and he would tell of
his early seaman's adventures. Frequently there were
Sunday cruises about the bay on sloop or schooner, the
party made up of friends with their families.

Henry George was not a member of any church, nor
did his family attend any regularly, though in his broadness of mind he left his wife entire freedom in this for herself and the children. He attached himself to no sect, yet
his nature was strongly reverent. He wished to have his
children say night and morning prayers, and often at twilight or before they went to bed he would lie on his lounge
in his library and have them and their mother mingle
their voices in the old hymns that he had heard as a child
in Philadelphia, and again "Praise God from whom all
blessings flow" seemed to swell and echo through old St.
Paul's. Out of the inquiry, why want goes with plenty,
religion had come to have a new meaning. In the conviction that he had discovered that it was not by God's
will, but because of violation of God's ordinance that men
suffered involuntary poverty in the heart of civilisation,
"a faith that was dead revived." He had turned from a
religion that taught either of a Special Providence on the
one hand or of a merciless fate on the other. Now all
the fervour of his spirit went forth in the belief that
social progress is governed by unchanging and benefi-
cent law.

His children's training began at this time to engage
his earnest attention. They had never attended any but
public schools, and travelling and moving had broken even

this schooling. His own method broke it more. He discouraged lesson-studying at home, saying that the regular school hours were long enough, and that the hours at home should be spent in recreation and other ways. But if his children, as a consequence, stood low at recitations, they stood high in general information and the independent use of their faculties, for he would talk or read to them on whatever topic arose which could be brought within their understanding; and at dinner table, when the family was alone, he would ask them in turn questions touching history, literature, public matters or elementary science—such things as may have come up in previous conversations. When they could not answer, he himself would do so. Reading was encouraged, and the boys, at least, were directed to such books as the father delighted in when of their age. A copy of "Robinson Crusoe" was the first book he gave to his eldest boy—a tale that all his life fascinated Henry George and is frequently referred to in his writings. Another book-present to his children was the "Arabian Nights," which he sent while they were in Philadelphia, and which, he wrote to his wife, he had, "like a goose, spent the night re-reading." Thus the children might constantly fail in the school lessons they were expected to study at home, but if asked, could recite from Tennyson, Browning or Macaulay, had heard of the buried cities of Egypt and Yucatan, and in their own way, could talk about the rotation of crops, the forms of water or the nebular hypothesis. From either parent a request was a command, with corporal punishment swiftly following delay or delinquency; yet affection blended with obedience.

Visitors added materially to the children's education; for at the table, where the children were brought when old enough and taught to be silent, the guests were drawn towards topics most congenial to themselves, good feeling was let loose, and anecdotes, strange adventures, curious bits of information, flashes of wit and tales of humour poured forth. The host had the habit of politely withdrawing to the place of questioner. This was most agreeable to his personal modesty. It also gratified a never-ceasing desire for information—information, apparently, of any kind and every kind, which, like his miscellaneous reading, was to be drawn on when needed, many a dinner talk later serving him with happy illustrations in his writings. Men from various parts of the world came, and as it were, poured out their contributions to the varied and instructive symposium.

Mr. and Mrs. George had now grown closer than ever before. In the early days of their marriage, when they were struggling along in poverty, she had refrained from inquiring into the matters outside of domestic affairs that interested her husband. Believing her mission to be to look after his health, his rest and recreation, she avoided all matters of business and tried to draw his mind into other channels. But as he advanced as a writer and their manner of living improved, she entered the council of his general affairs and came to be his close adviser.

The Georges had a small number of intimate friends. They never desired to move in the fashionable circles. Formal social occasions always had their snares and pitfalls for the husband. On one occasion when he was led to attend a reception at the Ralston residence alone, his wife being ill, he returned disgusted. "Such people live in a frivolous atmosphere," he said. "There was Mrs. —— for instance. She had nothing to talk about but the weather." "The weather!" exclaimed Mrs. George, somewhat doubtfully. "Why, yes," answered the husband; "she asked me what kind of a season we were likely to have, and I told her the indications were for a wet season!" Mrs. George broke into merriment. "Your social butterfly," said she, "wanted to know about the outlook for social events—receptions, concerts, balls, weddings, and the like!"

But if Mr. George disliked formal social gatherings, he deferred to his wife in other particulars. He took her to the theatre, even when he himself cared little or nothing for the performance; and to concerts, though he had no taste for any but the simplest music. On ladies' night, when his newspaper friend, Daniel O'Connell, or his actor friend, Henry Edwards, presided over the fun, he took her to "high jinks" at the Bohemian Club, of which he was one of the earliest members.

The dream of wealth, indeed, the desire for it, had long since departed. The dream of increasing the world's happiness and of raising the mass of men out of the slough of poverty had taken its place. But the wish to get beyond the anxieties of a hand-to-mouth way of living drew Mr. George into mining investments now and again, when the atmosphere became surcharged with the mining fever. When in 1872 silver bonanza discoveries occurred on the Comstock lode in the Washoe Mountains, Nevada—principally in the Crown Point and Belcher mines—he was drawn into investments during the general excitement, and came out with losses. His wife's letter to him from Philadelphia (May 17, 1872) touching the matter ran:

"I won't blame you. You feel it as much as I do. It was a risk at any rate, and I'm not surprised. You know I'm far off and can look at these matters coolly, while you have all the excitement. Don't gamble in anything else than newspapers. That is the only way you make anything."

But in 1875 he went in again. There was at the time the wildest and most general excitement that San Francisco had ever seen. It grew out of the discovery in the up to that time practically unproductive Consolidated Virginia mine on the Comstock lode of a bonanza that it was said would yield fifteen hundred millions. The mine was managed, under the firm name of Flood & O'Brien, by four men—James C. Flood and William S. O'Brien, who had kept a drinking saloon on Washington Street, San Francisco, and themselves served customers; and John W. Mackay and James G. Fair, who were practical miners on the Comstock, and who, with some real or fancied knowledge of conditions, drew the other two men with them into the purchase of the Consolidated Virginia mine. They paid for it less than $100,000. During the first half of 1875 the monthly output was more than a million and a half of silver, and the shares that had been purchased for less than one tenth of a million rose towards one hundred and fifty millions. Contagion of speculation "bulled" the whole market of mining stocks, during which, the managers unloaded their shares, reaction set in and the whole list fell with a rush. Mr. George's investments were in Ophir and Consolidated Virginia. He reaped a loss, which cramped his circumstances.

And as his wife was his counsellor in his mining losses, so was she when the break came on the "Evening Post" and he went out penniless. He quickly recovered his self-poise in the latter disaster, so that he could write from Sacramento shortly afterwards (March 14, 1876):

"Mills[1] tells me that they are willing to sell the 'Post,' lock, stock and barrel, for $35,000 over its receipts. Jones, he says, is heartily disgusted, and the chances are that he will soon drop the thing. For my part I would not touch it, unless it was given to me outright."

---

[1] William H. Mills, of the Sacramento "Record-Union."

Mr. George received strength from his wife when he needed it, and in return supported her when occasion called, for instance writing to her (February 24) touching the condition of her uncle, Matthew McCloskey, who was on his death bed:

"I am sorry to hear about Matt. I do not think much of the new doctor that will talk that way—that is if he talks so to his patient, as the most potent thing in medicine is hope. But however it may be, you must not suffer it to make you blue. We must all die, and what, after all, signifies a few years more or less. It is not Christian or reasonable to grieve about what God has appointed, nor is it wise to borrow trouble. I wish when you feel so you would go out somewhere."

They read much from general literature together and discussed what they read; and besides this, Mr. George now read some law, which he thought would be useful to him in understanding and discussing public affairs, even though he should never follow law as a profession. A letter dated Marysville, May 26, 1876, while he was on a meter inspecting trip with his brother Vallance touches on this:

"I have a good square day to loaf in, as Val is at work, and one can get ahead as well as two. Going to bed at nine o'clock, and right off to sleep, six in the morning at this season of the year seems late. After breakfast I went up-stairs and took a tussle with Kent. I was making fine progress till all of a sudden he threw me, and stretching out on the bed, I snoozed for an hour—very pleasant those sleeps are. . . . It is a nice day here—warm, but yet not oppressive. There is nothing particular though to see or to do and I shall put in my time this morning reading and writing. I feel encouraged by my progress in law, and really interested, though it does put me to sleep, and I think I can in a year make as much progress as ordinary students do in three or four."

There were times when his over-wrought, highly strung nerves brought a flash of irritability; but this was all—a flash—so that there was never anything like a lasting disagreement. The current of devotion ran even stronger and freer now than when, entering manhood, he went courting the girl who had just come from the convent school. And what affection and the marriage tie were to him only his own words can adequately tell—letters written by him from Sacramento to his wife in San Francisco during a few days' separation in the fifteenth year of wedlock.

Sacramento, March 18, 1876.

"I have been sitting in the Senate listening to a debate on the divorce bill—Pierson's bill to limit cause for divorces to adultery. I think the bill is in the right direction. We have found out, as Pierson said, that it was dangerous to talk of divorces in mixed company. He also said that there was one divorce granted in San Francisco for every three marriages, and that divorces were often got in a single day.

"If I ever had any leaning to the modern doctrine in this matter I have entirely got over it. Marriage is not only the foundation of society; it is the divinely appointed state which confers the highest and purest happiness, and I have no doubt that if people knew that they could not separate from each other, the result would be to make them try harder to live comfortably with each other."

Sunday evening, March 27, 1876.

"I have wanted to write to you all day; but I have been moving around, and though I have thought volumes, I did not have a chance to write them.

"I got at noon to-day your letter of last night. Many thanks. I hardly expected it, but thought it would be so nice if I should get a letter, and when I went down to the 'Record-Union' after the train got in, there it was.

"You are a dutiful little woman, my darling. By my own feelings, I know how hard it was for you to have me stay away; but it pleased me to think you approved of it, and it made the separation lighter. I have felt happy all the afternoon. In all the pauses of the talk the face of the woman I love rose up before me. A man is a bundle of inconsistencies. It delights me to think that you are wholly and absolutely *mine*. There is a pride and pleasure in feeling that I am really your 'lord and master'; and yet your approbation, it seems to me, outweighs that of all the world. What a blessed thing it is to be truly married, as we are married—in body and mind and soul. I often thank God for it, and when I hear, as I often do, how married men sin against their vows, I think what poor fools they are, not to realise how much more real pleasure there is in the love of one virtuous woman. If my darling is mine, I also am hers. If I have the right to her, she also has the right to me. All that I can achieve she must share; my full possession of her involves just as complete a possession on her part of me. The old ideas are right and are founded on the depths of human nature. The 'love, cherish and protect' on one side, and the 'love, honour and obey' on the other, are more than any other contract; and when the binding force of the obligation is felt, the touch of the chain, instead of galling, is a pleasure.

"How much fresh delight there is in our love. From the time I first saw you and was captivated by that something in face and voice and manner, which I never could explain in words, it has gone on increasing and increasing. Husband and father, I am still more lover than when I used to stop in my work to take out your picture and steal a glance at it. Satisfaction only crowns desire, and the love of the mature man is not only deeper, but more passionate than that of the boy. And this love is the great thing with me. All outside ups and downs are trivial compared with that."

March 30, 1876.

"Mills was saying the other night that if a man and woman kept up their love, they never grew old to each other, and I told him he was right. You are to me prettier, more loving and more tempting than when you were a little delicate slip of a girl. Do you know that it is a keen delight to me to think how you have improved. I always have felt towards you a good deal as Abelard must have felt towards Héloïse—as though you were my pupil as well as wife."

March 31, 1876.

"Did you ever notice one thing about the higher pleasures—they don't pall, as the grosser ones do. On the contrary, they become more exquisite. The very regularity of the letter gives it new delight. There is such a proud satisfaction in feeling you are not mistaken. I like even that boy[1] to know that 'my girl' thinks so much of me. And then they weave such links between us, and keep us together in spirit, even though we are separated in space. I once read a little story—I don't know where it was—of how a husband was beginning to wander in thought a little from his wife when he was away, and how her letters held him and brought him back to her, more her lover than before. And is there not something in this which goes even beyond the present life? Others may, but it is not for you and me, my darling, to doubt the goodness of God. The more I think of it, the more I feel that our present life will not bound our love."

Upon such a foundation of affection was reared a noble superstructure. One day as his wife sat close beside him in a low chair, the husband while lying on his sofa said: "What do you most admire in a man?"

"Courage," the wife answered.

---

[1] Reference to a hotel boy, who, bringing his letters, would say, " Another letter from your girl, Mr. George "

"Courage," he repeated, jumping up and walking the floor. "I thought you would say virtue."

"No, not virtue, because I have come to perceive that the world sets up separate standards for men and women, and that what would be a breach of virtue in the woman might not be considered as such in the man. I do not say that that is right, but I do recognise that the world so holds it."

"But why courage?" asked the husband.

"Because it is the manly quality."

"But courage might seem to go with physique—and I am a small man. How do you find this courage in me?"

"I do not mean physical courage," replied the wife, "but moral courage; the courage that impels a man who sees his duty to follow it, though it mean to make sacrifices—to stand up against the world."

The husband said that this strengthened as well as gratified him, and that some day he might have to ask her to support him when duty called him to stand up against the world.

CHAPTER VI.

FIRST SET POLITICAL SPEECH.

WILLIAM S. IRWIN, Democrat, the new Governor of California, was sworn in at the State Capitol at Sacramento on January 1, 1876, and one of his first acts was to appoint Henry George to what was regarded as among the most lucrative offices within the Executive gift —State Inspector of Gas Meters. He did this partly from a motive of assisting a man who had through the "Evening Post" and the "Morning Ledger" done much to help his election. But E. W. Maslin, who was the Governor's private secretary, says that another motive played an important part in the matter.

"Henry George was recognised as nominally a Democrat, but not a partisan. He had no political backing and was regarded to be without political claims upon the Governor. It was therefore a political surprise when he was appointed Gas-Meter Inspector. The appointment was more than anything else a tribute to intellect.

"I was the Governor's private secretary, and in the leisure hours of the office we were accustomed to discuss books, public men and measures. The Governor was chary of giving praise, yet not once but many times he expressed his strong admiration for Mr. George's intel-

lectual ability, and laid peculiar stress upon his logical
mind, power of statement and clear and brilliant style.
In one of those conversations he declared that George
possessed the clearest and finest style of all English
writers.   I was not surprised that the Governor should
speak of the logic and power of statement, for this arose
from the character of his own mind.   He had little
imagination, but he was logical, well read and highly
trained.   I was not surprised that he should speak of
similar qualities in George; but I was astonished that
the latter's style should have attracted his attention.
I myself had in 1871, when Secretary of the State
Board of Equalisation, supplied George with some statistical matter which he used at the time in his pamphlet, 'Our Land and Land Policy,' and I had read a
number of things, long and short, from his pen afterwards; but though I recognised his ability, I did not
appreciate his mode of expression, as did the Governor.
The fact that this cold, unimpassioned man should so
often break into praise of George's 'elegant and brilliant
style' made a profound impression on me."

Henry George took official charge on January 13 and
within a few days began to "test" the registry of meters
by forcing a measured quantity of air through them in
place of gas, fastening a brass seal on all that met the
lawful requirements.   A set fee was allowed on every
meter so tested and sealed.

The office of inspector of gas meters had been established for the protection of gas consumers and did much
to correct impositions.   But a loop-hole had been left,
perhaps inadvertently, by which the law did not reach
some of the towns scattered over the State, where large
numbers of meters, purchased from or through the San
Francisco Gas Company or its officials, had without being
inspected and sealed been put into use.   George, or rather
his friends who were most zealous for his interests, had

an amendment introduced into the legislature which should compel companies to submit for inspection all unsealed meters in use or intended for immediate use. The gas companies, and particularly the San Francisco company through its president, raised hot opposition. After cutting off some features to which the companies particularly objected, the measure went through and the inspector during the next few months went to the chief cities throughout the State and demanded that all unsealed meters be brought to him to be tested, his brother, John V. George, going with him to assist in the work. Though at first by virtue of this amendment of the inspection law, Mr. George obtained what seemed to him like large sums of money from places like Marysville and Grass Valley where numbers of untested meters were in use, the office of inspector yielded only an intermittent revenue and on the whole only enough to live on comfortably and without extravagance. Mr. George for a while entertained the expectation of going East in the summer to visit the old folks and to see the international exposition then to be opened with great ceremony at Philadelphia in commemoration of the hundredth celebration of the nation's independence. This had to be given up, as for the time the receipts from the office fell off.

"Though my official duties were light," said Mr. George when reviewing this period,[1] "I never ate the bread of idleness, but was always very hard at work." Among the matters engaging him were a number of measures before the State legislature and chief of these were two bills introduced by William M. Pierson in the Senate, both relating to the publication of newspapers, one to compel the retraction of false or defamatory articles and the other

---

[1] Meeker notes.

requiring the signature of all original articles or correspondence. Mr. George was particularly interested in the latter and wrote in support of it two bright, vivacious, signed articles for the "Sacramento Bee," which were afterwards printed in pamphlet form. His contention was that the march of concentration was putting newspapers more and more into the hands of massed capital, making newspaper workers more and more dependent upon special interests and utterly helpless to get outside recognition so long as they should work anonymously.

> "The effect of the present anonymous system is to make the newspaper everything, the writer nothing. The tendency of the personal system would be to transfer importance and power from the newspaper to the writers—to diffuse instead of to concentrate; to make the men who see for the people and think for the people independent of capital, instead of dependent on capital; and to facilitate the establishment of new papers whenever the old ones abandoned the popular cause."

He got some personal satisfaction from this article, for he wrote to his wife (March 14) : "I spent a good part of the afternoon listening to the debate in the Senate upon the signature bill. Uncle Phil [Philip A. Roach. one of the editors and part proprietor of the "San Francisco Examiner"] threw himself in opposition, though he made a very handsome allusion to me, as all the principal speakers have done." Both the signature and the retraction bill, while they passed the Senate, had the powerful opposition of the San Francisco papers and were killed in the House.

As helping to make his ideas known, the articles in support of the signature bill were probably worth the effort he made, but a few months later there was an occurrence of much greater importance to Mr. George personally—the first set speech. At various times, beginning as far back as 1865 when a member of the Sacramento Lyceum, he had got upon his feet for a few impromptu remarks. Now came a chance for a formal effort. The Presidential campaign was opening, with Governor Rutherford B. Hayes of Ohio, candidate of the Republican party, and Governor Samuel J. Tilden of New York, for the Democratic. Mr. George entered on the campaign with lively feelings, for Hayes, he considered, represented the reactionary policy of his party, while Tilden, he believed, was a free trader, and while demanding the remission of war-tax burdens, would take the side of the industrial masses, just now idle in thousands all over the country.

Animated by something akin to the admiration Governor Irwin had for George's abilities, a number of energetic young men of radical opinion in San Francisco; enrolled in what was known as the "Tilden and Hendricks Central Club," asked Mr. George to speak under its auspices, hoping, as one of them, Walter Gallagher, said, "to make this speech the keynote of the canvass in California." George was thereupon formally invited. He spoke before a big meeting in Dashaway Hall on the evening of August 15, on "The Question Before the People." He stood beside the reading desk on which he had his manuscript spread out, read by glances and spoke slowly and distinctly. He avoided the usual political declamation and struck a high tone at once.

> "Remember this, the political contest is lifted above the low plane of denunciation and demagogism, and becomes not a contest for spoils in which the people are simply permitted to choose which gang shall plunder them; but a solemn, momentous inquiry, demanding from each voter a conscientious judgment."

The kernel of the speech was this:

"The Federal tax-gatherer is everywhere. In each exchange by which labour is converted into commodities, there he is standing between buyer and seller to take his to'l. Whether it be a match or a locomotive, a dish-cloth or a dress, a new book or a glass of beer, the tax-gatherer steps in. He says to Labour as the day's toil begins: 'Ah! you want to do a little work for yourself and family. Well, first work an hour to pay the interest on the national debt and defray the necessary expenses of government; and then another hour for the national banks and subsidised corporations, and the expenses of governing the Southern States! Then an hour for the army and navy and the contractors thereof; then an hour for the manufacturers of New England, and an hour for the iron millionaires of Pennsylvania; half an hour for the Marine Corps and the various comfortable little bureaus; and then, after you have done a little work for your State Government, and a little work for your county and municipal government, and a little work for your landlord—then you can have the rest of the day to work for yourself and family.' . . .

"Fellow-citizens, negro slavery is dead! But cast your eyes over the North to-day and see a worse than negro slavery taking root under the pressure of the policy you are asked as Republicans to support by your votes. See seventy thousand men out of work in the Pennsylvania coal-fields; fifty thousand labourers asking for bread in the city of New York; the almshouses of Massachusetts crowded to repletion in the summertime; unemployed men roving over the West in great bands, stealing what they cannot earn. . . . It is an ominous thing that in this Centennial year, States that a century ago were covered by the primeval forest should be holding conventions to consider the 'tramp nuisance'—the sure symptom of that leprosy of nations, chronic pauperism. . . .

"Be not deceived! You might as well charge the bullet or the knife with being the cause of the death of a murdered man as to think that all the things of which you complain result from the accident of having had bad men in office. What can any change of men avail so long as the policy which is the primary cause of these evils is unchanged?"

Ex-District Attorney Thomas P. Ryan was president of the club. He presided at this meeting and says of the speaker and the speech:

"At that time he looked to me to be about thirty years of age. He impressed me then, as he always did, as being a man of naturally nervous temperament, but one who had so schooled himself as to give no expression as a rule to that fact by his manner. In repose his habit was calm, almost placid, and age sits lightly upon those so blessed. In action there was no want of fire, and when the situation required, it was fittingly displayed. If we rate his speech that night by the standard of eloquence of the great French orator, Bishop Dupanloup—a thorough knowledge of one's subject— he was indeed eloquent. That the address was extraordinarily able and convincing was the universal opinion of those who heard it. The impression it left on me is lasting and the best evidence of its force and effect is to be found in the fact that at this late day I am, almost without effort, able to recall in the main most of the facts then presented and the circumstances surrounding the speech's delivery.

"At its conclusion, Mr. James G. Maguire, since so devoted a disciple of Henry George, and distinguished as an upright judge and Member of Congress, arose and said that it was the ablest political address to which he had ever listened, and moved that it be printed for distribution as a campaign document, which was done.

"The audience was a large and most appreciative one, Governor Irwin, among other distinguished men, being present.

"Touching this speech, and indeed, of everything else Henry George said and wrote subsequently, I have carried in my mind the thought so happily expressed by Mommsen in speaking of Renan: 'He is a savant in spite of his fine style.'"

This Dashaway Hall speech was carefully prepared. Mr. Gallagher tells of an unprepared one that Henry George made very soon afterwards.

"Some days after the Dashaway Hall meeting Mr. George was present at a very large and enthusiastic meeting at the Mission in Humboldt Hall. I was expected to speak at that meeting and did not expect to see Henry George there. Cameron H. King, I think, presided. Mr. George, who was familiar to a large number in the audience, was vociferously called for. He was very backward about responding and hesitated quite a while before he was finally persuaded to go upon the rostrum. I think I can picture him now in my mind's eye as he appeared on that night. He was sitting close up to the front where he could easily see and hear all that was going on. He held a little old soft felt hat crumpled up tightly in his hand. When he finally made up his mind to respond to the cheers and calls he went with a rush. It seemed to me that he ran to the rostrum and immediately in a loud, full voice, at a very high pitch, entered into a discussion of the issues before the people—all the time holding his hat in his hand. The audience expected a different kind of speech from him than from the rest of us. The audience was not disappointed, for what he said was full of thought and force. But I remember that his elocution was not of the best. He was earnest and sincere, but his manner and gesticulation were not to be commended as accompaniments of oratory. He did not have the proper control of his voice, and there appeared to be in his manner an absolute disregard for those little arts of the orator which have so much effect upon a crowd."

But it was the speech on "The Question Before the People" that attracted chief attention and the Democratic

State Committee invited him to "stump" the State and deliver it in the principal cities and towns. From no speaking reputation whatever, he sprang through this one address to the place of a leading speaker in California, and was given the honour of making the final speech of the campaign in Platt's Hall, San Francisco. Dr. Shorb was chairman and knew George well, but amused himself by introducing him as "Colonel Henry D. George." Mr. George, somewhat disconcerted, protested that he had neither a title nor a middle initial, whereupon somebody in the audience shouted: "Oh, go ahead, Harry. We all know who you are."

So the campaign passed; election day came and went, and the decision was not yet clear when Mr. George wrote to his mother (November 13) touching his personal interests:

> "Well, the campaign is over, though its result is as yet unsettled. I cannot say that I am glad that it is over, for although I think Tilden is President, the way this coast went is a great disappointment to me; but at any rate I shall now have a resting spell—a longer one and a better one than I have had before.
>
> "I did my best, for my heart was in it, and that is a consolation. And personally what I accomplished was very gratifying. I have shown that I could make myself felt without a newspaper, and shown that I possessed other ability than that of the pen. I have always felt that I possessed the requisites for a first-class speaker, and that I would make one if I could get the practice; and I started into this campaign with the deliberate purpose of breaking myself in. It was like jumping overboard to learn to swim. But I succeeded. I think no man in the State made as much reputation as I have made. From not being known as a speaker I have come to the front. I wanted to do this, not as a matter of vanity or for the mere pleasure of the thing; but to increase my power and usefulness. Already well

known as a writer, I knew that this kind of a reputation would aid me immensely in the future. And so it will—whether I go into politics, into the law or into the newspaper business again. I do not intend to rest here; but to go ahead step by step.

"You need not be afraid of politics doing me harm. I do not propose to mix in lower politics, nor do I propose to chase after nominations. I shall wait till they seek me. I propose to read and study, to write some things which will extend my reputation and perhaps to deliver some lectures with the same view. And if I live I shall make myself known even in Philadelphia. I aim high.

"So far as my personal interests are concerned, defeat is as good to me as a sweeping victory—in fact, I think better, as a man of my kind has a chance of coming forward more rapidly in a minority than in a majority party. However, about all such things, I am disposed to think that whatever happens is for the best. Talent and energy can nearly always convert defeats into victories. I could easily have started a paper during the campaign, and could, I think, readily do so now. But I don't feel like going back into newspaper harness. The best thing for me, I think, is to keep out of newspapers for a while."

Thus he wrote of himself. What he meant by wanting to be a speaker "not as a matter of vanity or for the mere pleasure of the thing," but to increase his "power and usefulness," he could not bring himself to tell any one as yet. He must wait for time to show even his mother the exalted purpose he had in his heart of hearts.

When he wrote to his mother, Mr. George believed that Tilden had been elected President. It was conceded that the Democratic candidate had received the largest popular vote, and that from the States where the returns were undisputed he had received one hundred and eighty four electoral votes, so that he lacked just one vote of the number required to elect, while Hayes lacked twenty. The difficulty lay with the returns of Oregon and three Southern States—Louisiana, South Carolina and Florida—which were contested. This condition of things, involving such great consequences, could not fail to stir to the depths an active participant in public affairs like Henry George. As weeks passed without a settlement and the time fixed by the constitution for the inauguration of the new President approached, he became so aroused that in January he wrote a long presentation of the matter and put it in the form of an eight paged pamphlet entitled, "Who shall be President?—A Survey of the Political Situation," saying that the fact that who should be President should be treated as an open question was "both scandalous and dangerous"—scandalous because the uncertainty imimplied "a doubt of the efficacy of law"; and dangerous "because when law fails, force is the necessary resort." He made a careful analysis of the matter to show why he believed Tilden was entitled to the office, giving his explanation of the persistent contention by the Hayes partisans that "a coup d'état was contemplated."

It was Mr. George's intention to send this paper East, where he thought it would get consideration; but before he could carry out his plan news came that Tilden had given his consent to remand the question of returns to the decision of an electoral commission—a tribunal specially created by Congress. This commission, composed of eight Republicans and seven Democrats, by a party vote decided in favour of the Republican electors in every case, thus awarding 185 electoral votes to Hayes and 184 to Tilden, and placing Hayes in the Presidential chair.

Nine years after this, in the pages of his "Protection or

Free Trade," Henry George gave expression to a great
change of feeling towards Mr. Tilden.[1]

"A wealthy citizen whom I once supported, and called
on others to support, for the Presidential chair, under
the impression that he was a Democrat of the school of
Jefferson, has recently published a letter advising us to
steel plate our coasts, lest foreign navies come over and
bombard us. This counsel of timidity has for its hardly
disguised object the inducing of such an enormous expenditure of public money as will prevent any demand
for the reduction of taxation, and thus secure to the
tariff rings a longer lease of plunder. It well illus-
trates the essential meanness of the protectionist spirit
—a spirit that no more comprehends the true dignity
of the American Republic and the grandeur of her pos-
sibilities than it cares for the material interests of the
great masses of her citizens—'the poor people who have
to work.' "

---

[1] Chap. XXX, (Memorial Edition, p. 327).

CHAPTER VII.

LECTURE AT THE UNIVERSITY OF CALIFORNIA.

1877.   AGE, 38.

AS by distinct stages, Henry George's mind showed development. In the first half of 1877 came the last two stages before it was to break into full flower. The first of these took the form of a lecture on political economy before the University of California; the second, of an oration on the Fourth of July.

Scarcely had the Presidential question ceased to absorb him when he was invited to deliver several lectures before the students and faculty of the University of California which now had been established permanently at Berkeley, adjacent to Oakland. He was to be one of a number of prominent men to give a course of addresses on various topics, and the first subject that it was agreed he should treat was "The Study of Political Economy."

There was no separate chair of political economy in the University and now came talk of establishing one, with George to fill it. His Chinese article; his pamphlet, "Our Land and Land Policy"; and many of his "Evening Post" editorials marked him as qualified to hold such a position. It was thought that the lectures he was about to deliver would make the ground of his appointment

Touching this he never afterwards had much to say, in the family observing that there had been talk of a chair and of him to fill it. He never mentioned who of his friends were interested in the project. At the time, possibly from his old habit of secretiveness, but more probably from a feeling of modesty until the project should take definite form, he said nothing about the matter to his wife, except indirectly remarking that there was no title in the world he cared to have save that of "Professor."

At any rate, on March 9, accompanied by his friend, Assemblyman James V. Coffey, he lunched with Professor John Le Conte, the President of the University, after which the three men proceeded to the hall where the students and most of the faculty were gathered. The lecturer read from his manuscript and occupied about three quarters of an hour—probably three quarters of an hour of astonishment for regents and faculty.

He said that as his lecture was to be more suggestive than didactic, he would not attempt to outline the laws of political economy, nor even, where his own views were strong and definite, to touch upon unsettled questions. He wished to show the simplicity and certainty of a science too generally regarded as complex and indeterminate; to point out the ease with which it may be studied, and to suggest reasons which make that study worthy of attention.

"The science which investigates the laws of the production and distribution of wealth concerns itself with matters which among us occupy more than nine tenths of human effort, and perhaps nine tenths of human thought. In its province are included all that relates to the wages of labour and the earnings of capital; all regulations of trade; all questions of currency and finance; all taxes and public disbursements—in short, everything that can in any way affect the amount of wealth which a community can secure, or the proportion in which that wealth will be distributed between individuals. Though not the science of government, it is essential to the science of government. Though it takes direct cognisance only of what are termed the selfish instincts, yet in doing so it includes the basis of all higher qualities."

A hundred years had elapsed, the lecturer said, since Adam Smith published his "Wealth of Nations," yet political economy had made little progress. This he thought "referable partly to the nature of the science itself and partly to the manner in which it has been cultivated."

"In the first place, the very importance of the subjects with which political economy deals raises obstacles in its way. The discoveries of other sciences may challenge pernicious ideas, but the conclusions of political economy involve pecuniary interests, and thus thrill directly the sensitive pocket-nerve. For, as no social adjustment can exist without interesting a larger or smaller class in its maintenance, political economy at every point is apt to come in contact with some interest or other which regards it as the silversmiths of Ephesus did those who taught the uselessness of presenting shrines to Diana. . . . What, then, must be the opposition which inevitably meets a science that deals with tariffs and subsidies, with banking interests and bonded debts, with trades-unions and combinations of capital, with taxes and licenses and land tenures! It is not ignorance alone that offers opposition, but ignorance backed by interest, and made fierce by passions.

"Now, while the interests thus aroused furnish the incentive, the complexity of the phenomena with which political economy deals makes it comparatively easy to palm off on the unreasoning all sorts of absurdities as political economy. . . . But what is far worse than any amount of pretentious quackery is, that the science even as taught by the masters *is* in large measure disjointed and indeterminate. As laid down in the best text-books, political economy is like a shapely statue but half hewn from the rock—like a landscape, part of which stands out clear and distinct, but over the rest of which the mists still roll. . . . Strength and subtilty have been wasted in intellectual hair splitting and super-refinements, in verbal discussions and disputes, while the great high-roads have remained unexplored. And thus has been given to a simple and attractive science an air of repellent abstruseness and uncertainty."

And from the same fundamental cause had arisen an idea of political economy which had arrayed against it the feelings and prejudices of those who had most to gain by its cultivation.

"The name of political economy has been constantly invoked against every effort of the working classes to increase their wages or decrease their hours of labour. . . . Take the best and most extensively circulated text-books. While they insist upon freedom for capital, while they justify on the ground of utility the selfish greed that seeks to pile fortune on fortune, and the niggard spirit that steels the heart to the wail of distress, what sign of substantial promise do they hold out to the working man save that he should refrain from rearing children?

"What can we expect when hands that should offer bread thus hold out a stone? Is it in human nature that the masses of men, vaguely but keenly conscious of the injustice of existing social conditions, feeling that they are somehow cramped and hurt, without knowing what cramps and hurts them, should welcome truth in this partial form; that they should take to a science which, as it is presented to them, seems but to justify injustice, to canonise selfishness by throwing around it the halo of utility, and to present Herod rather than Vincent de Paul as the typical benefactor of humanity? Is it to be wondered at that they should turn in their ignorance to the absurdities of protection and the crazy theories generally designated by the name of socialism?"

What he wished to impress upon his hearers was the "real simplicity of what is generally deemed an abstruse science, and the exceeding ease with which it may be pursued."

"For the study of political economy you need no special knowledge, no extensive library, no costly laboratory. You do not even need text-books nor teachers, if you will but think for yourselves. All that you need is care in reducing complex phenomena to their elements, in distinguishing the essential from the accidental, and in applying the simple laws of human action with which you are familiar. Take nobody's opinion for granted; 'try all things: hold fast that which is good.' In this way, the opinions of others will help you by their suggestions, elucidations and corrections; otherwise they will be to you but as words to a parrot. . . . All this array of professors, all this paraphernalia of learning, cannot educate a man. They can but help him to educate himself. Here you may obtain the tools; but they will be useful only to him who can use them. A monkey with a microscope, a mule packing a library, are fit emblems of the men—and unfortunately, they are plenty—who pass through the whole educational machinery, and come out but learned fools, crammed with knowledge which they cannot use—all the more pitiable, all the more contemptible, all the more in the way of real progress, because they pass, with themselves and others, as educated men."

And then addressing himself directly to the students, he said:

"I trust you have felt the promptings of that highest of ambitions—the desire to be useful in your day and generation; the hope that in something, even though little, those that come after may be wiser, better, happier that you have lived. Or, if you have never felt this, I trust the feeling is only latent, ready to spring forth when you see the need.

"Gentlemen, if you but look you will see the need! You are of the favoured few, for the fact that you are here, students in a university of this character, bespeaks for you the happy accidents that fall only to the lot of the few, and you cannot yet realise, as you may by and by realise, how the hard struggle which is the lot of so many may cramp and bind and distort—how it may dull the noblest faculties and chill the warmest impulses, and grind out of men the joy and poetry of life; how it may turn into the lepers of society those who should be its adornment, and transmute, into vermin to prey upon it and into wild beasts to fly at its throat, the brain and muscle that should go to its enrichment! These things may never yet have forced themselves on your attention; but still, if you will think of it, you cannot fail to see enough want and wretchedness, even in our own country to-day, to move you to sadness and pity, to nerve you to high resolve; to arouse in you the sympathy that dares, and the indignation that burns to overthrow a wrong. . . .

"Political economy alone can give the answer. And if you trace out, in the way I have tried to outline, the laws of the production and exchange of wealth, you will see the causes of social weakness and disease in enactments which selfishness has imposed on ignorance, and in maladjustments entirely within our own control. . . .

"You will see that the true law of social life is the law of love, the law of liberty, the law of each for all and all for each; that the golden rule of morals is also the golden rule of the science of wealth; that the highest expressions of religious truth include the widest generalisations of political economy."

So much for the nature of the address. The lecturer read his audience correctly, for when he went home he told his wife that his utterances had been well received by the students, but by the authorities with a polite and dignified quietness that made him think that he might not be invited to lecture again.

What wonder! Was this a sample of what the man was to preach? Perhaps much of what he said was as plain and fair as common sense; but did he propose to go wide of the beaten path—to set up a new scheme of things? Were the faculty and regents to be committed to new principles—principles that they had not yet even considered; that wrenched at old things, that jarred to their centre institutions which, right or wrong, had come down through the generations? Was this Inspector of Gas Meters, this warring newspaper editor, this political speech-maker, who had never given an hour's study inside a university to continue to proclaim among them that "all this array of professors, all this paraphernalia of learning, cannot educate a man," and prate of "a monkey with a microscope" and "a mule packing a library" as emblems of men "passing through the educational machinery"? And then were they—the professors and the regents—to find themselves *willy-nilly* bumping against new problems at every turn? Starting in this way, where was the thing to stop?

This fear of heresy and revolutionary utterance seemed to govern some. Others had a more material reason for opposing the San Francisco man. Through a charge by George in the columns of the "Evening Post" in 1874 of peculation in connection with the building of North Hall or the College of Letters, and a legislative investigation that followed, the Chairman of the Building Committee of the Board of Regents, was requested by the Governor of California to resign, which he did. But he left behind him for the "Post's" editor the resentment of his friends and of those on or connected with the Board whose lax attention to duty had permitted the scandal to occur.

Thus for perhaps personal and impersonal reasons Mr. George was quietly forgotten. Nothing was said about a chair by those who had the power to confer it. He was not even invited to speak again, although brief notes in his diary lead to the inference that he had commenced work on a second lecture. Yet whatever disappointment arose from this could not have been lasting, as there was uninterrupted interchange of social visits with Professor John Le Conte and his brother, Professor Joseph Le Conte, the physicist, and with other friends at Berkeley.[1] And his high regard for universities as institutions of progressive thought could not have been much, if any, diminished by this incident. Indeed, two years later, when about to launch "Progress and Poverty," it was his expectation that at least some of the professed teachers of political economy would take up the truths he endeavoured to make clear and "fit them in with what of truth was already understood and thought." It was not until subsequently that a change came "o'er the spirit of his dream."

---

[1] His friend Prof. William Swinton had resigned three years before, and going to New York, had entered upon a remarkably successful career of text-book writing.

CHAPTER VIII.

A FOURTH OF JULY ORATION.

1877.   AGE, 38.

NOW came the last stage before the writing of "Progress and Poverty."

The oration on the Fourth of July, 1877, like the lecture before the University of California, showed the broad sweep that Mr. George's mind was taking. "Our Land and Land Policy" regarded politico-economical conditions primarily from the standpoint of the Californian; his mind now enveloped the world. Not the progress of California, but human progress, was what engaged him; not particulars, but generals; not a question of policy, but the enunciation of the eternal law of "each for all and all for each."

And as the lecture was the exordium, the Fourth of July speech became the peroration. One pointed to the simplicity of the natural order, the other to the necessity of following it. One turned to the fundamentals of the science relating to the social conditions under which civilised men should get their daily bread; the other sounded the war clarions and gave the battle cry of "liberty and equality." One came from the solitary—the man of the closet; the other from the man of the practical world of struggle and conflict. Each was the complement of the

282

other—the two primary elements in "Progress and Poverty"—the reflections of the thinker who hands down the law; the call of the leader who marshals the hosts.

A season of depression having set in, and the income of the Inspector of Gas Meters having diminished very considerably, husband and wife decided to reduce domestic expenses. They gave up the San Francisco house, and storing part of the furniture, moved the remainder to Saucelito, a pretty little village on the north side of the bay. There they took a six-roomed cottage, where they lived comfortably during the summer months, the wife doing the domestic work herself. During these Saucelito days Mr. George did a good deal of reading and thinking. He also spent much time with his wife, frequently taking little walks or rides; and with his children, taking them swimming or sailing, or helping to make or float toy boats. Moreover, there was the frequent interruption of friends from San Francisco. But the matter of chief importance was the Fourth of July speech.

It was the custom for the city of San Francisco to have a military parade and civic exercises in celebration of the nation's birthday, and towards the middle of June Henry George was notified that he had been chosen to be "the Orator of the Day" for that year. He had been expecting this; had, in fact, begun work on his oration—"The American Republic."

The afternoon of the Fourth was sultry, but the old California Theatre where the exercises were held was crowded. First came the reading of the Declaration of Independence and the poem of the day, and then the oration. There had been a miscalculation as to length, and the speech was long for the exercises. Nevertheless the effort—the greatest that Henry George had yet made—was well sustained.

It did not take him long to come to the consuming thought that would not give him rest.

"We are yet laying the foundations of empire, while stronger run the currents of change and mightier are the forces that marshal and meet. . . . For let us not disguise it—republican government is yet but an experiment. That it has worked well so far, determines nothing. That republican institutions would work well under the social conditions of the youth of the Republic —cheap land, high wages and little distinction between rich and poor—there was never any doubt, for they were working well before. . . . The doubt about republican institutions is as to whether they will work when population becomes dense, wages low, and a great gulf separates rich and poor. Can we speak of it as a doubt? Nothing in political philosophy can be clearer than that under such conditions republican government must break down. . . .

"Six hundred liveried retainers followed the great Earl of Warwick to Parliament; but in this young State there is already a simple citizen[1] who could discharge any one of thousands of men from their employment, who controls 2,200 miles of railroad and telegraph, and millions of acres of land; and has the power of levying toll on traffic and travel over an area twice that of the original thirteen States. Warwick was a king-maker. Would it add to the real power of our simple citizen were we to dub him an earl? . . .

"Here is the test: whatever conduces to the equal and inalienable rights of men is good—let us preserve it. Whatever denies or interferes with those equal rights is bad—let us sweep it away. . . .

"Wealth in itself is a good, not an evil; but wealth concentrated in the hands of a few, corrupts on one side, and degrades on the other. No chain is stronger than its weakest link, and the ultimate condition of any people must be the condition of its lowest class. If the

---

[1] Leland Stanford.

low are not brought up, the high must be brought down. In the long run, no nation can be freer than its most oppressed, richer than its poorest, wiser than its most ignorant. This is the fiat of the eternal justice that rules the world. It stands forth on every page of history. It is what the Sphinx says to us as she sitteth in desert sand, while the winged bulls of Nineveh bear her witness!"

The oration closed with a majestic apostrophe to Liberty, that became the key-note, indeed, with but few changes, the very language of "Progress and Poverty."[1]

"They who look upon Liberty as having accomplished her mission, when she has abolished hereditary privileges and given men the ballot, who think of her as having no further relations to the every-day affairs of life, have not seen her real grandeur—to them the poets who have sung of her must seem rhapsodists, and her martyrs fools! As the sun is the lord of life, as well as of light; as his beams not merely pierce the clouds, but support all growth, supply all motion, and call forth from what would otherwise be a cold and inert mass, all the infinite diversities of being and beauty, so is Liberty to mankind. It is not for an abstraction that men have toiled and died; that in every age the witnesses of Liberty have stood forth, and the martyrs of Liberty have suffered. It was for more than this that matrons handed the Queen Anne musket from its rest, and that maids bid their lovers go to death!

"We speak of Liberty as one thing, and of virtue, wealth, knowledge, invention, national strength and national independence as other things. But, of all these, Liberty is the source, the mother, the necessary condition. She is to virtue what light is to colour, to wealth what sunshine is to grain; to knowledge what eyes are to the sight. She is the genius of invention, the brawn

---

[1] "Progress and Poverty," Book X, Chap. v
(Memorial Edition, pp. 543–545).

of national strength, the spirit of national independence! Where Liberty rises, there virtue grows, wealth increases, knowledge expands, invention multiplies human powers, and in strength and spirit the freer nation rises among her neighbours as Saul amid his brethren—taller and fairer. Where Liberty sinks, there virtue fades, wealth diminishes, knowledge is forgotten, invention ceases, and empires once mighty in arms and arts become a helpless prey to freer barbarians!

"Only in broken gleams and partial light has the sun of Liberty yet beamed among men, yet all progress hath she called forth.

"Liberty came to a race of slaves crouching under Egyptian whips, and led them forth from the House of Bondage. She hardened them in the desert and made of them a race of conquerors. The free spirit of the Mosaic law took their thinkers up to heights where they beheld the unity of God, and inspired their poets with strains that yet phrase the highest exaltations of thought. Liberty dawned on the Phœnician Coast, and ships passed the Pillars of Hercules to plough the unknown sea. She broke in partial light on Greece, and marble grew to shapes of ideal beauty, words became the instruments of subtlest thought, and against the scanty militia of free cities the countless hosts of the Great King broke like surges against a rock. She cast her beams on the four-acre farms of Italian husbandmen, and born of her strength a power came forth that conquered the world! She glinted from shields of German warriors, and Augustus wept his legions. Out of the night that followed her eclipse, her slanting rays fell again on free cities, and a lost learning revived, modern civilisation began, a new world was unveiled; and as Liberty grew so grew art, wealth, power, knowledge and refinement. In the history of every nation we may read the same truth. It was the strength born of Magna Charta that won Crecy and Agincourt. It was the revival of Liberty from the despotism of the Tudors that glorified the Elizabethan age. It was the spirit that brought a crowned tyrant to the block that planted here the seed of a mighty tree. It was the energy of ancient freedom that, the moment it had gained unity, made Spain the mightiest power of the world, only to fall to the lowest depth of weakness when tyranny succeeded Liberty. See, in France, all intellectual vigour dying under the tyranny of the seventeenth century to revive in splendour as Liberty awoke in the eighteenth, and on the enfranchisement of the French peasants in the Great Revolution, basing the wonderful strength that has in our time laughed at disaster. . . .

"Who is Liberty that we should doubt her; that we should set bounds to her, and say, 'Thus far shall thou come and no further!' Is she not peace? is she not prosperity? is she not progress? nay, is she not the goal towards which all progress strives?

"Not here; but yet she cometh! Saints have seen her in their visions; seers have seen her in their trance. To heroes has she spoken, and their hearts were strong; to martyrs, and the flames were cool!

"She is not here, but yet she cometh. Lo! her feet are on the mountains—the call of her clarion rings on every breeze; the banners of her dawning fret the sky! Who will hear her as she calleth; who will bid her come and welcome? Who will turn to her? who will speak for her? who will stand for her while she yet hath need?"

Who would stand for liberty, indeed! *his* kind of Liberty? There was general wonderment at the orator's fine imagery and eloquent periods, but who comprehended his philosophy? The stage was crowded with men distinguished in the city and the State. Some of these were conspicuous representatives of the institutions which Mr. George more than vaguely threatened, though they made no sign. The great audience applauded the flowing and lofty language, but who save the personal friends scattered about understood that the speaker was striking at the castle of vested rights—private property in land? As for the press, its attitude was not very encouraging, the friendliest paper, the "Examiner," saying faintly that "the oration was good throughout and full of food for thought," while the most hostile, the "News Letter," observed that the "gas measurer . . . kindly spoke for several hours on the Goddess of Liberty and other school-reader topics." Privately the newspaper men expressed surprise that "Harry George" could write so well.

Shortly following this event the family moved back to San Francisco, taking a house on Second Street, Rincon Hill, just around the corner from the former Harrison Street residence. The new house was dusty in the dry season from the heavy travel through the street to and from the wharves, but it was comfortable withal, and the rent low—an important consideration in that period of general depression.

Mr. George was in the troubles of moving when suddenly he found himself pitchforked into politics. In his diary he noted on August 20, "Found I had been nominated for the State Senate at Charter Oak Hall," an independent political organisation. Five days later the diary showed that he was "nominated last night by Anti-Coolies," a workingmen's anti-Chinese movement. But he was not to be drawn from his seclusion just then, and on Sunday, August 26, he made this entry: "John M. Days at house in morning. Went to office and wrote declination to Anti-Coolies. Home and wrote declination to Charter Oak, and sent it to Days by Harry."

And so for the first time in a number of years, Henry George was a spectator of political affairs, and there is little to note up to election day early in September other than that he stayed at home and read, among the books being German history, Code of Civil Procedure and Knight's "History of England."

CHAPTER IX.

"PROGRESS AND POVERTY" BEGUN.

1877-1878.   Age, 38-39.

UNDER date of September 18, 1877, the pocket diary bears the simple entry: "Commenced 'Progress and Poverty.' "[1]

Another child was expected soon to be added to the family circle. In the period preceding and following its advent the husband was tenderly attentive. He spent his time chiefly with his wife, for a whole month not leaving the house more than half an hour each day. He conversed on all manner of cheering subjects and read much aloud—newspapers in the mornings, and magazines or books later. George Eliot's "Daniel Deronda" had just reached the Pacific Coast. Mr. George was not much of a novel reader, yet he read this to his wife, and afterwards "Middlemarch," which he liked better. He regarded George Eliot as a woman of great powers.

---

[1] Although the work was begun on Sept. 18, the diary entry was not made until later, as the title, "Progress and Poverty," selected from among several, as one of his note books shows, was not decided upon until the writing had begun to take form. In a speech in 1893 (on "the Single Tax," Art Institute, Chicago, Aug. 29) Mr. George said: "I remember how much the name of 'Progress and Poverty' bothered me when it first suggested itself to my mind, for when I talked to my friends about it some thought it was too alliterative, while others thought that with what followed, it was too much like Benjamin Franklin's sign."

But in the parts of the day when he was by himself in his workroom, and he had taken his favourite thinking position—stretched out on his lounge, smoking—his mind reverted to the old problem that "appalled and tormented" and would not let him rest. The whole country was suffering an industrial depression. In many of the larger centres were social disorders. Great railroad strikes occurred in the East, and in six States troops were under arms. A riot broke out in Baltimore, and in Chicago artillery was used; while at Pittsburg more than two hundred lives were lost and wealth aggregating $12,000,000 destroyed.

In California the depression was deepened by a drought during the preceding winter months and by a heavy decline in the output of the silver mines on the Comstock Lode, which brought down all the stocks on the California exchanges and for the time stopped the speculation of the outside world through this market. At this period when workmen all over the State were idle, the Central Pacific Railroad, controlling practically every mile of track in the State, proposed to reduce wages. In San Francisco workmen held mass meetings, to denounce on the one side the great monopolies, and particularly the railroad, as oppressing the masses of labouring men; and on the other, Chinese immigration, as subjecting them to starvation competition. But there was no disorder. The railroad magnates—Stanford, Crocker, Huntington and Hopkins—were by name stigmatised, and in some few instances Chinese laundries were stoned by boys. But there was no head or form to the discontent until timid Privilege, under pretext of restraining anarchy, organised under the leadership of William T. Coleman five thousand men in what was called a Committee of Public Safety, armed them with pick handles; obtained a reserve of 1,700 rifles and

500 carbines from the United States War Department, and supported them with United States vessels, which were sent down to the metropolis from the Navy Yard at Mare Island with Gatling guns and other arms.

The uprising among the society savers tended to bring to a head discontent among the disorganised working classes. All that was needed was a voice to ring out, and the voice that came—in clear, though harsh tones—was that of a drayman named Dennis Kearney, an uncouth, illiterate young man who had a facility for rough, profane speech. He had denounced working men and had carried a club in the Committee of Public Safety, but now jumping to the other side, he arraigned the aristocrats and monopolists, and Chinese immigration, and in the tide of passion that was flowing expressed for the moment the strong feeling of his hearers. The hungry and discontented flocked to his standard and in August of 1877 he organised the "Working men's Party of California," which, strengthening in organisation and numbers, by the commencement of 1878 threw general politics into chaos. The social discontent had changed into a political upheaval.

It was amid these circumstances inspiring serious thought that Henry George sat down on the 18th of September, 1877, to commence what resulted in a momentous work. The question that engaged his mind was the phenomena of industrial depressions. One had thrown him out of employment when a boy in Philadelphia in 1858 and sent him forth to seek his fortune in the new country. Others had overtaken him while he was a struggling young man. Now came a greater than all the others, manifesting itself all over the United States in discontent, turmoil and suffering.

Mr. George's purpose was to write a magazine article on the subject of progress and poverty. It was to be, more than anything else, an inquiry into the cause of industrial depressions and of increase of want with increase of wealth, and was to indicate a remedy. Using all opportunities, he pursued the writing, and when the article was in form he read it to his close friend, Dr. Edward R. Taylor, who had formerly been Governor Haight's private secretary and was now his law partner in San Francisco. Taylor was much impressed; so much so that he urged George to reserve publication of the article and to give the subject a more extended treatment. After consideration, Mr. George decided to yield to the suggestion, concluding at length to make this the more extended politico-economic work, which, soon after the publication of "Our Land and Land Policy" in 1871, he realised would be necessary if he were to present his views properly. Those views had cleared and strengthened during the years of debate in his newspaper work, by his speeches, and through private conversations among his friends and acquaintances; while much, if intermittent, reading had made his mind a very arsenal of information; so that with quickened and sharpened powers of perception, statement and argument, and a new driving force in the widespread turmoil and distress, the elements were set in action to produce from the acorn of "Our Land and Land Policy" the oak of "Progress and Poverty." He realised that this would require elaborate and difficult work; that from his point of view so much confusion enshrouded political economy that he would have to clear away before he could build up; and that he would also have to write at once for those who had made no previous study of such subjects and for those who were familiar with economic reasonings.[1]   In accordance with this decision to expand the

---

[1] Preface to fourth edition and all subsequent editions
of "Progress and Poverty,"

writing, we find in the diary on November 5 an entry: "Started on 'Rent.'"

Meanwhile had come an important interruption. On October 2 the fourth child had been born—a girl. The other children—Harry, Dick and Jennie—were now fifteen, thirteen, and ten years old, respectively. The baby was named Anna Angela—Anna, after her mother, and Angela, as suggested by her aunt Sister Theresa Fox, because her birth came on the Feast of the Angels. The husband was all tenderness during this time of trial and he went to market daily for some dainty that might tempt his sick wife. From the pleasure he showed in providing these and other small luxuries, it was evident that his mind kept reverting to the terrible time when baby Dick was born and there was not a mouthful of food in the house to give to the mother.

Yet even now Old Adversity once in a while made his presence known. The year 1877 closed in hard times for the family, and memoranda among his papers show that Mr. George was personally $450 in debt. The meter inspector's office which was thought to be so lucrative was at the time yielding next to nothing. It was perhaps the necessity of eking out his livelihood during the work of writing on his book that caused him to turn to the idea of lecturing.

This idea held out some hope for him, for there was now an organisation composed of his friends and based upon his principles to support him. In the latter part of 1877 a few men, among them William M. Hinton, James G. Maguire, John M. Days, John Swett, Joseph Leggett, Patrick J. Murphy and A. L. Mann, met a few times with Henry George and his brother, John V. George, in Maguire's law office on Clay Street, above Montgomery, to discuss the economic parts of "Our Land and Land

Policy." These discussions resulted one Sunday afternoon early in 1878 in a meeting in the City Criminal Court room, in which on other days of the week, Robert Ferral, formerly on the editorial staff of the "Evening Post," sat as judge. At this meeting, perhaps thirty persons attending, "The Land Reform League of California" was organised. It had for its purpose "the abolition of land monopoly," and it was the first organisation of any kind in the world to propagate Henry George's ideas. Joseph Leggett, a lawyer, who was born in the county of Dublin, Ireland, and who came to California in 1868, was elected president; and Patrick J. Murphy, a newspaper writer trained on the "Evening Post," became secretary.

About the first thing the League did was to invite Henry George to deliver a pay lecture under its auspices in one of the large halls of the city, and to take for his text the prevailing industrial depression and labour troubles. Accordingly he laid aside work on his book to lecture at Metropolitan Temple, on March 26, under the title of "Why Work is Scarce, Wages Low and Labour Restless." He was very nervous about his manner and voice, and in the afternoon went to the hall for practice, inviting his wife to go with him. He went upon the platform and made a few trials, reading from the manuscript of his intended lecture. Mrs. George sat midway in the auditorium, and their old friend, George Wilbur, who had also come, sat up in the gallery. Rev. Isaac S. Kalloch, who delivered Sunday discourses in the hall, came in while Mr. George was practising and said that if those were the sentiments he intended to utter that night he would talk over the heads of the workingmen whom he expected mainly to compose his audience, since their selfish instincts must be appealed to. Mr. George drew himself up and replied: "Working men are men and are susceptible of lofty aspirations. I never will consent to appeal to them on any but high grounds."

By eight o'clock that night the lecturer was seized by "stage fright"; though for that matter he never in the rest of his life, even after his long election campaigns and lecturing trips, was free from high nervous tension before speaking. There was reason enough that night for nervousness. He told no one, yet he was about to prove the ends for which he had desired to be a speaker. As the book on which he was at work was to contain his written message to the world, so now he intended to commence with this lecture his spoken word—to set forth his perceptions, thoughts, convictions, philosophy; to proclaim the equal rights of all men to the land as one potent means of ridding civilisation of involuntary poverty.

His expectations of a big audience were badly disappointed. All his friends had been interested in the lecture, and advertisements and notices had appeared in the daily papers, but the house, the largest and finest of the kind in the city, was only partly filled. Yet though his audience was small, his words were the words of hope, in this way closing his lecture:

"Only a little while ago nations were bought and sold, traded off by treaty and bequeathed by will. Where now is the right divine of kings? Only a little while ago, and human flesh and blood were legal property. Where are now the vested rights of chattel slavery?

"And shall this wrong that involves monarchy and involves slavery—this injustice from which both spring —long continue? Shall the ploughers forever plough the backs of a class condemned to toil? Shall the millstones of greed forever grind the faces of the poor?

"Ladies and gentlemen, it is not in the order of the universe! As one who for years has watched and waited, I tell you the glow of dawn is in the sky.

Whether it come with the carol of larks or the roll of the war-drums, it is coming—it will come!

"The standard that I have tried to raise to-night may be torn by prejudice and blackened by calumny; it may now move forward, and again be forced back. But once loosed, it can never again be furled!

"To beat down and cover up the truth that I have tried to-night to make clear to you, selfishness will call on ignorance. But it has in it the germinative force of truth, and the times are ripe for it. If the flint oppose it, the flint must split or crumble!

"Paul planteth, and Apollos watereth, but God giveth the increase. The ground is ploughed; the seed is set; the good tree will grow.

"So little now, only the eye of faith can see it. So little now; so tender and so weak. But sometime, the birds of heaven shall sing in its branches; sometime, the weary shall find rest beneath its shade!"

A gleam was in the speaker's eye, hope shone in his face; his shoulders were squared, his head was up. Intense earnestness and intense conviction were in his manner. It was as if he spoke with his soul. Yet when his voice sank to the deep tones and he uttered the words, "So little now, only the eye of faith can see it," it seemed as though he spoke in an empty hall. He had started out to preach his word to the world. His voice was like a "cry in the wilderness."

Mr. George drew little money from this lecture, as the expense very nearly equalled the receipts. Moreover, the city newspapers dismissed it with few words. But as some of the State papers noticed it favourably, he delivered it in Sacramento and several of the other cities, under the short title of "The Coming Struggle." But he nowhere attracted large or even moderate sized audiences.

Measured in material results, the return from this lecturing effort was meagre, but he had made a start to

preach that faith which came from his heart's core; and
that counted for more than all else to him.

Nor did he let this effort stand alone. He delivered
another lecture a few months later, in June; one that
must be considered to be in many respects the most finished address he ever gave. The Young Men's Hebrew
Association of San Francisco, had just then been organised. It was composed of a number of bright, intelligent
young men. They invited Mr. George to deliver their
opening address. He accepted, but surprise and something like embarrassment seized the progressive members
when he announced "Moses" as his text, as they had looked
for some live topic of the day. Their feelings changed
when they heard the discourse. The leader of the Exodus
was held up as the colossal ancient figure of the Hebrew
nation. More than that, he was hailed as "one of those
star souls that dwindle not with distance, but, glowing
with the radiance of essential truth, hold their light while
institutions and languages and creeds change and pass";
a "lawgiver and benefactor of the ages," who pointed the
way for the new exodus—the exodus of the people of
this modern age out of the bondage of poverty, and laid
down a code for the observation of common rights in the
soil and the establishment of a commonwealth, "whose
ideal was that every man should sit under his own vine
and fig-tree, with none to vex and make him afraid."
The discourse abounded in vivid passages and exquisite
imagery, so that at its close Dr. Elkan Cohen, Rabbi of
the Temple Emanuel, turned to Max Popper, chairman
of the lecture committee, and said with deep feeling,
"Where did you find that man?"

Nevertheless Dr. Edward Taylor, who also had heard
the address, observed to Mrs. George as they walked to a
car on the way home: "Considered in itself, that lecture

was a fine effort, but Mr. George is writing a book that is so much superior in importance that to stop for matters like this is like wasting time."

But if just now he gave no more time to lectures, he did give it to other things. Besides contributing an article entitled "Each and All" to a volume of miscellaneous essays published for the benefit of the Youth's Directory, a benevolent institution of the city, he gave much thought and labour to the organisation and establishment of the Free Public Library of San Francisco. As early as 1872 he had talked with State Senator Donovan in advocacy of this means of popular amusement and education, and in 1878 with other public-spirited citizens worked for the passage of a State law providing for the establishment of a number of public libraries in California. He became a member and the first secretary of the original Board of Trustees of the San Francisco library, the records showing the minutes in his handwriting and the same blue ink which he was using at the time in writing "Progress and Poverty."[1]

But the chief interruption to the work on the book grew out of politics. In obedience to a popular demand, the legislature had passed an act providing for the holding of a convention for the general amendment of the State constitution, delegates to which were to be elected in June. Seeing in this convention a possible opportunity to graft into the organic law of California his principles touching the taxation of land values, Mr. George issued early in May an address to the citizens of San Francisco, announcing himself as a candidate "for the support of such voters, or bodies of voters," as might deem that as a delegate he would fitly represent them. After declaring his general

---

[1] This library, with its several city branches, is the most complete west of the Rocky Mountains.

principles, he told in what particulars he would endeavour, so far as he had power, to amend the constitution, giving chief place to this:

> "That the weight of taxation may be shifted from those who have little to those who have much, from those who produce wealth to those who merely appropriate it, so that the monopoly of land and water may be destroyed, that wealth may be diffused among the many, instead of stagnating in the hands of a few; and an end put to the shameful state of things which compels men to beg who are willing to work."

The Land Reform League, of course, became active in support of George and of his principles, and it moreover issued a list of questions to be put to all candidates for the convention. Mr. George was nominated by the Democratic party and afterwards by the new Working men's party, which, rising from the discontent with social and political conditions, and drawing from both of the two old parties, had a strength that no one pretended to ignore.

With the double nomination, Mr. George seemed sure of election. All that remained was for him to go before the Working men's ratification meeting, and acknowledging the leadership of Kearney, subscribe to their party platform. But there the difficulty lay. He went before the meeting where others had gone before him, and was asked the questions in which others had smoothly and quietly acquiesced. His reply was almost a shout, "No!" He said he would acknowledge no man leader to do his thinking for him; that moreover there were some planks in their platform that he did not believe in and must oppose. He would receive their nomination as a free man or not at all. Hisses greeted his speech and the nomination was revoked.

This left him with the single nomination of the Democratic party, and with small prospects of election, for that party was known to be greatly weakened by the political upheaval. The whole Democratic ticket was beaten at the polls, but George received more votes than any other Democrat. His friend, Assemblyman Coffey, who had run on the same ticket, on the following morning called at the meter inspector's office. Not finding him in, he pinned a card on the door bearing the message: "Accept congratulations on leading the Democratic party to the devil!"

Thus, for the second time standing for the suffrages of the people, Mr. George had been beaten; but he had the consolation now, as in 1871 when he ran for the Assembly, of knowing that he had kept faith with himself.

He turned once more to work on his book and did not again suffer any important interruption.

CHAPTER X

"PROGRESS AND POVERTY" FINISHED.

1878-1879.   AGE, 39-40.

ENTERING his library, one might witness the author, slightly inclined over an ample table in the centre of the room, writing on his book. Perhaps wearing a little house jacket, he sat, one hand holding the paper, the other moving a soft gold pen over it. And as he roused at sound of your entrance and turned and sank back, with one arm still on the table, the other thrown over the back of his chair, he raised a countenance not to be forgotten—a slight smile on the lips, a glow in the cheeks, tense thought in the brow and a gleam in the deep-blue eyes that looked straight through and beyond you, as if to rest on the world of visions of the pure in heart.

It was in a house on First Street,[1] near Harrison, to which the restless family now moved, that the main work on "Progress and Poverty" took place and the book was finished. For a while there was no parlour carpet, because the family could not afford to buy one, but the library, which was the workroom, was sufficiently furnished and was large and light and comfortable, and had three windows looking out on the bay.

Mr. George by gradual accumulation had acquired a

---

[1] No. 417 First Street.

library of nearly eight hundred volumes. They were his chief possessions in the world. They related to political economy, history and biography, poetry, philosophy, the sciences in popular form, and travels and discovery, with but few works of fiction. But these were only a few of the books he used, for he drew from the four public libraries of the city—the Odd Fellows, Mercantile, Mechanics and Free—and from the State Library at Sacramento; while he also had access to the books of his friends and acquaintances. Dating from the time of his leaving the "Evening Post," he had applied himself assiduously to reading, adding to a natural taste the sense of duty of storing his mind. His method or order of reading suited the needs of his work or the bent of his fancy, though he most frequently read poetry in the mornings before beginning labour, and after the midday and evening meals. He had not what would be called a musical taste or "ear," yet he said that all poetry that appealed to him—and it took a wide range—set itself to music in his mind.

He read mostly reclining, a pile of books drawn up beside him. He devoted himself with care to the reading of the standard works of political economy, yet freely confessed that of all books, these gave him the greatest labour. At night, if wakeful, he would ask his wife to, or would himself, take up some solid work, preferably some law treatise, which would invariably send him to sleep. He would frequently mark passages, and at times make notes; but he could generally with little difficulty turn to whatever in his past reading would serve an argument, fit as an illustration or adorn his diction. To most of his friends he seemed a browser rather than a deep reader, because he spent so little time on a book: and in truth, to use his own expression, he read "at" most books, not through them. Yet in this dipping he had the art of culling the particular parts that were useful to the purposes of his mind.

He needed eight hours sleep nightly, and what he lost at one time he would make up at another. He arose about seven, took a cold bath and dressed, careless about his outer clothes but invariably donning fresh linen. After breakfast he smoked a cigar and looked over the newspaper, then he stretched out on his lounge and read poetry for perhaps half an hour. And lying on his back he would do most of his thinking; but he also thought as he walked and smoked. He seldom sat in his chair except to write.

As he wrote much by inspiration, especially on the more elevated parts of his book, he could not always work at a set time or continuously. When his mind would not act to his suiting he would lie down and read, or go sailing or visit friends. To the casual observer his brain must have seemed intermittent in its operation; whereas, there really was an unconscious, or half conscious, cerebration when all the faculties seemed wholly occupied with outward trifles, for after such diversion he could write freely on the point that before was confused.

His writing, therefore, he did at any hour—early or late—suiting the state of his mind. Sometimes it fell in the middle of the night, when sleep was coy and thought surged. Brilliant passages of his book came in these hours, as by voluntary gift, and his pen ran rapidly over the paper. The analytical sections he wrote slowly and with labour, since this could not be dashed off, but required thought in conception, thought in construction, thought in the use of every word. Throughout the work he applied himself without saving, and if genius is the art of taking pains, his application bespoke consummate genius.

First came the rough drafting, in which he used a system of simple marks to represent the smaller common words. Numerous revisions and re-writings followed for sense, arrangement and diction, the requirements of the latter being clearness and simplicity, with a preference for short, Saxon words. Over and over again he wrote, arranged, expanded, contracted, smoothed and polished, for his motto was, "What makes easy reading is hard writing." When finished, the matter was submitted to the criticism of his friends, and strengthened wherever, to his view, they could find weak spots, so that eventually— in the preface to the fourth edition of the book—he was enabled to say that he "had yet to see an objection not answered in advance in the book itself." Indeed, so un-remitting was his toil that it might almost be said that the labour of writing was with him finished only when the book was printed and beyond further work.

Careless about his personal appearance, the greatest neatness distinguished his manuscript. He wrote on ser-mon paper, for the most part in dark blue ink, with a straight margin on the left-hand side. The words, in large, clear letters, were separated by wide, even spaces. The manuscript when finished was inviting and easy to read. The influence of his father's plain, clear, direct manner of thinking and speaking and of his mother's fine nature and lofty language showed in his style so early that he may be said to have been a born writer. And when he sat down to write his book, common sense and melody mingled harmoniously as the events of his restless life rolled before him like a varied panorama—a panorama to which books brought the parallels and contrasts of shade and colour. As without knowledge of the schools, he had read the suggestions of scenes about him, drawn his own deductions and constructed his own philosophy; so without training in the rules of style, he followed the quick, nervous action, and force and cadence of his own mind. And type and illustration came as a natural consequence from life around—no man too common, no incident too trivial, to make a picture or grace an argument.

Points to treat and forms of speech to use were frequently set down, mostly on loose sheets, though two small blank books exist containing such notes, among them being two early ideas for a title—one of them, "Must Progress Bring Poverty?" another "Wealth and Want."

The eldest son had reached the top grade in the grammar school, which was thought to be enough schooling, so that he was taken away and became amanuensis to his father, at the same time studying shorthand with the view of taking dictations and in other ways becoming more helpful. Mrs. George gave every encouragement in her power and verified fair with marked copies of the manuscript. It was perhaps with this period taking chief place in his memory that Dr. Taylor, after his friend's death, said:

> "Surely, never were man and woman closer to each other in affection and sympathy than were Mr. and Mrs. George—companions ever till death stepped between them; companions, too, of the noble sort that breasted together not only their own sufferings, but the sufferings of the world around them."

And so, too, the relations between Henry George and his friends were extremely warm; perhaps singular. As if in pursuance of his father's early injunction, to "make friends and use them," few men with close friends ever drew more from them. No matter how they differed among themselves, to him each offered earnest devotion. None of them was what could be called a political economist; yet for that matter George held that political economy is the one science that cannot be safely left to specialists, the one science which the ordinary man, without tools, apparatus or special learning, may most easily study.[1] At the beginning, at least, it was not so much the principles he proclaimed as it was two personal qualities he possessed that drew his chosen friends closely about him and commanded their strong support. One of these qualities was courage—described as "his sublime courage in attacking the most gigantic vested right in the world." The other quality was sympathy.

This quality of sympathy was, perhaps, Henry George's predominant trait of character. It had made him heartsick at sight of the want and suffering in the great city; it had impelled him to search for the cause and the cure. In the bonds of friendship it carried him into the other's thoughts and feelings. Intuitively he put himself into the other man's place and looked at the world through those other eyes. Rarely demonstrative in such circumstances, he did not speak of his sympathy, but it was as plain as if the word was written on his face. He had not studied man from the closet. He had all his rugged life been at school with humanity, and to him the type of humanity was the common man. Civilisation built up from the common man, flourished as the common man flourished, decayed and fell with the common man's loss of independence. He himself had climbed out on swaying yards like the commonest man, carried his blankets as a prospector and common miner, felt something of the hardships of farming, tramped dusty roads as a pedlar, had every experience as a printer, and suffered the physical and mental tortures of hunger. Learning and pride and power and

---

[1] This idea is expressed in all of his books, but most explicitly and fully in " The Science of Political Economy," General Introduction, p. xxxv.

tradition and precedent went for little with him; the human heart, the moral purpose, became the core thing. Towards him, from this very quality of sympathy, each friend—blacksmith or lawyer, man of little reading or lover of *belles-lettres*—had a singular consciousness of nearness—a feeling that this man could see *what* he himself saw and *as* he saw—could understand *his* labours, *his* sufferings, *his* aspirations. Nor was this condition peculiar to the "Progress and Poverty" period. It developed at that time and continued to Henry George's death. On the part of most of the men with whom he came in close contact, in California and in other parts of the world, there were feelings of attachment which if unspoken, were deep, solemn and lasting.

Among the friends closest to him during the writing of "Progress and Poverty" and whose criticism or counsel he asked in one particular or another were Assemblyman James V. Coffey, Ex-Assemblyman James G. Maguire, William Hinton and his oldest son, Charles; State Senator P. J. Donovan and Ex-State Senator John M. Days, John Swett, Principal of the Girl's High School; A. S. Hallidie, Regent of the University of California and Trustee of the Free Public Library; James McClatchy of the "Sacramento Bee"; H. H. Moore, the bookseller; and Dr. Edward R. Taylor. Two of them were Englishmen born, the others came from various parts of the United States. Not one of them had received a finished education in the European sense. All were positive, aggressive, independent men, representing distinct opinions, tastes and habits of life. Each had made his way in the community chiefly by the force of his own nature. George made requisition upon these different men for different purposes. But Taylor was the mainstay—the only man who read all of the manuscript and subsequently all of the proofs.

Edward R. Taylor had worked as purser on a Sacramento steamboat, set type and written for a newspaper, studied and practised medicine, served as private secretary to Governor Haight, and afterwards studied law and entered on a profitable practice in partnership with him. With it all he had found time to attain many of the refinements of life, had read carefully and widely, made himself master of polished verse and a competent judge of the fine arts. To him George made constant reference, and he responded with tireless zeal. After his friend's death, Taylor said:[1]

"When 'Progress and Poverty' was in process, as on its completion, it occurred to me that here was one of those books that every now and again spring forth to show men what man can do when his noblest emotions combine with his highest mentality to produce something for the permanent betterment of our common humanity; that here was a burning message that would call the attention of men to the land question as it had never been called before; and that whether the message was

---

[1] The following lines were written by Mr. George in a copy of the original edition of "Progress and Poverty" that he gave to Dr. Taylor:

TO

E. R. Taylor

this copy of a book which he knows from the first

and in the production of which

he has aided not only as compositor, proof-reader, critic and poet,

but still more

by the clearness of his judgment, the warmth of his sympathy, the support of his friendship and the stimulation of his faith

is

on the day when the long, hard struggle breaks into the first success,

presented by Henry George

in token of feelings which it could but poorly

symbolise were it covered with gold and crusted with

diamonds.

San Francisco, Oct. 20, 1879.

embodied in an argument of absolute irrefragability or not, it was yet one that would stir the hearts of millions.

"And similarly, the author of the book never for a moment doubted that his travail had resulted in a great deliverance; and he firmly believed (this faith never once faltering up to the moment of his death) that he had pointed out the one true road for burdened humanity to follow."

During the work on "Progress and Poverty" the author gave many proofs of his preoccupation. This appeared mostly at table. He was impatient of service and was willing to commence and finish with anything, so long as he did not have to wait. One day at lunch he sat down in a dreamy way, drew a dish of cold stewed tomatoes towards him and helped himself bountifully, for he was very fond of them. By the time he had eaten them the other edibles were served. Presently his eyes fell upon the tomatoes at the farther end of the table. "Well," he said with some asperity, "am I not to have any tomatoes? Don't you know I like them?" At another time one of the boys on a Sunday evening went to the cupboard and took out a cake with the intention of eating some, for the family was accustomed on that day to take an early dinner. He had the knife in hand and was about to cut a slice, when he was caught in the act, so to speak, by his father's entrance. Instead of reproving him, as the boy half expected, the father took the knife, cut himself a slice and sat down to eat it, all the time in a reverie, holding the knife and forgetful of the boy. When that was eaten, he cut himself another and afterwards a third slice, still holding the knife. It was only then that he noticed that his son was not eating. "Here, have a piece," he said. "It is good."

As he was in these respects, so was he in others. While

contending with the loftiest problems possible for the human mind and writing a book that should verily stir the hearts of millions, there was no more personal show or pretence in or out of his workroom than if he were engaged daily in filling out government weather reports. Thoughtless of dress, and often abstracted, he was unconventional in speech, at times even to lapses in syntax. There was an utter absence of anything that was stiff or pompous. He could work with his boys over a toy boat in the yard and then go and help sail it; unbend to his older girl and talk doll and party until her eyes shone; sing and coo to the new baby and call her "sunshine"; discuss lighter literature with his wife as if it shaped his daily course; defer to a visitor who came to break bread as with an absorbed purpose to learn; lead in the merriment of a mild practical joke among his friends and laugh with the ring and cheer of boyhood over a comical story. There were times in the family when the strain of following the long examination and argument and of watching the multitude of details told on the strong, quick, high-strung nature with bursts of impatience; but they passed as April showers.

Though writing a book that was quickly to become famous, he could not absolutely foresee this. He believed he was writing the truth and this urged him on, yet constantly came the disheartening thought, how hopeless the effort, how futile the sacrifice; for what could avail against such stupendous odds? And while waged this inner conflict, there was outward stress and struggle, debts and difficulties. At one time just for a little ready money he pawned his watch. But despite all, he pressed on, until by the middle of March, 1879, almost a year and a half after he first sat down to it, the task was done. "On the night in which I finished the final chapter of 'Progress

and Poverty,'" he subsequently wrote,[1] "I felt that the
talent intrusted to me had been accounted for—felt more
fully satisfied, more deeply grateful than if all the kingdoms of the earth had been laid at my feet."

The full meaning of these words, and what reveals the
living fire that burned in the breast of him who uttered
them and the religious zeal that possessed and drove him
on, is to be found in a postscript to a letter he wrote four
years later (February 1, 1883) to Rev. Thomas Dawson
of Glencree, Ireland—a letter which in a former chapter
we have quoted in part.[2] Written in his own hand, it was
attached to a letter he had dictated to his eldest son and
was never seen by any eye but Father Dawson's until after
death had claimed its author.

"There is something else I wanted to say to you that
I can only write with my own hand. Don't be disturbed because I am not a Catholic. In some things
your Church is very attractive to me; in others it is
repellent. But I care nothing for creeds. It seems to
me that in any church or out of them one may serve the
Master, and this also that faith that is the soul of your
Church holds. And in my way, in the line that duty
has seemed to call me, that I have tried to do. Because
you are not only my friend, but a priest and a religious,
I shall say something that I don't like to speak of—
that I never before have told to any one. Once, in
daylight, and in a city street, there came to me a thought,
a vision, a call—give it what name you please. But
every nerve quivered. And there and then I made a
vow. Through evil and through good, whatever I have
done and whatever I have left undone, to that I have
been true. It was that that impelled me to write
'Progress and Poverty' and that sustained me when else
I should have failed. And when I had finished the
last page, in the dead of night, when I was entirely

---

[1] Preface to "The Science of Political Economy."　　　[2] Page 193.

alone, I flung myself on my knees and wept like a child. The rest, was in the Master's hands. That is a feeling that has never left me; that is constantly with me. And it has led me up and up. It has made me a better and a purer man. It has been to me a religion, strong and deep, though vague—a religion of which I never like to speak, or make any outward manifestation, but yet that I try to follow. Believe this, my dear father, that if it be God's will I should be a Catholic, he will call me to it. But in many different forms and in many different ways men may serve Him.

"Please consider this letter to *yourself alone*. I have only said this much to you because you wrote my wife hoping I would become a Catholic. Do not disturb yourself about that. I do not wish you not to be a Catholic. Inside of the Catholic Church and out of it; inside of all denominations and creeds and outside of them all there is work to do. Each in the station to which he has been called, let us do what is set us, and we shall not clash. From various instruments, set to different keys, comes the grand harmony. And when you remember me in your prayers, which I trust you sometimes will, do not ask that I shall be this or that, but only for grace, and guidance, and strength to the end."

From daguerreotype taken about the time that
Henry George, less than fourteen, left
school and went to work.

Henry George when learning to set type in Philadelphia.
From daguerreotype, 1857.

From daguerreotype taken in 1865, showing Mr. George at 26, just after job printing office experience.

Mrs. George.

From photograph taken in 1898.

THIRD PERIOD

PROPAGATION OF THE PHILOSOPHY

What I tell you in darkness, that speak ye in light: and what ye hear in the ear, that preach ye upon the housetops.

And fear not them which kill the body, but are not able to kill the soul: but rather fear him which is able to destroy both soul and body in hell.　　　　　　　　　　　　　　　　　　　　Matthew x. 27, 28

CHAPTER I.

"PROGRESS AND POVERTY" PUBLISHED.

1879-1880.   AGE, 40-41.

THE diary shows that on March 22, 1879, a copy of
"Progress and Poverty" in manuscript was shipped
to D. Appleton & Co., Publishers, New York. No West
Coast house was judged to have facilities for placing a
book of this kind on the market. Moreover, the Appletons were the American publishers of the works of Herbert Spencer, whose "Social Statics" Mr. George regarded
as having in some degree ploughed the ground for his
own book. They also published "The International Scientific Series" which he had in his library and to which
he thought "Progress and Poverty" might perhaps be
added. But about the middle of April he received word
from the Appleton Company:

> "We have read your MS. on political economy. It
> has the merit of being written with great clearness and
> force, but is very aggressive. There is very little to
> encourage the publication of any such work at this time
> and we feel we must decline it."

However, the author had meanwhile asked his brother,
Thomas L. George, to go on from Philadelphia and confer
on publication with Professor William Swinton, Henry

George's old California friend, now living in New York, and with A. S. Hallidie, a member of the Board of Trustees of the San Francisco Free Library, who had gone East to buy books. The three gentlemen called on William H. Appleton, the senior member of the firm, and found him disposed to reconsider the matter, though his strong feeling was that the publication of such a book would not pay. And there he halted, so that the manuscript was submitted to other houses. Thomas George wrote to his brother on May 13:

> "I have just telegraphed you after consultation with Professor Swinton, and by his advice, that it 'seems impossible to get publisher without plates.' Appleton rejected the MS. and Harper, also, the latter emphatically, considering it revolutionary and all that sort of thing. Swinton and I called at Scribner's this morning . . . and were much pleased with our interview. In the event of Scribner refusing we shall try Boston."

Meanwhile, and before Appleton had written the first letter of rejection, Henry George, not wishing to remain idle, and for that matter urged by necessity to do something to make a living which his office of meter inspector had not recently afforded, re-entered public affairs. He started a four-paged weekly paper, "The State"—"A journal of politics and opinion." It was printed by William M. Hinton, who had opened a printing office on Clay Street. Mr. George did most of the writing, but Dr. Taylor, James V. Coffey and other friends made contributions. The paper was high in tone and temperate, though strong in language. It forcibly opposed the new constitution that the convention had drawn up and which was to be submitted to a popular vote early in May. Mr. George

held that such an instrument would strengthen the land
and railroad monopolies and that it had many other serious faults. The masses of the people thought otherwise,
however, so that it was adopted by a large vote.

"The State" afterwards dealt with a number of matters
of public interest in California, and took a vigorous adverse position to General Grant, who purposed completing
a circle of the globe by way of San Francisco, to the end,
as many like George believed, of becoming candidate for a
third term of the Presidency. To Henry George, Grant
was distinguished as the President who had had the worst
of all political rings and corruptionists about him.
George's attack was so sincere and so strenuous that later,
when Grant arrived, and John Russell Young, who was of
the General's party, offered to arrange for a private interview, George refused.

"The State" had a short life, suspending with the
eleventh number. Not that it was losing money, for while
it did not have much of a circulation, it was just about
paying for itself. Mr. George stopped it because, having
undertaken to make plates of his book, he found that that
far more important matter demanded all of his available
time.

It is an old story how the copyright of Milton's "Paradise Lost" was originally sold for five pounds, and it goes
with the history of literature how many famous books from
"Robinson Crusoe" down to "Uncle Tom's Cabin" were
at start thought to be such poor business ventures as to
have to struggle for publication. "Progress and Poverty" had fallen into the same category. The ability it
showed was conceded, but aside from its doctrines to
which some objected, the book was thought unlikely to pay
the expense of handling. In truth, no works of political
economy up to that time had paid. There was nothing

for the author to do but himself to make his plates and then try again for a publisher.

But to a man who had no money—who indeed, was in debt—the expense of making plates was a serious matter. The way cleared, however. "My old partner, Mr. Hinton," said Mr. George later,[1] "who had got himself a printing office, thereupon said that he had faith enough in anything I should do to make the plates; and I put the manuscript in his hands." The diary on May 17 contains the note: "Commenced to set type on book. Set first two sticks myself."

But with characteristic pains, the author revised his manuscript, chapter by chapter, before the printers received it. Not a page or a paragraph escaped until it met whatever new questions had arisen in his mind. And he made many changes, but not one affecting principle. Most of them related to terseness, expression and arrangement.[2]

Those competent to judge will perhaps hold with the author that taken altogether the changes made in the

---

[1] Meeker Notes, October, 1897. See also "The Science of Political Economy," p. 203.

[2] A comparison of title pages will illustrate this :

As submitted to Appleton :	As revised and printed :
" Progress and Poverty	" Progress and Poverty
" An inquiry into the Cause of Recurring Paroxysms of Industrial Depressions and of Increasing Want with Increasing Wealth.	" An inquiry into the Cause of Industrial Depressions and of Increase of Want with Increase of Wealth.
" A Remedy Proposed."	"The Remedy."

There was also an important rearrangement and addition. As submitted to Appleton, the work consisted of eight grand divisions or books. The revision cast it into ten. The original Book VI, entitled, "The Remedy," and consisting of ten chapters, he divided into three books, as follows : Book VI, "The Remedy," two chapters (one of them, entitled, "The True Remedy,") being new; Book VII, "Justice of the Remedy," five chapters; and Book VIII, "Application of the Remedy," four chapters. The numbering manuscript at the time of putting the work into type made a marked improvement in "Progress and Poverty," as still further clearing and smoothing an already graceful, lucid style; but it is to the termination of the work that chief attention will turn. The manuscript ended with the closing words of Book VIII, or what by subsequent numbering became Book X. The author had ended his task, he had answered the riddle of industrial depressions, shown the cause of increase of want with increase of wealth and pointed to the remedy. But thought still mounted, his heart still moved him; so that while the printers were busy setting type on what he had previously written, he now wrote a chapter entitled "The Problem of Individual Life" to form the conclusion. This was not a mere rhetorical flourish, a splendid peroration to an elevated argument. His soul's message was going out to the world. He had made the long, hard struggle to find the Truth and to tell it. Would the Truth prevail? He understood the conditions that beset it and he answered: "Ultimately, yes. But in our own times, or in times of which any memory of us remains, who shall say?" He made a supreme appeal to those "who in their heart of hearts have taken the cross of a new crusade"; to those who seeing the Truth, "will toil for it; suffer for it; if need be, die for it." It was a trumpet call to those who would fight with Ormuzd! And he followed this up later, at the first formal publication of the work,[1] with a dedi-

---

of former Books VII and VIII was changed to IX and X, respectively. Besides the motto to precede the general work, one was now set at the head of each book, that heading Book VIII, being written by Dr. Taylor. It was ascribed to "Old Play," which, however, gave place to Taylor's name in the fourth edition, as George heard it highly commended and wished its author to have full credit.

[1] First Appleton edition.

cation of it "to those who, seeing the vice and misery that spring from the unequal distribution of wealth and privilege, feel the possibility of a higher social state and would strive for its attainment."

During all this labour of making plates, Taylor was of inestimable service to his friend, encouraging and suggesting, reading proofs, and even, like George, going back to the printer's case to set a few sticks of type. Nor did George forget his other friends. He now did as he had done during the previous work of writing—called for their aid whenever they could give it. For instance, John Swett has said:

"It was when he was putting 'Progress and Poverty' in type that Mr. George came, saying that some criticisms had been made by a friend respecting syntax, and that as he [George] depended more upon his ear than upon a knowledge of rules, he may have fallen into some gross errors. He, therefore, wanted me, as a friend, to read a set of proofs—the same set, in fact, on which the grammatical critic had made marks. I found that these marks related almost entirely to 'so's' and 'as's.' According to my liberal view, Mr. George's use of these marked words was in almost every instance correct. Indeed, as I now remember, the only incorrect use of them was in a single instance, which by some chance the critic had overlooked.

"Mr. George did not ask me to pass upon the subject matter of the work. Nor would I have felt in a position to do so, because I had made no special study of such matters. He asked me to read for grammatical slips; and from what he said, I expected to find here and there a break. I was greatly surprised to find practically nothing to criticise. His ear was as good as the rules of syntax."

One of his friends had originally suggested that the book be published by subscription, and the author concluded to follow this idea to the extent of an informal "Author's Edition" of five hundred copies. He printed a descriptive circular or prospectus of the work announcing that he would issue in August a small "Author's Proof Edition," under the title, "Political Economy of the Social Problem."[1] He sent this circular to those of his friends who he thought would take an interest in the matter, and he sold enough copies at three dollars apiece to enable him to pay part of the cost of printing the edition.

One of the first copies he sent to his father in Philadelphia, who had reached his eighty-first year. With the book he sent this letter (September 15):

"It is with a deep feeling of gratitude to Our Father in Heaven that I send you a printed copy of this book. I am grateful that I have been enabled to live to write it, and that you have been enabled to live to see it. It represents a great deal of work and a good deal of sacrifice, but now it is done. It will not be recognised at first—maybe not for some time—but it will ultimately be considered a great book, will be published in both hemispheres, and be translated into different languages. This I know, though neither of us may ever see it here. But the belief that I have expressed in this book—the belief that there is yet another life for us makes that of little moment."

A fortnight after writing this letter, the author received from D. Appleton & Co. of New York a proposal to publish the book. This was in response to an effort

---

[1] The title, "Progress and Poverty," was the name used when the book was first submitted to Appleton and the other Eastern publishers, as shown by the original manuscript. Why Mr. George announced a totally different one in this circular perhaps came from a desire to protect the former title until it had been printed with the book and copyrighted. He showed similar care with his later books.

he had again made to find a publisher. "I sent," he said, "copies of the author's edition without binding to publishers both in America and England, offering to put the plates at their disposal for printing. I received but one proposal, that of Appleton & Co. They offered to take it and bring it out at once, and I acceded to this."[1] The publishers proposed to issue the book at two dollars a copy and agreed to give a royalty of fifteen per cent.

To his friend, John Swinton, of New York, brother of Professor William Swinton, Mr. George wrote in satisfaction:

"So, at last, I feel sure of getting the book published! This is a very great relief to me. I was from the first apprehensive about finding a publisher and Somers brought to me a message from you as to the difficulties that was anything but encouraging. Turning aside from everything else, I worked hard and faithfully to get the book through, only to feel when the writing had been finished that I was but on the threshold of the real difficulty. When, in spite of your brother's efforts, I could get no one to publish from the manuscript, I had to work on an uncertainty and make the plates. To do this I had to stop the little paper that I had started."

Soon following this letter Mr. George wrote another to John Swinton:

"If the book gets well started, gets before the public in such a way as to attract attention, I have no fear for it. I know what it will encounter; but, for all that, it has in it the power of truth. When you read it in its proper order and carefully, you will see, I think, that it is the most important contribution to the science of political economy yet made; that, on their own

---

[1] Meeker notes, October, 1897.

ground, and with their own weapons, I have utterly broken down the whole structure of the current political economy, which you so truly characterise. The professors will first ignore, then pooh-pooh, and then try to hold the shattered fragments of their theories together; but this book opens the discussion along lines on which they cannot make a successful defence."

Mr. George also received some cheer through complimentary copies of the "Author's Edition" which he sent to such distinguished persons as he thought would be interested in it; one copy going to Gladstone, who had just made a speech or two with radical tendencies on the land question, another to Sir George Grey, the master spirit of New Zealand; and others to Herbert Spencer and the Duke of Argyll, both of whom, the one as author of "Social Statics" and the other of "The Reign of Law," would, the author presumed, welcome a work harmonising with principles they had enunciated. Spencer does not appear to have responded, but the Duke sent a courteous acknowledgment. Gladstone on one of his customary postal cards said (Hawarden, November 11, 1879): "Accept my best thanks for the copy of your interesting work, which reached me to-day, and which I have begun to examine. There is no question which requires a more careful examination than the land question in this and other countries, and I shall set great store on whatever information you may furnish under this head." Sir George Grey wrote in a still more gratifying way (Auckland, N. Z., January 27, 1880). "I have already read a large part of the book," he said. "I regard it as one of the ablest works on the great questions of the time, which has come under my notice. It will be of great use to me. . . . It has cheered me much to find that there is so able a man working in California, upon subjects on which

I believe the whole future of mankind now mainly hangs."

Early in 1880 John Russell Young went to London and carried a number of copies of "Progress and Poverty" with him which he presented with personal letters to notable men of his acquaintance, among them being W. Fraser Rae, L. H. Courtney, M. P., Dean Stanley, and Henry Labouchere, M. P., Thomas Hughes and Henry Fawcett, M. P., as well as the Irish Members of Parliament, A. M. Sullivan and J. O'Connor Power, and he wrote back to Mr. George that most of these copies of the book were getting read and that some would probably produce results.

But if such messages were beginning to come in from the outside world, recognition at home was slow. Friendly newspapers like the "San Francisco Examiner" and the "Sacramento Bee" said complimentary things, without attempting to discuss or even to notice extendedly. Most of the papers, if they did not treat the book with contemptuous silence, sneered at the "hobby" of "little Harry George," and said in substance with the "Alta California" that the book never would be heard of. This belief found expression beyond the newspapers, as indicated by an incident related by Mr. George in his "Science of Political Economy":[1]

"When the first few copies of my 'Progress and Poverty' were printed in an author's edition in San Francisco, a large land-owner (the late General Beale, proprietor of the Tejon Ranch, and afterwards United States Minister to Austria), sought me to express the pleasure with which he had read it as an intellectual performance. This, he said, he had felt at liberty to enjoy, for, to speak with the freedom of philosophic frankness, he was

---

[1] Pages 170,171.

certain my work would never be heard of by those whom
I wished it to affect."

The Sacramento "Record-Union," the railroad organ,
was really the first representative of the hostile newspaper
interests to honour the book with a serious and extended
criticism. The author was moved to reply. He filled four
and a half columns, incidentally making some personal explanations that we should note.

"If [in replying] I shall seem to show any of that
absence of diffidence which you deem one of the remarkable characteristics of my book, do not charge it
to any want of respect or lack of proper modesty, but
to the fact that when a man has so thought out and
tested his opinions that they have in his mind the highest certainty, it would be but affectation for him to
assume doubts he does not feel. . . .

"For my own part I am not lacking in respect for
authority. Like everybody else, I am disposed to believe whatever I am told by those reputed wise and
learned, and if I have been enabled to emancipate myself from ideas which have fettered far abler men, it is,
doubtless, due to the fact that my study of social problems was in a country like this, where they have been
presented with peculiar directness, and perhaps also to
the fact that I was led to think a good deal before I
had a chance to do much reading."

Mr. George was depressed by hearing from the Appletons that they would not attempt publication until after
the Christmas holidays. They wrote, moreover, that their
London agent had failed to induce any of the English
houses to take the book, one publisher saying that "if the
plates were sent free of cost" he would not publish it.
The Appleton agent had concluded that English publishers
generally would not look with much favour on the book

because it antagonised the tenets of the current political economy. Nor did the Appletons themselves see any advantage for the author in putting in the American edition of the book the words "rights of translation reserved," since to their view there was small chance of anything of importance being done in the way of translation.

This dashed the hopes that had begun to rise, and what increased the author's depression was that though it had brought comparatively little return to him during the last two years, he was about to yield up his office of inspector of gas meters, George C. Perkins, a Republican, having been elected to succeed Governor William S. Irwin. While friendly with him, Mr. George would not ask, nor did he expect, anything from Mr. Perkins, and a few days after taking his chair in January, 1880, the new Governor appointed a Republican to the office of gas meter inspector.

Henry George had written a book which he was confident would some day become famous; but in writing it, he had chosen the hard road of the social pioneer, and in the fall of 1879, when his friend John Russell Young was in San Francisco with the General Grant party, he was beginning to realise with secret bitterness the difficult task he would have from now forward in making a living; for the world regards as an impractical man and a dreamer him who is in advance of his time. To a man with such a mission as Mr. George had set before himself, the making of a living would have been a difficult task even under good general circumstances; but California now was industrially under a cloud. He said later: "I could hardly walk a block without meeting a citizen begging for ten cents."[1] Eighteen years later Mr. Young said:

---

[1] "The Land Question," Chapter XV.

"I saw much of George in these California days. He talked of his career, was swimming in heavy seas. This could only be divined bit by bit, for the proud, self-respecting, sensitive gentleman made no sign. Then came the knowledge of the book, the new gospel. I never see 'Progress and Poverty' without recalling the pathetic circumstances under which it was written and honouring the courage of the author. The clouds were heavy over George. Proud, brave, smiling, hopeful—San Francisco did not appreciate him; had never given him recognition. He would speak of it as cold and barren, ruled by strenuous men too busy with mines and wheat and empire building to listen to prophecy."[1]

About the time he was talking to Young, George expressed kindred sentiments in a letter to Charles Nordhoff, one of the chief editorial writers for the "New York Herald," whom he had met early in the seventies in San Francisco and whose strong belief in immortality made a deep impression on his mind. The letter (December 21) ran:

"Your kind letter reached me last Monday, but until now I have not had time to acknowledge it. It has given me a great deal of pleasure—more than you can think. It pleases me that you remember me, and it pleases me that you like my book. Your friendship and your opinion I value very much. You know how earnest men are drawn towards those for whom they feel an intellectual sympathy, and I have derived so much from you that it pleases me *very* much that my book interests and pleases you.

"As for the book itself, I believe it sets forth some very great truths that have been hitherto ignored and slurred over, and I think they will grow on you as they have grown on me. To write the book was not an easy

---

[1] Signed article by John Russell Young in "New York Herald," October 30, 1897.

task for me, and I could not have done it but for the animation of a very deep and very strong feeling, and when I got through it was with such a deep thankfulness that I cannot express it. I had hard work, too, to get it into print and to get it a publisher, and it has been weary waiting. But now Appletons write me that they will publish it in January.

"With all deference to your judgment, I think you are wrong in your opinion that I should have briefly stated the economic laws. That would have been sufficient if I had been writing for men like you. But I have aimed to reach a very much larger audience. I have tried to make a book which would be intelligible to those who have never read and never thought on such subjects before, and to do that in such a way as to get the primary truths firmly established in their minds. And it is astonishing and appalling how few there are capable of logical thought—or, rather, who are willing to undertake it.

"In the latter parts the book is too much condensed, I know, and I had to omit a good deal I should like to have said. The fact is it covers too wide a scope for one volume. The chapters, for instance, relating to the development of civilisation are but a bare skeleton of what I should like to say, and do not begin to present the argument as strongly as I feel it. But at least an outline seemed to me essential, and I did not know, even if I lived, if I should ever find opportunity to write again.

"If this book makes success enough to insure it a reception . . . and if opportunity is given me, there are two books I should like to write—one a brief political economy, which, without controversy, should lay down the principles of the science, and make of it a harmonious whole; and the other a dissection of this materialistic philosophy which, with its false assumption of science, passes current with so many.

"You speak of the intellectual poverty of this coast. You can hardly understand how deep it is, for of course you came in contact with the highest people, and they must have seemed to you relatively far more numerous than they really are. This is bad enough; but what is worse is the moral atmosphere—at least in the circles in which I have moved and lived. Do you know what impressed me so much with you and made me want to talk with you, was that you actually believed in the immortality of the soul. It made you to me almost a curiosity, and I thought of it over and over again. It was like meeting a man whose opinion was worth something who told you he saw something which you would very much like to see; but which you could not make out for yourself and which every one around you whose opinion was worth anything said did not exist at all. At that time I should have gladly hailed any assurance that was to be found in spiritualism, but I found in it nothing but humbug, and in its believers, fools.[1]

"But now I really, and for myself, believe with you. Out of the train of thought which is set forth in that book; out of the earnest, burning desire to do what I might to relieve human misery and make life brighter, has come to me a faith, which, though it is not as definite and vivid and firm as must be the Christian's faith, when it is really felt, is yet *very* much to me. The opportunity to write that book came out of crushing disaster, and it represents more than labour. But I would not forego this satisfaction for any success. And I feel that there is much, very much, of which I get only vague glimpses or rather suggestions of glimpses.

"I should like very much to talk with you. There are so many things on which I should like to compare notes with you. Sometime I may have the chance."

Thus it is clear that Henry George did not look for the initial advancemennt of his ideas in California. As John Russell Young subsequently said: "George never for a moment—never when under the grinding heel of bitter

---

[1] Three years later he wrote from Brooklyn to Taylor: "There is evidently something in spiritualism; but I am the more convinced that it is a bad thing to have anything to do with."

conditions—doubted the truth of his mission to mankind
and its ultimate success.   But this obviously was not to be
attained in Eldorado."

All was not against him, for now two circumstances
occurred that were of importance to him.   One of these
concerned the translation of "Progress and Poverty" into
German by a cultured man named C. D. F. von Gütschow,
who, having lost a fortune in Germany, had recently come
to California to begin life anew, and who, chancing to
read a copy of the "Author's Edition," was so impressed
with the work that he at once asked for permission to
translate it.   Consent was gladly given on the single condition that the translation should be faithful.   Mr. George
could read no foreign tongue, but he afterwards had assurance that this translation was excellent—by far the
best of three soon published in Germany.

The other circumstance of importance was the conversion of a scholarly Englishman, Dr. Montague R. Leverson,
who had personally known and studied under William
Ellis and John Stuart Mill, and who had in 1876 published in New York a primer of political economy for
grammar and high schools and the lower colleges.   He had
come to California to arrange for the publication and
introduction of the book on the Pacific Coast, but learning
of "Progress and Poverty" through Professor Joseph Le-
Conte of the University of California, he declared, immediately on reading it, that he had met his master in the
study and that not another copy of his primer should be
issued until the work had been re-written.   This manifestation of rare intellectual honesty was never forgotten
by Mr. George.

But George's gaze was turned eastward.   To Dr. Taylor, who had gone to Washington, D. C., on business, he
wrote (February 17, 1880) :

"I got yesterday the first European notice of our book. It is in the Parisian 'Revue Scientifique,' signed by Emile de Laveleye. I got Phil Roach to translate it for me. It is first-class—says the book has instructed him and led him to think; indorses substantially the whole programme; says the chapter on Decline of Civilisation is worthy of being added to 'De Tocqueville's immortal work,' etc. So, my friend in need, your judgment is being verified. The 'Graphic' of February 4, had a very fine notice. I am told also that there have been fine notices in the 'Boston Transcript' and in some of the Cincinnati papers; but have not yet seen them.

"By the bye, there is one thing I would like to have you do for me in the East which I forgot to mention. Among the many projects which I have been vaguely meditating is that of lecturing through the East. I wish if you can get time, you would go and see Redpath or some other of the Lecture Bureau people. I had a card from Redpath some time since asking about the publisher of the book. Possibly that will soon get advertised enough to enable me to begin to draw a little, and I have faith in my own ability if I once get started. I know you don't share that—but I have always felt it, and on two or three occasions have tested it. For the present I am doing a little hack work—and waiting. But soon my time for waiting will be past."

Mr. George sent his California University lecture, "The Study of Political Economy," to the "Popular Science Monthly," owned by the publishers of his book, D. Appleton & Co. It was accepted and appeared in the March number (1880). For the same periodical he wrote by invitation on "The Kearney Agitation in California," which appeared in August. The lecture on "Moses" was not suited to that magazine, but under the title of "The Leader of the Exodus," it was sent to another American, and afterwards to an English, periodical. The author was unknown and the article, though one of the most brilliant pieces of writing that ever came from his pen, was in both instances rejected.

Again George wrote to Taylor (March 12):

"I am sorry you have not seen or heard of my book. . . . I wish you would go into one of the Washington bookstores and inquire whether they have it or have had it. You know how I feel about the ultimate fate of the book. That does not worry me. What I am concerned about is the meeting of my obligations to Hinton. I have been calculating that by the early part of next month I could get a return or an advance from Appleton which would enable me to square up with Hinton. There will be no difficulty if the book is selling; but it will be hard if it has not yet begun. Well; we shall see.

"I have been sick and am far from well—the old trouble of which I have several times spoken to you, growing more intense. The doctor says I must rest. That is the best prescription, but often the hardest to take."

The illness of which he spoke was writer's cramp and biliousness, with bladder trouble; all proceeding from overwork and nervous strain. First had come the year and a half of hard writing and then the long months of striving and waiting for results. He had written in December (1879) to John Russell Young:

"What a book of this kind, so much out of the usual run, really needs is such a service as Mill in his autobiography speaks of having rendered to Carlyle's 'French Revolution' in a first review. But whether it is at first applauded or denounced makes little difference, provided it is treated with attention. The book fairly started, will go. This is not merely my judgment; it is my experience. I have put out enough copies to thoroughly test it, and I am more than satisfied of that."

Towards the middle of March (1880) a brilliant review, that covered most of a page, appeared in the "New York Sun," from the pen of M. W. Hazeltine. What it meant to the author he wrote to John Swinton (March 22):

"A year ago to-day I finished my book and shipped it off to seek a publisher. After the toil and the pains of the writing came the anxiety, the rebuff, the weary waiting; and I have longed that by this day at least there might be some sure sign that the seed I tried to plant there had not fallen by the wayside. This review is that sign; it secures for my book that attention which is all I ask."

Important reviews soon followed in other Eastern newspapers and periodicals, so that the gaze in that direction was stronger than ever. Moreover, the Appletons wrote that if the author would consent to a reduction in copyright, they would issue a dollar, paper-covered edition of the work, to which he gladly agreed. One of the instruments in bringing this about was a young man in the Appleton employ, A. J. Steers, who had read the book and was enthusiastic about it. Mr. George wrote (April 4) in reply to a letter from him:

"I cannot tell you how grateful your letter is to me and how much I thank you for it. I have wanted a cheap edition very much. . . .

"But it is not this of which I speak so much as the sympathy and interest your letter expresses and which makes me feel that the book has spoken to you as I knew there would be some men to whom it would speak. This is my reward—the verification of my faith. It is very, very much to me—more than profit, more than fame. I knew when I wrote it that my book would sometime find such men, but whether I should ever know it, that I could not tell; for many a man does his work and in this life sees no result. And no matter how much of a success the book may become in my lifetime, I do not think I shall be proud of it, as men are proud of writing a successful history or novel. The feeling is one of deep gratitude that it has been permitted me to do something. And this, already, I know—your kind letter is one of the proofs of it—that every here and there is a man on whom these ideas have taken hold, as they have taken hold of me, and who in his turn will be a fresh centre.

"You speak of how little you can do. Did you ever think of it, how little we know of what we can do, or of what we do? Sometimes a word, a little act, starts a train that, if we could follow it, we should see leads to the widest results. But it is not the result so much as the effort to do what we can, with which we are concerned."

At length John Russell Young wrote hopefully of being able to get George a writing position in New York on the "Herald" that would permit him to do his work away from the office and give him much time to himself. Young perceiving his circumstances, voluntarily sent him money with which to go East. Having nothing to keep him, and arranging to pay those to whom he owed money at the earliest opportunity, in August of 1880 Henry George took train for New York, leaving his family behind him. His purse was so light that he was compelled to travel third class. But no sooner had he got well started than his spirits threw off their depression, and although he was going into practically a new world where he had not half a dozen friends, confidence came, for the time of waiting had passed. From Winnemucca he wrote back to Taylor, who had returned to San Francisco: "I am enjoying the trip and am full of hope. The spell is broken and I have taken a new start."

CHAPTER II.

COMMENCING THE NEW YORK CAREER.

1880-1881.   Age, 41-42.

IT was towards the middle of August, 1880, that Henry George set foot in New York almost as poor in the money sense as any immigrant who ever landed in the great city. He had but three personal friends there—the two Swintons (William and John) and Charles Nordhoff of the "New York Herald." John Russell Young, who had spoken hopefully of getting him a place on the "Herald," was away. On returning, he, with Nordhoff, recommended George for a vacant writing position on the paper. No action was taken in the matter for some time, and word eventually came that there was no chance for the San Francisco man. The book, first fixed at two dollars and afterwards at one dollar (when the author cut his copyright to ten per cent.), was selling; but as yet it yielded little. William H. Appleton, at the head of the publishing firm, was very friendly, and so also was Professor E. L. Youmans of the "Popular Science Monthly." The latter invited a political article and paid for it; though it was not used, owing to a change in editorial policy. But there was little to do at writing just now, and the eyes of the California man turned to politics.

The Hancock-Garfield Presidential fight had commenced,

and from a visit with William Swinton and William C.
De Witt of Brooklyn to Hancock at Governor's Island,
headquarters of the Department of the Atlantic, which
the General commanded, Mr. George was favourably impressed with the candidate's simplicity and manly bearing.
He believed that as two generals of the Civil War were
contesting, the old "bloody-shirt" issues could not be used
by either side, and therefore that there would be a chance
for new ideas and radical sentiments. Suddenly the Republicans raised the tariff issue, declaring for protection
and denouncing the Democrats for free traders. The
Democratic managers responded with a straddle. Just
then Henry George entered the campaign.

"I was not then very well known in New York, but
just before the election, when the tariff issue was sprung,
the Democratic Committee sent for me and told me
they had heard that I was the best man in all the country to talk to the working men on the question of the
tariff. I told them I didn't know about that, but that
I could talk to working men and that I should like to
talk to them about the tariff. They asked me if I
would go out and make some speeches. I said, 'Certainly I will'; and they made a great list of engagements
for me that ran close up to the day of election, so that
I went out. Well, it seems that what they were after
was somebody to tell the working men that the Democratic party was as good as the Republican party for
the tariff. I went to a crowded meeting. The gentleman who spoke before me made that kind of a speech
and then I was put on the platform. I told them that
I had heard of a high-tariff Democrat, though I could
not conceive how there could be such a thing; and I
knew there were men who called themselves revenue-
tariff Democrats; but there was also another kind of
Democrat, and that was a no-tariff Democrat; and that
what was wanted was to sweep away the custom houses
and custom house officers and have free trade. Well,

the audience applauded, but you ought to have seen the men on the platform there; and I went off without a man to shake my hand. I got that night as I was going to my next engagement, a telegraphic despatch asking me to go by midnight train to New York. The chairman of the committee met me and begged me not to make any more speeches."[1]

But there was one place in New York State where Henry George could talk out plainly for free trade, and that was in Brooklyn. Thomas Kinsella, editor of the "Brooklyn Eagle," William C. De Witt and a number of other influential Democrats were busy fighting the Democratic machine in the city, holding lively meetings in Jefferson Hall. There Mr. George was invited to speak, and he fearlessly demanded the abolition of custom houses. Andrew McLean, then managing editor of the "Eagle," but now editor of the "Brooklyn Citizen," says of that meeting:

"I had read 'Progress and Poverty' with deep pleasure and had reviewed it in the 'Eagle.' Time and again I discussed it with the more thoughtful men in the office. We greeted it as giving clear expression to those vague and misty thoughts that had been floating in our minds. I had not met Mr. George and did not know what he looked like. One night during the Hancock campaign I dropped into Jefferson Hall while a mass meeting was being held, without knowing precisely who were to speak. I was tired out with newspaper and election work and was glad to find a seat out of the way, and must admit that I drowsed during the remarks of some of our more or less familiar Brooklyn men. Presently a new voice commenced, and the abrupt, direct, clear-cut sentences, together with the radical meaning they bore, startled me. I stood up and looked at the new

---

[1] Speech in Birmingham, England, Jan. 23, 1884.

speaker. He was a short, sturdy man, with scant hair and full reddish beard. I had never before seen him. But I could not mistake his style of speech. I said to myself: 'Thou art the man! There most certainly is the author of that book "Progress and Poverty."' I did no more drowsing, and after the speech was over I went and introduced myself to Mr. George."

This speech of Henry George was a rarity in the campaign. Democratic speakers generally dodged the tariff question, and General Hancock himself pronounced it a "local issue." Mr. George believed that Hancock's defeat, which was by a very narrow vote, was due to this evasion.

After election Mr. George was still at sea about his plans. His wife, in California, wishing to lighten his burden had taken boarders, and his oldest boy was working in a printing office there. George wrote to Taylor (October 12): "I shall not go back to California, unless for something. I don't know precisely what I shall do, but something will open. . . . Don't think me a Micawber. I shall go to work if I have to go to the case."

He did not have to go to the printer's case; yet for a time he had to break a resolution not to seek or to accept employment that would require the publication of any of his work unsigned. Shortly before his death he said of this 1880 period:

"Mr. Appleton informed me that among the men he esteemed of great reputation who had expressed admiration of 'Progress and Poverty' was Abram S. Hewitt, a wealthy man and a Member of Congress; and when Mr. Hewitt came from Europe I got a communication from him asking to see me. I responded. He said some good things of the ability shown in 'Progress and Poverty' and that he would like to get me to do some work that he had not time to do himself, on an investigation commission's report that he intended to make to Congress. I needed work and could not refuse to put what ability I had at his service, with the understanding that I was to do faithfully what he required of me and to keep the matter secret, allowing him to make whatever use of it he might see fit over his own signature in his report."[1]

To Taylor, George wrote confidentially at the time (November 20, 1880) :

"I have taken a job from Hewitt to prepare a Congressional report—the labour investigation. Have agreed to give him three hours a day for $50 per week, till the thing is done, or either of us is dissatisfied. So, raising a little money in advance, I have taken a room. . . . My job begins to-morrow. Before it gets through, unless it should terminate suddenly, I shall have got my feet down. I shall get, first thing, a suit of clothes, and make some acquaintances."

As will be seen, other writing interrupted the Hewitt work, which ended, as noted in a letter to Taylor (March 6, 1881) :

"I took my matter down to Hewitt and read it to him. He was *much* pleased with it and laid out what he wanted done in the further steps; but when I asked him for another $100 he changed his tune, thought it was costing too much, and that he would stop. I told him I was very glad, that I felt I was working too cheap, but that having undertaken it I had not wished to say anything. So I stopped, though it was inconvenient to do so right then, as I had laid my plans on getting another $100 to-day. I got the first $100 of

---

[1] Roused by some public remarks made by Mr. Hewitt during the 1897 New York Mayoralty campaign, Mr. George dictated this statement to a stenographer, but subsequently concluded that its publication then was not appropriate. His death soon followed and it never appeared.

course. It really ought to have been more under our agreement, but I had that uncomfortable feeling that prevents you from making out your bills in first-class style, and though I had intended the $100 to be only on account, said nothing about any more."

The best information as to the way "Progress and Poverty" was going and other matters of interest is found in correspondence with Taylor.

November 20, 1880.

"I did feel depressed when I wrote you before. But it was not so much on account of circumstances. I am in my way of thinking a good deal of a Stoic. Adverse fortune does not much depress me. What always worries me is the thought that *I* might have done better—that it is myself who is to blame—and it seemed to me then as if I had been fooling away my time very largely. The fact of course is that I have been labouring under many disadvantages. However, there is no use in talking about that.

"I found when I got here that the book had had nothing like a fair start in the East, and the political campaign seemed to check its sale. I think now that it is going to start off. The first copies of the paper [75 cent] edition were received in the store this afternoon, and one will go to you by the mail which follows this. The preface bothered me very much. I wrote two or three—possibly enough for ten—and finally throwing it all aside, came down to a simple summary of the book.[1]

"I suppose you saw the 'Atlantic Monthly's' double-barrelled notice. . . .

"I got to-day a letter from Wm. D. LeSueur of Ontario, who has an article in the July 'Science Monthly.' I gave him a copy of the book when I met him here, and I attach a good deal of importance to his opinion, for he is a man of weight. . . . He started in, of

---

[1] Preface appearing in the fourth and all subsequent editions of " Progress and Poverty."

course, all against it, for, in addition to previous pre-dilections, Goldwin Smith, for whom he has a good deal of respect, sat down on it. But he writes me that he has *never* read a book with so much interest; that during the last few days while he was reading the last part he could think of nothing else; that he is a thorough con-vert, with the exception that he thinks the men to whom the State has sold lands ought to get some recom-pense, though he admits that there would be infinitely less injustice in giving them nothing than in continuing the present system; and that now his most ardent desire is to be a co-worker for the destruction of private prop-erty in land. . . .   In short he wants to be counted in, and proposes to begin the campaign in Canada. Now here is a man who in my opinion is worth half the college professors in the United States.

"I showed the letter to Youmans, who has a very great opinion of LeSueur, and he at the same time was reading a letter from another man, Professor Ellis, I believe, of whom he has also a great opinion, and to whom he had given a copy of 'P. and P.'   Ellis also said it was a *most* remarkable book—the most profound and original book on such subjects yet produced in America; that it ought to be immediately translated into German (he had just returned from three years there) and that for his part he proposed to write a review for —— (some unpronounceable name).   Youmans proposed to have these letters copied, that he might send them to Kegan Paul [publisher] of London, to whom he wrote a few days ago in reference to an English edition.

"Did I tell you that Michael Davitt pledged the Land League to push it in Great Britain? I shall send him copies by Tuesday's steamer. . . .

"I lecture in Hudson (N. Y.) on the 6th, beginning a 'star course.'   I am to be followed by David A. Wells, Park Godwin and Eaton (Civil-Service Reformer).

December 18, 1880.

"I got to-day copies of the German translation, as far as out—8 numbers to beginning of Book XI. It is very neatly and tastefully gotten up. I also got a long letter from the publisher. He says it will be a success, and that a number of long reviews are being prepared. The whole will be out this month. . . .

"I dined with Albert S. Bolles, author of 'Financial History,' etc., on Tuesday. Last night I dined with Dana of the 'Sun,' the company consisting of his family, Hazeltine, the reviewer, John Swinton and myself. He lives in magnificent style. I have plenty of chance to go into company, but have hitherto kept out of it; for until last week I had only my old clothes, and last night felt rather out of place, when seated on the right of the hostess, yet the only man in the room in a business suit. However!

"My wife thinks she can get along cheaper at boarding than keeping house, and so I have told her to sell out. . . . So life goes. My pleasant little home—that I was *so* comfortable in—is gone, and I am afloat at 42, poorer than at 21. I do not complain; but there is some bitterness in it."

January 4, 1881.

" . . . About the book. *At last*, it begins to look as though it had really taken hold. When I came East I found that it had hardly got started here. And during the campaign and until the last two weeks in December it went very slow. But then a movement began, and on the last day of the year every copy of the previous editions and every copy of the 1,000 of the cheap edition were gone, and orders and inquiries came piling in from every quarter. Appleton & Co. begin to realise for the first time that I have been telling them the truth, and that they have got hold of a book capable of an enormous sale; and now they are beginning to open out. . . .

"Comparatively speaking, the success of the book is already tremendous—for, so far as I can learn, no book on political economy has ever yet been published in the United States (or to my astonishment, I learn in England either) that has sold 1,000 copies in the first year (unless forced into the schools), and in fact the entire sales of most of them are to be counted in hundreds, not thousands. My book is getting to be regarded here as *the phenomenal* one, and such publishers as Holt are already regretting that they did not take it when they had a chance.

"And to-day I get the first ringing note from the radicals of England in a copy of the Leeds 'Independent,' which declares it a book which every Englishman ought to read, and proposes to receive subscriptions for it.[1] The future of the book is, I think, secure.

" . . . I want to go and see John Russell Young. His wife is dying. Poor fellow! his cup seems filled to the brim.

"P. S.   Mrs. Young is dead. I add this in Young's room, where I am staying to receive his brother-in-law from Philadelphia. . . . General Grant has left, after a long stay. That is one good thing about the old fellow; he is true to his friends."

January 21, 1881.

"The book is a success. The sale sems now to have commenced in good earnest, and orders are coming from all parts of the country—in ones, two and tens and twenties. Better still, Kegan Paul, who has hardly more than got his 500 [from Appleton] writes that he will probably want more and arranges a cypher so that he can cable. The German notices are *way* up. It has at last got a show in Europe. . . .

"You will see by the 'Popular Science' this month that Youmans has at last read Book X. of 'Progress and Poverty' ['The Law of Human Progress']. He himself is the best example of the need of that book. He would not take the trouble to vote at election time, said that he should have to slowly evolute, and has told me several times that there was no use in trying to fight evils of which he himself is as conscious as any one, as to get rid of them is a matter of thousands of years!"

---

[1] The editor of the Leeds "Independent" was Dr. F. R. Lees, the distinguished temperance advocate. He had read while on a visit to United States a copy of the "Author's Edition" of "Progress and Poverty."

January 23, 1881.

"Slowly but steadily everything seems opening to me. If I live I am going to fill a large place and do a large work—that now is clear.

"Do you see how the 'Sun' is opening up the taxation question and advertising me? Chip in, if you have leisure, with some short communications. There is some satisfaction in writing for a paper that prints over 120,000. I suppose you have seen the 'Popular Science' for this month. Youmans says I don't make converts; I find them in all directions. Every day I get letters."

To the picture of conditions at this time, which these letters from George to Taylor give, must be added a description from memory which John Russell Young wrote the day following his friend's death.

"These early New York days were of extreme and honourable poverty. I saw Henry George a great deal —was almost a daily companion. It was a daring experiment—this unknown gentleman, with no aid but his own high spirit, nothing in his carpet-bag but one book of gospel, coming at 42 to make his way into the heart of mighty Babylon. The more I studied George under heavy conditions the more I admired him. His ability and his courage; his honesty, independence and intellectual power were those of a leader of men.

"We took walks on the Battery, whither we went under the flush of strenuous midnight work, the great city at peace and no companions this side of the stars; strolls in the Park, in Westchester and the suburbs of Brooklyn—the brave, intrepid soul wrapped up in his book and smiling upon fate. . . .

"George was resolute in his creed. He gave it to you as the truth to be accepted, in a sense of worship, a dogma of political infallibility. 'Does this not mean war? Can you, unless when dealing with craven conditions among men, hope to take land from its owners without war?' 'I do not see,' said George, 'that a mus-

ket need be fired. But if necessary, war be it, then.
There was never a holier cause. No, never a holier
cause.'

"Here was the gentlest and kindest of men, who
would shrink from a gun fired in anger, ready for universal war rather than that his gospel should not be
accepted. It was the courage which as has been written makes one a majority."

Mr. George had for a while stopped work on the Hewitt
report to write an article on the Irish Land Question for
"Appleton's Journal." The subject growing on him, he
kept on with his writing until he had a little book of seventeen chapters. In this brief work he gave the first striking
evidence of a high order of practical ability, showing that,
besides the genius to formulate a philosophy, he had the
wisdom to avail himself of passing events to apply it.

On April 20, 1879, the month after the completion of
"Progress and Poverty," Michael Davitt, fresh from seven
years of penal servitude in an English prison for devotion
to the principle of Irish independence, had organised a
mass meeting in Irishtown, County Mayo, Ireland, for
John Ferguson and Thomas Brennan to address, in denunciation of the landlord tyranny and rack-renting that were
driving the western peasantry into starvation. With the
cry of "The land for the people," he struck a spark that
kindled a spreading fire. The failure of physical resistance to the English power, on the one hand, and of Parliamentary action by Parnell and his legislative colleagues,
on the other, drove all the Irish faction into Davitt's
movement, to make common war on the landlords. This
landlord class, though comparatively small and living for
the most part in England, not only made a heavy rent
charge upon the toil of the labouring masses, but wielded
pretty much all political power, filling all local offices,

such as sheriffs', grand jurors', and justices of the peace, besides through their class interests controlling legislation in the Imperial British Parliament.   In the fall of 1879 the Irish National Land League was formally organised in Dublin, with Parnell as president and Davitt as one of the honorary secretaries.   It was to supersede the Home Rule League, of which Parnell had been the head, and was to be the official organisation of so much of the Irish Parliamentary party as acknowledged his leadership.   Its immediate purpose was to "bring about a reduction of rackrents."   It was also, at least, so far as Parnell and his particular adherents were concerned, to facilitate the creation of a peasant proprietary, in enabling tenants to become owners of their holdings by paying a "fair" rent for a limited number of years.   There was division over this latter purpose, however.   Davitt, the fire and soul of the extending organisation, continued to proclaim the principle of "the land for the people," including in its benefits, though somewhat vaguely, not only all the tenant farmers, but the much greater class of agricultural labourers as well.   And Patrick Ford, of the "Irish World," a weekly newspaper published in New York and devoted to Irish and Irish-American affairs, the great organising factor in the United States, took his stand on the old Irish doctrine that the land of Ireland "belongs to the whole Irish people .   .   .   without exception of persons," and he demanded that it "be restored to its owners with all possible speed."

While these differing principles and purposes were put forward by the respective factions, all united to defend those Irish agricultural tenants who were threatened with eviction for refusing to pay "unjust" rents.   This was striking the ruling class on the "sensitive pocket nerve," and both sides prepared for war.   The Irish Land League needed money. Parnell, with Dillon, came to the United States, and with the truly powerful backing of the "Irish World," spoke to great meetings in sixty-two cities, addressed the House of Representatives at Washington, collected a war chest of $200,000, and before leaving in March, 1880, formally organised the auxiliary American Land League.

Knowing that Parnell was a land-owner, with views and feelings of the land-owning class, and that he had been educated in a conservative English university, George did not expect much in the way of radical action from him, though he believed radical public opinion would sweep him along. But to Davitt, born a Mayo peasant, and by instinct a "man of the people," George looked with high hope, and when Davitt came to America on Land League business, towards the fall of 1880, George met him, with the result, as we have seen in the letter to Taylor: "Davitt pledges the Land League to push it ["Progress and Poverty"] in Great Britain."

Mr. George perceived that the Irish rent-war was fast making that country the theatre in the world-wide drama of the land question. He therefore addressed himself to it in his pamphlet, under the title of "The Irish Land Question: What It Involves, and How Alone It can be Settled." He aimed to show that the only solution lay in observing the principle of common ownership in land, by taking, through the medium of taxation, the rental value for all the people. Thus the advantage that the rack-renting landlord class had hitherto possessed would be transferred to the people as a whole, and no one would get any advantage as a mere landholder. But he did not have Ireland alone in his mind. Said he:[1]

---

[1] "The Land Question," Chap. XVII (Memorial Edition, pp. 106, 107).

"What I urge the men of Ireland to do is to proclaim without limitation or evasion, that the land, of natural right, is the common property of the whole people, and to propose practical measures which will recognise this right in Great Britain as well as in Ireland. What I urge the Land Leagues of the United States to do is to announce this great principle as of universal application; to give their movement a reference to America as well as to Ireland; to broaden and deepen and strengthen it by making it a movement for the regeneration of the world—a movement which shall concentrate and give shape to aspirations that are stirring among all nations."

The pamphlet was finished at the end of February and was at once published by Appleton in New York, and a month later by William Reeves in London, John Haywood & Sons in Manchester and Cameron & Ferguson in Glasgow.

Mr. George had meanwhile brought his family East, and was with them boarding at Fort Washington in the upper part of New York. At times he was very hard pressed for money and once drew on Taylor in far-off San Francisco for the sum of twenty dollars. We quote again from the Taylor correspondence.

"'The Irish Land Question' has been noticed magnificently: 2½ columns in 'Times,' 2½ in 'Sun,' 1 in 'Express,' 2¼ in 'Star,' 2½ in 'Charleston News,' etc. And the astonishing thing is the goodness of the comments. Nothing like the back action of the early notices of 'Progress and Poverty.' I am getting famous, if I am not making money. I have two magazine articles and a cyclopedia article to write[1] and if that 'Herald' thing does not turn, can, I think, go on the

---

[1] On " Chinese Immigration " for Lalor's " Cyclopedia of Political Science, Political Economy," etc.

'Brooklyn Eagle.' I am going to give the 'Moses' lecture before long.

"About the railroad people: McClatchy of Sacramento told my wife that Leland Stanford (to whom he sent 'Progress and Poverty') read it while sick, and told him that he had become 'a disciple of Henry George.' If that means anything, it will tell."

May 12, 1881.

"Inclosed find check for $20. . . . You do not know, and I cannot readily tell you how much this little accommodation has been to me. It is not so much the want of money as the mental effect it produces—the morbid condition. The man who does not understand that, does not know how it is possible for people to commit suicide. This thing has weighted me very much. Could I have felt free and been relieved of the terrible anxiety, I could have in the same time accomplished many times as much. But yet it has seemed as though a Providence helped me through.

"When I drew on you for this $20 it seemed my darkest hour. I was weak and weary in mind and body. . . .

"Article of mine in 'Appleton's' for this month. Got pay for that—$50. 'Scribner's' will have an article pitching into me, which I hear privately is by Professor Sumner. None of those people have dared attack openly yet."

May 25, 1881.

"Why do you allow the papers there to abuse me without sending me a copy? To be abused and not to know of it is almost as bad as not to be abused at all. . . .

"Yes: look at the Republican party, and also look at the Democratic party! It is pot and kettle. I am done.

" . . . I shall have article in 'Appleton's' for June and in 'North American' for July—'pot boilers' both."[1]

---

[1] "The Taxation of Land Values," "Appleton's Journal," June, 1881; "Common Sense in Taxation," "North American Review," July, 1881.

Meanwhile Mr. George had begun to lecture. Early in May (1881) he spoke in Chickering Hall, New York, and shortly afterwards in Historical Hall, Brooklyn; in both places, of course, on the land question. The weather on both occasions was warm, but nevertheless he made $130 on the first and nearly $200 on the second. A lot of young converts managed the New York lecture. Rev. R. Heber Newton, of All Soul's Episcopal Church, introduced Mr. George, having a few days before found that this was the friend of his boyhood. Andrew McLean, of the "Eagle," arranged for the Brooklyn lecture. Through him Thomas G. Shearman, who had won a reputation at the New York bar, as a skilful corporation lawyer and as the successful defender and devoted friend of Henry Ward Beecher, was interested in this lecture and met Mr. George for the first time. It was the beginning of a life-long friendship. Mr. Shearman had but just read "Progress and Poverty" and had been deeply impressed with it; but he doubted whether rent alone would suffice to pay all taxes, while he objected to the use of the word "confiscation." He was an aggressive free trader and had spent much time and money in agitating against the protective tariff idea. But he had not yet fully grasped the fact that *all* tariffs and all indirect taxes were unjust, because they tax poverty far more than wealth; nor did "Progress and Poverty" call his attention to this. He now studied the subject on statistical lines; and in a few months starting from an opposite point of view and on an entirely independent line of reasoning he arrived at substantially the same conclusions with Henry George. Soon after their meeting, by his invitation, Mr. George addressed the Brooklyn Revenue Reform Club, of which Henry Ward Beecher was president; and before long the distinguished lawyer was in his own way working on the same radical lines as Mr. George, with an energy that caused the latter to write to him: "You suggest to me what was said of Brougham, 'a steam-engine in breeches.'"

In this connection it may be mentioned that Mr. George joined the New York Free Trade Club through one of its active young men, Poultney Bigelow, son of John Bigelow, ex-United States Minister to France. Young Bigelow was a convert to "Progress and Poverty" and of his abilities and prospects for influence in the community Mr. George thought highly. Soon after joining the club the author attended a Free Trade Club dinner. He was surprised and disgusted at the lack of radical spirit manifested in the speeches, it being evident that with the generality of members "free trade" meant only "tariff reform." He wrote to Bigelow, who could not get there, that being called upon to speak, he gave them "four minutes' worth of horse sense."

It was with important results that Henry George now began to lecture before the Land League organisations, writing Taylor (June 13), "I talk here [Saint Albans, Vermont] to-morrow night, and then go to Montreal (two lectures), Ottawa and Toronto, and four or five places in New York on the way back. Rutland and this place are $25 each; Montreal and Ottawa, speculation; Toronto, $50, and the others $25 each. Good enough though to see the country and get my hand in." But "getting his hand in" involved, as most other things did with him, concentrated effort. Here, for instance, are two of the casual diary notes:

"Montreal, June 16.—Lecture 'Irish Land Question' a total failure. Don't know whether to attribute it to bad physical condition, or that I cannot get up enthusiasm in going over same ground twice. This certain, that I should have written it beforehand. Will try to do better to-morrow. Feel very bad, but must try to pluck victory from defeat."

"Montreal, June 17.—Did it. Best ever have done. Astonished and pleased them all."

The lecture programme in the North was cut short and diverted West—Mr. George making a trip to San Francisco with his wife and younger daughter to attend to some private business of a friend.[1] On August 11 he lectured there on the land question in Metropolitan Temple, but now instead of the "beggarly array of empty benches" which had greeted him while he was writing "Progress and Poverty," a large audience was attracted by the world-renown his book was winning. The early friends and believers were there and were filled with cheer and enthusiasm over this, to them, remarkable manifestation of change in the public mind. But even this was not without its shadow for the lecturer. On the afternoon preceding the discourse he sent a note to Taylor: "One of my creditors has been after me, and I fear some of them may make an attempt to garnishee proceeds to-night. I should like to consult you, but cannot go down." However, this

---

[1] Mr. George had found in the spring that he was not without honour in California, for at the time that John F. Miller, Republican, was elected by the California legislature to the United States Senate, Henry George received two complimentary votes, those of George C. Gorham of San Francisco and Warren S. Chase of Santa Barbara and Ventura, the latter saying, in making the nomination : " I shall name neither a lawyer nor a soldier, but a political economist who has distinguished himself and acquired a national reputation ; who is throughout the world recognised as the peer of such intellects as Ricardo, John Stuart Mill and Malthus." Though Mr. George wrote to James V. Coffey, who apprised him of the occurrence, " I presume that is about as near as I shall ever come to being elected to anything," yet he appreciated the compliment.

matter was arranged and before Mr. George left San Francisco he had paid off all but a small portion of the old debts there. On the eve of his departure for the East his intimate friends gave him an informal little dinner at Campi's restaurant on Clay Street, in the centre of his old activities, and sent him off with a fervent God speed.

On his return to New York the Appleton people had surprising news for him. One thousand copies of the best edition of "Progresss and Poverty" had been ordered by Francis G. Shaw, a man of means and advanced years, living quietly on Staten Island, New York Bay. One of his daughters had married George William Curtis, the distinguished author, editor and orator, and another into the family of James Russell Lowell, the poet and United States Minister to England. Mr. Shaw was best known in some circles for the substantial nature of his benevolent works. George wrote to Taylor about him (September 7) :

"The book they tell me has been selling splendidly. One item is that Francis G. Shaw ordered one thousand copies to place in the libraries throughout the country. I saw him to-day   He is the father of the Colonel Shaw who was killed leading coloured troops in the war and was 'buried with his niggers.'[1] He says he had become hopeless on social questions till sixty days ago he got my book. 'The light broke upon him,' and he wants to spread it.

"You, better than any one else, can understand how this gratifies me. He did not want to be known; but I told him it was the highest compliment and best advertisement of the book, and the knowledge of it would spread as many copies as the donation.

"I see too, by the English papers that Alfred Russell Wallace has been indorsing 'Progress and Poverty'

---

[1] The Colonel Shaw to whom the splendid bronze memorial has been raised in Boston, Mass.

which he says 'is undoubtedly the most remarkable and important work of the present century.'

"So the seed has begun to sprout."

Following hard upon the Shaw matter came what Mr. George considered of even greater importance. To Taylor (September 12) he said:

"I have concluded an arrangement with the 'Irish World,' by which I shall go to Ireland and England in about two weeks: I will take my wife and two daughters with me, leaving the boys here in New York. The engagement is for three months, but of course, when I get over there I may stay longer. My terms with the 'World' are very good, considering how much I want to make the trip. I am to get passage both ways for myself and family and $60 per week. Thus the chance I have long waited for opens. It will be a big thing for me. I think the biggest I have had yet."

A crisis had now come in Irish affairs. The Conservative Government going out, had left the legacy of the agrarian trouble in Ireland for the incoming Liberal Government, headed by Gladstone, to cope with. Lord Cowper was the new Irish Viceroy, and William E. Forster, who had done so much for popular education in England by the extension of the board schools, became the Chief Secretary. The Irish landlords went clamouring to them about the difficulty of getting rents from old tenants and the intimidation of, and in some instances violence to, new tenants, through the workings of the Land League. Forster and Cowper had both sought to secure some legal relief for tenants; but both urged the passage of coercive measures to repress the violence of injured tenants. The writ of habeas corpus was suspended; and hundreds of men, known or "suspected" to be connected with the popular movement, were imprisoned without trial. Davitt had some time before been arrested and sent back to Portland prison on the ground of violation of the conditions of his ticket-of-leave. And now the arrest of Parnell was threatened.

The proposal for correspondence with the "Irish World," had come to Mr. George, but he had been unable to accept until Mr. Shaw, seeing in this an opportunity to help the new cause in which he had enlisted, put at his disposal a little money that enabled him to meet some small obligations and make the start. But he was delayed until the middle of October and meanwhile he wrote to Mr. Shaw (October 9):

> " 'Truth' to-day commences the republication of 'Progress and Poverty.' I am very glad of this. From all I hear its circulation is between 75,000 and 100,000. This gives an enormous audience, and largely of a kind that cannot be reached in any other way. . . .
>
> "One of the firm of Kegan Paul & Co., the London publishers of 'Progress and Poverty,' was in Appleton's yesterday. He says the book at first was dead as a log; but has now picked up and is selling rapidly. He anticipates a very large sale."

"Truth" was a New York, one cent, poor man's daily paper. Its chief editorial writer was Louis F. Post, a young man bred to the bar and possessing an extremely fair and open mind. He had skimmed "Progress and Poverty," formed hasty and loose opinions and written flippantly about it; but returning to a closer examination, he had gradually changed his views, until the book whispered to him, "Leave thy nets and follow me," and he obeyed. Thenceforward Henry George had no more devoted friend or thorough and stanch disciple. The author was asked to permit "Truth" to republish the book serially. Though compensation was not offered, he consented, glad in this way to "spread the light" among working men.[1]

But a matter of domestic consideration engaged Mr. George's mind before setting off. His two sons were to stay behind; the problem was how to employ them during the separation. The younger one, Dick, it was settled was to return to school, and with the elder, Harry, the question was whether he should be put in a newspaper office or be sent to Harvard College, where special considerations at the time had let down the bars to poor men's sons. In talking the matter over with the boy the father weighed it in this way: "Going to college, you will make life friendships, but you will come out filled with much that will have to be unlearned. Going to newspaper work, you will come in touch with the practical world, will be getting a profession and learning to make yourself useful." So the decision was for newspaper work. An opening was made on the "Brooklyn Eagle" by Andrew McLean, and the boy was put to the first small reporting. To assist him in learning to write, the father gave his son four rules: First, to make short sentences; second, to avoid adjectives; third, to use small words; and fourth—a general rule—not to attempt "fine" writing; to say as simply and as briefly as possible all that should be said, and then to stop.

Before sailing Mr. George went to Philadelphia to bid good-bye to his parents, who were now advanced in years. He was accompanied by his boys part of the way and was in a meditative mood, saying, as if half to himself: "When I had finished 'Progress and Poverty' I was certain that

---

[1] Afterwards the "Chicago Express" followed "Truth's" example and printed the book serially.

I had written a great book and that the time would come when the truth in it would set the world afire. But I could not feel confident of seeing in my own lifetime more than perhaps a hundred persons who would grasp it and believe in it. Yet now, only two years after its publication, it is being talked of all over the world; and men are rising up everywhere to hail it!"

All the preparations being at length made, Henry George, with his wife and his two daughters, on Saturday, October 15, 1881, sailed on the steamship *Spain* of the National line, for Liverpool.

CHAPTER III.

THE IRISH LAND LEAGUE MOVEMENT.

1881-1882.   AGE, 42-43.

TWO days before Mr. George sailed for Europe news had come that Parnell and two other Parliamentarians, John Dillon and J. J. O'Kelly, had been sent to jail, which swelled the list of political prisoners under the crimes or coercion act to something like five hundred. While George was on the sea, Patrick Ford of the "Irish World," cabled to Patrick Egan, the Land League treasurer, suggesting that the League retaliate with a manifesto calling upon agricultural tenants to pay no rent whatever until the Government would withdraw the coercion act. Egan approved of the idea and transmitted it to Parnell in Kilmainham jail. The latter disliked to strike so radical a blow at the landlord interests, but nevertheless he yielded to the necessity of using the only weapon left in his hands. The no-rent manifesto was accordingly sent out in the name of the Land League. At that the Government advanced another step and suppressed the League; whereupon Patrick Egan went to Paris to protect the war chest, while the women, headed by Miss Anna Parnell, organised the Ladies' Land League to carry on the field-work.

As has been said, Mr. George sailed for Liverpool, but

he changed his plans and got off at Queenstown when the ship put into that Irish port. He hurried to Dublin, after stopping a few hours in Cork.

"With an area of only 32,000 square miles and a population of little more than five millions," Mr. George said at one time, "Ireland now required for its government in a time of profound peace 15,000 military constables and 40,000 picked troops." The regular army and the Royal Irish Constabulary, the soldier-police, he described in a few words in his first letter to the "Irish World" (November 3) :

"The police are a stalwart body of men, clad in comfortable, dark-green uniforms; the soldiers are the pick of English and Scotch regiments—strong, active men, in the very prime of life, wearing smart, clean uniforms. . . . Every now and again you meet a detachment marching down the street with rifles on their shoulders and blankets on their backs, on their way to the country to guard somebody's castle, or help evict somebody's tenants."

Touching the nature of the government, he said:

"It is not merely a despotism; it is a despotism sustained by alien force, and wielded in the interests of a privileged class, who look upon the great masses of the people as intended but to be hewers of their wood and drawers of their water. . . .

"I leave out of consideration for the moment the present extraordinary condition of things when constitutional guarantees for personal liberty are utterly suspended, and any man in the country may he hauled off to prison at the nod of an irresponsible dictator. I speak of the normal times and the ordinary workings of government."

But, wrote Mr. George, "the people have become accustomed to act together" in wielding the weapon of passive resistance. It is from his private letters to Patrick Ford that we get the clearest and most intimate view of some phases of the movement. For instance, on November 10 he wrote:

" . . . The truth is that I landed here at a most unfortunate time for my purpose, and have found more difficulty in 'getting my feet down' than I could have imagined would be possible. . . .

"The first intimation I got was on the tender [in Cork Harbour] when the agent who had the passenger list from the steamer, called me aside and asked if I was Henry George, and telling me he was a Land Leaguer, told me I was expected. He wanted to change my name [on our trunks] telling me I should certainly be dogged from the moment I landed and possibly be arrested. I, of course, refused any such kindness, telling him that I did not propose to disguise myself and that the whole detective force was welcome to listen to all I had to say.

" . . . As I said before, it seems hard for a stranger to get to the bottom, and things change. But one impression has not changed. I got indignant as soon as I landed, and I have not got over it yet. This is the most damnable government that exists to-day out of Russia—Miss Helen Taylor [step-daughter of John Stuart Mill] says, 'outside of Turkey.'

" . . . As to the clergy: Croke struck a harder blow than Gladstone. It was as Dr. Nulty said to me, '*Et tu Brute.*'[1]

"If I had told you what the general statement of the men I met at first was, it would have been that the clergy were the greatest force the Land League had to meet. It is really better than that. The majority of the clergy are, I am inclined to think, with the people

---

[1] Archbishop Croke became radical later and gave encouragement to the popular cause.

and the no-rent fight, but they are for the most part
'bull-dozed' and the others are most active. . . .

"Miss Helen Taylor came [to Dublin] last week to
propose that she should . . . take charge, letting
Miss Parnell go to Holyhead and direct from there.
Her idea was that as soon as the Government found
that the Ladies' League was really doing effective work
in keeping up the spirit of the people they would swoop
down on the women, too, and that it would hurt the
Government more to arrest her [an English woman]
in Ireland than it would to arrest an Irish woman, and
would hurt them much more to arrest Miss Parnell in
England than it would to arrest her in Ireland. (Miss
Taylor, who is one of the most intelligent women I
ever met, if not the most intelligent, says the existence
of the Gladstone Government is involved; that they will
stop at nothing, rather than lose power.) . . . Miss
Parnell's objection was that she could not be spared.

" . . . I am certain that everything is working
together to the end we both desire—the radicalisation of
the movement and the people. . . .

"Bishop Nulty told me that . . . the English Catholics
and the Irish Catholic land-owners had been deluging
Rome with complaints.   But, he said, the Pope is a man
of strong common sense, and had refused so far to interfere."

Mr. George had not been long in Dublin before four
committees waited on him to ask him to deliver a public
speech.   Edward Dwyer Gray, proprietor of the "Freeman's Journal," advised him to speak in England first,
as that would give him more influence; but writing Ford
on the matter (November 10), George said: "My sympathies go so strongly with this people that it would seem
to me cowardly to refuse anything that might encourage
them; and besides at this time it is *extremely* important
to get them into line. . . . I will not talk politics;
but I will not stint the truth."   Mr. George had not yet

come to his full powers as a speaker and his wife wrote to their sons (November 10) that she was very anxious about the lecture. "I earnestly hope it will be a success," said she, "but somehow I think he will suit an English audience better, as he is unimpassioned like them, and not demonstrative like Irishmen." Mr. George spoke on the 14th. The result satisfied him, as he wrote to Ford (November 15):

> "My lecture last night was a grand success, and I had the hardest work possible to avoid being dragged through the streets. It was, in fact, the only chance the Dublin people had had since the suppression of the Land League to show their enthusiasm."

The demonstration after the lecture to which Mr. George alludes was a custom with which he became abruptly acquainted when a crowd surged about his carriage and attempted to unhitch the horse, with the intention of themselves drawing the vehicle. He got almost indignant. He ordered the driver to whip up and gave him a liberal fee when he cleared the crowd. When addressing another Dublin audience some months afterwards Mr. George referred to the incident. He said the custom was undemocratic and savoured too much of the subservience to which through the long generations they had been habituated in giving rent and thanks for the privilege of living on the common soil. The audience applauded to the echo. The people were ready to hear plain speech and to embrace new ideas. A few days after the Dublin lecture (January 1, 1882) George wrote to Taylor: "The majority of the Irish don't know yet how to get at what they want. Like all great movements, it is a blind groping forward. But it is the beginning of the revolution, sure."

Bishop Nulty had been made to feel the displeasure of

the higher Catholic authorities for his by this time famous pastoral letter declaring common rights in land, and was probably secretly reproved for an interview with him which Mr. George had published in the "Irish World," and which in garbled form was cabled back to a London paper. Following this George wrote to Ford (December 28):

"I presume we have at last got Dr. Nulty into the trouble he has been so anxious to avoid. One of the reasons I went to Mullingar was to sound him about the publication of his platform [from the pastoral letter].[1] I believe I told you that I got the Ladies [Land League] to order a lot printed just as it appeared in the 'Irish World.' Alfred Webb, who was printing them, suggested to me that perhaps the Doctor would not like it, and that he was doing such good work that we ought to be very careful not to embarrass him.

"So I did not ask his permission, for I did not want

---

[1] This passage from the Rt. Rev. Dr. Thomas Nulty's pastoral letter to the clergy and laity of the Diocese of Meath, ran :

"The land of every country is the gift of its Creator to the people of that country ; it is the patrimony and inheritance bequeathed to them by their common Father, out of which they can, by continuous labour and toil, provide themselves with everything they require for their maintenance and support, for their material comfort and enjoyment. God was perfectly free in the act by which He created us ; but, having created us, He bound himself by that act to provide us with the means *necessary* for our subsistence. The land is the only means of this kind now known to us.

"The land, therefore, of every country is the common property of the people of that country, because its real owner, the Creator who made it, has transferred it as a voluntary gift to them. *Terram autem dedit filiis hominum.* Now, as every individual in that country is a creature and child of God, and as all His creatures are equal in His sight, any settlement of the land of a country that would exclude the humblest man in that country from his share in the common inheritance would be not only an injustice and a wrong to that man, but, moreover, would be an impious resistance to the benevolent intentions of his Creator."

to commit him. I merely told him it was being done, and he made no objection.

"Well, the thing is beginning to tell. It is going all over the country and some of the priests are distributing it, and it is getting pasted up, and the Tory papers and all the English papers are reprinting it as an outrageous *official* declaration of communism from a Catholic bishop; and from all I have heard of their temper, I shall be surprised if the English prelates don't try to raise a row at Rome about it.

"But it is going to do an immense amount of good."

In the same letter George made some comments from his inside point of view upon persons in the movement and its management.

"There is a great amount of 'whigging' in this Land League movement, more than I thought before coming here. And I think this is especially true of the leaders. With very many of those for whom it is doing the most, the 'Irish World' is anything but popular. And I have felt from the beginning as if there was a good deal of that feeling about myself. We are regarded as dangerous allies. I have, of course, never pretended to see or notice this, though I have had some curiosity about it, as to how much was due to conservatism and how much to influences from America. But come what may, this movement is going to assume a much more radical phase. In spite of everything, the *light is* spreading."

Mr. George then related how when "United Ireland," the official league organ, was seized, the plates of the number just to be issued were got off to his lodgings and hidden under his bed, whence they were sent in a trunk to London, where the League managers, instead of putting them to press at once, lost several days and much money in negotiating about the matter. Ultimately "one paper was got out in London, and another totally different in

Dublin, and an edition from the Dublin plates worked off in Liverpool." He observed to Ford in a letter from London:

> "Some of them told me that this was splendid, as showing the Government that when one paper was suppressed three would spring up; but I told them that in my opinion the Government would laugh at such work and see how easy it was to make them spend their resources.
>
> "   .   .   .   To sum up: It appears to me that there is in many things a lack of management, and consequently, waste both of opportunities and resources.
>
> "Sometimes it seems to me as if a lot of small men had found themselves in the lead of a tremendous movement, and finding themselves lifted into importance and power they never dreamed of, are jealous of anybody else sharing the honour.
>
> "I do not refer to Parnell, who, I think from all I hear of him, is a first-class man, though he lacks qualities and powers in which Davitt is strong.
>
> "I wish I had got here before the suppression, that I might have seen the thing in free play.
>
> "Miss Parnell, from all I learn, is really an extraordinary executive and organiser, and the Ladies are and have been doing their work wonderfully well, considering all the difficulties.   .   .   .
>
> "Miss Taylor urged me not to return to Ireland, saying that I was greatly needed, and that the Government will certainly arrest me before long.   But while I won't put myself in the way of that, I don't feel like turning aside for fear of it.   My sympathies are so strongly with this fight against such tremendous odds of every kind that it is impossible for me not to feel myself in it."

It was at this time, when Mr. George was in London and his wife and daughters in Dublin, that Miss Parnell got word from a confidential source inside Dublin Castle that the Ladies' Land League was to be proscribed; that she and her able assistant, Miss Nannie Lynch, were to be arrested at once; and that one of the Dublin jails was actually being cleared out for the reception of the women. These two ladies needed no further hint; they immediately sped for London, Miss Lynch sending her official books to Mrs. George for safekeeping. The remaining ladies invited Mrs. George to preside that day over the regular business meeting of the Ladies' League. She never before had attempted to preside at any kind of a meeting and her embarrassment was heightened by the presence of men, whom she afterwards was told were Government detectives, and a number of reporters and correspondents. But the women triumphed. The absence of Miss Parnell and the appearance of an American woman in the chair completely nonplussed the Dublin Government officials and the Ladies' Land League escaped proscription.

Mr. George's post of special correspondent of the "Irish World," the mouthpiece, so to speak, of the Land League in America, the chief source of the "sinews of war," gave him an introduction to all the prominent men in the Irish movement, from Parnell in Kilmainham jail to Justin McCarthy in London and Patrick Egan in Paris, while his reputation as the author of "Progress and Poverty" and of "The Irish Land Question" gave him a standing outside political circles. He therefore had little difficulty in making acquaintances. But he quickly discovered that the members of the Irish Parliamentary party, while cordial enough at dinner parties and on other social occasions, and polished and polite under all circumstances, were always guarded in speaking with him on the affairs of the movement, and many of them absolutely uncommunicative. As time passed on this condition of aloofness grew.

Aside from these formal acquaintances, Mr. George while in Dublin formed some friendships of a deep and lasting kind. One of these was that of Dr. James E. Kelly, who, upon the American's arrival in the city in the period of national despondence consequent upon the arrest of the leaders, was one of the first persons to welcome him to Ireland. Dr. Kelly was thoroughly in sympathy with and made many sacrifices for the popular cause. During the Georges' stay in Dublin he frequently entertained them at his house and almost daily saw and talked with Mr. George on social or political matters, or on questions of philosophy.

Another warm Irish attachment formed at this time was with Rev. Thomas Dawson of the Catholic order of the Oblate Fathers, who then lived at Glencree. He had read "Progress and Poverty " and had become imbued with its spirit and with the belief that no matter what its author called himself, the final chapter of the book proved him to be essentially a Catholic. It was to Father Dawson that Mr. George subsequently wrote the letter touching his religious faith which has already been quoted.[1]

As we have seen, Miss Helen Taylor was another of the important acquaintances made in Dublin. Acquaintance strengthened into warm friendship, and when the Georges went to London in January they accepted her hearty invitation to share her hospitality at South Kensington. She possessed sufficient means to make her independent, and for years had been doing all in her power, with voice, pen and purse, to advance public ideas along the lines taught by her famous step-father, John Stuart Mill. She believed that were Mr. Mill alive he would have been heart and soul with the Irish in their struggle and would have

---

[1] Pages 311-312.

been among the first to greet "Progress and Poverty" as containing the truth, notwithstanding its contradiction of much that he had previously taught.

After spending several weeks with Miss Taylor, the Georges visited Mr. and Mrs. Henry M. Hyndman in Portland Place, and afterwards Mr. and Mrs. Thomas Briggs at Dulwich. Mr. Hyndman had long been one of the leading writers on the London press, but a too active sympathy with the Irish movement had caused him to be "boycotted." An intense socialist, he was president of the Democratic Federation, which propagated those doctrines in England. For a time he seemed hopeful of converting Mr. George to his views, while the American thought socialism in his friend was weakening. Hyndman had found at the British Museum a copy of a lecture by Thomas Spence on "The Real Rights of Man," delivered before the Philosophical Society of Newcastle, November 8, 1775, a year before the publication of Smith's "Wealth of Nations," and for which the Society, as Spence said, did him "the honour to expel him." In the lecture Spence proclaimed common rights in land and proposed that land values be taken for public purposes, all other taxes to be remitted. George had never heard of Spence and was delighted at the discovery. He urged Hyndman to publish the lecture in tract form, believing that it would do much good. Mrs. George suggested that this might prove disadvantageous to Mr. George, for people might say that if the idea of taxing land values had been proposed a hundred years before and had since been ignored by the world, there was little use of George in his "Progress and Poverty" trying to popularise the principle now. Her husband answered that most people hesitate to accept an idea thought to be new; that if the proposal in "Progress and Poverty" could be shown to be really an old one, it might make much more rapid way. And so he urged Hyndman to publish the lecture, which the latter did; while George himself sent a copy to Patrick Ford for publication in the "Irish World."

It was while they were guests of the Hyndmans that Mr. George met Herbert Spencer. Through the Hyndmans, Mr. and Mrs. George were invited to a reception at Mrs. (since Lady) Jeune's. It was a "London crush," the drawing-rooms thronged and many notables present, among them, Tennyson, tall, careless and dreamy—in appearance every inch a poet; and Browning, on this occasion at least, smart and dapper, and so far from appearing a great poet, looked, as Mrs. George said, "like a prosperous merchant draper." Mr. George admired both of these men, but was introduced to neither. He met Spencer, however, as soon as the latter appeared. This gave him real pleasure. He had been hearing stories of vanity in the English philosopher that he could scarcely credit, as he put him on a high plane, not because of the evolutionary philosophy, for it was that to which George referred when, in writing to Charles Nordhoff before leaving San Francisco, in 1879,[1] he said he would like sometime to write a book dissecting "this materialistic philosophy, which, with its false assumption of science, passes current with so many." But he had all along held Spencer as immovably against the institution of private property in land, and had in "Progress and Poverty" quoted from the English philosopher's scathing ninth chapter of "Social Statics." He, therefore, expected to find a man who, like himself, saw in the agrarian struggle in Ireland the raising of the question of land ownership and fundamental economic principles. Their conversation quickly

[1] Page 328.

turned to Ireland, for scarcely had they exchanged civilities when Spencer bluntly asked what George thought of Irish matters. The American condemned the Government and praised the League. Spencer burst into vehement dissent. "They," said he, meaning the imprisoned Land Leaguers, "have got only what they deserve. They are inciting the people to refuse to pay to their landlords what is rightfully theirs—rent." This speech and the manner of its delivery so differed from what was expected of the man who in "Social Statics" wrote, "equity does not permit property in land," that Mr. George was first astonished and then disgusted at this flat denial of principle. "It is evident that we cannot agree on this matter," was all that he could say, and he abruptly left Mr. Spencer. The meeting had proved a deep disappointment. Mr. George seldom outside the family circle spoke of it, but to Dr. Taylor he wrote soon after the occurrence (March, 1882): "Discount Herbert Spencer. He is most horribly conceited, and I don't believe really great men are."

It was about this time that Mr. and Mrs. Walter Wren entertained Mr. and Mrs. George at dinner. To put Mrs. George at her ease, Mr. Wren, in the American fashion, presented the other guests to her, among them Mr. and Mrs. Walter Besant. But Mr. George was made acquainted with the inconvenience of the English custom of not introducing. For after the dinner Mrs. George asked her husband how he liked Besant. He said he did not know. "Why, you were apparently on good terms with him?" "Good heavens!" he exclaimed. "Have I been talking with Walter Besant all evening without knowing him?"

A little while after this came a meeting with John Bright and Joseph Chamberlain, who were members of

the Gladstone Cabinet. To Ford, George wrote privately
(April 22) :

"I dined with Walter Wren at the Reform Club last
night and he had John Bright and Joseph Chamberlain
there to meet me. We started in on Irish affairs with
the soup, for Bright asked me point blank what I
thought of what I had seen in Ireland, and I had to
tell him, though it was not very flattering. We kept it
up to half past ten, when Mr. Bright had to go down
to the House, having left his daughter in the gallery,
but Chamberlain remained until nearly twelve.

"Bright has got to the end of his tether, and will
never get past where he is now; but Chamberlain is an
extremely bright man, and his conversation, which was
unreserved, was extremely interesting to me, and would
make a most interesting letter if I could use it, which
of course I cannot. . . .

"Chamberlain has evidently been reading the 'Irish
World,' for he alluded to some things in my letters, and
he told me laughingly to look out when I went back to
Ireland that I did not get reasonably 'suspected.'

"I told him that I wanted to see Michael Davitt; that
Harcourt had refused me; and asked him if he could
help me. He said he could not, as the Home Secretary
would be jealous of any interference by him; but he
added that he thought I should be able to see Davitt
before I went home, which I took to mean that Davitt
would be released before long. This I sincerely hope,
for he is badly needed in Ireland.

"Of course meeting a Cabinet Minister in that way I
could not catechise him about what the Government intended; but I gathered from what he said that he at
least was in favour of going further with the land-bill
and relieving the rigours of coercion, which I take it,
at least in the line of the suspect business, will be the
policy of the Government. . . .

"Kegan Paul told me this morning that he met Justin McCarthy at dinner last night, and that he told him
that the Irish members were getting frightened at the

length to which the movement was going, and were disposed to unite with the Government on fixing up the land bill. I only tell you this sort of stuff for what it is worth, but my notion is that there will be some sort of joint attempt all around to settle the Irish land question, and—that it won't settle! . . ."

Justin McCarthy's reported utterance and Chamberlain's reference to the probable future policy of the Government were of a piece. Although the "no-rent" movement was as strong as ever, if not stronger, Parnell and some of his immediate associates had had enough. Asserting for an excuse that the no-rent movement had failed, they had run up the white flag. Through Captain O'Shea and others, Parnell had entered into a pact with the Government, by which he was to "slow down" the Land League agitation, while the Government was to release the suspects and extend the existing land act, both of which it was glad enough to do. George wrote to Ford (June 6): "Kettle says that O'Kelly, who came over to Ireland to get Parnell to make some compromise, and got put into prison, to the amusement of all inside, gradually worked on his fears."

But there was at the time no public talk of a dicker with the enemy and no previous word that there was to be a liberation, so that when Parnell and his Parliamentary associate prisoners, Dillon and O'Kelly, walked forth from Kilmainham on May 2 there was general astonishment and rejoicing over what appeared to be the Irish leader's victory and Gladstone's defeat. But at least some of the insiders suspected, if they did not know of, the treaty. George wrote to Ford (June 6): "The evening Parnell was let out, the Ladies [Land League], instead of rejoicing, were like mourners at a wake."

On the other side, to liberate Parnell or in any way to

treat with the man who had been denounced as "steeped in treason to the lips" was to discredit the policy of the Viceroy and the Chief Secretary. So Cowper and Forster resigned. Earl Spencer and Lord Frederick Cavendish were appointed to the respective places, and on May 6 made their official entry into Dublin. At seven o'clock that evening the new Chief Secretary and Mr. Burke, the Under Secretary, were killed by a band of political assassins calling themselves "Invincibles."

Mr. George had hurried that day from Dublin to London to meet Michael Davitt, who as publicly announced, and evidently as a part of the Government's more lenient policy, was to be released from Portland prison. In his "Irish World" letter of May 9, Mr. George said that he had been with Davitt until late that night and was to meet him next day.

"We did meet, but earlier than either he of I expected. I was awakened early in the morning by a telegram from a friend in Dublin [Dr. James E. Kelly], telling me that the new Chief Secretary and the Under Secretary had been stabbed to death in Phœnix Park. But for the terms of the despatch and the character of my friend I should have thought the story a wild rumour, for Dublin is a good place for rumours. But these left no doubt, and getting out as soon as I could, while all London was yet asleep, I after awhile managed to find a cabman dozing on his cab, and rousing him with some difficulty, got him to drive me to the Westminster Palace hotel. I went at once to Davitt's room, woke him up, and handed him the despatch as he lay in bed. 'My God!' was his exclamation, 'have I got out of Portland for this!' And then he added mournfully: 'For the first time in my life I despair. It seems like the curse that has always followed Ireland.'

"I went and woke Dillon. He, though less surprised,

was hardly less impressed. It seems that before they went to bed on Saturday night, or rather on Sunday morning, word was brought to them of the murders by one of the reporters of the 'Central News'; but it seemed so incredible that both the Chief Secretary and the Under Secretary should be stabbed to death in Phœnix Park, that it was at once set down as a hoax. Davitt, his mind filled with the vivid impressions of the first hours of freedom, after fifteen long months of imprisonment, and with friendly greetings ringing in his ear, had gone to sleep without reverting to the report again; but Dillon said he had been thinking over it all, and that the more he brooded over it the more it seemed 'too strange not to be true'; its very improbability seeming, as he thought of it, proof that it could not be wholly invention.

"After waking up Mr. Dillon, I went at his request to Mr. O'Kelly's room with the same intelligence, and soon the only London Sunday paper, the 'Observer,' came with the confirmation of print. Mr. Dillon went out to find Mr. Parnell, who came to the hotel, and after a conference the manifesto to the Irish people was written by Davitt, and having been submitted to the Parnellite members, who nearly all gathered in the hotel towards the afternoon, was signed by Parnell and Dillon as well as Davitt, sent out to the papers, and telegraphed to Dublin, where Alfred Webb had been holding his printing office in readiness to strike it off, and whence prominent members of the party had been asking by telegraph for the issuance of something of the kind."

The manifesto that Mr. George speaks of was addressed to the Irish people. It denounced the crime as "cowardly and unprovoked" and hoped that the murderers would be brought to justice. George said in his "Irish World" letter of May 9 that Parnell's "first impulse was immediately to resign his seat, but after consultation with other members he contented himself with sending a message to Mr. Gladstone offering to do this if it would in any way make the Premier's position easier, but received a reply expressing a hope that he would do no such thing."

That Sunday was a day of confusion. Fearing that the English would rise in violent retaliation against the Irish residents, some counselled the Irish leaders to seek safety in France, and this was the sentiment among most of the guests at the dinner party at A. M. Sullivan's, where Mr. and Mrs. George had been invited. For when Mr. George put the question as to what Davitt should do, Mrs. George was alone in saying that Davitt "should go to Ireland by the first train, and be a leader to the people in this hour of dismay!" An exclamation went around the table, and some one said that if Davitt went there in the then state of passionate feeling he would be killed by the Government supporters. Mrs. George replied: "How could Michael Davitt die better than with his people?" Mr. George said little more than that his wife's words expressed his own feeling; but he never forgot those words, and he repeated them to her fifteen years later when his own supreme moment for decision came.

Contrary to expectation, no disturbances anywhere followed the news of the Phœnix Park murders, though the Government was compelled by public opinion to reverse its intended policy of leniency, and turned the screws of coercion even tighter than they had been at the height of the no-rent agitation. Parnell inside the House of Commons opposed this; yet outside he did all he could to kill the old movement. He had no intention of reviving the Land League in any form. Indeed, the day that Davitt was released from Portland, Parnell had denounced the Ladies' Land League to him, saying that it "must be suppressed" or else he would "leave public life,"[1] and he

---

[1] " Life of Charles Stewart Parnell," by R. Barry O'Brien, Vol. I, p. 364.

actually did kill it by refusing it money from the general
fund. Dillon thought that the land agitation should be
carried on, and he went to Parnell and asked: "What are
your intentions? Do you mean to carry on the war or
to slow down the agitation?" "To slow down the agitation," said Parnell.[1] By October he had succeeded so
effectually with the "slowing down" that he organised a
new league. It was the old Irish National Land League
with "Land" left out. He became president, and Home
Rule was made the primary aim. Nothing was heard of
the principle of "The Land for the People," with which
Michael Davitt had set Ireland aflame. On the contrary,
in his first speech under the new auspices Parnell said that
"no solution of the land question can be accepted as a
final one that does not insure the occupying farmers the
right of becoming owners by purchase of the holdings
which they now occupy as tenants."

It was the old peasant proprietary cry—a proposal to
swap landlords, and to swap largely on the terms of the
existing landlords. All thought of the agricultural labourers and of the great mass of the Irish nation who
were too poor to buy land—all reference to natural, equal
rights to land, was ignored.

But the fact of a Kilmainham treaty and of the sur-
render of the movement by Parnell to the Gladstone government came out only by degrees. In writing to the
"Irish World" George tried to put the best face on the
thing, refusing at first to write what he suspected; but in
his private letters to Ford he spoke without reserve. On
May 17 he wrote: "The whole situation is very bad and
perplexing. The Land League in its present form on
both sides of the water seems to me to be smashed. But

---

[1] "Life of Charles Stewart Parnell," by R. Barry O'Brien, Vol. I, p. 365.

the seed has been planted. . . . We who have seen the light must win because much greater forces than ourselves are working with us." Three days later he wrote, "Parnell seems to me to have thrown away the greatest opportunity any Irishman ever had. It is the birthright for the mess of pottage."

CHAPTER IV.

STARTING THE REVOLUTION IN GREAT BRITAIN.

1882.   AGE, 43.

A FEW months of immurement in Kilmainham jail,
even while mitigated by personal comforts, if not
luxuries, and the companionship of numerous political
friends, had sufficed for Parnell; and he came out to "slow
down" the great Land League movement that had roused
the enthusiasm of tens and hundreds of thousands on two
continents. But neither the seven years of hard penal
servitude nor the year or more of subsequent and lighter
solitary incarceration in the English prison had broken
the spirit of Michael Davitt. He had no thought of sur-
render to the Government. In a letter to the "London
Standard" he showed that while he had given up his old
idea of the efficacy of physical force and dynamite to bring
reforms, he did not wish to be a party to the Kilmainham
treaty; and on the 21st of May he made a speech at Manchester on these lines. Mr. George had been invited to
lecture on the Irish question in Free Trade Hall and Mr.
Davitt to preside. To Mrs. George her husband that
night wrote: "It was Davitt's lecture, not mine. He
wanted to make a pronunciamento, and had it all written
out, and got through only a few minutes before the time

378

when, according to the programme, I was to have closed—
so that I spoke for only about fifteen minutes, and as usual
under such circumstances, hardly did myself justice. He
was nice about it, though, and I was very glad to have
him take the time and sit down on the 'Treaty of Kilmainham.' "

"Disruption" was the cry at once raised by the Parnellites against Davitt in consequence of this speech—a
fatal cry in so many Irish struggles. They who had themselves made the real departure in setting themselves against
the Land League movement, audaciously charged Davitt
with aiding Ford and George in trying to make a split
in the ranks. Davitt could suffer imprisonment, but he
shrank from this. He told George a few days later when
they met in Dublin that he thought it wiser for them
not to travel together into the West of Ireland as they,
or at least as George, had contemplated. Mr. George
wrote privately to Patrick Ford from Dublin (May 27) :

"I have seen Davitt . . . at Dr. Joseph Kenny's.
I told him I would go into the west with him to-morrow,
but could plainly see he did not want me to go. . . .
I expressed my mind to him and to Kenny (a Parnellite
first, last and all the time). I told him I thought
you had been extremely moderate; that I was sick of
this undemocratic talk of 'leaders'; that Davitt did represent a much greater idea than Parnell; that it was
not merely now, but during Davitt's long imprisonment
that we had been holding him up as such; that instead
of making a break, you were doing your utmost to prevent it; that it was radical men's work and radical
men's money that had been the backbone of the American support, and that they would not consent to be
used, and to be told that what they had been sacrificing
for was a failure and a humbug; and that there was
no use of disguising the fact that between the programme on which American money had been largely

gathered and the programme now offered them was a
wide chasm; and that in America at least I believed
the smash had already come. I told them, of course, a
good deal more than I could begin to write. Healy
came in, and without resuming the conversation I left.

"With the exception of myself, Davitt has seen nobody since he came out but the Parnellites and the Whig
section of the Land League. He himself is all right, but
he is a very impressible man. He is to come to see me to-
morrow. I shall tell him what I think, but I won't go
down into the west with him, though I have been intending to do so ever since I have been here, only remaining because things were so volcanic. Of course I
know what they din into his ears—'George has captured
you for the "Irish World."' He as much as told me so
before. But whatever happens now, Davitt will be to
those moderates—what shall I call them—a bull in a
china shop. I am confident of that."

But if Davitt shrank from an open break, he certainly
had plans distinct from those of Parnell, as shown by a
letter from George to Francis G. Shaw (May 30):

"Davitt is all right. He believes just as we do, but
he is very much afraid of breaking up the movement,
and is sensitive to the taunt that he has been 'captured
by Henry George and the "Irish World."' . . .

"Michael Davitt is full of the idea of popularising
'Progress and Poverty.' That was the first thing he
said to me. He had read it twice before, and he read it
twice again while in Portland [prison], and as you may
see from his speeches and letters, he believes in it entirely. He says if a copy of that book can be put in
every workman's club and Land League and library in
the three kingdoms the revolution will be made. His
first act was to demand of Parnell and Dillon £500 to
use in the English propaganda, £300 of which he wanted
to put in my hands for as many copies of 'Progress
and Poverty' as it would bring. Parnell and Dillon at

first agreed, and he went to Paris to get Egan's consent. Egan refused; but afterwards wrote that what Davitt wanted would have to be granted, and then after the Manchester speech Parnell and Dillon refused.

"The fact is that the line is really drawn and the split made, but not publicly. They [the Parnellites] will not budge beyond extension of the purchase clause; Davitt is for nationalisation and our programme. And the whole strength of the Land League management is to be used—in fact, it has all along been used—against the spread of more radical ideas. Davitt says he is going to the United States for the purpose of getting money for the propaganda."

But the money that was wanted came suddenly from another quarter. Mr. Shaw had that very month (May 10) sent Mr. George $500, saying: "As you do not tell me how I can help the cause just now, I take my own way and inclose a draft which I hope may strengthen the hands of you, its representative." And nine days later Mr. Shaw wrote that he had received a pledge of $3,000 for the circulation of "Progress and Poverty" from a man richer than he was who did not want to be known. He said that some of the money he would hold until he could learn what Mr. George advised doing with it, but that meanwhile he had ordered of Appleton a thousand copies of the book specially bound in cloth covers to be sent to the members of the Society for Political Education who were men of importance scattered about the country, and that he had preceded this by sending to them copies of George's pamphlet, "The Irish Land Question." Mr. George was at first inclined to believe that this society was "a sort of mutual admiration affair," on the members of which it would be useless to waste money; but the fact of the distribution subsequently raising some contention in the columns of the Boston "Advertiser," he then wrote to Mr. Shaw (August 3): "You have kicked up a row. And of all the things we want to do, to kick up a row is first and foremost. For when the row begins then those who most bitterly oppose us serve the cause the most."

But to go back. On June 6, 1882, came an earthquake. Michael Davitt, despite Parnell's express opposition, made a dashing speech in Liverpool, came out squarely against the peasant proprietary scheme and declared himself flatly for "land nationalisation." Davitt did not espouse the George method of application, which was to absorb land values through taxation. He leaned rather to Alfred Russell Wallace's plan of buying the land from the land-owners (though at half the market valuation) and then exacting a rent from the holders, which seemed to the socialists to include their idea of "management." But *method* just then was a secondary matter with Henry George. What he was most interested in at this time was the assertion of the principle of common rights in land, and he took Davitt's speech to be the old Land League cry of "the land for the people," advanced a stage towards practical application. The speech created a sensation. George was filled with exultation and wrote to Shaw (June 8):

" 'Now, by St. Paul, the work goes bravely on!' I think we may fairly say that we have done something, and that our theory(!) is at last forced into discussion. I should have sent you a congratulatory despatch last night; but I knew you would read the 'Irish World' and would know I was thinking of you when sending the news. I have gained the point I have been quietly working for, and now those who oppose us most bitterly will help us most. Well, after all the toil and worry and the heart sickness, when the devil comes to whisper, 'You are doing nothing!' there are some half hours that pay for all. And because I feel that, I know that you must feel that, too."

On the same day George wrote to Ford:

"Davitt will be with you as soon as this letter. So there is no use of my saying anything about him. . . . For the moment the Kilmainham Treatyites are 'flabbergasted,' but they will rally and fight. It is a long fight and a wide fight—it is not won or nearly won; but it has commenced, and there is no more sailing under false colours. . . .

"Well, I feel like congratulating you. At last the banner of principle is flung to the breeze, so that all men can see it, and the real, world-wide fight begun. What we have been hoping and praying and quietly working for is so far accomplished.

"Davitt proposes compensation. Of course neither you, nor I, nor Bishop Nulty agree to anything of that sort; but that makes no difference. It is best that Davitt should propose it, for his great work from now on is to be rather in England than in Ireland. . . . I don't care what plan any one proposes, so that he goes on the right line. . . .

"I lecture in the Rotunda (Dublin) Saturday night. You can well imagine what I will say."

This lecture, Mr. George's second in Dublin, was delivered on June 10. It was on the "Irish Land Question" and was for the benefit of the Prisoners' Aid Societies. It took the line of and supported Davitt's Liverpool speech and was well received, for he wrote to Ford three days afterwards: "Sexton, who had been all the week in Dublin lying quiet, put in an appearance at the lecture, and on moving thanks to me essayed to defend somewhat the peasant proprietary business; but I went for that in my reply, and evidently carried the audience with me. . . . What was a most significant thing was that from beginning to end Parnell's name was not mentioned. . . . There was not a voice for him, not a cheer."

Nevertheless, as Mr. George had predicted, the "Kilmainham Treatyites" soon rallied and began to fight, and fight with effect. They attacked George covertly at first, aiming to arouse national jealousy against him by speaking of him as "an American" and a "cosmopolitan politician." But Davitt they attacked more openly, for having considerable influence on telegraphic and other large channels of news and political comment, they could and did harry him on both sides of the ocean at once.

Davitt's position was trying. Patrick Ford had arranged for a big reception to him in the Academy of Music, New York; but a committee from the Parnellite faction went down the bay, first reached him and made out such a case that he felt the necessity of giving a prominent place in his first speech in America to an explanation that he had not been "captured" by Henry George or anybody else.

Then again occurred the unlooked for. Some prominent prelates in the Catholic Church in the United States had condemned the Land League movement as attacking the rights of property. Rev. Dr. Edward McGlynn of St. Stephen's Catholic Church, one of the largest in New York, had privately expressed strong approval of the movement, but had never spoken publicly on this or any kindred subject. He had been widely known both for the eloquence of his utterances and the independence of his views, and yielding to the pressure to come out and take a public stand on the land question, he had laid prudential considerations aside, and consented to speak at the Davitt reception. He followed Davitt and made an extraordinary speech on the lines of the land for the people. Elegant in diction and oratorical in delivery, it flashed with wit and burned with enthusiasm. He spoke as a priest of the people, who bore witness to the everlasting truth.

He encouraged Davitt to "preach the gospel" and not to apologise for it or explain it away. His address made such a sensation that the Doctor was invited to speak at most of the meetings with Davitt during the short tour, and he did speak at three, at one of them saying:

"If I might take the liberty of advising him [Davitt] I should say: 'Explain not away one tittle of it, but preach the gospel in its purity!' [Cheers.] I say it is a good gospel, not only for Ireland, but for England, for Scotland and for America, too. [Great cheering.] And if in this country we do not as yet feel quite so much the terrible pressure of numbers upon the land, the same terrible struggle between 'Progress and Poverty,' as is felt in other lands, no thanks are due at all to our political system, but thanks only to the bounties of nature, and to the millions of acres of virgin lands with which God has blessed us. But when these virgin lands shall have been occupied; when the population shall have increased here as it has elsewhere in proportion to our extent of territory, we shall have precisely the same problem to solve, and the sooner we solve it the better. [Loud cheering.] And so I quite agree with Michael Davitt to the full, and with Henry George to the full [loud cheering, and three cheers for Henry George], and lest any timid, scrupulous soul might fear that I was falling into the arms of Henry George, I say that I stand on the same platform with Bishop Nulty, of Meath, Ireland. [Cheers.] But for that matter—to let you again into a secret—my private opinion is, that if I had to fall into the arms of anybody, I don't know a man into whose arms I should be more willing to fall than into the arms of Henry George." [Loud cheers.]

These speeches were too marked in their effects on popular thought in this country, the main source of Land League funds, to go unnoticed by those at Rome and elsewhere bent on suppressing the Irish cause; and the powers which had silenced so many of the clergy of Ireland, among them Dr. Nulty, for the same kind of utterances, now turned towards New York. They caused Cardinal Simeoni, Prefect of the Propaganda, in the name of the Pope, to write several letters to Cardinal McCloskey in New York complaining of "the priest McGlynn" who seemed "very much inclined to favour the Irish Revolution" and who was making speeches containing "propositions openly opposed to the teachings of the Catholic Church." The Cardinal Prefect ordered Dr. McGlynn's suspension, unless Cardinal McCloskey should deem another course advisable.   Dr. McGlynn after the first letter of complaint had an interview with Cardinal McCloskey. He explained his doctrine, and as he said five years later,[1] he defended it from the Cardinal's "misunderstandings and misapprehensions." "I told him substantially," said Dr. McGlynn, "that I knew my theology well enough not to sin against it ignorantly, and that I loved my religion too well to sin against it wilfully."   As a result of this interview Dr. McGlynn said he would not speak further for the Irish Land League cause. "I voluntarily promised to abstain from making Land League speeches, not because I acknowledged the right of any one to forbid me, but because I knew too well the power of my ecclesiastical superiors to impair and almost destroy my usefulness in the ministry of Christ's Church to which I had consecrated my life."

While to Patrick Ford, Dr. McGlynn was a revelation, to Henry George he was more than that, for never before had he heard of the clergyman. McGlynn was a new star in the sky; as George wrote to the "Irish World," a "Peter the Hermit" in the new crusade; and as he wrote to Ford

---

[1] Dr. McGlynn's review of his own case, "The Standard," Feb. 5, 1887.

privately: "If Davitt's trip had no other result, it were well worth this. To start such a man is worth a trip around the world three times over. He is 'an army with banners.'"

But it was of Davitt that George wrote chiefly to Ford at this time. Before any adequate report of the New York meeting had reached him, he said (June 20): "To-day there is a despatch that Davitt says that there is no dispute between him and Parnell, and that the latter's scheme will be carried first. It won't. Davitt has awakened the echoes both in Ireland and in England. He is first and Parnell is nowhere, if he [Davitt] will only stand firm and not get scared. Tell him so for me." George wrote ten days later, "It's a nice combination [against Davitt] —Government, Fenians, Whigs and Parliamentarians! When I say Fenians I mean only those of the Devoy stripe." But Davitt yielded to the pressure, both while in America and subsequently when he returned to the British side. He allowed the great work of his life to be subordinated to the comparatively trifling Parliamentary programme. George's views are reflected in letters to Ford:

London, July 1.

"I got the New York 'Tribune's' report of Davitt's speech, sent to me by Mr. Shaw. It is several shades more apologetic than I should like to see it. Think of a man having seriously to defend himself from the charges of being captured by Henry George and run by the 'Irish World'! . . . But whatever temporary events may be, we can afford to laugh at those who oppose us. They are simply drifting, while 'the stars in their courses are with us.' Don't lose heart for a moment, however much you may be tempted. Those who oppose us most bitterly will help our cause the most."

London, July 4.

"The Kilmainham treaty has gone to smash sure enough at last. The situation, though, is not a good one—the old fight in the dark is to go on again. Ireland has plenty of good minor officers and guerilla chiefs, but not a single general. Davitt is nearest, but he lessened his influence and injured his usefulness by what seems to me like weakness. . . . A great leader would not begin an important campaign by an apology, and I am well satisfied that you had nothing to do with that. Well, I am sorry for Davitt's sake, but the cause moves on no matter who falls."

Dublin, August 4.

"As for me, Davitt should have had sense enough to know that no one could have made him my 'trumpet.' He had too great a position. And surely he need not have been afraid of my trying to put him in the position of a disciple of mine. For in public and in private I have been engaged in pushing him to the front as the 'great leader.' But his enemies—O'Kelly first, I think—charged him with being captured by Henry George and the 'Irish World.' They saw that that annoyed and affected him, and then they pushed it. All he had to do was simply to go forward and not mind them. But their talk affected him so much that he was afraid to be seen with me or to have me go where he went. And so they made him morbidly afraid of the 'Irish World.' It seems to me pitiable weakness when a man's enemies can thus make him afraid of and unjust to his friends. Davitt has let his enemies turn him and swerve him in various ways; he has put himself on the defensive when he ought to have been on the aggressive, and has kept himself in hot water and dropped from the position he might have held.

"But he is a noble character, and by far the best of the lot."

The palpable fact was that Henry George felt increasingly lonely in the Irish movement—all the leaders save

Davitt and Brennan hostile to him in principle, and even Davitt now shunning close connection and Brennan gone off to the South of France in utter disgust with the Kilmainham business.   George had come in touch with many representative men in England like Joseph Cowen, proprietor of the "Newcastle Chronicle," Thomas F. Walker, manufacturer, Birmingham; and William Saunders, President of the Central News Agency in London.   He had also met on very friendly terms the new Chief Secretary for Ireland, George O. Trevelyan; and for John Morley he wrote a "Fortnightly" article.   But these men were of the general British radical movement and not of the Irish movement *per se*.

Yet on the other hand, such men as John Ferguson of Glasgow and Rev. Harold Rylett of Belfast joined with a host of Scottish and English radicals in wishing the war carried into Africa, believing that the most effective way to carry on the Irish land-for-the-people fight would be by raising the issue in England and Scotland.   To this end Mr. George was invited to deliver an address in Glasgow on St. Patrick's night, the 17th of March.   He accepted and spoke before a great public meeting in the City Hall. Three nights later he spoke before another big meeting in the National Hall.   John Ferguson took the chair at the first meeting and Richard McGhee at the second.   Many persons date the radical land movement in Scotland from these meetings, and it is clear that they put the spark to the agitation among the crofters, or small farmers, which soon blazed up.

Davitt had had something of this idea of spreading the war to the British side of the Irish Sea in wishing to circulate "Progress and Poverty," and now George, getting the Shaw money, obtained the means with which to carry the idea forward.   Shaw cabled that he would send

£300, and George replied by letter, "Now we shall start the revolution!"

He made an arrangement with James C. Durant, who had a printing office in Clement's Inn-Passage, for setting type and making plates of "Progress and Poverty" for a book of eighty-eight pages, quarto form, and paper cover, to sell at sixpence a copy. Durant was an enthusiastic admirer of the book and agreed to risk one third of the expense, and to take his pay out of the profits, if there should be any. George was to meet the other two thirds of expense. He did not look for any profit to himself after paying Durant; indeed, unless the sale should be very large they both stood to lose on the operation; but both were moved by the spirit of the propaganda.

Kegan Paul, Trench & Co. were to handle the sixpenny edition on commission. From thinking nothing at all of the book, they had come to have great expectations of it, George writing Shaw as early as February 11 (1882):

"Paul, of Kegan Paul, Trench & Co., says it is the most astonishing success he *ever* knew. When they first got it out no one would touch it. They laughed at the idea of selling an American book on political economy. It was a long while before they got rid of twenty copies. Then, as he says, purely on its own strength, the book to their astonishment began to make its way. Their first edition was out early in December (1881). They have got another; that is going faster, and they anticipate a big sale."

It was Mr. George's idea to push the reading of "Progress and Poverty" all over the three kingdoms. As a preliminary to this, he bought a set of plates of "The Irish Land Question" from the Glasgow publishers, Cameron & Ferguson—the Ferguson who had with Davitt and

Brennan begun the Land League movement. From those plates an edition of five thousand copies of the pamphlet was struck off and sold at threepence each. Copies of it, together with a little four-paged tract by Mr. Shaw, entitled "A Piece of Land," were sent to all the newspapers in the United Kingdom and to all the Members of Parliament. In a similar way copies of "Progress and Poverty" were sent out when it appeared. Sample copies were also sent to every Land League organisation and every working men's club with a circular offering to supply quantities at wholesale rates. This edition of the book was also advertised in some of the papers, so that the £300 from America was made to go as far as it would in the propaganda work, and Mr. George was enabled to write by June 30 to Mr. Shaw: "So, my dear friend, we are in the way of doing something—so much that I don't like to say what I really think. The big stone is really moving. All it wants is a little push to start it rolling. And that, I think we are about to give. It is not what we do so much as what we start other people doing."

As if in a measure to meet the "slowing down" policy of the Parliamentary party, Patrick Ford had asked Mr. George to stump Ireland; but he had dissented. "I am willing and anxious to do all I can," he wrote (June 22), "and I have done all I have been asked to do; but you must remember I am not an Irishman, and these people are jealous of advice or interference from an outsider. That is the reason they are thrusting me forward, saying I have captured Davitt, etc. You see how Harris alludes to me as a 'cosmopolitan politician.' I don't like to mix in Irish politics on this account."

Nevertheless, he now concluded to make a correspondence trip to Western Ireland. He set off early in August, accompanied by an Englishman, James Leigh Joynes, one of the masters of Eton College, who wished to see something of the popular side of the Irish movement and who was engaged to write some descriptive articles for the London "Times." Joynes started out with the average Englishman's idea that rural Ireland was a place of outrages and murders. As they rode along part of their journey on an open jaunting car, he appeared somewhat apprehensive of their being mistaken for landlords and shot from behind the walls or hedges that fringed the roads. But the most peaceable of rural country met their view, and many pictures of industry that gave rise to Mr. George's expression in an "Irish World" letter (August 22) that "of all the libels upon the Irish, that which stigmatises them as idlers is the worst. If there are on the earth's surface any people who will work harder and suffer more for those who cling to them, I do not know where they are to be found."

At length the travellers arrived at the little town of Loughree. It was "guarded by seven police fortresses," besides having "two police barracks and a large military barrack." "As we drove down the street to the only hotel," said Mr. George, "the police seemed to start from the houses on each side and follow us." And the moment the travellers sprang to the ground both were arrested under the Crimes Act as "suspicious strangers." Said Mr. George:

> "The whole thing struck me as infinitely ridiculous. There was, after all, a good deal of human nature in Artemus Ward's declaration that he was willing to sacrifice all his wife's relatives to save the Union. And in my satisfaction in seeing an Eton master lugged through the town as too suspicious a stranger to be left at large I lost all sense of annoyance at my own arrest. In fact, my only regret was that it was not Kegan Paul."

They were taken into a barred room in the barrack, and despite Joynes' profuse protestations that there must be some mistake, the police went through the baggage and examined all the papers. Mr. George says:

"A rough draft of a bit of poetry was scanned over by a knot of constables as though it had been a Moonlight general order or a receipt for making dynamite, while as for a little leaflet, 'A Piece of Land,' by our countryman, Francis G. Shaw, I think they must almost have got it by heart the way they stared at it. . . . I could not feel angry—the whole thing was too supremely ridiculous, but the Eton master could not see the joke. To come to Ireland only to be mistaken for an emissary of sedition, a would-be assassin of landlords, or maimer of cattle, was something that had not entered into his calculations."

Resident Magistrate Byrne who came to examine them apparently soon concluded that there had been a mistake, even if the police had acted upon telegraphic orders from some source. At any rate, after three hours' detention the suspects were released, not, however, without a formal protest from Mr. George against the proceedings as "needlessly annoying and insulting."

After spending that night at the hotel they visited Prior Corbett of the Carmelite Order and the stores of several "suspects." Then they drove to the town of Athenry, a few miles distant and within the same police district—"a town of one pump," an ordinary hand pump, from which the entire water supply of the place is drawn. Yet in so small a town, which furthermore could not support a single doctor, were quartered no less than twenty-six police constables and fifty-six soldiers. The travellers visited Father McPhilpin and then viewed the antiquities of the place, after which they went to the railway-station to take train for Galway. But the police, a great number of whom had appeared to be lounging around, closed in and arrested George, but not Joynes. After several hours' detention, Mr. George was taken before Magistrate Byrne —the same magistrate who had examined him at Loughree —and a lot of foolish testimony was presented touching the prisoner's movements and the nature of his printed papers and written notes. One of the papers put in evidence was a list of names, with the supposed letters "F. C." after some of them, which the Head Constable believed meant "Fenian Centre," but which the magistrate interpreted to be "T. C.," and to mean "Town Councillor." The upshot of the matter was Mr. George's discharge.

"The magistrate then summed up with a justification of the police for arresting me, and to my surprise finished by discharging me. Whether what had seemed to me the manifest purpose to require bail had been altered by the telegrams which Mr. Trevelyan stated in the House of Commons he had sent to Ireland on the subject, or whether it was the magistrate's own sense, I cannot tell."

The trip affected a radical change in Mr. Joynes' views of the state of Ireland, and he wrote letters to the London "Times" based upon what he had seen and heard that seemed incomprehensible to the editor, so that the arrangement between Joynes and the newspaper was cancelled.

When Mr. George got back to Dublin in the middle of August he wrote to Mr. Shaw: "I have just returned from a very interesting trip into the west, in which among other things I saw the inside of two 'British Bastiles.'" He also sent to the President of the United States a letter of protest at the uselessness of the American Ministerial representation at the Court of St. James, making his own case the occasion of his writing and saying that while he fully realised the duty of an American citizen "in a foreign country to conform his conduct to the laws of that country, and that he cannot expect exemption from such police regulations as its Government may deem necessary," yet "that it is due to their own dignity that the United States should claim for their citizens travelling in countries with which they maintain relations of amity, exemption from wanton annoyances, unreasonable inquisitions and imprisonment upon frivolous pretexts." He averred that American citizens had been imprisoned there "without trial, and even without specific accusation," while the only action taken by the United States so far as known and currently reported there was on the part of American consuls who "attempted to bribe them by offers of money into acknowledgment of the justice of their arbitrary imprisonment by agreeing to leave the country as a condition of release." The letter was aimed at James Russell Lowell, the United States Minister to the Court of St. James —"a place," as Mr. George often afterwards described it, "for the spoiling of good poets." To make the protest more direct seemed inadvisable on account of the relations existing between Lowell and Mr. Shaw. Nevertheless, the letter stirred up the Administration at Washington to call upon the Government representatives for proper action in such cases. When Mr. George returned to the United States he was invited by Secretary of State Frelinghuysen to put in a claim for damages, but he declined, saying that all he asked for was protection to the citizen in his proper rights abroad.

In a letter to Mr. Shaw (September 12) Mr. George wrote with some amusement:

"By the bye, I met William H. Appleton in London. He told me that Lowell had been talking to him about me, and asked, 'Why, who in the world buys such a book as that?'

"'Well,' said Appleton, 'one man who buys it is a friend of yours—Francis G. Shaw. He bought a thousand, and then he came back and bought another thousand.'

"'Goodness!' exclaimed Lowell—or words to that effect; 'he is a dear, good friend of mine, but—but, he *must* be getting eccentric!'

"I brought a letter to Lowell from John Russell Young, but never presented it."

The incident of Mr. George's arrest and the Parliamentary questioning relative to it were noticed by all the newspapers in Great Britain and Ireland, all of which fell in most aptly with George's plans to "start the revolution." The press had just been noticing "The Irish Land Question" pamphlet very liberally and now at last the English printers had the sixpenny edition of "Progress and Poverty" ready. Twelve thousand copies were printed in the first edition, and two thousand were distributed free. Within a few days there was, perhaps, reason for his joyous words to Shaw, "I feel as though we are really beginning to 'move the world,'" for the London "Times" set an example to the British newspapers and periodicals by seriously reviewing "Progress and Poverty" in a five-column article—an example that brought reviews tumbling in. Kegan Paul sold all the copies of the book he had on hand by the afternoon of the day on which the "Times" article appeared. John Russell Young, then United States Minister to China, sent George congratulations from Pekin, saying that the fact of such a lengthy review, was, regardless of its spirit, the "blue ribbon of critical approbation," and that it ranked George "at once among the thinkers of the age," whose words were "worth heeding in England." No one more fully appreciated the significance of the article than the author himself, and he wrote to his San Francisco friend, Dr. Taylor (September 16): "I send you the 'Times' notice. The book which the 'Alta California' said never would be heard of is at last, it is now safe to say, famous. The cheap edition is going off well. One house in Melbourne took 1,300 copies and 300 went to New Zealand." To Mr. Young, he wrote shortly after returning to New York (January 17, 1883):

"The review in the 'Times' gratified me very much. The 'Times' had alluded to me previously in several editorials, saying that I could no longer be ignored, and a good many other things not too flattering. I saw in a moment that the review was from a friendly hand. If you noticed it, you must have seen that it was written with great skill; for the purpose of directing attention to the book, slurring over those things that would be disagreeable to the British people and dwelling on those things that would attract them. The 'Atheneum,' alluding to it, said it was by Fraser Rae. I went to see him, delivering your letter; and had a very pleasant talk. He had got the book originally from you. He was very anxious for me to dine with him and meet a professor of political economy at one of the Scotch universities, who desired to meet me; but I was leaving London for Ireland and could not do so."

Then, too, came encouragement from another quarter. Early in 1882 the Land Nationalisation Society had been started in London. The eminent Alfred Russell Wallace was at its head and his recent book, "Land Nationalisation," ostensibly embodied its aim. It contained in its membership those who like Wallace desired to take possession of the land by purchase and then have the State exact an annual quit-rent from whoever held it; those who had

the socialistic idea of having the State take possession of
the land with or without compensation and then manage it;
and those who with Henry George repudiated all idea
either of compensation or of management and would recognise common rights to land simply by having the State
appropriate its annual value by taxation. Such conflict-
ing elements could not long continue together, and soon
those holding the George idea withdrew and organised on
their own distinctive lines, giving the name of the Land
Reform Union to their organisation. But meanwhile the
Land Nationalisation Society invited Mr. George to lecture under the auspices of a working men's audience in
Memorial Hall on September 6, Professor Wallace presiding. This was Henry George's first public speech in London and he addressed the class he was very anxious to
reach. For as he said in April in writing to Mr. Shaw:
"I have little hope of the literary class here—never at all
of the men who have made their reputations. It is the
masses whom we must try to educate, and they are hard
to get at through ordinary channels."

This working men's lecture was followed by a meeting
on the afternoon of the 19th that gave him real satisfaction—a meeting of Church of England clergymen. The
proceedings had much the nature of a conference, Mr.
George making a few preliminary remarks explanatory of
his principles and then answering questions. He wrote to
Mr. Shaw (September 21): "The meeting of clergymen
was most remarkable. It occupied three hours. The ball
has surely commenced to roll." That evening he was honoured with a two shilling working men's banquet, and then
he bade adieu to his English friends and started for Dublin and home.

On the eve of his departure from Dublin, Mr. George
was entertained at a banquet by T. D. Sullivan, M. P.,

Dwyer Gray, owner of the "Freeman's Journal," Michael
Davitt, Dr. James E. Kelly, Father Behan, Dr. Joseph
Kenny, and other well-known citizens; and then, the eldest
daughter who had been ill with typhoid fever being strong
enough to travel, the family proceeded to Queenstown and
on October 4 embarked on the National liner *Helvetia*
for New York.

But before leaving Dublin Mr. George wrote to Mr.
Shaw (September 26):

> "Sure as we live, we have kindled the fire in Eng-
> land, and there is no human power that can put it out.
> Thanks to you, and the friend who made the contribu-
> tion through you, I think I have in this year done a
> bigger work (or rather started bigger forces) than any
> American who ever crossed to the old country. I say
> this freely to you, because without you I could not have
> come or stayed.
>
> "Our English friends are very earnest for me to stay;
> but I know the movement will go ahead without me.
> No man is necessary to it now. We may help a little;
> but whether we help or not, it will go on.
>
> "Hope to have a twenty thousand new edition of
> 'Progress and Poverty' printed by next Monday."

CHAPTER V.

KINDLING THE FIRE AT HOME.

1882-1883.   AGE, 43-44.

A YEAR before Henry George had sailed away from New York scarcely noticed. Now he returned to find himself, as he said, "pretty near famous"; the newspapers heralding him, the labor unions crowding spacious Cooper Union for a formal welcome, and men notable at bench and bar, in politics, the ministry and commercial pursuits banqueting him at Delmonico's. Hon. Algernon S. Sullivan was toastmaster at the banquet, with Justice Arnoux, Justice Van Brunt, Henry Ward Beecher, Thomas G. Shearman, Andrew McLean, and Francis B. Thurber among the speakers. Mr. George alarmed his immediate friends by mistaking the hour and arriving late, and amused others by having forgotten to get his shoes polished. But the occasion passed with fine effect, the guest's speech being marked by quiet delivery, yet intense feeling, for he believed this to be but another indication that the world was awakening to the truth. That different feelings were also awakening elsewhere was manifest from the fact that amid the generally favourable notices of the press was one observing that a number of the persons present representing special privileges probably had

no notion of the ideas promulgated by the man they
honoured, since they acted like a lot of fat sheep who had
without realising their danger invited a wolf into the fold.
If Mr. George did not feel the force of this remark at
once, he did when, three years later, lines of interest were
drawn, and many of those who had fêted him at Delmonico's took front rank among the "Society Savers" arrayed against him. Then he said with a twinkling eye
to those about him: "Those gentlemen gave me a complimentary dinner once."

But no matter to what changed feelings some of the
banqueters afterwards awakened, the fact of such an event
gave evidence, as much as the working men's reception,
of a strong tide setting in the direction to which the
George ideas pointed, so that it was with a consciousness
of rising power that he wrote to Rev. Father Dawson of
Ireland (October 23) : "I find that the prophet is honoured, even in his own country"; and that he wrote to
Taylor at the same time: "It is a good deal like going to
sleep and waking up famous."

Charles Nordhoff of the "New York Herald" thought
the time had come for Mr. George to be most useful in
Congress; that there he could get the best hearing before
the country and make his influence felt in tangible laws,
primarily towards a liberation of trade, for Nordhoff was
a radical free trader. To Nordhoff's letter suggesting
that he talk with Patrick Ford about the matter, George
replied (October 29) : "I think I can be quite as useful
outside of Congress as in, and I should not now seek a
nomination in any way. So I shall not say anything to
the 'Irish World' people about the matter. But I quite
as fully appreciate your kindness and your esteem as
though I wanted the place."

One of the first things that Mr. George did after getting back was to call upon Rev. Dr. Edward McGlynn and pay his respects. The clergyman was a native of New York, of Irish parentage. At an early age he became a protégé of Archbishop Hughes, who sent him to the College of the Propaganda at Rome to study for the priesthood. He was distinguished as a student and was ordained at twenty-two, becoming at first the assistant, and at thirty, the successor to Rev. Dr. Cummings of St. Stephen's Church, New York. Dr. Cummings was a man of extensive learning and very liberal views. As such he had large influence in the community, an influence which his young successor, with like qualities, acquired and extended. Dr. McGlynn was two years Henry George's senior, and when they met was in his forty-sixth year. A copy of "Progress and Poverty" had been given to him by A. J. Steers, the young man in D. Appleton & Co.'s employ who had helped persuade that house to get out a dollar edition of the book in 1880.

On meeting Dr. McGlynn, Henry George found a large man physically, of urbane manners, many intellectual graces and remarkable conversational gifts; and with those qualities of heart and mind that made him the loved and venerated priest, confessor, adviser, leader—the father—among the poor of a great New York City parish. Dr. McGlynn subsequently speaking of this meeting, said: "Already captured by 'Progress and Poverty,' I was now captured by its author. I found united with his lofty intellect and virile character, the simplicity and sweetness of a child—in fact, that 'something feminine' which a Frenchman has said is to be found in all men truly great." The two men talked simply, yet they understood each other. That meeting began the intimate friendship between "the Priest and the Prophet."

There were many calls for lectures and some for articles from Mr. George's pen, and he was in the midst of his plans when death struck down his friend, Francis G. Shaw, after seventy-two years of usefulness to his kind. To Mrs. George, who was in Philadelphia, her husband hastily wrote (November 8) : "I got this morning a letter from Mrs. Lowell saying that her father, Mr. Shaw, was very sick and could not live. I went over there as soon as I could and found he had died last night. I have no sorrow for his sake, but I feel the loss of such a friend and deeply regret that I did not get an opportunity to see him again. Yet this is generally the way our last partings seem to us—partings for a day !"

Beautiful memorial sketches of Mr. Shaw were written by Sydney Howard Gay and George William Curtis and printed for private circulation. Mr. George made the dedication of a new book later in the year the wreath of his lasting tribute, but in the first days he expressed his sentiments to the daughter, Mrs. Lowell (November 15) : "There was between us something of that feeling that among the ancients was the closest of ties. I was, in some respects at least, his proxy, his younger man, whom he sent into the struggle he would have made himself; and this thought will always be to me a satisfaction and a strength."

Mr. George made a lecturing trip to St. Louis, Terre Haute and Wheeling, speaking on the land question. When he got back to New York he wrote to Taylor (January 17) :

"I have received $1000, which Mr. Shaw left me. This puts me at ease. I shall use it in the way I know he intended it—to give me leisure to do some writing—and before that is gone I shall have my feet well under me.

"What a curious life mine is—literally from hand to mouth; and yet always a way seems to open.

"I want to do something strong on the tariff; and then a popularisation—in the form probably of question and answer—of our doctrines, with special view to the farmers. And by that time the cheap 'Progress and Poverty' will have told, and I shall have made some paying lecture engagements.

"My article goes in the 'North American Review' next month (March number).

"Get the 'Modern Review' for January. It is the best review of 'Progress and Poverty' yet."[1]

Note should be taken of the "North American Review" article of which Mr. George spoke. It was entitled "Money in Elections." In it he advocated, as the corrective of purchase and intimidation of voters, the adoption of the Australian secret ballot system. In San Francisco twelve years before he had made the same proposal in the "Overland Monthly," and when in 1886 he became candidate for the New York Mayoralty, this principle formed one of the planks of his platform.

But this "North American" article was now merely by the way. The English cheap edition of "Progress and Poverty" was doing so well that the author was set on a cheap American edition. He thought of importing a duplicate set of the English plates, but abandoned this to put the book in the hands of John W. Lovell, a publisher of standard books in cheap form, who had just started a serial library, with a complete book in each number. They were paper covered, compact, attractive volumes. "Progress and Poverty," like the average number, was sold for twenty cents—more than the English edition, but there were compensating advantages in size and appearance and as to distribution. Mr. George was to get ten per cent.

---

[1] Signed article by George Sarson, M. A.

royalty, the same as from Appleton for the better edition; but this in effect amounted to very little, for the author gave away so many copies and made such large personal discounts to those who bought quantities for educational purposes, that the Lovell edition brought small return to him, considering the great sale.

"The Irish Land Question" also was put in Lovell's Library, and at ten cents a copy. In order to make it apply to the United States and the world, rather than to Ireland exclusively, the title was modified to "The Land Question," which the book has since carried.

The Land League organisation in the United States had since Parnell's change of policy pretty generally gone to pieces. What remained was used to push the cheap editions of the books. But a far greater agency was found in the Order of the Knights of Labour. This organisation had sprung from a local secret society formed by ten Philadelphia garment cutters in 1869. Not until the close of the seventies did it assume great proportions, and by 1883 it had local assemblies or branch organisations all over the country. Its more recent declaration of principles, though in some respects vague and confused, had a clear central purpose—that of equal rights for all and special privileges to none. Its "fifth demand" ran:

"The land, including all the natural sources of wealth, is the heritage of all the people, and should not be subject to speculative traffic. Occupancy and use should be the only title to the possession of land. Taxes upon land should be levied upon its full value for use, exclusive of improvements, and should be sufficient to take for the community all unearned increment."

While this had for several years been in the declaration of principles, nobody had paid much attention to it as a practical idea, and it had been allowed to lie dormant. But discussion of the Irish land question had, with other things, drawn attention to the land question at home; and T. V. Powderly, Grand Master Workman, made a personal declaration on the question and helped Mr. George, who had joined the order, to get "Progress and Poverty" and "The Land Question" into the local assemblies. George set high value on this and wrote Thomas F. Walker of Birmingham, England (April 21):

> "I inclose you a very significant clipping. Powderly is head of the great organisation of the 'Knights of Labour.' Up to this he (as most of the leaders of labour organisations) has considered the land question as of no practical importance. His change will have a very important effect. It is, moreover, only one indication of the general change that is going on.
>
> "The 20-cent edition of 'Progress and Poverty' got out in February and is working powerfully. We are gaining rapidly in every direction. It will not be long now before the movement will show in politics."

Mr. George and his little bunch of immediate friends in New York at this time started an organisation called the Free Soil Society. Besides being fairly descriptive of their purpose—to free the soil from speculation—the name had historical associations, having been used by an aggressive anti-slavery party before the civil war. The new organisation was federal in its plan, starting from local groups. Louis F. Post, formerly of "Truth" but now returned to his law practice, was president; Rev. R. Heber Newton, treasurer; and Charles F. Adams, a young lawyer of brilliant parts, secretary; with John P. Cranford, a prosperous city contractor in Brooklyn; T. L. McCready, A. J. Steers, who had given "Progress and Poverty" to

Dr. McGlynn; several members of the "Irish World" editorial staff, Professor L. E. Wilmarth, Clinton Furbish, William McCabe, John Beverly Robinson, and Henry George, his wife (for women were eligible), his sons and his eldest daughter were of the first members. The object was purely propaganda; the method, all means that would promote thought. The society proved effective for a time in getting together those who were already persuaded; but it brought in few new people and died a quiet death before a great while.

It resulted, however, in some informal, half-past six o'clock dinners in a small restaurant in the wholesale district on Duane Street, New York, kept by a Portuguese named Pedro D. Beraza. These dinners were occasional, and talk was informal. Mr. George, light-hearted and sanguine as a boy, generally sat at the head of the board and passed a question around to each by turn when he wanted an expression of views. They were essentially "experience" meetings. Nor was any allowed to pass without delivering his personal testimony to the progress of "the cause." In those days small events gave the brethren much cheer.

The thousand dollars left by Mr. Shaw enabled Mr. George to commence early in the year on the cherished plan of writing a book on the tariff question. To James McClatchy of the "Sacramento Bee," who in some alarm admonished him not to attempt too much, he wrote (March 28): "Don't be afraid that I shall get out of my depth. I am well conscious of the limits of human effort of which you speak, and there is too much in my own line to do for me to venture beyond it. My real purpose in treating the tariff question is to show workingmen that *the* question is the land question, and that they are to a great extent wasting their efforts in barking up the wrong tree."

When Mr. George had got well along in the writing two important proposals came to him. One was from Allen Thorndike Rice, proprietor of the "North American Review," for a political and economic weekly paper, to be edited and partly owned by George. The other was for a series of signed articles for "Frank Leslie's Illustrated Newspaper." He wrote Taylor (March 25):

> "As to the paper negotiations, they finally came to this. Capitalist to put up $25,000, to take fifty-five shares of stock, I to have forty-five. I to have control and a salary of seventy-five dollars a week until the thing paid, and then a hundred dollars a week, in addition to the earnings of my stock. They wanted to start on the 15th of May. After a good deal of consideration I refused. I think I shall go into a paper, though, about September or October, and believe I can make a combination that will assure success. This will solve the bread and butter question for good.
>
> "In the meantime I have made an arrangement to write a weekly article for thirteen weeks for 'Frank Leslie,' the articles to be two columns and a half and I to get $100 for each.
>
> "My free-trade matter I think of selling to a newspaper in the same manner before bringing it out in book form."

So he laid aside work on the tariff book to write the "Frank Leslie" articles. They were intended by the paper's managers to be a counter-attraction, as it were, to a series of articles just started by "Harper's Weekly" from the pen of Professor William G. Sumner of the chair of political economy at Yale. George's articles were to deal with current social questions from his own standpoint, under the title of "Problems of the Time." His purpose was, as he wrote in the preface to their book form afterwards, "to present the momentous social problems of our time, unencumbered by technicalities, and without that abstract reasoning which some of the principles of political economy require for thorough explanation."

The fifth article dealt with "The March of Concentration." It spoke of the obvious increase in size of land holdings, incidentally stating that a mere glance at the United States Census reports for 1870 and 1880 showed that the general figures utterly contradicted the deductions that the average size of farms was decreasing, and that the reports were, therefore, unreliable and worthless. This brought to the front the man who had superintended both censuses—Professor Francis A. Walker, who had held the chairs of political economy in two colleges and was author of a text book on the subject. In a curt letter to "Frank Leslie's" he offered if the reports were not clear to Mr. George to supply "a more elementary statement, illustrated with diagrams," in support of the official statement that the average size of farms was decreasing. George at once replied, Walker made a surrejoinder, and George a rebutter, all of which served to show George's keen, analytical powers. The "New York Sun" in subsequently reviewing the case said: "It is amusing because, while there is no lack of suavity and decorum on the part of Mr. George, his opponent squirms and sputters as one flagrant blunder after another is brought forward and the spike of logic is driven home through his egregious fallacies." Nor was the matter cleared up until the Census Bureau explained—what at the time of the controversy it had not realised—that the tables for 1870 were based on *improved* area and those of 1880 on *total* area, thus making Walker's comparison of the two censuses impossible, and proving George's charge of carelessness.[1]

---

[1] See "Statistics of Agriculture." U. S. Census for 1880, issued 1883, p. xiv.

In the summer Mr. George put the "Leslie" articles together with the view to publication in book form. He made each article a chapter, and added eight more and a conclusion. He named the book "Social Problems" and dedicated it to the memory of Francis G. Shaw, with the quotation from Revelation: "Yea, saith the Spirit, that they may rest from their labours; and their works do follow them." With the book he printed as appendices, Mr. Shaw's little tract, "A Piece of Land"; a letter on "The Condition of English Agricultural Labourers," by William Saunders of London; and the Walker Census controversy. The book was put into the hands of Belford, Clarke & Co., publishers, of New York and Chicago, but was not brought out until January.

In April, 1883, a proposal had come before the New York Legislature for the establishment of a State Bureau of Labour Statistics. Before the bill was passed—before he had decided whether or not he wanted it—Mr. George's name was urged by a number of labour unions for the place of Commissioner. But when the bill creating the Bureau was passed, Governor Cleveland appointed a polit ical supporter.

At the end of July Mr. George wrote to Mrs. Lowell in connection with some other matters: "I have met with a loss that bites out a big piece of my work and quite disarranges my calculations as to what I should accomplish. All the manuscript that I have been making for a book to be published this fall has gone—where I cannot tell, but I presume into an ash barrel." It was the free trade book, and was equal to about a hundred printed pages. The family had been boarding on Fourteenth Street, near Seventh Avenue. Thence they moved to a furnished house on Hancock Street, Brooklyn. The manuscript was lost in the Fourteenth Street house, Mr. George

ultimately settling down to the conclusion that he had
inadvertently included it in a lot of waste papers that he
told a servant to carry off and destroy. This was a loss
in several senses. Taylor early in August became his
confidant.

"For past two weeks I have been staying home pushing doggedly at work. I find there is considerable I
want to add to 'Social Problems,' though for my own
exigencies I should hurry it into print. And I have
found it hard to make headway. Writing well on exact
subjects is of all work the hardest. Yet I should be delighted if I could see my way clear to keeping at it.
How blessed are they for whom the pot boils of itself!
I have now just $25 in the world, about half a week's
living with economy; no, not that. However, this is no
new experience to me.

"That MS. is a very serious loss even in the financial
aspect.

"I shall get out this book, and I have several other
things in mind.

"One suggested to me by William Swinton is to take
Smith's 'Wealth of Nations,' cut out the parts not
necessary to a clear understanding of Smith's economy
(giving a synopsis of such parts), annotate it, and publish at a popular price. I have nearly finished a reading
—really the first thorough one I ever gave the book—
with this view, and think I could make an exceedingly
useful volume, rendering Smith much more intelligible to the general reader, and pointing where he goes
astray and all his successors have followed him.

"What do you think of it? Write me how it strikes
you. I would give $20 of my available assets for a good
Saturday afternoon talk with you."

As the latter part of this letter shows, there was no
sitting down for repining. And the idea he threw out
for an annotated "Wealth of Nations," was later on taken

up and the work begun, though more pressing things prevented it from being carried forward any considerable distance, and it was never finished.

That summer he went with his family and Louis F. Post and family to Budd's Lake in New Jersey for a two weeks' camping trip, which gave him, he told Taylor, "more of a dead rest," than he "had had for years." But he continued (August 12):

> "There is, it seems to me, an undertone of sadness in life which engulfs a man—at least a thoughtful man—who does not keep moving. Pleasure is in action—and the highest pleasure in action directed to large and generous social objects. . . .
>
> "How it is all passing! I have been lying under the trees thinking of that, and of the infinite mystery with which we are surrounded. What fools are these positivists. *Our* positive knowledge! More and more certain it seems to me that this life *must* be only a stage, a passage. You are right, conduct *is* the one thing."

The problem of individual life—it was the constant problem with Mr. George in the seasons of quietness. Yet the abstraction of the philosopher did not in his case work the result so often shown in history—make the man on the domestic side less attentive and tender, as witness the note written by the husband on the night of October 12 for the wife to find on waking next morning:

> "It is twenty-three years ago to-night since we first met—I only a month or two older than Harry, and you not much older than our Jen. For twenty-three years we have been closer to each other than to any one else in the world, and I think we esteem each other more and love each other better than when we first began to love. You are now 'fat, fair and forty,' and to me the mature

Poverty" had come too late for them. The father read it, and pride of his son's valiant courage and high purpose filled his heart. He saw at once that it was based upon justice and equality, and he pronounced it a great book. But he was in his eightieth year when it was printed. He was living in the past; he did not give enough heed to the pressing, struggling world about him to see the full purpose and strength of the book. It was the brave, sturdy son that he thought of, rather than of the son's book. And to the mother, the son had been still the child, to be encouraged and guided in the moral ways. "I am too old to read the book," she said when it came; and though a calm smile overspread her face at the sound of the public applause of her son, it was sweeter to her devout mind to have him join the morning prayers when the father read as of yore from the Scriptures; or to have him sit with her and the family in old St. Paul's and listen to the preaching of the Blessed Word.

"Their deaths were as beautiful as their lives," Henry George wrote to Dr. Taylor; and death seemed much nearer to him than before. Yet he did not shrink. His heart's most precious desire was at last safe. "Yes, I could die now," he exclaimed one day as he was crossing Broadway with his son, Richard. The street was clear for the moment. He had stopped short in the middle of the roadway and spoke as if musing, his eyes turned upward, as though intently regarding the building tops. "Why do you say that?" asked the son in amazement. The question brought the father out of his reverie with a start. "I was thinking," he answered, walking to the sidewalk, "that I could die now and the work would go on. It no longer depends upon one man. It is no longer a 'Henry George' movement—a one-man movement. It is the movement of many men in many lands. I can help it while I live; but my death could not stop it. The Great Revolution has begun."

But if he felt this way, his friends in the cause felt that there was need of his fiery zeal everywhere. So that in answer to the increasing calls from England he set sail four days before Christmas with his son, Harry, on the *City of Richmond* of the Inman Line. As when a boy on his first voyage before the mast, he entered in his pocket diary, "East wind and smooth sea."

CHAPTER VI.

BRITISH LECTURE CAMPAIGN.

1884.　　　　　Age, 45.

THE scenes into which Mr. George was hurrying exceeded his fondest wishes. Next to Gladstone, he was at the moment the most talked of man in England. This was chiefly because more than forty thousand copies of the sixpenny edition of "Progress and Poverty" had been sold. The book was the burning theme. It engaged the critical reviews and the newspapers; it entered into lectures, debates and mock parliaments. It had stormed the redoubts of conservatism—the great seats of learning. Rt. Hon. Henry Fawcett, M.P., Postmaster-General and Professor of Political Economy at Cambridge, had grappled with the book's chief proposal and afterwards incorporated his views in his "Manual of Political Economy." For Oxford spoke one of its professors, Arnold Toynbee, M.A., a young man of high character and brilliant parts, who in two lectures before fashionable West End London audiences essayed to answer the book.[1]

---

[1] Mr. Toynbee died of brain fever soon after these lectures. Failure to carry conviction to all those present, and especially to some socialists who made rude and noisy opposition, is believed to have preyed on the intense, sensitive, high-purposed mind, until chagrin induced the fatal fever. The lectures were published after his death by his close friend, Sir Alfred Milner.

So wide had become the interest in it, that timid Privilege grew alarmed and the landlord "Liberty and Property Defense League," through Lord Bramwell, one of its council, made a furious attack; while the "Edinburgh Review" linked Herbert Spencer's "Social Statics" with "Progress and Poverty" in a common condemnation, and brought from the English philosopher his first indirect denial of the truth he had proclaimed in the unequivocal words that "the right of mankind at large to the earth's surface is still valid; all deeds, customs and laws notwithstanding."[1]

And well might the special interests take alarm. Not only had no work on political economy excited such general attention, but no book of the kind had ever struck so boldly at the mother of vested rights—private property in land. "Abolition, without compensation," was the cry. A fleeting curiosity in an audacious and brilliantly written work might perhaps account for its circulation among the educated classes; but how explain its popularity among the labouring masses who could rarely afford to buy or find time or inclination to read a book of any kind? Yet certain it was that literature could furnish no precedent for the way this book was going the rounds of working men's unions, clubs and societies; and indications were not wanting that its sentiments with time must crystallise political and social discontent among the file leaders of the all-pervading army of the poor and rouse a demand not to be satisfied with the trifling reforms that hitherto had been conferred with much show and condescension.

True, no less a personage than the Prime Minister, Mr.

---

[1] "Social Statics," p. 134. Spencer made his denial in a letter to a London Tory newspaper, "St. James's Gazette." Referring to this Spencer letter, George at the time wrote Taylor: "Spencer is going the way of Comte — going insane from vanity."

Gladstone, had pronounced as "in form and substance the best answer to George," an address delivered by the Government Statistician, Robert Giffen, who proved by figures the "progress of the working classes in the last century." But on the other hand, those missionaries among the miserably poor, the Congregational Union, gave voice to "the bitter cry of outcast London" in a pamphlet that showed with startling vividness that a vast part of the population lived in homes "compared with which the lair of a wild beast would be a comfortable and healthy spot"; while the "Pall Mall Gazette," helped by the Salvation Army, soon afterwards revealed indubitably the existence of a horrible traffic in young girls. Even so-called Radical leaders could see what might come. "If something is not done quickly to meet the growing necessities of the case," cried the Rt. Hon. Joseph Chamberlain, "we may live to see theories as wild and methods as unjust as those suggested by the American economist adopted as the creed of no inconsiderable portion of the electorate."[1] Chamberlain, like a shrewd politician, had his ear to the ground. Nor did he overlook the subsequent fact that a typical English audience crowded into St. James's Hall, in West End London, late in December to hear the Irish patriot, Michael Davitt, lecture on "The Land for the People" under the auspices of the Land Reform Union. As Mr. Chamberlain said: social reform was in the air.

It was on the last day of December (1883) that Henry George arrived in Liverpool. He was met by Davitt and Richard McGhee, of Glasgow. Davitt was now without let or hindrance preaching the doctrine of land nationalisation and paying no more attention to the Parnellites

---

[1] "Laborers' and Artisans' Dwellings," by Rt. Hon. Joseph Chamberlain, "Fortnightly Review," December, 1883.

(who for the time were in eclipse) than to those physical-force men, who were trying dynamite explosions in England as a means of compelling public recognition of Irish claims. After stopping off over night at Birmingham to consult with Thomas F. Walker, who had been distributing "Progress and Poverty" extensively among the members of the Liberal Association, the political sponsors for Joseph Chamberlain and John Bright, Mr. George went up to London; which however he left again, to make a formal entry on Sunday afternoon, January 6, when he was received just outside Euston Station by a concourse of labour organisations; and from the top of a four-wheel cab he made a short speech, thanking them for their welcome and explaining the purpose of his coming.

The conspicuous movers in the Land Reform Union were William Saunders, Miss Helen Taylor, Thomas F. Walker, Rev. S. D. Headlam, James Durant, Rev. Phillip A. Wicksteed, Richard McGhee, Thomas Briggs, Dr. Gavin B. Clark, H. H. Champion, R. P. B. Frost, J. L. Joynes, Rev. J. E. Symes and William Reeve, the publisher. These and others made up a fund to meet the expenses of the George campaign, for, unlike the custom of pay-lectures in the United States, most lectures in Great Britain are delivered practically free, only a few front seats being charged for and reserved. Arrangement had been made for George to lecture in most of the important cities and towns of Great Britain, the campaign to be opened in St. James's Hall, London, on January 9.

But before he opened the course, Mr. George had to settle two important questions. The first affected his attitude towards socialism. Mr. Champion, the treasurer, and Mr. Frost, the secretary of the Land Reform Union, were in reality not wholly in harmony with the individualism of "Progress and Poverty," but believed rather in the collectivism of Karl Marx, who had a few months before died in London after a long residence there. These two men, with one or two others, waited on Mr. George and plainly said that if he did not make the socialistic programme part of his own and call for nationalisation of capital, including all machinery, the socialists would be compelled to oppose his campaign. Mr. George replied with some sharpness that he had come across the sea on invitation of the Land Reform Union to lecture on the principles with which his name was identified and no others; that his principles were clearly explained in his books; and that the socialists could support or oppose, as they pleased. As a matter of fact Champion and Frost made no further objection and quietly acquiesced in George's plans, but men like Hyndman at the head of the socialistic movement *per se* made covert opposition.

The other question for settlement was as to "confiscation."[1] This was the most common objection to the George proposal, and even some of the members of the Land Reform Union urged him to be as mild as possible and to say nothing against compensation to landlords, for, said they, the English nation will never consent to take property from the landlords without paying for it. His answer to them was short and clear. The land of right belonged to all the people, or it belonged to those who

---

[1] August Lewis on this point says : " In a conversation with Mr. George one day, I said : 'Thomas G. Shearman thinks that it was a grave error and a great detriment to the progress of the movement that the word "confiscation" should ever have been used. You should have called it instead the gradual absorption of rent. What is your opinion about that? Would you avoid the term "confiscation" were you to write "Progress and Poverty" to-day?' His face assumed a sort of a troubled and displeased expression, and he said : 'I don't know what I should do to-day ; but when I wrote the book, I was not in the humour to have much consideration for anybody's feelings.' "

called themselves landlords. If it belonged to the land-lords, they might do what they pleased with their own; and no one could have basis for complaint. If it be-longed to all the people, then it should be restored at once; nor could they in justice be called upon to pay one penny for getting back what was of right theirs. To give com-pensation, would be to concede the landlords' right of title. He himself did not want confiscation—he wanted to stop confiscation—to stop those who called themselves landlords from taking rent, which did not belong to them, and to give it to the community to which it did belong, which he proposed to do by means of taxation. However, he said he would tell his audience that they could com-pensate if they pleased, but that he did not think it would be just to do so. Thus Mr. George had to contend with two sets of his own supporters before he met the common enemy. But he hesitated no more with the one than with the other.

As showing the habits and temperament of the man, it may be interesting to note the way he prepared himself for what he believed was to be the most important address in the tour—the lecture in St. James's Hall. Most of the day before he kept to his lodgings near Russell Square thinking out the line of his discourse, which was to be on the subject of "Progress and Poverty." Slowly and with labour he dictated to his son. In the afternoon he sent for another stenographer and worked late into the evening alternately with the two writers. In this way he used his son up and sent him off to bed, continuing with the other shorthand writer. Early next morning when the son waked he found that his father had been up and at work betimes. The father announced, somewhat to the young man's dismay, that he had cast aside all the work of the day before and that since rising he had commenced on a new, and the true, line. Proceeding along this new line, Mr. George dictated to his son and the other stenographer who was again called in, all that day, except when interrupted by members of the committee. He was in fact busy almost up to the moment when the committee called to conduct him to the hall. Then there was a scramble to get papers together, to dress and get off. And the upshot of it all was that the notes were not used, for only in main points and general sequence of ideas was that which was delivered like that which had been dictated with so much labour.

The great hall was packed; every seat and every foot of available standing room was filled. The platform even was crowded, mostly with members of the Union, and Michael Davitt conspicuous. All classes and vocations were represented there—nobles and commoners, men noted in politics, literature, the ministry and the professions, or leading in the world of manual labour. Ill health prevented John Ruskin from presiding or even attending, but Henry Labouchere, M.P., editor of "Truth," filled the chair with capital effect. He said that the country had in the last two centuries four Georges who had meddled with and muddled public affairs. Now came George the Fifth who did not wear a crown, but who came with keen intelligence and a generous impulse—a man whose sympathies were with the poor and lowly, instead of with the high and mighty.

Just before rising Mr. George whispered to his friend, Thomas F. Walker: "If I speak too long, pull my coat-tail. I have the habits of a writer, rather than those of a speaker. When I get thinking, ideas come with a rush; so that when I am on my feet I lose the sense of time." But Mr. Walker forgot the suggestion in the charm of the finished address. The pre-eminent qualities of the lecture were sincerity and confidence. As in California he had said to the early California reviewer that "when a man has so thought out and tested his opinions that they have in his mind the highest certainty, it would be but affectation for him to assume doubts he does not feel," so now, as he stood up before the great and distinguished audience in the capital of the world, he had that dead certainty of air, which, accompanied by a direct, sympathetic manner, a flow of clear language, a logical order, quick response and complete command of the subject, captivated his listeners, and caused the arch Tory newspaper, "The Standard," next morning to say sarcastically: "He is perfectly simple and straightforward; a man with a mission; born to set right in a single generation the errors of six thousand years."

The climax of the lecture was reached when Mr. George said that charity could not lift the poor of London from the misery and squalor of the slums—that resort must be made to justice. Cheers interrupted, and a voice cried: "Who brought them into the world?" "God Almighty, in my opinion," cried the lecturer, electrifying his audience; "and whom God Almighty brings into the world who shall dare to put out?"

Justice, he went on to say, compelled the returning of the land to the people without cost—but if doing this should work a hardship upon some—the helpless widow, for instance—whose case was constantly being brought forward—he would favour some provision for that. Statistics showed some two hundred thousand widows in England of all kinds and ages. Every widow, from the lady who sat on the throne down to the poorest labourer's widow, could receive, not as a matter of charity, but as a matter of justice, a pension of £100 a year   Laughter, cheers and some hissing followed this, and the Tory papers next day denounced George for disrespect to the Queen. In response to calls at the close of the lecture, Michael Davitt made a short, spirited speech, thus again publicly associating himself with Henry George.

The London lecture was to the press throughout the three kingdoms like a spark to gunpowder. Mr. George wrote to his wife, "I can't begin to send you the papers in which I am discussed, attacked and commented on, for I would have to send all the English, Scottish and Irish press. I am getting advertised to my heart's content, and I shall have crowds wherever I go. . . . I could be a social lion if I would permit it. But I won't fool with that sort of thing."

The new book "Social Problems," British rights to which the author sold to Kegan Paul, Trench & Co., was now out in various editions; and this, with his former books, was to be seen on every bookstall of any pretensions in the British Islands. He had received £400 for "Social Problems," which he sent home to pay some debts in New York and California.

The first provincial lectures were at Plymouth on the 15th and Cardiff on the 16th of January, touching both of which Mr. George wrote Mr. Walker of Birmingham, from Cardiff: "My lectures both at Plymouth and here were, I think, *telling* successes." Then relative to "confiscation," he said:

"I believe I am wise in taking the advance ground clearly and plainly. No matter how moderate I had been, there would have been precisely the same denunciation. The real cause of this is that the land-owning classes begin to realise the danger, not any particular thing I say.

"The advance, whatever it may be, will draw the fire; and I am doing a service to more moderate men in draw-

ing that fire so much ahead of the ground they occupy.
It will make them seem and feel quite moderate.

"As for your Radicals who have got into a flurry,
don't mind that. In a very short time they will rally
again. In a few months from now you will see many
of the men who are now so fearful of confiscation openly
avowing themselves 'confiscators.'

"The Tory press are doing our work. *They* will do
more for us than we could by any exertion do for
ourselves."

A fortnight afterwards George wrote to Walker: "The
thing to do is for you to pose as a compensationist, and
me as a confiscationist, just as Snap & Gobble join different churches. With you and Miss Taylor representing
the conservative wing, the landlords may well ask to be
preserved from their friends."[1]

After Cardiff, Mr. George spoke in Bristol and Birmingham. The Birmingham "Owl" said of the latter
lecture:

"It was a magnificent audience that gathered to hear
Henry George, and one which gave forth no uncertain
sound. It was one of the most unanimous and enthusiastic audiences I have seen in town for years. When

---

[1] While on a visit to Birmingham, Mr. George, in company with Mr.
Walker, Edward McHugh, lecture agent for the Land Reform Union, and
young George, went to hear Miss Helen Taylor address a big working
men's meeting at Smethwick, a suburb. As they entered the hall she
had reached the compensation point in her address and said in substance :
"Compensation ? Yes, I am in favour of compensation to the landlords.
And this can be easily arranged. First let the landlords pay to the nation the back taxes of four shillings in the pound on the actual value of
their land from the time of Charles II.— from which time they have been
paying little or nothing — and, moreover, let them pay to the nation interest and compound interest on the money thus withheld, and then out
of this great fund we can compensate the present individual cases." Mr.
George joined heartily in the general laughter and applauded vigorously.

Mr. George first came forward the cheering was tremendous. And again, when, after a portrayal of the evils consequent on the present state of things, the lecturer asked 'Was it not time that a missionary came from somewhere?' the applause was deafening, as the crowded audience recognised and accepted the missionary in Henry George."

Hard upon the London lecture, the official Liberals had followed suit of the Tory and Parnellite parties, and tabooed George. Evidence of this was given in each place where he spoke; but it was most marked in Liverpool, where he appeared on January 25. The Junior Reform Club, which had invited him to be its guest at dinner, withdrew the invitation; Mr. Samuel Smith, M.P., a wealthy and distinguished citizen of Liverpool, who had spent much in public benevolence, delivered a set lecture against the American; and the papers were united in condemnation. So that, although a large audience gathered in the Rotunda to hear the radical land reformer, the customary platform support had to be dispensed with. He wrote to Walker:

"My lecture here was a victory that would have done your heart good. The set against me in Birmingham was nothing to the set against me here. Poor Jackson, on whom all arrangements devolved, seemed utterly demoralised. . . . He had not ventured to send out any complimentary tickets—said no clergyman or man of note would accept one. Not a soul was to go on the stage with me save Dr. Cummins, M.P.; and I urged him not to, but he insisted that he would. Samuel Smith's relatives and family were in the audience, which was evidently largely in sympathy with him, and warmly applauded his name when I mentioned it. But the consciousness of opposition, which always rouses me, gave me the stimulus I needed to overcome physical weakness, for I was in bad trim from loss of sleep, and I carried the audience with me, step by step, till you never saw a more enthusiastic crowd. Jackson has told me since that he believed organised opposition had been planned; but that before I got to the place where they could object I 'had the audience, and the fuglemen left in disgust. At the close I called for a vote on compensation, and there were only three hands held up against it—two of which Jackson afterwards told me were those of land speculators. A rush was made for the platform as soon as I got through, and I could not get away for some time for the handshaking. Of the effects at the time there could be no doubt, and I hear of the most gratifying effects upon those who did not go."

The Liverpool "Post" next day said editorially: "Mr. George's lecture in Liverpool last night had all the sweet and seductive beauty which has stolen away the judgment of many a reader of his famous book. . . . He apparently has convinced a large number of persons that thieving is no theft, for his great audience last night pronounced unanimously in favour of appropriating the land of the country and giving the present owners no compensation."

But if Mr. George was making conquests, his opponents were not idle, the most conspicuous among them being Frederic Harrison, the Positivist, and John Bright. After George had spoken in Birmingham, Bright made a speech there on "the most extraordinary, the greatest, the wildest, the most remarkable" social proposition "imported lately by an American inventor." George read Bright's speech in Scotland, whence he wrote Walker (Dundee, February 3):

"I can fancy your disgust if you heard Mr. Bright. The old man is utterly ignorant of what he is talking about. If John Bright would meet me on the platform and discuss the matter, I would be glad of the opportunity. If you think it would be a good thing to do, write to him to that effect.

"Frederic Harrison is lecturing against me. Has delivered two lectures in Edinburgh, and lectures again to-night at Newcastle. His is the very craziness of opposition, if I can judge by the reports.

"We are certainly getting the animals stirred up, and before the Liberals know it will have the Radical rank and file, no matter what may become of their leaders. I am glad it was Bright and not Chamberlain that came out against us—not that I care for any one's opposition, but that I am glad that he has not taken a stand which might injure his future usefulness."

Mr. George's confidence of getting the "Radical rank and file" came not only from what he had seen in England, but from what he was observing in Scotland, which he had entered after lecturing in Bolton and Newcastle.

If England had discontent among her slum population to make her ripe for the consideration of the land question, so Scotland had her own condition, perhaps more directly traceable to the land problem. Two years previously the crofters in the Western Island of Skye, had centred attention by resisting, for a time with force, the inclosure, by a large land-owner, of a piece of land that had been a common grazing ground from time immemorial. Physical resistance was put down only when the crofters had been brutally clubbed by a body of police sent up from Glasgow for the purpose. Public opinion sided strongly with the peasants, and the incident blew into live sparks again the seemingly dead ashes of wrath originally set into fierce glow by clearances and evictions in many parts of Scotland, some of them within comparatively recent times. Sheep and deer of large pro-

prietors had become the solitary occupants of regions once
studded with the habitations of a hardy people. A Royal
Commission had been appointed to examine into crofter
grievances and the still worse cotter troubles. This Commission subsequently effected what had been brought
about in Ireland—a reduction in rents. But this could
not be a complete remedy. The questions of property,
ownership, equal rights, justice had been raised. It only
needed a man like Henry George, with a simple, clear-
cut proposition to give point and force to the general conviction of wrong, by turning all thought into a single
channel—which he proceeded to do by demanding the
restoration of the common rights in land. The opening
of the Scottish course with a lecture in Dundee was therefore under auspicious circumstances. The lecture was
in Newsome's Circus. Rev. David Macrae, a vigorous no-
compensationist, was in the chair, and three or four other
clergymen and several councilmen among those on the
platform.

Yet there was the fly in the ointment. To many minds
Henry George had desecrated the Lord's Day by participating in a mass meeting in London on the Sunday of his
public entry into the Metropolis. But this lapse was
quickly forgotten in the glow of religious fervor he excited
when, by invitation, he delivered in Rev. Mr. Macrae's
temporary church, in the Kinnaird Hall, the lecture on
"Moses" which, while at work on "Progress and Poverty,"
he had delivered, in San Francisco, before the Young
Men's Hebrew Association of that city. Its eloquence
and fire and vivid picturing spoke to the hearts and minds
of a people still possessing many of the traits of the
Covenanter of old, and as it were, gave the active, speaking support of the Scriptures to the proclamation of
equal rights to the land. Mr. George repeated the "Moses"

lecture several times in Scotland during this and subsequent trips, and latterly had it put in pamphlet form for free distribution. This lecture and other things tended in the minds of many to give a religious benediction to all his utterances; and a number of his lectures in the Highlands on the land question were opened or closed with prayer, pronounced by some devout person on the platform or in the audience.

The lecture course was north to Wick and Keiss, and incidentally Mr. George visited John o' Groat's house at the extreme northeastern point of Great Britain. Then he retraced his steps and turned west to the Island of Skye. He lectured at Portree and made informal speeches on the land question at Glendale and Uig. Edward McHugh, who was acting as Mr. George's lecture agent, says of the Portree lecture:

"McDonald of Skeabost, an important landlord in the island, was present and showed a lively interest. After the address proper he took the floor to ask what Mr. George recommended the people to do with the landlords if their lands should be taken from them. Mr. George replied that he would do with the landlords as the fisherman does with the oyster—open it, take out the fish and throw the shells away. The answer made a sensation and McDonald stalked out of the hall. Mr. George did not learn until afterwards of the singular aptness of his reply, since this same McDonald had taken from the people of Skye the immemorial privilege of fishing for oysters in the shallow waters of the island and had thereby increased his own and his fellow landlords' income by sending the supply to the London market."

From Skye, Mr. George proceeded to Glasgow, Inverness, Aberdeen and Edinburgh. But of all the lectures in Scotland, that in Glasgow proved to be the most important. He spoke there twice, on February 18 and again on February 25, both times in the City Hall. The first lecture was of the regular course. There were some empty seats in the hall, but the audience was anything but apathetic, for at the close five hundred persons remained to take part in the formation of an organisation to propagate the ideas held by the lecturer. To launch this organisation in good style, the second meeting was held, with Mr. George as the chief spokesman, John Murdock in the chair, and William Forsyth, proprietor of the Cobden Hotel of the city, to move the resolutions formally establishing the Scottish Land Restoration League —a title suggested by Richard McGhee, one of the active workers in the plan. The hall was jammed, and enough people were turned away to have made another big meeting. Mr. George was at his best, as were all the other speakers. The audience was hot with enthusiasm and gave itself up to wild cheering when a couple of pipers in costume came pressing through the throng playing national airs. In a word, the Scottish Land Restoration League started off with a furor, and 1940 signatures were handed in to the committee for enrollment on the membership list. William Forsyth was elected President, and Mr. George wrote the League's proclamation to the people of Scotland. The action in Glasgow was contagious. Similar societies were formed very quickly in Dundee, Aberdeen, Inverness, Edinburgh, Greenock and several other cities.

Entering England again, Mr. George lectured in Leeds, Oxford, Cambridge and Hull, and then went back to London. He had set out on the tour expecting to meet with all manner of opposition arising from frightened special interests, class feelings, local prejudices and other circumstances. Yet strange as it may appear, it remained for Oxford, that ancient and famous seat of learning, to earn the distinction of discreditable conduct. Michael Davitt, who came there shortly afterwards to lecture, was locked in his hotel chambers by a body of the University students, and did not get out in time to speak. Mr. George did not suffer this treatment, but his lecture in this intellectual centre was attended by the turmoil of the hustings. There were honours, for during his two days' stay in Oxford he was the guest of Professor F. Max Müller; and at the lecture, which was held in the Clarendon Assembly room, F. York Powell, M.A., lecturer in law, presided, and a number of ladies and men prominent in the University attended. But in the midst of the audience, which consisted chiefly of under-graduates, sat a bunch of unruly young aristocrats, who, by shouting, ironically cheering and general noise, kept up a disturbance throughout the proceedings. This made a smooth and connected discourse impossible; but when the lecturer, assuming his audience for the most part to be well grounded in economic subjects, cut short his address proper to answer questions, one man after another took the floor, not to put simple interrogatories, as invited, but, possibly following the University debating habit, to make a speech, often with the harsh manner and strong epithets of a special pleader.

Alfred Marshall, lecturer on political economy at Balliol College, was the first to rise. He observed, among other things, that not a single economic doctrine in Mr. George's book was both new and true, since what was new was not true, and what was true was not new. He announced that he had repeatedly challenged any one to disprove this, but that no one had come forward. Moreover, he was of opinion that Mr. George in his book had not understood a single author whom he had undertaken to criticise; but he (Marshall) offered no censure, because Mr. George had not had the special training necessary to understand them. Interspersed with asseverations of this kind was a shower of questions.

The lecturer's chief reply was that he was willing to subject "Progress and Poverty" to Mr. Marshall's test— that it contained nothing that was both new and true. Because, said Mr. George, the book was based upon the truth; and the truth could not be a new thing; it always had existed and it must be everlasting. He endeavoured to pick out and answer a number of Marshall's questions, and he really succeeded in winning the support and applause of a considerable part of the audience. But there were cheers from others for the Balliol man; and he, after rising very often and engaging much time, turned to his supporters and announced that the lecturer had failed to meet his queries; whereupon he sat down.[1]

But the climax of disorder was reached when Mr. Conybeare, son-in-law of Professor Müller, denounced Mr. George's remedy as a "nostrum" that was "scandalously immoral." He delivered this with a tone and manner that called forth mingled cries of dissent and approval from the divided audience and that excited the lecturer himself to say—for he did not recognise the speaker—that he must withdraw the compliment he had paid early in the evening to the University's learning and good manners. This remark increased the uproar for a time; and Professor Müller sat on the platform, an uncomfortable, yet outwardly calm, witness to this caustic interchange between a member of his family and his guest. The tur-

---

[1] George's final views of Marshall as a political economist may be found in "The Science of Political Economy." See Marshall in index.

bulence was stilled when Mr. Conybeare arose and said that he intended no reflection upon Mr. George's character—that he intended only frankly to criticise ideas. Mr. George had met the young man before, but had lost sight of his relationship to his host. When attention was drawn to the matter after the lecture, he was pained and mortified and expressed to Professor Müller his sorrow that he had shown weakness in allowing the young man's words to chafe him. The professor on his side was much moved. He apologised for what he called a public insult to a guest by a member of the family; the offence being the more flagrant he said, since the one who had caused it had not read "Progress and Poverty" and could not properly judge of its doctrines. Nothing could have added to the sincere and graceful bearing of the eminent scholar in the difficult circumstances.

The Cambridge lecture proved to be as quiet and orderly as the Oxford lecture had been noisy and disorderly. The audience was very large; and though the questions indicated that opposition to the principles enunciated was not wanting, the proceedings were stamped with every mark of propriety.

When Mr. George got back to London he found that his managers could not again obtain St. James's Hall for him—that on one pretext or another it had been refused; but he spoke four times in other halls, and so closed his triumphal tour. He had been speaking with fiery zeal for the best part of three months; had travelled from Plymouth in the South to John o' Groat's House in the North, and from Hull in the East to the Hebrides in the West. On the 5th of April he was given a farewell banquet at the Criterion by the Land Restoration League, when he said in his address that a flame had been lit in Great Britain that would be fanned by every wind.

On invitation, chiefly of Michael Davitt, Mr. George crossed to Ireland and lectured to a large audience in the Ancient Concert Rooms, Dublin, on "The Land for the People," Mr. Allingham, the Mayor of Waterford, in the chair. On Sunday morning, April 13, Mr. George embarked at Queenstown with his son on the Guion liner *Oregon* and sailed for New York.

Although the several months in Great Britain had been, as a whole, strenuous, there were intervals of relaxation. One of these was when Wilfred Meynell, editor of the Catholic "Weekly Register," took Mr. George to meet Cardinal Manning. Mr. Meynell said after the death of both men:

> "It was my great privilege to introduce Henry George to Cardinal Manning. I have a vision of the two profiles facing each other in the dim light of the growing dusk, and I recall the emotion of tone in which each man made frankly to the other a sort of profession of faith. They had travelled to the same goal from opposite directions. 'I loved the people,' said Henry George, 'and that love brought me to Christ as their best friend and teacher.' 'And I,' said the Cardinal, 'loved Christ, and so learned to love the people for whom He died.' They faced each other in silence for a moment—in a silence more eloquent than words."

There were also lighter moments, when Mr. George's sunshiny nature gave itself free play. Humour was one of his salient qualities, and there were many amusing incidents in passing. For instance, on reaching Cardiff, he went to a Turkish bath to relieve his fatigue. When the bath itself was over and he lay resting in the cooling room, he was treated to a discussion of "this American, Henry George," between an attendant and a visitor; neither of whom apparently had the least idea that Mr.

George was in the apartment with them. In whatever else they differed, the talkers were agreed that "the American" was preaching robbery; that he wanted to take property away from people; that Americans were "all a set of liars." "All except the Canadians," said Mr. George, getting into the conversation. Continuing, he said: "Those American busybodies like Henry George should be sent back to America to try their doctrines there before they try to force them upon us."

"Yes, yes," answered both the other men.

"Why, just to think what he teaches," exclaimed George, with show of indignation. "Here is the Marquis of Bute, who owns so much of the land of Cardiff. Of course the land is his."

"Yes," said the men.

"And he can do what he pleases with his own property."

"Yes," was the response.

"And, of course, since the land is his and he can do what he pleases with his own property, he can, if he wants to, clear off a large part of the population of Cardiff— can, if he should choose to do so, destroy an important section of the city."

At this the men made protest; and as Mr. George pressed for the rights and privileges of the Marquis of Bute, the men became more and more radical, until they asserted that the nobleman really had no better right to the land there than anybody else in Cardiff—the very principle they had previously condemned in "the American." Mr. George played the staunch conservative to the last and left the building without revealing himself.

At another time, while on a train to Aberdeen, he fell into conversation with the only other occupant of the compartment—a man who talked well and freely, and who said he was a newspaper writer. Various subjects were passed under contribution until, with a bright and airy way, the stranger came to the subject of "Henry George and his lecture trip." "Ah, what do you think of him?" said Mr. George. "A Yankee with a Yankee money-making scheme," said the other. "Our trans-Atlantic cousins are clever at such things. The man writes well; he puts things in a plausible way. He makes a proposition which for very hugeness has the charm of novelty. And really, the fellow is as entertaining as a speaker as he is as a writer."

"Then you have heard him lecture," said Mr. George calmly.

"Oh, yes," was the gay reply, and then in response to questions that drew him on, he gave a ludicrous description of Henry George's personal appearance, his companion joining in his laughter over it. The entertainment continued until the journalist left the train. Just as he was stepping out of the compartment, Mr. George said: "I owe you an apology; but you interested me so deeply that I did not like to stop you. Please accept my card." The gentleman gave one glance at the bit of pasteboard and then almost fell out on the platform.

Thus while at times he might pass for a native, he did not always. "Watch me play Englishman," said he one day to his son as their train pulled into Euston station. "Here, porter," he called, "get my luggage." "Is it an American trunk, sir?" said the man. Mr. George turned to his son and silently admitted the failure of the experiment.

It was while travelling in a third-class carriage in England that a poor woman got in at a way station and brought with her a jute or hemp satchel, such as is commonly seen in the hands of school children. She put this satchel down on the seat beside her, doubtless not noticing that one just like it was already there—a satchel which belonged to Mr. George and which was one of many receptacles for books and papers that he had, as by custom, accumulated on his travels. Presently the woman got out; and later Mr. George, thinking of some notes, put his hand into his satchel to get them. Instead of the notes, he found a strange and dilapidated pair of shoes. He was thrown into a sea of wonder, from which he did not emerge until thought recurred of the woman passenger who had just before gotten out. At a station where he had a few minutes' time, he telegraphed back along the line in hope of hearing of his papers, and word came that a complaint had been lodged by an indignant woman who protested that she had been robbed of a pair of shoes by a man who stuffed her satchel with a lot of paper trash. The philosopher was glad enough to forward her bag and a day later got his own in exchange.

CHAPTER VII.

"PROTECTION OR FREE TRADE?"

1884-1886. AGE, 45-47.

HENRY GEORGE at home had passed beyond the world of letters into the world of practical things. Besides being an author, he was recognised as a leader among the restless labouring classes—to be with the House of Want, rather than with the House of Have. The working men honoured his return with a mass meeting in Cooper Union. But men who made a business of politics or who moved in the privileged and fashionable world, held aloof, for instead of standing for glittering and unmeaning generalities, Henry George began to be understood to menace a revolution in political and social affairs. They instinctively drew away; and hence it was that a complimentary dinner given to him on the 30th of April, 1884, at the Cosmopolitan Theatre, New York, lacked the lustre of the Delmonico banquet of the year before; and a lecture in the Academy of Music proved a total failure, scarcely enough people being present to pay for rent and advertising. This lecture was given under the management of the theatrical and lecture firm of Brooks & Dickson, who made a six months' contract with Mr. George for a tour of the United States and Canada, he to get his expenses and sixty per cent. of the profits. Mr.

Brooks had been in England and had witnessed Mr. George's great success there, and both men looked for like success in this country. The utter fiasco attending the first lecture threw the firm into gloom, as they could see nothing but failure all along the line. Mr. George no sooner learned of their views than, with characteristic promptness, he released them from their contract and without consideration. Whatever lectures he delivered during the next year were under other management, generally his own.

Mr. George had during the British tour won great laurels as a platform speaker. Yet there were many who had spoken of his power as commonplace. The fact was that he was not even. He did not memorise, nor, except in the single lecture on Moses, did he read. He sometimes used a skeleton of heads, but his common practice was to speak without written notes of any kind. For this he prepared by meditation shortly before speaking; lying down, if possible, and perhaps smoking. He merely arranged a line of thought, and left the precise form of expression to inspiration when on his feet. This subjected him largely to conditions; a quiet audience, no matter how friendly, drawing forth a subdued speech, while a lively audience, friendly or hostile, provoked animation. He himself was conscious of this and said he could do best when facing opposition. Charles Frederick Adams tells how his friend returned from a lecture in Massachusetts one day and said: "Come out to lunch, Charley; I am so ashamed of that lecture as an artistic performance that I want to spend the money I got for it." Louis F. Post supplies an illustration of Henry George's two ways of speaking. He went to the working men's welcome meeting in Cooper Union on Mr. George's return in 1884.

"It was there that I had my first taste of his power as an orator. His London speech at St. James's Hall had been described by the English press in such superlative terms as an oratorical effort that I wondered. The London 'Times,' in a column editorial, had compared him as an orator with Cobden and Bright so much to their disadvantage that I began to question the standards of English oratory. George had seemed to me the best writer I had ever read, but no orator at all—at best only a plain speaker. And when he responded to the speech of welcome at Cooper Union I was still much puzzled by the estimate the London 'Times' had made. It was far from oratory in any sense. In matter it was excellent. George's oratory never failed in that respect. But in manner it was tame and unimpressive. After he had finished, and while some one else without oratorical ability was speaking, I went out for a ruminative smoke. Upon returning after possibly an hour's absence, a voice came up to me through the subterranean corridors as I entered the street door of Cooper Union, which made me think that now an orator had certainly come forth. As I descended, and a burst of applause followed a period, this impression grew. The voice was strange to me, and I wondered as its volume swelled what prodigy of platform eloquence this man could be. Hurrying forward with that impression deepening, and coming to one of the doors which disclosed the stage and a large part of an enthusiastic audience, there I beheld upon the platform, with one arm extended and head thrown back, his voice filling the hall and his sentiments stirring the blood of his auditors, no one else but Henry George. He had again been called upon to speak, and for nearly an hour he held his audience entranced, myself among the rest. Long before he had finished I knew why the London 'Times' thought him as great or greater than Cobden or Bright."

While he did some intermittent lecturing and speaking, Mr. George's chief purpose at this period was to apply himself to writing. The first thing he took up was an attack made on him and his principles by the Duke of Argyll in an article in the "Nineteenth Century" for April, entitled, "The Prophet of San Francisco." The article had appeared during the closing days of the British lecture trip, and the "Nineteenth Century," the "Fortnightly," and the "Pall Mall Gazette" hastened to offer their columns for reply. When Mr. George decided to answer he chose the same periodical through which he had been attacked.

But Mr. George was reluctant to enter the lists. He treated the attack as chiefly abusive, and abuse he believed not worth heeding. Whatever of principle appeared he considered to be answered in advance in "Progress and Poverty." But the active men in the Scottish Land Restoration League pointed out that, besides being a Peer of the Realm, close in rank to Royalty itself, the Duke was titular chief of the great Campbell clan. A controversy between the "Peer" and the "Prophet" would, the League advisers argued, carry the land question into every household in Scotland and arouse the highlanders. So Mr. George set himself to the task of replying in the brief moments of leisure that remained to him during his tour. He sat up a considerable part of the night in Cork, previous to sailing for America, working on the article. He actually had it written, and the ordinary critic would perhaps have said, completely written; but it did not satisfy its exacting author. He said to his son: "I'll not send it off now, but take it to New York and polish it like a steel shot." And with the title of "The 'Reduction to Iniquity,'" the reply appeared in the July number of the "Nineteenth Century."

The Duke had dropped as suddenly and as far in Henry George's estimation as had that other philosopher, Herbert Spencer. George acknowledged his obligations to the Duke as the author of the "Reign of Law," and as pointing out "the existence of physical laws and adaptations which compel the mind that thinks upon them to the recognition of creative purpose." Like the Duke, he had beheld "the grand simplicity and unspeakable harmony of universal law." But he now learned with amazement that the Duke's splendid philosophy broke down when it trenched on social affairs, and that "a trumpery title and a patch of ground" fettered "a mind that had communed with nature and busied itself with causes and beginnings." How little he cared for the Duke's unfairness and personal bitterness is shown by his passing them with contemptuous silence. But he considered the Scotsman as untrue to his own philosophy; and a dishonest philosopher kindled his wrath. For an intellectual leader who would consciously mislead, he had no mercy; so that in his reply, he coupled false philosopher and false philosophy, and together held them up to general scorn.

This one article, "polished like a steel shot," seemed to suffice. It was received by the Duke of Argyll in silence; nor did he ever attempt to make rejoinder. It was accepted by the reading world with the mixed feelings excited by the other writings from George's pen. But by all those in sympathy with the objects of the Scottish Land Restoration League it was hailed with demonstrations of joy. Accompanied by the Duke's article, it was soon published in pamphlet form under the caption of "The Peer and the Prophet," and in the hands of the League, was carried into the homes and factories of the cities, while it became a kind of "fiery cross" through the Highlands and Islands of Scotland, summoning the clansmen to the great struggle for natural rights. A similar pamphlet was published in the United

States with the title of "Property in Land," and became an effective instrument for propaganda.

The reply to the Duke of Argyll Mr. George regarded as a mere thing in passing, compared with the work to which he now settled down—the tariff book, or pamphlet, for he did not determine beforehand what size he would make it. A year had passed since the loss of the manuscript of the first book. Mr. George with his family spent the summer on a farm on Long Island, near Jamaica, worked by Walter Cranford, son of John P. Cranford of Brooklyn, an early and ardent advocate of the Georgeian ideas, and who with his purse gave much help to their spread. There on the Cranford farm Mr. George applied himself with steady industry to his task.

The book, intended primarily for working men, aimed, as he said in his preface, not only to examine the arguments commonly used, but, carrying the inquiry farther than the controversialists on either side had yet ventured to go, sought to discover why protection retained such popular strength in spite of all exposures of its fallacies; endeavoured to trace the connection between the tariff question and those still more important social questions, then rapidly becoming the "burning questions" of the times; and sought to show to what radical measures the principle of free trade logically led. In a letter to Walker of Birmingham (September 25) the author explained: "I first knock all the claims of protection; then turn around and show that the mere abolition of protection would accomplish nothing for the working classes; but that to accomplish anything for them, the principle of free trade must be carried out to its full extent, which means, of course, the abolition of all taxes and the appropriation of land values."

When the writing was well advanced, Mr. George had

some correspondence about it with Dr. Taylor of San Francisco, who suggested employment of the inductive method. George replied (September 14): "My view of the matter is the reverse of yours. I do not think induction employed in such questions as the tariff is of any use. What the people want is theory; and until they get a correct theory into their heads, all citing of facts is useless."

Mr. George was much interested in the animals on the Cranford farm and particularly in a fine blooded bull that was often tethered in a grass field just outside the window. The animal was much annoyed by flies, and in walking around would wind his rope short until his head was drawn close to the stake, and he could do little more in the hot summer sun than switch his tail and bellow. Often and often the philosopher stopped work to go out and drive the bull in the opposite direction and free his rope. This commonplace incident, oft repeated, suggested the opening illustration in the introductory chapter, which, instead of first, was about the last part of the book to be written at the Cranford farm.

In the fall the family moved to a house in Brooklyn, on Macon Street. Soon after that, on the urging of his boyhood friend, Rev. Dr. R. Heber Newton, Mr. George accepted an invitation to attend the Ninth Congress of the Episcopal Church, at Detroit, and speak to the topic, "Is our civilisation just to working men?" Rev. John W. Kramer, of New York, who was secretary of the Congress, afterwards said.

"Mr. George's first words were in answer to the question asked. He said: 'It is not. Try it by whatever test you will, it is glaringly, bitterly and increasingly unjust.' I remember the emphatic fervour with which this opening was uttered. It attracted the audience; it

startled men. But hearty applause came, given by
many hearers who were not ready to agree with the
strong statement, but who were for the moment captured
by the sublime courage of the speaker. The address
was published in full in the proceedings of the Congress."

The presidential campaign had for some weeks been in
full swing, but for the first time in many years Mr.
George could not warm up. Blaine, the Republican candidate, had avowed himself a champion of what George
called the "protection humbug," and Patrick Ford was
out with the "Irish World" strongly in Blaine's support.
Benjamin F. Butler of Massachusetts was running as a
Greenback-Labour candidate, but George quickly concluded that Butler was insincere in this and a mere "de-
coy duck for the Republican party." Yet the Democrats
avoided the issue. George wrote Taylor as early as August: "I am utterly disgusted with the attitude of the
Democratic party. It is a mere party of expediency, and
as such can never win. Cleveland's nomination was an
expediency nomination." George, however, in effect voted
for Cleveland. Leaving for Scotland before election day,
he paired with a friend who had intended to vote for
Blaine. And after the election was over and Cleveland
was known to have won, George wrote a signed article
for William Saunders' London paper, "The Democrat,"
stating among other things that events had shown that
now the tariff issue could no longer be avoided, that it
would split the Democratic party in two and that it
would raise the underlying question of why some grow so
rich while others, though they work hard, are yet so poor.

The managers of the Scottish Land Restoration League
had sent a pressing call to Mr. George to come and make
a lecture and speaking campaign through the lowlands

which contained the important political centres, for it was the purpose to force the land question into politics. And in order that he might the easier do this, they raised a fund with which to meet the heaviest expenses. Mr. George decided that this would be the most important work he could do for the time and in October he crossed the Atlantic alone.

In order to draw general attention to the campaign, a big meeting was held under the auspices of the English League in St. James's Hall, London. The hall was packed. Mr. George, of course, was the central figure, and Miss Taylor, Michael Davitt, William Forsyth, President of the Scottish League, and others spoke. George had now come to full powers as a speaker and his address was thought by many to be the finest he had yet delivered in Great Britain. The effect of this meeting was to set the press, and particularly the Scottish press, agog on the subject.

The Scottish campaign opened in the City Hall in Glasgow on November 21. The hall was crowded with a pay audience and people were turned away. Lectures in other towns followed in close succession, the one in Kilmarnock on Christmas Eve being appropriate to the night and particularly fine.

Trouble had again broken out between the crofters and the half dozen or less landlords in Skye and the other Western Islands. Police from Glasgow and Royal Naval Marines had been sent there to keep the peace. The League arranged for several meetings in Skye for Mr. George, all of which were eminently successful, some of the soldiers attending and applauding the lecturer's sentiments. On returning to Glasgow, Mr. George was interviewed at length by a representative of the "Pall Mall Gazette" of London. In answer to the question what, apart from his radical remedy, could he suggest in the way of immediate measures of relief for the crofters, he said:

"The withdrawal of the army of invasion, the suspension, at least as to crofter holdings, of all laws for the collection of rent; the suspension of all laws for the preservation of game, and of the law requiring gun licenses. The enactment of a short bill of this kind would greatly relieve the crofters, while larger measures were being considered, and would obviate the necessity for any charitable fund, such as the Earl of Breadalbane and the Rev. Mr. McDonald of Inverness, are raising, which could be turned to the relief of the landlords, if any of them really suffered by not getting rents. The suspension of the gun license and of game laws would enable the crofters to protect their crops, and vary their diet, while accustoming them to the use of arms, a thing in itself much to be desired among a free people."

The campaign was closed as it began, with an address in London. The English League had asked the Lord Mayor for the use of Guildhall. Being refused that, they decided to hold a meeting of the unemployed outside the hall, or more precisely, in front of the Royal Exchange. The meeting took place Saturday afternoon, January 17. It was estimated that seven thousand people were in the gathering. William Saunders, Rev. Stewart Headlam, Rev. Mr. Hastings, Rev. C. Fleming Williams, William Miller, Peter Hennessy (tailor), A. Pike (shoemaker) and A. Brown (joiner) were among the speakers. The strongest point in Mr. George's speech was when he pointed to the inscription in great letters across the front of the Royal Exchange and said: "Look up there. 'The Earth is the Lord's.'" [A voice: "The landlords'!"] "Aye, the landlords'. They have substituted the land-

lords for the Lord above all; and the want of employment, the misery which exists from one end of the kingdom to the other—the misery which encircles society
wherever civilisation goes, is caused by the sin of the
denial of justice."

Before sailing for home, Mr. George was induced to
lecture in Liverpool and also to cross the Irish Sea and
address a North of Ireland audience at Belfast, the capital of Ulster. Both gatherings were large, the latter, filling Ulster Hall, numbering between four and five thousand people. Enthusiasm in both cities was very great.

The result of the trip across the Atlantic was summed
up by Miss Taylor in a note to Mrs. George: "Mr. George's
name is in our papers every day for praise or blame, and
he has more warm friends here than bitter enemies."
She might also have said that Joseph Chamberlain, the
then leading Radical, had in a speech taken such advanced
ground for the taxation of land values that his name
was very frequently coupled with Mr. George's. The
visit had a further significance in that some of the friends
urged George to return and stand for Parliament, assur-
ing him that he could be elected in any one of a number
of constituencies. He wrote to Durant in the matter
(February 11): "I am at heart as much a citizen of Old
England as of New England, but I think that from the
accident of my birth I should be under disadvantage on
your side of the water. At any rate, I should not deem
it prudent to go over there, unless there was such a considerable call as made it seem clearly my duty. When
this point is reached it will be time to talk about it."
Within that year a general election took place under
the new franchise act and redistribution of seats, and
to use Mr. George's words "a little knot of thorough-
going 'Land Restorationists'" were "returned" to the new

Parliament, "with quite a large fringe of men sufficiently advanced for immediate purposes." However, Irish matters engaged British politics for some time afterward and little more than educational work could be done along land restoration lines in Parliament.

In addition to the foregoing signs of progress in Great Britain was one to which, if not Mr. George's recent trip, at least his former visits and the extensive reading of his books might reasonably be supposed to have been a contributing cause. It was the truly extraordinary report made in spring of 1885 by a "Royal Commission on the Housing of the Working Classes," which recommended that a local tax of four per cent. of its selling value be placed upon vacant or inadequately used land, as tending to relieve general "rates" (i. e., local taxes), and by forcing new land into use, to bring down the price of general building land.[1] The members of the Commis-

---

[1] This passage of the report ran as follows: "At present, land available for building in the neighbourhood of our populous centres, though its capital value is very great, is probably producing a small yearly return until it is let for building. The owners of this land are rated [taxed locally], not in relation to the real value, but to the actual annual income. They can thus afford to keep their land out of the market, and to part with only small quantities, so as to raise the price beyond the actual monopoly price which the land would command by its advantages of position. Meantime, the general expenditure of the town on improvements is increasing the value of their property. If this land were rated [taxed locally] at, say, four per cent. on its selling value, the owners would have a more direct incentive to part with it to those who are desirous of building, and a twofold advantage would result to the community. First, all the valuable property would contribute to the rates [local taxes], and thus the burden on the occupiers would be diminished by the increase in the rateable property. Secondly, the owners of the building land would be forced to offer their land for sale, and thus their competition with one another would bring down the price of building land, and so diminish the tax in the shape of ground rent, or price paid for land, which is now levied on urban enterprise by the adjacent land-owners — a tax, be it re-

sion were, Sir Charles W. Dilke, Bart. (chairman),
H.R.H. the Prince of Wales, Cardinal Manning, Lord
Salisbury, Lord Brownlow, Lord Carrington, George J.
Goschen, Sir R. A. Cross, Rt. Rev. W. Walshaw How,
Bishop of Bedford; Hon. E. Lyulph Stanley, W. McCul-
logh Torrens, Henry Broadhurst, George Godwin, F.R.S.,
Samuel Morley, Sir George Harrison, E. Dwyer Gray and
Jesse Collings. The large majority of the commissioners
seem to have approved of this proposal. At any rate,
but three formally dissented from it—Salisbury, Goschen
and Cross.

While on this trip to Great Britain Mr. George, as on
former occasions, met many people interesting to him,
but one of particular interest was the Rt. Hon. James
Bryce, notable in literature and politics, and who, the
American found on personal contact, bore out his reputation for broadness of mind and democracy of spirit. The
two men had a long talk on subjects of common interest
to them. Mr. Bryce says of this meeting:

> "Mr. George quite won the heart of my sister by ad-
> miring her cat which was quite a privileged character in
> our household—so privileged that it walked over my
> papers with impunity and spoiled many of 'The Ameri-
> can Commonwealth' proofs by lying down on them while
> the ink was fresh."

Mr. George intended to do some lecturing on reaching
home, but the general lecture season had been bad and
two or three that he tried proved unprofitable financially.

---

membered, which is no recompense for any industry or expenditure on
their part, but is the natural result of the industry and activity of the
townspeople themselves. Your Majesty's Commissioners would recommend that these matters should be included in legislation when the law
of rating comes to be dealt with by Parliament."

He therefore settled down to writing, which engaged him mainly until the close of the summer of the next year, 1886. Articles for the "North American Review" constituted much of this writing. First appeared in the July number, 1885, a "conversation" on the subject of "Land and Taxation" between him, representing his own ideas, and the eminent jurist, David Dudley Field, speaking for the established ideas. The managing editor of the "Review," Lorettus S. Metcalf, brought the gentlemen together at luncheon and explained that in order to place in juxtaposition the two views he would ask them to converse, each from his own standpoint, on the subject of "Land and Taxation," while a shorthand writer should take down all that was said. Of this matter Mr. Metcalf later said:

"The gentlemen had not met before, but they quickly measured each other and fell into cordial, easy, deferential interchange of thought. The remarkable feature of this meeting was the exhibition on both sides of the art of exact expression. So accurately did each speak that, except to catch typographical errors, not a single change was made in either manuscript or proof. The conversation was a marvel of clear thinking and precise utterance."

Mr. George always considered that he had by far the better part of the conversation; indeed, later he had the article reprinted in tract form for general circulation.

In the "North American Review" for February, 1886, the author had an article treating of trans-Atlantic social and political affairs under the caption of "England and Ireland"; and in the April number one entitled, "More about American Landlordism," showing the concentrating tendency of ownership. Mr. Metcalf had now with-

drawn from the management of the "North American
Review" and James Redpath, who took his place, engaged
Mr. George to write a series of articles on "Labour in
Pennsylvania"—Pennsylvania, the home of "protection"
and strikes. The author visited the State and presented
in four numbers between August, 1886, and January,
1887, his findings, based largely upon official statements
and the evidence of the labourers themselves. The articles related chiefly to the great coal and iron regions
owned by a comparatively few men, each in his own district as autocratic as a baron of old, for, said the writer,
reaching the bottom of his conclusions, "the power of the
sole landlord enables the operator or superintendent to
exercise such control as he cares to and may deem prudent. He may enact dog laws, goat laws, chicken laws,
liquor laws, or any other laws that he pleases, short of
the point of producing a general revolt; may regulate
trade and control amusements."

But though these magazine articles engrossed much of
his time, what chiefly absorbed him after his return from
Scotland up to the middle of 1886 was the completion
and publication of the book, "Protection or Free Trade?"
Some of the chapters of this work had appeared in serial
form in a combination of newspapers in the fall and
winter of 1885. From this the author obtained nearly
$3,000, which more than paid for the printing in book
form early in 1886. The latter he concluded to do himself under the name of Henry George & Co., his son,
Richard, being, in James Redpath's language, "Co." The
office was in Astor Place, New York, in joint occupancy
with an agency of Porter & Coates, Philadelphia publishers, the representative of which was Gaybert Barnes,
whose acquaintance had been made through William
Swinton. Besides handling the new book, Henry George

& Co. became the sole publishers of the cloth editions of the other George works.

It was while he was putting the new book through the newspapers that the acquaintance with Tom L. Johnson began. Mr. Johnson was a young man of just thirty-one, flushed with success as an inventor and Western street railroad manager and owner. He was born in Kentucky of a line famous in that State's politics. His father had been a planter and had lost all in the Civil War. Young Tom, with little more than a year's schooling, went to work at fifteen and quickly developed a mechanical and managing genius, which, with the acquisition of street railroad franchises in Cleveland and other cities, rapidly led to fortune. One day in a railroad car he bought and read Henry George's "Social Problems." That led him to read "Progress and Poverty," and to accept the doctrines that these books taught, even though their fundamental principle was based upon the destruction of monopolies, the very things that were the source of his rapidly increasing wealth. It was when he came to Brooklyn to purchase a street railroad that he called on Mr. George. He says of this interview:

"I had looked forward with more intense interest to the meeting than I was aware of, for when I tried to speak in a manly way of what was in my heart, I was conscious of much emotion. I said that I should rather have it to say to my children that I had met Henry George and had entertained him under my own roof as my guest than to be able to transmit to them any worldly blessing.

"I did not want to talk about myself. I did not go there for that. I went to talk to Mr. George about his cause; and I wanted in some way to call it my cause, too. But he stretched out on a lounge and I sat in a chair and I found myself telling him the story of my life.

"Then I said: 'Mr. George, your book on the tariff question will soon be out. I want to help to do good with it. I want 200 copies so as to send one to each lawyer and clergyman in Cleveland.' I also said to him: 'I cannot write, and I cannot speak. The least I can do is to make money with which to push our cause.'

"Mr. George answered: 'You do not know whether or not you can write; you have not tried. You do not know whether or not you can speak; you have not tried. Take an interest in political questions. It is well enough to make money, but the abilities that can make money can do other things, too.'"

CHAPTER VIII.

CANDIDATE FOR MAYOR OF NEW YORK.

1886.   AGE, 47.

BUSY during the summer of 1886 in pressing the circulation of his new book, "Protection or Free Trade?" and in preparing the series of articles on "Labour in Pennsylvania" for the "North American Review"; proposing towards the end of the year to start the long thought of weekly, and contemplating before that another short lecturing trip through Great Britain, as friends there suggested, Mr. George saw his time well laid out. But one day, while in his office talking with Tom L. Johnson and Gaybert Barnes, young Richard George entered with a newspaper that announced that the labour unions of the city proposed to enter politics in the fall in the hope of bringing about better political and social conditions and intended to invite Henry George to be their candidate for mayor. The little group thought the story entertaining, but none regarded it seriously. Nor did Mr. George think much of the matter even when waited upon by a committee from a conference of trade and labour unions, which, representing nearly all the labour organisations in New York, was being held with the view to political action. Mr. George was qualified to run for the office, having moved to Pleasant Avenue, New

York, but he told the committee that he had planned important work that he would not like to interrupt. Nevertheless, the committee after a few days returned and was more urgent. Mr. George told them that he was in sympathy with the trade unions and that he believed that the remedy for the evils of which they complained lay through the ballot, but that trade union candidates the year before had not only met with ignominious defeat, but had not received anything like the united support of the trade union members themselves. He was willing to stand for principle, he said, but did not wish to be made ridiculous by a miserably small vote. Therefore, he did not care to consider the matter. Yet again the committee returned, this time to assure him that, whereas, the unions the year before had not been harmonious, they were entirely so now; and that though there was a long list of offices to fill in the fall election, the unions would concentrate their entire efforts on the single candidate for Mayor.

Mr. George had meanwhile been talking quietly to some of his friends, most of whom seemed extremely flattered over the recognition he was getting. They were anxious to use the occasion to preach the land question and the many things that it involved. Charles Frederick Adams argued that the great majority of working men held various and confusing views and that if George stood he would supply a clear, concise, coherent body of principles, which, while educating and rallying the working men themselves, would appeal even more strongly to the book-reading, thoughtful elements of the community. Tom L. Johnson said that he was not acquainted with conditions in New York, but that if George decided to fight, he would heartily support. In the emergency Mr. George consulted Dr. McGlynn, who possessed a large knowledge of political affairs and manifested a lively interest in this particular matter. The Doctor counselled him to run.

Matters were in this state when the labour committee for the third time waited upon Mr. George and urged him to consider the matter and to write a formal letter to James P. Archibald, Secretary of the Labour Conference, either accepting or declining the proposition. Mr. George consented, for he believed now that a large proportion of the men in the unions were earnestly looking to him for leadership in a fight against their hard living conditions. Then he conceived what Dr. McGlynn called his "master stroke." At the end of August he wrote the letter to Archibald. In it he set forth fully and clearly his own views and stated that his sense of duty would not permit him to refuse any part assigned to him by the common consent of earnest men really bent upon carrying into politics the principles he held dear. Yet failure would hurt the very cause they wished to help. "For this reason," he wrote, "it seems to me that the only condition on which it would be wise in a Labour Convention to nominate me, or on which I should be justified in accepting such a nomination, would be that at least thirty thousand citizens should, over their signatures, express the wish that I should become a candidate, and pledge themselves in such case to go to the polls and vote for me. This would be a guarantee that there should be no ignominious failure, and a mandate that I could not refuse. On this condition I would accept the nomination if tendered to me."

Unusual and difficult of fulfilment as this condition was, it was nevertheless hailed by the labour bodies not only in New York but elsewhere with many marks of satisfaction and enthusiasm. This was particularly shown at the annual Labour Day parade early in Sep-

tember, which Mr. George was invited to review in Union
Square with the then mayor of the city, William R.
Grace.

The working men were without political machinery
and the election laws at the time made party machinery
greatly advantageous. The laws were such as to make
bribery, intimidation, and miscounting so common a
practice as to give singular force to the cynical observation of a Democratic subordinate manager, who said:
"How can George win? He has no inspectors of election!" Nevertheless, the way signatures to George
pledges were rolling in daunted and even frightened the
Democratic leaders; for a large part of George strength
was developing in what had been Democratic strongholds.

New York City was, and under one name or another had
been for the most part since the organisation of the Tammany charitable and political society a hundred years before, strongly Democratic. That society had started out
with Jeffersonian principles and an opposition to aristocracy and Hamilton's federalism, but long years of political power had corrupted its principles and made it the
instrument of the unscrupulous, until the Tweed exposures in the seventies made its name synonymous with
political debauchery.[1] Tammany went into eclipse and a
regenerated party under the name of County Democracy
arose triumphant. But power corrupted that, too, and
it fell into the hands of professional politicians, though
it retained in its membership list many of the respectable
names with which it had started out. In the last preceding city election the County Democracy party had

---

[1] In exposing the naturalisation frauds, Dr. Montague R. Leverson
struck the first blow at Tammany, though it was not until later, when
evidences of the theft of public money were obtained, that the Tweed
ring fell.

elected William R. Grace to the mayoralty. Now both factions saw a common danger in the rise of George. They, therefore, sent a joint emissary to wait upon the proposed labour candidate. About this interview Mr. George a few days before his death said:[1]

"Before my nomination had formally taken place I received a request from Mr. William M. Ivins, then Chamberlain of the city, and a close political friend and representative of Mr. Grace, to privately meet him. I did so at Seighortner's, on Lafayette Place. We sat down in a private room, unattended, and smoked some cigars together. Mr. Ivins insisted that I could not possibly be elected Mayor of New York, no matter how many people might vote for me; that the men who voted knew nothing of the real forces that dominated New York. He said that I could not possibly be counted in. He offered on behalf of Tammany Hall and the County Democracy that if I would refuse the nomination for mayor they would run me for Congress, select a city district in which the nomination of the two was equivalent to election; that I should be at no expense whatever, but might go to Europe or anywhere I willed, and when I came back should receive a certificate of election to the House of Representatives. I said to him finally: 'You tell me I cannot possibly get the office. Why, if I cannot possibly get the office, do you want me to withdraw?' His reply was: 'You cannot be elected, but your running will raise hell!' I said: 'You have relieved me of embarrassment. I do not want the responsibility and the work of the office of the Mayor of New York, but I do want to raise hell! I am decided and will run.'"

It was not the office he was after; he wanted to plant the seed. He wrote to Taylor (September 10): "It is by no means impossible that I shall be elected. But the

[1] Published reply to statement made in the newspapers by Abram S. Hewitt, October, 1897.

one thing sure is that if I do go into the fight the campaign will bring the land question into practical politics and do more to popularise its discussion than years of writing would do. This is the only temptation to me."

Election really looked more than possible—even probable. With four other candidates in the field—Republican, Prohibitionist, and one for each of the Democratic factions—it was estimated that George would require for election little more than twice the thirty thousand votes guaranteed in the pledges now being rapidly signed; whereas, the labour organisations themselves were supposed to have a membership of sixty-five thousand. The nominating convention of the Trade and Labour Conference took place in Clarendon Hall on September 23. It adopted a platform written by Henry George, which the "New York World" characterised as "an epitome of Mr. George's popular essay entitled 'Progress and Poverty.'" One hundred and seventy-five labour organisations were represented by 409 delegates, from whom George received on the first ballot 360 votes, while 31 votes were cast for a popular furniture dealer named J. J. Coogan; and 18, purely by way of compliment, for William S. Thorn, Superintendent of the Second Avenue Railroad, who had treated his men extremely well. The proceedings were remarkable for enthusiasm and harmony among the usually hostile and warring factions of the labour bodies. Seldom before had labour representatives manifested such confidence of success in a political contest.

And interest in the nomination extended beyond the labour unions. It sprang up among "that great body of citizens," said Mr. George, "who, though not working men in the narrow sense of the term, feel the bitterness of the struggle for existence as much as does the manual labourer, and are as deeply conscious of the corruptions of our politics and the wrong of our social system." These had not to any number signed the pledge to vote for George, but they gave voice to their support by a meeting in Chickering Hall on October 2, at which Rev. John W. Kramer presided, and Rev. Dr. R. Heber Newton, Professor Thomas Davidson, Daniel DeLeon, Ph.D. of Columbia College; Charles F. Wingate, Professor David B. Scott of the College of the City of New York, and the Rev. Dr. Edward McGlynn spoke. The meeting packed the hall and with a roar of approval passed resolutions indorsing George's nomination by the Trade and Labour Conference.

Dr. McGlynn spoke, said one who heard him, "as if he expected that night to be his last." And it was a mighty moment in his life. He had been forbidden by his ecclesiastical superior to speak. Some days before Archbishop Corrigan had written Dr. McGlynn expressing anxiety about the latter's "relations with Henry George" and hoping that he would "leave aside" anything that would seem "to coincide with socialism." In order to show what manner of man Henry George was and the true nature of his teachings, Dr. McGlynn suggested that Mr. George call on the Archbishop, which he did, bearing a letter of introduction from Dr. McGlynn. The Archbishop received Mr. George courteously, but was not prepared to hear him explain the land doctrine, as he said, after giving a history of the case, that Dr. McGlynn had violated an understanding made in 1882 that he was to make no more public utterances. "The Archbishop told me," said Mr. George afterwards,[1] "that he had called his council to meet at twelve that day for the purpose of taking into consideration the case of Dr. McGlynn, and

---

[1] "The Standard," January 8, 1887.

as I understood at the time, of suspending him." "On leaving the Archbishop," continued Mr. George, "I called on Dr. McGlynn and informed him of the result of my interview. He said that his understanding of the promise he had felt himself obliged to make in 1882 was that he should deliver no more speecnes on the Irish question, which promise he had kept; that he had since made speeches on behalf of Mr. Cleveland [during the presidential canvass] to which there had been no remonstrances whatever, and that he had not up to that time received any inhibition from speaking at the Chickering Hall meeting; yet even should one come, he could not, now that he had been announced to speak, refrain from doing so consistently with his own self-respect and without publicly renouncing the rights of an American citizen."

Then it was that Dr. McGlynn received a letter from the Archbishop forbidding him to take part in the Chickering Hall meeting or "to take any part in future in any political meeting whatever without permission of the Sacred Congregation of Propaganda Fide." Other priests who were expected to attend the meeting and speak had been warned and stayed away. But the pastor of St. Stephen's attended and spoke as never before in his life. Nor did any—not even Mr. George—know for many days after the campaign was over that on the morning following the meeting Archbishop Corrigan had suspended Dr. McGlynn for two weeks.

The formal nomination of Henry George having been made by the labour conference and indorsed by business and professional men in public meeting, a formal acceptance was arranged to take place in the historic Cooper Union Hall on October 5. The multitude was so great that Mr. George had some difficulty in squeezing in, and an immense overflow meeting took place outside. Several large bundles containing the signatures of more than thirty-four thousand voters who had pledged themselves to support George at the polls were, amid much excitement, passed in over men's heads and placed upon the edge of the platform in general view. Rev. Mr. Kramer first presented the resolutions of the Chickering Hall meeting to John McMackin, Chairman of the Executive Committee of the Labour Party, and then Mr. McMackin tendered the nomination with its indorsement to Mr. George, who on rising was received with a long ovation of cheering. When quiet was restored he said:

"The step I am about to take has not been entered upon lightly. When my nomination for Mayor of New York was first talked of I regarded it as a nomination which was not to be thought about. I did not desire to be Mayor of New York. I have had in my time political ambition, but years ago I gave it up. I saw what practical politics meant; I saw that under the conditions as they were a man who would make a political career must cringe and fawn and intrigue and flatter, and I resolved that I should not so degrade my manhood. Another career opened to me; the path that I had chosen—that my eyes were fixed upon—was rather that of a pioneer—that of the men who go in advance of politics, the men who break the road that after they have gone will be trod by millions. It seemed to me that there lay duty and that there lay my career, and since this nomination has been talked about my friends here and through the country and beyond the seas have sent me letter after letter, asking me not to lower, as they are pleased to term it, the position I occupied by running for a municipal office. But I believe, and have long believed, that working men ought to go into politics. I believe, and I have long believed, that through politics was the way, and the only way, by which anything real and permanent could be secured for labour. In that path, however, I did not expect to tread. That, I thought, would de-

volve upon others, but when the secretary of this nominating convention came to me and said, 'You are the only
man upon whom we can unite, and I want you to write
me a letter either accepting or refusing to accept and
giving your reasons,' that put a different face on the
matter. When it came that way I could not refuse, but
I made my conditions. I asked for a guarantee of good
faith; I asked for some tangible evidence that my fellow-
citizens of New York really wanted me to act. That
evidence you have given me: All I asked, and more."

The office of Mayor of New York, he said, important
though it was, was fettered by commissions, the occupants of only two of which he could remove. But still
he had the power of visitation and inquisition—of finding out how things were going—and the further power
of appealing to the people; and those powers he proposed, if elected, to use to their utmost and to destroy
political corruption. But the mayoralty movement meant
even more. Chattel slavery was dead; there now devolved
upon them the task of removing industrial slavery.

"We have hordes of citizens living in want and in vice
born of want, existing under conditions that would appall
heathen. Is this by the will of our Divine Creator? No.
It is the fault of men; and as men and citizens, on us
devolves the duty of removing this wrong; and in that
platform which the convention has adopted and on
which I stand the first step is taken. Why should there
be such abject poverty in this city? There is one
great fact that stares in the face any one who chooses to
look at it. That fact is that the vast majority of men
and women and children in New York have no legal
right to live here at all. Most of us—ninety-nine per
cent. at least—must pay the other one per cent. by the
week or month or quarter for the privilege of staying
here and working like slaves. . . .
"Now, is there any reason for such over-crowding?

There is plenty of room on this island.   There are miles
and miles and miles of land all around this nucleus.
Why cannot we take that and build houses upon it for
our accommodation? Simply because it is held by dogs
in the manger who will not use it themselves nor allow
anybody else to use it, unless he pays an enormous price
for it—because what the Creator intended for the habi-
tation of the people whom He called into being is held
at an enormous rent or an enormous price. . . .

"But what do we propose to do about it? We propose,
in the first place, as our platform indicates, to make the
buildings cheaper, by taking the tax off buildings. We
propose to put that tax on land exclusive of improvements, so that a man who is holding land vacant will
have to pay as much for it as if he was using it, just
upon the same principle that a man who should go to a
hotel and hire a room and take the key and go away would
have to pay as much for it as if he had occupied the
room and slept in it. In that way we propose to drive
out the dog in the manger who is holding from you what
he will not use himself. We propose in that way to remove this barrier and open the land to the use of labour
in putting up buildings for the accomodation of the
people of the city. . . .

"I am your candidate for Mayor of New York. It is
something that a little while ago I never dreamt of.
Years ago I came to this city from the West, unknown,
knowing nobody, and I saw and recognised for the first
time the shocking contrast between monstrous wealth
and debasing want. And here I made a vow, from
which I have never faltered, to seek out and remedy,
if I could, the cause that condemned little children to
lead such lives as you know them to lead in the squalid
districts. It is because of that that I stand before you
to-night, presenting myself for the chief office of your
city—espousing the cause, not only of your rights but of
those who are weaker than you. Think of it! Little
ones dying by thousands in this city; a veritable slaugh-
ter of the innocents before their time has come. Is it
not our duty as citizens to address ourselves to the ad-

justment of social wrongs that force out of the world those who are called into it almost before they are here— that social wrong that forces girls upon the streets and our boys into the grog shops and then into penitentiaries? We are beginning a movement for the abolition of industrial slavery, and what we do on this side of the water will send its impulse across the land and over the sea, and give courage to all men to think and act. Let us, therefore, stand together. Let us do everything that is possible for men to do from now until the second of next month, that success may crown our efforts, and that to us in this city may belong the honour of having led the van in this great movement."

The press gave large reports of the meeting. All of them confessed that George, because of his high character and personal abilities, and because of the unprecedented signs of harmony among the labour unions in support of him, would be an important factor in the municipal contest. Most of the papers did not seem to know exactly what attitude to assume as yet. Only two of them showed downright ill will, "The Daily Illustrated Graphic" calling George another Jack Cade and the "Evening Post" saying that while not apprehending his election, he might "get a vote large enough to demoralise the officers of the law and diminish the protection we now enjoy against mob violence."

By voluntary contributions and assessments, the labour unions raised some money for the uses of the election committee, though the amount was inadequate to meet even the necessary and legitimate needs imposed by the election laws, which, among other things, required each party to print and distribute its own tickets. The campaign on the working men's side began and ended with few brass bands and little red fire. The working men's headquarters on Eighth Street were anything but garish; nor

was there any show or pretence about Mr. George's headquarters in the Colonnade Hotel, around the corner on
Broadway. Most of the work was done by volunteers,
and hall rent for some of the larger meetings, at least,
was, contrary to all political usage, collected from the
audience by "passing the hat." Other money came from
some of Mr. George's close friends, chiefly from Tom
L. Johnson; and some, in small sums, came through the
mails from unknown sympathisers in the city and outside.

A notable contribution was a cheque for $100 from a
stranger, August Lewis of August Lewis & Co., straw
goods importers and manufacturers on Greene Street, New
York. The cheque was accompanied by a short note of
good will, and Mr. Lewis soon afterwards followed this
by a personal visit. He was born in Aix-la-Chapelle,
Germany, of Jewish parents and received an ordinary
grammar school education. Coming to this country in
1869, whither some members of his family had preceded
him, he joined one of them in business. As a member of
the Society for Political Education he had in 1882 received one of the complimentary copies of "Progress and
Poverty" presented to that organisation by Francis G.
Shaw; but not until Mr. George was a candidate and
began to be vigorously discussed in the newspapers did
Mr. Lewis read the book. It immediately did for him
what it had done for Mr. Shaw—brought him hope where
before had been despair of the social problem. And
feeling so, though it ran counter to his political habits
and social affiliations, Mr. Lewis gave Henry George his
moral and material support. He quickly took his place
as one of Mr. George's closest friends, and in the end
he shared with Tom L. Johnson the honour of the dedication of the philosopher's last book.

Mr. George's refusal to withdraw from the mayoralty

contest, and his rapidly gathering strength left little hope
of victory for the Democracy, save in the course some of
the party papers urged—the union of the two factions.
But it was evident when the Tammany convention met
on October 11, that a considerable number of the delegates were for George and would have favoured his indorsement. But the little group controlling the machine
had no thought of such a thing. Yet they did not see
hope in a candidate from their own factional ranks. They
therefore selected a man identified with the other faction
—Abram S. Hewitt. Hewitt's name was presented to
the convention and the perfunctory form of nomination
was gone through with by the delegates, though few of
them had had a hint of what was coming and astonishment for a time was supreme.

Abram S. Hewitt was of the large iron manufacturing
firm of Cooper, Hewitt & Co. He was son-in-law of the
then late philanthropist, Peter Cooper, and brother-in-
law of Edward Cooper, sometime Mayor of New York.
For years he had been Congressman from New York.
He was the same Abram S. Hewitt who in 1880 had
spoken in praise of "Progress and Poverty" to William
H. Appleton, the publisher, and who, through Mr. Appleton, had invited an acquaintance with Mr. George, whom
he engaged privately to work on a Congressional report,
which work was discontinued on Hewitt's refusal longer
to pay what George regarded as reasonable compensation.
Their agreement had been for privacy on both sides, as
the Congressman intended to use the report as his own;
but Hewitt now, during the mayoralty campaign, broke
the seal of confidence, and gave to one of the newspapers
a story that George had once been his secretary, but had
to be discharged because he would run the land tax into
everything. No response was made to this at the time,

but eleven years later, during the second mayoralty canvass, when Mr. Hewitt was reported to have made some personal statements about him that called for reply, Mr. George dictated to a stenographer a statement of the 1880 episode, although afterwards he concluded that the occasion was inappropriate to publish it.

Mr. Hewitt in his letter of acceptance took the ground that he had been called upon to save society.

"An attempt is being made to organise one class of our citizens against all other classes, and to place the government of the city in the hands of men willing to represent the special interests of this class, to the exclusion of the just rights of the other classes. The injurious effects arising from the conclusion that any considerable portion of our people desire to substitute the ideas of anarchists, nihilists, communists, socialists, and mere theorists for the democratic principle of individual liberty, which involves the right to private property, would react with the greatest severity upon those who depend upon their daily labour for their daily bread, and who are looking forward to a better condition for themselves and their children by the accumulation of capital through abstinence and economy. The horrors of the French Revolution and the atrocities of the Commune offer conclusive proof of the dreadful consequences of doctrines which can only be enforced by revolution and bloodshed, even when reduced to practice by men of good intentions and blameless private life."

Mr. Hewitt seemed to believe that since he was undertaking to defend social order and institutions against "anarchists, nihilists, communists, socialists and mere theorists," the Republicans should make common cause with him and support him. But the Republicans cleaved to themselves and nominated for mayor an able young man of large personal fortune and artistocratic connections and ideas—Theodore Roosevelt.

Practically all the politicians and all the daily press except the "Volks Zeitung" and a little paper called "The Leader," which had started for the campaign and of which Louis F. Post was made the editor,[1] were now in full cry against George; and the lies, intentional and accidental, that one paper started the others took up and circulated. For instance, George was reported by the "Sun" to have said in a speech that with all its horrors the great epoch of the French Revolution was about to repeat itself, and the "Evening Post," with a seeming *malice prepense*, repeatedly in editorials (and "Harpers Weekly," with letterpress and a cartoon) quoted this in the face of its obvious inconsistency with George's known principles and direct denials. Mrs. Lowell, Francis G.

---

[1] Mr. Post says: " 'The Leader' was the only newspaper support that the George party had after the campaign opened, except the 'Volks Zeitung,' the socialist paper, printed in German. At first the 'Volks Zeitung' opened its editorial columns to articles in support of George in English, and I did the work. But early in the campaign 'The Leader' was started. It jumped at once to a circulation of 35,000 daily, and was self-supporting from the beginning. But to make it self-supporting all the editorial and reportorial work had to be contributed without pay. And this was done. Though the other newspapers unanimously opposed George, their sub-editors and reporters almost unanimously supported him. As they could do nothing for him in their own papers, they volunteered in large numbers for work upon 'The Leader.' After doing a full day's work on their respective papers, they would turn in and do another day's work, in the same twenty-four hours, for us. And this they continued to the last. Where all were so devoted it would be invidious to mention names, even if I could remember them. But the managing editor's and the city editor's chairs were filled in this way; and as fine a body of reporters as ever came together on any paper joined with the rest of us in working for 'The Leader' without pay throughout the campaign. Editorial writers on other papers also contributed to this unpaid work by sending in editorials and special articles."

Shaw's daughter, wrote in some alarm to Mr. George about the reported utterances, and he replied: "I not only never *meant* to encourage lawlessness or disorder, but never *did*, by direction or indirection. On the contrary, I have told my people in the most emphatic way that I would preserve order and enforce the law."

But George did not have much time for explanations of this kind. His campaign was not defensive, but offensive; not one of excuses, but of aggression. He addressed an open letter to the Democratic candidate pointing out that Hewitt himself represented the dangerous and unscrupulous classes, as personified by Richard Croker and the many other professional politicians about him; whereas he (George) represented the great working mass of the community—the workers with head as well as with hand; and that as an English statesman had happily phrased it, the working men's movement was one of "the masses against the classes." Finally he proposed that Hewitt and he discuss the various questions of the campaign in joint debate.

Hewitt's reply was quite as spirited. He ascribed George's candidacy to his "peculiar views as to the nature of property"; and asserted again that he was supported by "all the anarchists, nihilists, communists and socialists in the community," with whom he (Hewitt) did "not wish to confound the men supporting him whom" George had "stigmatised as politicians." He also regretted that he could not "accommodate in debate a gentleman for whose 'remarkable acuteness, fertility and literary power' [he had the] highest respect."

Two other open letters passed between the candidates, one from George, in which he offered Hewitt half his time at a meeting to take place that week at Chickering Hall; and one from Hewitt declining the proffer and declaring it George's purpose "to array working men against millionaires."[1]

This was the kernel of opposition from press and platform to George. He was denounced as a "marauder," an "assailant of other people's rights," a "leveller," a "robber of the poor," a "revolutionist," an "apostle of anarchy and destruction," a "man who attacks the sacred foundations of property," and a "recreant to liberty"—so that that came to pass which Mr. George predicted in his speech of acceptance, when he said: "This, in my opinion, will be one of the fiercest contests that ever took place in this or any other American city. Every influence that can be arrayed against me will be used. There will be falsehoods and slanders, everything that money and energy and political knowledge can command."

One instance of this was given when a story was published that Dr. McGlynn had withdrawn his support from George. At the risk of further displeasure to his ecclesiastical superiors, the Doctor gave out a statement to the newspapers in which he said that his "admiration and affection for Henry George's genius and character" were, "if possible, increasing every day." Though it was not yet known, Dr. McGlynn had been "disciplined" for disobeying his Archbishop's order, which was literally, not to speak at the Chickering Hall meeting, but which was really, as subsequent events proved, not to help George. But now towards the close of the contest, when the last supreme efforts were being made, and when McGlynn's great influence was strongly felt, the higher resident dignitaries in the Church did not hesitate

---

[1] For the full text of this correspondence and a sketch of the contest, see a small compilation by Louis F. Post and Fred C. Leubuscher, entitled "The George-Hewitt Campaign," formerly published by John W. Lovell Company, New York.

themselves to enter the conflict. For, in answer to a letter from one of Mr. Hewitt's chief managers, Rt. Rev. Monsignor Preston, Vicar-General of the Diocese, made a formal, written reply condemning George's principles as "unsound, unsafe and contrary to the teachings of the Church," and averring that if "logically carried out," they "would prove the ruin of the working men he professes to befriend"; adding that "although we never interfere directly in elections, we would not wish now to be misunderstood at a time when the best interests of society may be in danger." This letter was promptly given to the press and distributed at the Church doors the Sunday preceding election day, and it strengthened the denunciation launched in sermons from several Catholic altars against Henry George and what he was declared to represent.

A single furtive attempt was made on George's personal character. A story was published in some San Francisco papers, and telegraphed to some New York papers, that he was once connected with a piratical expedition. This referred to the Brontes Mexican Revolution enterprise, with the details of which the reader has already been made acquainted.[1] The tale of piracy was seen to be ridiculous and was quickly dropped. As by common accord, George's enemies spoke of him as of pure private life and unquestionable abilities—an honest and dangerous fanatic.

Yet the cries of threatened machine politicians and corruptionists and an opposing press frightened into co-operation the timid rich and a large commercial class, who always fear changes, even though they be the sweeping away of long-standing abuses; so that Henry George

---

[1] Pages 165–67.

had a tremendous combination of forces, good and bad, respectable and disreputable, arrayed against him. But if such powers opposed, he had the intense, burning enthusiasm of the great working masses behind him—"a power," to use his own words, "stronger than money, more potent than trained politicians"; something to meet and "throw them aside like chaff before a gale."

Louis Prang, the Boston art publisher, who feared for George's dignity as an author and teacher of a great idea if he should enter upon a speaking campaign, urged him to follow General Grant's custom and make no speeches. But George replied: "I appreciate all you say. Nevertheless, I have been called into this fight, and I propose to go through with it. While it was perfectly proper for Grant to make no campaign speeches, that is the very thing I must do; and I look forward to a month of speaking every night."

And never before in New York, and perhaps nowhere else in the country, had there been such a speaking campaign. In halls and from "cart-tails," at the noon dinner hour or at midnight, before exclusive audiences and before street throngs, in the commercial centres and through the tenement regions, Henry George spoke. Rather than a seeker for office, he was a man with a mission, preaching the way to cast out involuntary poverty from civilisation. Rather than a politician ready to pare away and compromise, he pressed straight for equality and freedom, and in a breath-taking way struck at the ignorant prejudices of his own followers as sharply as at those of his fiercest antagonists. While it was, for instance, the rule to temporise on the tariff and liquor questions, George called for the abolition of custom houses and of excise and licenses. He made speeches, frequently as many as twelve or fourteen a day, of a variety, strength,

clearness, fire and human sympathy that amazed and
thrilled the multitudes that flocked to hear him, and that
inspired with increasing energy the scores and hundreds
of all walks of life who sprang up to talk for him and
his cause. Among these were Patrick Ford, who, though
he did not actually speak, sat upon the Cooper Union
platform and gave the strong editorial backing of the
"Irish World"; General Master Workman Powderly of
the Knights of Labour; Samuel Gompers, President of
the American Federation of Labour; and Rev. J. O. S.
Huntington, son of the Protestant Episcopal Bishop of
Central New York, and head of the Episcopal Order
of the Holy Cross. There had been many municipal elections in New York before, but none like this. They had
been purely political; this involved social questions as
well. The sure sign of internal interest was the registration of voters, preparatory to the formal balloting. This
year, with no accompanying State or national contests to
augment it, the registration was extremely heavy.

Outside, the press of the country noted, discussed and
divided, as though they were active participants; while
beyond the broad seas, men at the antipodes watched and
waited, and the British public, in placid ignorance of
most things American, was by cable reports in its newspapers daily informed of each important event in this
New York mayoralty struggle, as though it involved the
advancement or downfall of a sovereign State. The truth
—the vital spark—the expression of hope of a less bitter
struggle for subsistence for all men, even the meanest
and lowest, that had raised the California writer from
obscurity, that had given his book on political economy
a world-wide circulation, that had gathered throngs to
hear him speak from one end of Great Britain to the
other, was now infused into a city election and centred

the gaze of millions—made the world its audience. Letters of God-speed poured in upon the candidate from a thousand sources—from organisations whose hearts beat responsive to his trumpet call; from isolated individuals he never saw and never could expect to see. "The great question"—he dashed off in a note of cheer to Mr. Gutschow, German translator of "Progress and Poverty," who had sent money out of his small purse for the campaign— "The great question is at last in politics and the struggle has begun."

The campaign closed with the Republicans deprecating both Hewitt and George, and the Democrats crying that a vote for Roosevelt was a vote for George, while the policy of those who feared the rise of the labour power was "anything to beat George." The last and most signal proof to them that their fears were well founded was a parade of labour unions on the Saturday night three days before election. Through a cold, drenching rain, without brass bands, uniforms or any of the usual political trappings, bearing aloft their trade-union banners, and with here and there a few torches, but mostly in darkness, the long, dense line of men, headed by William McCabe, a journeyman printer, were two hours in marching past the reviewing platform in Union Square, and made one continuous, fervid shout of salutation to the man, their candidate, standing there.

So the campaign closed, and election day came. Then was seen the great disadvantage of the working men's party. It had no representatives in the polling places to count the votes. Moreover, under the election law it had to print its own ballots and distribute them to voters, and some of the election districts were actually without distributors and ballots. The law worked for the benefit of the party "machines." Yet men without pay and without

food stood from dawn till nightfall working for George.
Late in the evening the returns showed that Abram S.
Hewitt had been elected Mayor, with George second, and
Roosevelt third; the official canvass subsequently showing
for Hewitt, 90,552; for George, 68,110; and for Roosevelt, 60,435. Mr. George believed at the time, and many
circumstances afterwards confirmed his belief, that he
had really been elected, but had been "counted out."

But he had got all that he really wanted—a big vote.
At twelve o'clock election night, when the event was no
further in doubt, he made a speech at the working men's
headquarters on Eighth Street, crowded with the more
active among his supporters. Disappointment was written on most faces there. They had fought with the confidence of winning. Defeat was bitter. But George's
voice rang out bell-like and clear:

> "I congratulate you to-night upon the victory we have
> won. The future is ours. This is the Bunker Hill.
> We have been driven back as the continental troops were
> from Bunker Hill. If they won no technical victory,
> they did win a victory that echoed round the world and
> still rings. They won a victory that made this Republic
> a reality; and thank God, men of New York, we in this
> fight have won a victory that makes the true Republic
> of the future certain. We have lit a fire that will never
> go out. We have begun a movement that, defeated, and
> defeated, and defeated, must still go on. All the great
> currents of our time, all the aspirations of the heart of
> man, all the new forces of our civilisation are with us
> and for us. They never fail who die in a good cause.
> This has been but a skirmish that prepares our forces
> for the battles that are to follow."

These words of courage thrilled all who heard and
called out round after round of cheers.

CHAPTER IX.

"THE STANDARD" AND THE ANTI-POVERTY SOCIETY.

1886-1887.   AGE, 47-48.

AFTER an undisturbed night's sleep, Henry George on the morning following the mayoralty election was back at his Astor Place office. To a "Sun" reporter who came to ask him of his plans, he said: "I shall buy a bottle of ink and a box of pens and again go to writing."

The press, abroad as well as at home, recognised in him a new power in the public world. The London papers were thoroughly alive to this, the Tory "St. James's Gazette" observing that "the election should cause all respectable Americans to forget the trumpery of party fights and political differentism and face the new danger threatening the commonwealth." On the other hand, the Radical "Pall Mall Budget" said:

"The two words 'Henry George' on the voting paper against which 68,000 persons put their mark did not even to these 68,000 mean only the five feet, nine inches of commonplace flesh and blood, thatched with sandy hair and shod with American leather. They meant much more than that. They meant an embodied protest against the kingdom of this world, which after nineteen centuries, alike under democracies and monarcies and empires, is still ruled by Mammon 'the least erected spirit that fell from heaven.' He stood as the incarnation of a demand that the world should be made a better place to live in than it is to-day; and his candidature was a groan of discontent with the actual, and therefore of aspiration after the ideal."

The "New York Times" expressed the views of many thoughtful persons at home in saying: "That a new party should suddenly have been called into existence in this city, and without an existing organisation, without a party fund, and under the leadership of men inexperienced in political work, should have given its candidate a vote nearly equalling that cast in recent years by any of the existing political parties is at once seen to be an event demanding the most serious attention and study."

And well might the press so speak. For letters of congratulation poured in upon Mr. George from all parts of the country, and in many places he was talked of as labour candidate for the presidency in 1888. Moreover, four days after the election a crowded meeting for rejoicing was held in the large hall of Cooper Union. Mr. George's speech was fine in tone. "It is not the end of the campaign," said he; "it is the beginning. We have fought the first skirmish." They must go on, pressing forward the land question and the kindred ideas.

And he now demanded a radical reform of those voting laws which, as he believed was instanced in the recent contest, enabled the unscrupulous to manipulate elections. He demanded the Australian ballot system. He had advocated this reform in magazine articles in 1871 and 1883; he had inserted it, though not in express terms, in the platform he had written and stood on in the mayoralty fight. But at this Cooper Union congratulation meeting on November 6, 1886, began the agitation of the idea for the first time seriously in American politics.

It was taken up by the trade unions and labour movements in various parts of the country, and acquiring support from other sources, was, in one form or another,
within a few years adopted by most of the States in the
Union, and ultimately by all.

With a view to carrying the land reform, ballot reform
and lesser principles into practical effect, resolutions were
passed at the Cooper Union meeting declaring that a permanent political organisation be effected in New York
and elsewhere. It was also resolved to carry on syste-
matic educational work through the medium of lectures
and speeches and reading matter. A committee to direct
this consisting of John McMackin, Rev. Dr. McGlynn and
Prof. David B. Scott was named. The latter, on account of ill health, soon gave place to James Redpath,
managing editor of the "North American Review." This
committee opened an office in the Cooper Union building,
and with Gaybert Barnes as secretary, at once commenced the organisation through the country, and especially through New York State, of "Land and Labour
Clubs."

But more important than this, at least to Mr. George
personally, was the announcement of his intention to
start a weekly newspaper—the first number to be issued
on January 8 of the new year. A prospectus he sent out
brought in many yearly subscriptions, with money in advance; and with this money and $500 borrowed from a
deeply interested English friend, Thomas Briggs of London, the paper was started, the printing being done on
the presses of the "New York Herald," by courtesy of
James Gordon Bennett. Mr. George had thought of naming his paper "Light," but on the suggestion of John
Russell Young, he adopted the title of "The Standard."

The paper started with high expectations and a large

salaried staff. Besides Mr. George as editor and proprietor, there were Wm. T. Croasdale, a trained newspaper man, as managing editor; Louis F. Post as editorial
and special writer, Rev. John W. Kramer as special
writer, J. W. Sullivan as labour editor and special writer,
W. B. Scott as stenographer to Mr. George and exchange
editor, Henry George, Jr., as correspondence editor; T. L.
McCready, John V. George and Richard F. George in the
business department, and William McCabe as foreman of
the composing room—eleven men in all, besides the type-
setters.

Mr. George said in his salutatory that he established the
paper with the hope of aiding in the work of abolishing
"industrial slavery." "Confident in the strength of
truth," he said, "I shall give no quarter to abuses and
ask none of their champions. . . . I shall endeavour
to conduct this paper by the same rules on which a just
man would regulate his conduct. . . . I hope to make
this paper the worthy exponent and advocate of a great
party yet unnamed that is now beginning to form, but
at the same time to make its contents so varied and interesting as to insure for it a general circulation."

The first issues of the paper contained many well written articles on political and economic matters—in fact
were "varied and interesting." But everything was
thrown into eclipse by signed articles from Mr. George's
pen on "The McGlynn Case," which was now attracting
international attention.

As has been said in the previous chapter, Dr. McGlynn
was suspended from his priestly office for two weeks during the mayoralty campaign for refusing to absent himself from the George meeting in Chickering Hall, while
the Vicar-General of the diocese a few days before election wrote a letter that was published in the newspapers

condemning Mr. George's principles as "unsound, unsafe
and contrary to the teachings of the Church." A fortnight
or more following the election the Archbishop, in a pastoral
letter that was read in all the Catholic churches in New
York, attacked "certain unsound principles and theories
which assailed the rights of property." Though not naming
Henry George, it was clear that the principles were those
with which he was identified. A few days later an interview with Dr. McGlynn appeared in the "New York
Tribune" avowing the very principles that the Archbishop
had condemned, and taking direct issue in asserting that
they were not contrary to the doctrines of the Church.
For this the Archbishop suspended Dr. McGlynn for the
remainder of the year and wrote a letter to the Cardinal
Prefect of the Propaganda laying the matter before him.[1]
This letter procured a cable ordering Dr. McGlynn to
Rome. When the Archbishop by letter informed him of
this, Dr. McGlynn by letter replied that several grave
reasons, among them his physician's orders (he had heart
trouble, which, with other complications, ultimately
caused his death) would prevent his undertaking the journey. But he added:

> "As I cannot go to Rome to give an account of my
> doctrine about land, I would say that I have made it
> clear in speeches, in reported interviews and in published
> articles, and I repeat it here: I have taught and shall
> continue to teach in speeches and writings as long as I
> live, that land is rightfully the property of the people in
> common and that private ownership of land is against
> natural justice, no matter by what civil or ecclesiastical
> laws it may be sanctioned; and I would bring about
> instantly, if I could, such change of laws all the world

---

[1] Statement of Rt. Rev. M. A. Corrigan, "The Standard,"
January 29, 1887.

over as would confiscate private property in land, without one penny of compensation to the miscalled owners."[1]

The Archbishop responded to this declaration by extending Dr. McGlynn's suspension until such time as Cardinal Simeoni or the Pope should act.

Meanwhile, Mr. George had early in December (1886) addressed an open letter to the Archbishop answering that part of the pastoral "taken by the press as placing the Catholic Church in the attitude of a champion of private property in land." The article did not pass beyond a quiet discussion of economic principles. But when Archbishop Corrigan procured the order for Dr. McGlynn to go to Rome, Mr. George came out in a blazing article in the first issue of "The Standard." He presented the importance of the subject in this style:

"The case of Dr. McGlynn brings up in definite form the most important issues which have ever been presented in the history of the Catholic Church in the United States. It has in fact an interest far transcending this country, in so much as the question which it involves is the attitude of the greatest of Christian Churches towards the world-wide social movement of our times, and its decision will be fraught with the most important consequences both to the development of that movement and to the Church itself."

He reached the heart of the matter when he said:

"What Dr. McGlynn is punished for is for taking the side of the working men against the system of injustice and spoliation and the rotten rings which have made the government in New York a by-word of corruption. In the last Presidential election Dr. McGlynn

---

[1] Dr. McGlynn's review of his case, "The Standard," February 5, 1887.

made some vigorous speeches in behalf of the Democratic candidate without a word or thought of remonstrance. His sin is in taking a side in politics which was opposed to the rings that had the support of the Catholic hierarchy."

Some of Dr. McGlynn's friends, said George, advised the clergyman's obeying the summons to Rome, "in order to present the case of those Catholics who believe in the common right to land, and to force the question to an issue, which would forever still any pretence that this doctrine was condemned by the Church."[1] To this Mr. George replied:

"This might be all very well if Dr. McGlynn could go to Rome after some such unequivocal popular expression as would convince the Roman authorities that he was the ambassador of American Catholics, and that they did not propose to be trifled with. But for him to go to Rome as a suspended priest with any expectation of getting a hearing as against an Archbishop, backed by all the influence of the rich Catholics of the United States, and by all the powerful influence of the English Colony and English intriguers at Rome, would be folly. Dr. McGlynn would have no chance in Rome to make any presentation of the case, even if the Propaganda were a perfectly impartial tribunal. . . . Is it likely that they would give any hearing now to the 'priest McGlynn,' whom they condemned four years ago because of his partiality to the 'Irish revolution'?"

Mr. George quoted Vicar-General Preston to the effect that Dr. McGlynn was "not sent for to be complimented,"

---

[1] This was Mr. George's own view at first, but he yielded to the judgment of Dr. McGlynn, who, from what he had seen in Rome while at the College of the Propaganda, believed he would be unable to get a hearing at the Vatican.

but "to be disciplined." Proof, if any was needed, that the plan was to have the case prejudged came a little later when the Archbishop published, as coming from Cardinal Simeoni, a cable message directing him to "give orders to have Dr. McGlynn again invited to proceed to Rome and also to condemn in writing the doctrines to which he has given utterance in public meetings or which have been attributed to him in the press."

The first issue of "The Standard," or more particularly Mr. George's article, made a sensation, and two extra editions of the paper, or in all seventy-five thousand copies, were struck off. But "The Standard" was practically alone in the fight for Dr. McGlynn. Even papers with a strong Protestant bias and generally ready to seize upon any circumstances disadvantageous to the Catholic Church, now, because of the social and political upheaval threatened by George and McGlynn, were glad to side with an Archbishop who used tyrannical power against a liberal and public-spirited priest and with a foreign power that dared to interfere with and curtail the rights of a citizen of the United States. And the newspapers approved of the Archbishop's action when, in the middle of January, he removed Dr. McGlynn from the pastorate of St. Stephen's Church. Nor did they make any derogatory comments at the unseemly manner in which the order was executed, Rev. Arthur Donnally, until then of St. Michael's Church, the appointee, going to St. Stephen's rectory, without notice of any kind, and in the absence of Dr. McGlynn, walking into the latter's private room and attempting to take instant possession, notwithstanding the fact that clothes, books and papers scattered about gave evidence that the man who had occupied the chamber for twenty years was yet its occupant and would need a brief time to remove his effects. Fa-

ther Donnally afterwards went into the Church proper
and tore Dr. McGlynn's name from the confessional, and
later still, attended by a police captain, ruthlessly broke
in upon the solemn duties of confession, and in a loud
voice ordered two of the assistant priests, and the people
who had come to devotions, out of the place; and this and
much more against the all but violent protestations of a
great congregation by whom for a generation Dr. Mc-
Glynn had been deeply loved and venerated.

A chorus went up from the press that Henry George in
"attacking the Catholic Church" had destroyed his political
future and hope of "The Standard's" success. He replied
that he did not attack "the Church," but the men who misused the Church; that he had no political aspirations, else
he would not have re-entered journalism; and that if the
time came when "The Standard" could not "freely and
frankly take a stand on any question of public interest,"
then it would be "high time for it to give up the ghost."

The case of Dr. McGlynn now seemed to be in the
hands of the Church authorities at Rome. Yet strangely
enough at this very time Cardinal Gibbons wrote from
Rome to Rev. Dr. Richard L. Burtsell, of the Epiphany
Church, Dr. McGlynn's lifelong friend and legal adviser,
that in personal interviews with Cardinal Simeoni and
the Pope, both had stated to him that they had not passed
judgment, much less condemned Dr. McGlynn. Cardinal Gibbons therefore urged Dr. McGlynn to go to
Rome. As we have seen Dr. McGlynn had reluctance to
going to Rome as he felt that he would get small chance
of a hearing. Nevertheless he now sent word through
Dr. Burtsell that he would go as soon as the weak state
of his heart would permit, on condition that he should
first be reinstated and that a public statement be made
by some one in authority that no judgment had been

passed upon the case and that his land doctrines had not been condemned at Rome. But Cardinal Gibbons for some reason or other failed to place before the Propaganda or the Pope Dr. Burtsell's letter and no effort at reinstatement or correction of public utterances was made.

Dr. McGlynn had not the least idea of receding from his position. He held that there was no conflict between the doctrine of the land for the people and the fundamental truths of the Church. Towards the end of March he repeated his land doctrines in a most emphatic and eloquent manner in a lecture in the Academy of Music on "The Cross of the New Crusade," before a very large audience, that was composed chiefly of Catholics and largely of St. Stephen's parishioners; and which marked every period with a burst of applause.

This led almost immediately to a movement to awaken in the hearts and minds of the poor and outcast of the great city a hope for a civilisation that should be based on social justice and bring peace and plenty to all. The idea had originated some time before with Thomas L. McCready of "The Standard" staff. His plan was to form a militant society against poverty, and with it to go into and rouse the New York tenement regions. It was a new scheme to educate the masses on the land question. After Dr. McGlynn's lecture on "The Cross of the New Crusade," the McCready idea took fire. The first steps towards organisation were taken at a little meeting in "The Standard" office, and a name suggested by McCready was chosen—"The Anti-Poverty Society."[1]

---

[1] The declaration of the Anti-Poverty Society consisted of a single paragraph, viz: "The time having come for an active warfare against the conditions that, in spite of the advance in the powers of production, condemn so many to degrading poverty, and foster vice, crime, and greed, the Anti-Poverty Society has been formed. The object of the Society is

By common voice Dr. McGlynn was named president, and Henry George, vice-president; with Benjamin Urner, a commission merchant, for treasurer, and Michael Clark, an editorial writer on the "Irish World," for secretary.

The first public meeting took place in Chickering Hall on Sunday evening, May 1. The hall was crowded and thousands were turned away. Dr. McGlynn's address was the chief feature of the meeting. Of it Mr. George said in his signed editorial in "The Standard":

> "Never before in New York had a great audience sprung to its feet and in a tumult of enthusiasm cheered the Lord's Prayer; but it was the Lord's Prayer with a meaning that the Churches have ignored. The simple words, 'Thy kingdom come, Thy will be done *on earth* as it is in heaven,' as they fell from the lips of a Christian priest who proclaims the common fatherhood of God and the common brotherhood of man; who points to the widespread poverty and suffering not as in accordance with God's will, but as in defiance of God's order, and who appeals to the love of God and the hope of heaven, not to make men submissive of social injustice which brings want and misery, but to urge them to the duty of sweeping away this injustice—have in them the power with which Christianity conquered the world. And in New York to-day, as by the sea of Galilee eighteen centuries ago, though the Scribes and Pharisees are filled with rage and the high priests and rich men are troubled and dismayed, the people hear them gladly."

Men and women of all religious denominations and of no religion at all came in flocks to enroll as members of

---

to spread, by such peaceable and lawful means as may be found most desirable and efficient, a knowledge of the truth that God has made ample provision for the need of all men during their residence upon earth, and that involuntary poverty is the result of the human laws that allow individuals to claim as private property that which the Creator has provided for the use of all."

the Anti-Poverty Society, and the next meeting on the following Sunday evening was in a larger place, the Academy of Music, when Henry George made the chief address. The press turned loose denunciation and ridicule, but that only served to extend the membership and to advertise the meetings which came to be held regularly every Sunday evening in the Academy.

The Archbishop early in May had apparently received a letter from Cardinal Simeoni, summoning Dr. McGlynn to Rome and giving him forty days from receipt of the letter in which to do so, under pain of excommunication, "to be incurred by the act itself and also by name," if he should fail.

Dr. McGlynn contented himself with his former reply that grave reasons would prevent his making the journey then. The conspicuous signs in the Anti-Poverty movement were that for his personal character, his doctrines on the land question and his consequent attitude towards his ecclesiastical superiors, Dr. McGlynn had a large and strong following—indeed, that a large part of his former parishioners had joined the movement and hung on every word that dropped from his lips. If these signs failed there could be no mistaking the size and character of a parade and demonstration held in his honour and in protest against the impending excommunication. It was composed mainly of Catholic working men. A not-friendly newspaper—the "New York Herald"—estimated that seventy-five thousand persons took part. But in anticipation of what seemed certain to occur, Henry George wrote in "The Standard" (June 25):

"There stands hard by the palace of the holy inquisition in Rome a statue which has been placed there since Rome became the capital of a united Italy. On it is this inscription:

GALILEO GALILEI

was imprisoned in the neighbouring palace
for having seen
that the earth revolves around the sun.

"In after years when the true-hearted American priest
shall have rested from his labours, and what is now
being done is history, there will arise by the spot where
he shall be excommunicated such a statue and such an
inscription.   And days will come when happy little children, such as now die like flies in tenement houses, shall
be held up by their mothers to lay garlands upon it."

The term of forty days having expired on July 3, the
threatened penalty fell. The Archbishop did not attempt
to make any ceremony of it. He merely wrote two letters, one to Dr. McGlynn and one to a Catholic newspaper addressing the clergy and laity of the diocese, saying that the Doctor having failed to comply with the
order from Rome within the time set, had thereby incurred excommunication. Dr. McGlynn had already been
stripped of his church and the right to perform his
priestly offices, so that excommunication so far as the
outside world could see went for little. And the loving
regard of the Catholic poor of St. Stephen's parish remained unaltered. They continued to crowd into the
Anti-Poverty meetings and wherever else their "soggarth
aroon" publicly appeared. Nor did the excommunication
in the least change Dr. McGlynn's own belief that he was
still a Catholic and a priest, or lessen his sense of obligation
to be true to the Catholic faith. Not only did he continue
strictly to follow in private life that course which had
made it impossible for searching enmity to breathe against

his character as a priest or a man, but in the addresses before the Anti-Poverty Society and elsewhere he invariably opened with the reverent spirit of a devout minister of the gospel, and at the heart of every discourse was religion. "Once a priest, always a priest," he cherished in his heart of hearts as among the most precious of the ancient sayings.

Not content with the excommunication of Dr. McGlynn, Archbishop Corrigan, in the interpretation of general instructions he had received from Rome, based upon his own presentation of matters in New York, punished, by transferrence to less important missions in the diocese, a number of priests who failed to give outward sign of condemnation of Dr. McGlynn. Even Dr. Burtsell, eminent in the United States as an ecclesiastical jurist, was deprived of an important office in the diocese and eventually of his church in New York City, being sent in 1890 to the little Church of St. Mary, at Rondout, up the Hudson. The Archbishop in his reasons to the Propaganda for this latter action said: "Dr. Burtsell has the name of being, and is held by public opinion, as well as by the followers of Dr. McGlynn, as by the clergy and the faithful of New York, to be not only a personal friend of Dr. McGlynn, but also the leader of those few discontented priests who more or less sustain Dr. McGlynn, and moreover the counsellor, defender and abettor of the latter." Nor did the Archbishop stop here. In two instances he prevented burial of persons in the Catholic Calvary Cemetery, because, while these persons were known to be strict in their duties to the Church, they attended the Anti-Poverty Society lectures of Dr. McGlynn.

Meanwhile Henry George had been doing some lecturing in other cities on what now began to be called the

"Single Tax" question.[1] He made an important trip, under the auspices of Major James B. Pond's bureau, to Madison and Milwaukee, Wis., Burlington, Ia., Saginaw, Mich., and Chicago. But work on "The Standard" engaged most of his time up to the middle of summer of 1887.

Discussion over the excommunication had not entirely subsided when a new excitement commenced—a political contest for State and municipal offices. A State convention called by the United Labour Party of New York City, met in Syracuse on August 17, with representatives from political labour parties or Land and Labour Clubs in all the important centres in the Empire State. This was the direct outcome of the great vote for Henry George's candidacy for mayor the year before. George and most of his immediate supporters were confident that the labour movement would draw out a very large vote in the State this year, which would permanently establish the new party and make it a factor in the presidential campaign in 1888.

But weeks before the convention met it became evident that the socialists, who had supported George in 1886 and raised no objection to the platform on which he

---

[1] The term "Single Tax" may be said to have been anticipated in "Progress and Poverty" (Book VIII, chap. iv ; "Memorial Edition," p. 425), but the commencement of its general use probably dates from early in 1887 ; Mr. George, in a speech at a single tax conference in Chicago in 1893, saying that no one had been able to devise a suitable title for the cause until one day Thomas G. Shearman of New York remarked to him : "It seems to me that the proper title should be 'The Single Tax.'" "And then," said Mr. George, "an article was published under that title and somehow or other the name stuck." The article referred to was a report in "The Standard" of a speech by Mr. Shearman (See "Standard," May 28, 1887). Mr. George never regarded the term as describing his philosophy, but rather as indicating the method he would take to apply it.

stood, and which he had himself written, were now bent on getting their principles to the front. They consisted of comparatively few men in New York City, but what they lacked in numbers they made up in earnestness and activity. They now undertook to steer the new political movement. They not only wished to keep their socialistic organisation intact while they acted as members in the larger United Labour Party, but their executive committee issued a statement insisting "that the burning social question is not a land tax, but the abolition of all private property in instruments of production." It was the same kind of opposition that George had encountered from the London socialists at the outset of his 1883-84 lecture campaign in Great Britain. He wrote in "The Standard" the week before the convention met that there could be no place for the socialists in the new party if they pressed their principles. "Either they must go out," said he, "or the majority must go out, for it is certain that the majority of the men who constitute the United Labour Party do not propose to nationalise capital and are not in favour of the abolition of all private property in the 'instruments of production.'"

The matter came to a head in the convention, to which the socialists sent contesting delegates from three of the New York City districts. They were given a hearing, but they were refused seats because they belonged to another political party. During that hearing they insisted on putting socialism forward and on the right to be members of the Socialistic Labour Party while active in the United Labour Party as well. They became very bitter about their exclusion and taxed George with throwing them over from motives of policy. They and their associates and supporters put in the field a list of their own candidates on a purely socialistic platform.

Thus Mr. George was compelled in public action to draw a line of demarcation which in writing "Protection or Free Trade?" in 1885 he had been at pains to make very clear as separating his own philosophy from that of socialism.[1] It also happened that occasion arose for him to draw a line on anarchy, or rather on the Chicago anarchists sentenced to death for being accessory to the killing of several Chicago policemen in 1885. The breaking up in October, 1887, by the police of a public meeting in New Jersey called to express sympathy with the Chicago anarchists caused Mr. George to protest in "The Standard" in behalf of free speech, but at the same time to say that he believed after reading the review of the testimony which was given in the Supreme Court decision[2] when the cases were appealed that the Chicago anarchists were guilty under the laws of Illinois. However, he thought mitigating circumstances and the fact that a "tragical death always tends to condone mistakes and crimes" would plead the commutation of the sentence of death to a sentence of imprisonment. He wrote this publicly in "The Standard," and privately he wrote a letter to the Governor of Illinois urging clemency on the same grounds.

But to return to the convention. Henry George and Dr. McGlynn, who also was a delegate, were the central figures. Henry George drafted the platform, in principle the same as that he had written for his mayoralty campaign the year before. It soon became evident that he would be pressed to accept the nomination for the

---

[1] "Protection or Free Trade?" chap. xxviii. (Memorial Edition, pp. 299-312), "Free Trade and Socialism."

[2] Some of Mr. George's friends have believed that had he read the full testimony of the case, and not what they believed to be the Supreme Courts' very unfair view of it, he would have come to a different conclusion.

chief place on the ticket—that of Secretary of State. He shrank from this because he did not like to appear as an office hunter and because he thought it bad party policy to run him just then. But an intimation that it might be said that he held back and wished another put forward because he saw small hope of election decided him to accept. The rest of the State ticket was filled out with men known in the labour movements of their respective localities, but little known in general politics.

Mr. George early entered on an active speaking campaign through the State and was accompanied by correspondents of the "Herald" and "World" of New York City, who gave fair reports of his speeches and their apparent effects. The Governor of the State, David B. Hill, having in a public speech made some reference to the labour party candidate and his principles, Mr. George invited him to joint debate, but the Governor ignored the challenge. However, Sergius E. Shevitch,[1] an able representative of the socialists—one of the unseated Syracuse convention delegates—challenged Mr. George to debate their respective principles. The latter accepted and they met in Miner's Theatre on Eighth Avenue, New York City. Dr. McGlynn also travelled over the State making speeches, as did Louis F. Post, Judge James G. Maguire of California, Rev. Hugh O. Pentecost of Newark, and many others. Moreover, a million tracts, mostly on the land question, were distributed. It was a canvass remarkably widespread and effective, considering the lack of money and organisation. Collections were made at many of the meetings, and small sums came from individual sources, but most of the scant fund obtained for

---

[1] A few years afterward Mr. Shevitch accepted a position in Russia under the Czar's government.

the campaign came from a fair held under the auspices of the Anti-Poverty Society and the superintendence of William T. Croasdale in Madison Square Garden during the first three weeks in October.

All the while opposition was not asleep. The politicians in both the great parties considered that this election involved the fate of New York, a pivotal State, in the national contest the next year, and therefore were bent on making strong party showings. The hierarchy of the Catholic Church of New York City of course set the seal of condemnation upon the new party and openly and secretly stirred up opposition everywhere. But what proved a great surprise to both George and McGlynn was that Patrick Ford broke with them and took the side of the Catholic Church authorities. He set aside the underlying land question, upon which in the past Henry George himself had not taken more radical ground, nor given a deeper foundation in ethics. He ignored the fact that Dr. McGlynn had on his invitation in 1882 made the very speeches that brought the first censures of the ecclesiastical authorities. He made no distinction between the officers or human representatives of the Church, whom they opposed, and the doctrines or spiritual part of the Church, which they did not oppose. He professed a continuance of personal friendliness to both men, but said that he must separate himself from their public course because they were warring on the Catholic Church. He set forth his views in three long, signed, double-leaded articles in the "Irish World," special editions of which were distributed widely over the State.

Then, too, George's attitude towards the socialists and the Chicago anarchists, while losing what support their small numbers represented, together with the far wider and more important support they were able to influence for the time being by charging him with mean motives,[1] did not draw to him the privileged classes, who had the year before charged him with preaching blood and revolution.

But notwithstanding opposition his courageous, sanguine nature soared. He was filled with high hopes. Neither the Democratic candidate for Secretary of State,

---

[1] Mr. George wrote after election (November 25) to C. D. F. Gütschow of San Francisco, the German translator of "Progress and Poverty": "I have no doubt whatever that the notion that I had turned on the socialists as a mere matter of policy was widely disseminated among our German population and did me harm, for this was the socialists' persistent cry through their German papers, and I had no way of correcting it. The truth, however, is just the reverse. Beginning about January of this year, they made the most persistent efforts to force socialistic doctrines upon us. I did not resist, and refused even to enter into controversy with them until it became absolutely necessary. There was no alternative other than to consent to have the movement ranked as a socialistic movement or to split with the socialists. Although this lost us votes for the present, I am perfectly certain that it will prove of advantage in the long run. Policy, however, did not enter into my calculations; I was only anxious to do the right thing.

"Second, as to the anarchists. The article to which you refer [averring that the accused men had not had a fair trial], published in the second issue of the paper, was not written by me, but by a gentleman in whom I have confidence, Mr. Louis F. Post. The opinion there expressed was my opinion, simply because I had received it from him, until I found that the Supreme Court of Illinois had made a *unanimous* decision. Our bench is not immaculate, but I could not believe that every one of seven men, with the responsibility of life and death hanging over him, could unjustly condemn these men. In spite of all pressure I refused to say anything about the matter until I had a chance to somewhat examine it for myself, and a reading of the decision of the Supreme Court convinced me, as it did everyone else whom I got to read it, that the men had not been condemned, as I had previously supposed, for mere opinion and general utterances. Not satisfied, however, with this, I sought the opinion of Judge Maguire, who expressed the same opinion which you say he has expressed in California. At my earnest request he said he would read the papers. The result on his mind you see in the last copy of 'The Standard' (November 19, letter of Judge Maguire to S. R. M.). [His

Fred. Cook, nor the Republican candidate, Colonel Fred. D. Grant, son of the late General U. S. Grant, made any particular canvass; whereas George spoke everywhere and to large audiences. He therefore became confident, as did those about him, of a big vote—he hoped 150,000. But fate decreed otherwise. He received only 72,000 votes, as against 459,000 for the Republican and 480,000 for the Democratic candidate, respectively. In New York City he received less than 38,000, as against 68,000 the year before. Louis F. Post, who was candidate for District Attorney on the local or county ticket of the labour party, was with Mr. George when news of the crushing defeat came. He has said:

"He and I went to the Astor House to watch the returns on the 'Herald' bulletins across the way. They were frightfully disappointing. It was soon evident to both of us that the United Labour Party movement had that day collapsed. In that frame of mind we went uptown, and just as our car was about to start, we standing on the front platform, I said: 'Well, George, do you see the hand of the Lord in this?' He looked at me with an expression of simple confidence which I shall never forget, and answered: 'No, I don't see it; but it's there.' Then he went on to say how he had thought a way of bringing back the people to the land had opened in the labour campaign of the preceding year, but now that way had closed; yet another way would open, and when that closed still another, until the Lord's will on earth would be done."

---

finding was that the condemned anarchists were "all guilty of wilful, deliberate, premeditated murder."]

"It is in the nature of things that the man who acts solely by conscience must often be misunderstood and seem to others as if he were acting from low motives, when in reality he is acting from the highest. This cannot be avoided, but I so much value your esteem and friendship that I want to make this personal explanation to you."

Mr. George left the car to go to the labour party headquarters. There he found a crowd of men struck dumb and utterly disheartened with the defeat. He sprang upon the platform and words of hope and courage came from him, which loosed in his hearers a flood of emotions that showed themselves in frantic cheer on cheer and a pressing forward to grasp the leader's hands.

CHAPTER X.

PROGRESS THROUGH DISSENSIONS.

1887-1889.   Age, 48-50.

"WHO is there to whom 'years have brought the philosophic mind,' who, looking back over his own career, may not see how often what seemed at the time to be disaster has really proved a blessing in disguise; that opportunity has come out of disappointment; and that the thing which he at the moment most strove to gain would have proved the thing which it would have been worst for him to have?"

Thus wrote Henry George in "The Standard" immediately after the election of 1887. He expected a new hope to rise out of the great defeat. It was a repetition of the thought he had uttered to Louis F. Post on election night, that, though the old road had closed, a new way would open. And the new way did open within a few weeks, for President Cleveland sent to Congress a message advising a reduction of the tariff. It was not a free trade message; it expressly repudiated free trade. It was the weak little cry of "tariff reform." But it was a crack in the tariff dike that discussion would wear larger. The hitherto dominant rings and reactionary protectionist powers inside the Democratic party, and Mr. Blaine and the Republicans outside, made dire threats against

this policy. But the President was firm. He prepared
for a hard, stubborn fight. This could only be educational and bear upon the campaign in the fall of 1888,
as a Republican Senate stood ready to checkmate anything the Democratic House of Representatives might
choose to do in the matter.

This laying aside of the old war issues and raising the
tariff question was precisely what Henry George had
hoped for since 1876, when he made free trade speeches
in California for Tilden, and to bring on which he several years later wrote "Protection or Free Trade?" For
the abolition of the tariff was necessary to establish the
single tax as a national policy. And because parties at
all times had been nothing to him, but principles everything, he quickly announced that while he thought it
unwise for single taxers to commit themselves to a line
of policy so far in advance of possible changes in the
political situation, yet it seemed to him that he would
have to vote with the Democratic party and support Cleveland should Cleveland be renominated and should he continue his assault on the tariff.

Post, Croasdale, Johnson, Lewis, Shearman, Garrison
of Massachusetts, Maguire of California and a great number of active single taxers in New York and over the
country viewed the matter in the same light; and many
so expressed themselves in "The Standard."

But there were others who wished to avoid the tariff
issue. They desired to put an independent single tax
candidate in the field. Some of these had left the Republican party, yet thought little good could come from
the Democratic party. Others, headed by John Mc-
Mackin and Gaybert Barnes, plainly said they favoured
an independent campaign in the "doubtful" States of
Connecticut, New York, New Jersey and Indiana. When

drawn into the debate in the columns of "The Standard" over the matter, Mr. George said that this did not look like standing up even for the single tax, but rather like leading the "United Labour Party into the same ignominious death trap into which Butler led the Greenback-Labour Party" in 1884—Butler going into the field ostensibly as an independent candidate, but towards the end of the canvass showing an undisguised purpose to defeat the Democratic candidate, Cleveland, and elect the Republican candidate, Blaine.

This independent movement probably would have had no standing whatever but for the support of Dr. McGlynn. He had made speeches for Cleveland in 1884 and was still on friendly terms with him. Moreover, he was a thorough free trader. But he could not endure the idea of even the loosest kind of an alliance with Tammany Hall, the representative of Democracy in New York City. Tammany Hall had worked hand in hand with Archbishop Corrigan and his advisers in seeking to crush the land or single tax movement and those who headed it. Hence association with it was for him intolerable.

Barnes and McMackin had control of the central machinery of what was left of the United Labour Party. They also controlled the executive committee of the Land and Labour clubs. The names of both of these organisations were used in February in a call for a national convention. George was aspersed for refusing to join. And here, indeed, to the superficial was the spectacle of the prime mover in the single tax cause refusing to continue in the direct line of the single tax movement. Friction was bound to arise, and friction did arise, between those who were for George's policy and those against it. A split occurred in the Anti-Poverty Society. Not to make scandal, Mr. George and his supporters withdrew.

At this time, when feeling among single taxers all over the country was running high, Mrs. Frances M. Milne, the California poet, wrote a letter of approval to "The Standard" office in which, quoting a taunt that Henry George "belonged to a party," she exclaimed: "Belonged to a party! No! not even a nation, not even an era can claim him—he belongs to the world! to all time!" Mr. George replied (March 7, 1888), and none but Mrs. Milne saw this letter till after his death:

> "I am very glad to know that you approve of my course, and I thank you for your good opinion; but, to speak frankly, I do not like the extravagance of your praise. This is not affectation. Such praise is the deadliest poison that can be offered to the human soul, and were I ever to accept it, my power would soon be gone. What power I have had comes from the fact that I know my own weakness; and when duty lay on me, have neither feared blame nor sought praise. If you shall survive me, as in the order of nature will be the case, then, when you have heard that I am dead, and it can be said of me, he 'has fought the good fight, he has kept the faith,' write me a requiem song of gladness and hope." [1]

Before the Presidential battle opened other things of prime importance to Mr. George occurred. In January, 1888, "The Standard" had entered its second year. With subsidence of the excitement arising from Dr. McGlynn's excommunication and the State campaign, the circulation ran down to between 20,000 and 25,000. Though this was several times as large as other weeklies that were regarded as "good advertising mediums," its radical doc-

---

[1] A few days after his death a requiem by Mrs. Milne, entitled "From the Battle," appeared in the San Francisco "Star."

trines made advertisers shy and the journal had to follow the pathway of the elder Garrison's "Liberator" and of almost all social reform papers (go almost without advertising—the mainstay of a newspaper). It was being read by thinking people in the various walks of life and was having strong intellectual influence; but its large staff was expensive and Mr. George was financially drawing less and less from it. Lecturing, however, now began to yield something, yet this, like his books, did not return what many of his friends doubtless supposed. Only the year before (January 29, 1887), he wrote to his friend Gütschow of San Francisco:

"That you should share in the notion that I have made so much money somewhat surprises me and not a little amuses. I allow all such newspaper statements to go uncontradicted and do not publish my real condition to the world; but the truth is, I have made very little out of my books—a few hundred dollars a year, that is all. With the exception of $2,000 I got for the English edition of 'Social Problems,' I have had almost nothing from abroad—and I am not a good saver, and besides my living expenses, have large demands to meet. But the net truth is that on the day I started 'The Standard' I was some thousands of dollars poorer than when I left San Francisco, owing that much more money. The sort of work that I have done does *not* pay. In lecturing, for instance, I have never made anything. The times that I have lectured for nothing and given up my fee have eaten up all I got in at other times. I merely mention this that you may know the real truth."

Mr. George sacrificed his copyrights or gave away books whenever he thought one or the other would help to spread his principles; and as for lecturing, he wrote to his wife from the West in 1887: "The working class won't come to high priced lectures and there is not enough of the other." At another time he wrote: "I can't go around assessing the people."[1] Happily this improved with time, for his pay lectures became increasingly attended. Yet 1888 was like many a year preceding—one of financial concern. Mr. George removed "The Standard" office up-town to 12 Union Square, and his residence from Harlem to East Nineteenth Street, the one in this way being brought within a short walk of the other.

What may have widened the belief that Henry George enjoyed ample means were frequent references in the newspapers to his obtaining a substantial bequest, some setting the figures as high as $30,000. Cynics marked how the philosopher "progressed from poverty." The truth of the matter is that this bequest, first and last, brought little but expense and trouble.

George Hutchins of Ancora, Camden Co., New Jersey, a retired farmer, dying in the fall of 1886, left the bulk of an estate officially appraised at something less than $10,000 to Henry George in trust for the dissemination of the George books. Mr. George had never before heard of this man, but regarded the bequest as a sign of the times and was prepared to enter upon the terms of the trust, when he learned from the widow that she had not been adequately provided for. Concluding that the entire estate was not more than she morally ought to have, he took legal advice with the view of refusing, in her favour, the bequest to him. But he found this step to be impossible, for the collateral heirs opposed. Indeed, they wished to break the will, hoping thereby to get two-thirds of the estate for themselves. They brought action

---

[1] One of these letters to Mrs. George calls attention to a marked characteristic — preoccupation. "I flatter myself," he wrote, "that I lost nothing until to-night, when I found I had left my nice new dress boots somewhere."

and saddled big expenses for lawyer's fees upon the estate. Vice-Chancellor Bird in May, 1888, held the will void on the ground that Mr. George's books were opposed to public policy in declaring private property in land to be robbery.[1] Mr. George was indignant and disgusted over this condemnation of his principles, but notwithstanding his desire to vindicate them, he offered to forego appeal if the collateral heirs would allow the property to go to the widow. They refused. He therefore appealed and won,[2] his attorneys at this stage being James F. Minturn, Corporation Attorney of Hoboken, N. J., and L. A. Russell of Cleveland, O., neither of whom, as Mr. George himself said, "asked nor received even the cost of printing their briefs." Mr. George then tried to have the widow made trustee in his stead. Failing in this, he instructed his attorney not to oppose any claims made by her, and her share was thereby largely increased at the expense of the bequest. This left Mr. George as trustee a claim to the real estate (which he made over for nothing to Mrs. Hutchins) and $584 from the personal property. This money had been paid for him to John T. Woodhull of Camden, his former attorney. Woodhull handed George $256, of which the latter gave $70 to the widow and retained $186, to pay for the actual cost of paper, presswork and mailing of some of his books to fulfill the letter of the bequest. But George had to bring suit against Woodhull to recover money still in the latter's hands, and this suit dragged along for several years. The sequel came in 1892, when Mrs. Hutchins, the childless widow, was forced upon public charity. Her mind had been weakened by her troubles, and she had lost every

---

[1] Hutchins vs. George, 44 N. J. Equity Reports, p. 124.
[2] William S. Braddock exec. vs. George, 45 N. J. Equity Reports, p. 757.

penny she had obtained under the will and through Mr. George's efforts. The announcement was made in some of the newspapers that the woman whose husband had left Henry George $30,000 was in the almshouse! But this was corrected as soon as the real facts became known. Mr. George now quietly sent little sums of money for the care of the heartsick and brain-weary old woman; and when she died, which she did soon afterwards, he bore the expense of her simple interment in a grave beside her husband at Ancora.

But to go back to 1888: Grover Cleveland, despite strong opposition of the protectionists in the party, was renominated by the Democrats for the presidency, with United States Senator Allen G. Thurman of Indiana for the vice-presidency. Ex-United States Senator Benjamin Harrison of Indiana and Levi P. Morton of New York, were the Republican candidates. In his letter of acceptance, Cleveland stood by his guns, and the tariff became the main issue in the fight. "The Standard" went with might and main for absolute free trade. Mr. George made a number of speeches in New York State and several in New Jersey and Pennsylvania, and he and his friends held a series of crowded mass meetings in Cooper Union. One of these latter meetings was of unusual nature in politics. The entire time was devoted by Mr. George to answering questions from the audience on the tariff issue. Another of these meetings marked the appearance of William Lloyd Garrison, the younger, in the cause. He had come to be interested in the single tax question by reading the controversy with the Duke of Argyll. He subsequently said:

"It was at Cooper Union in New York, August 27, 1888, at a great free trade meeting, that I formally and publicly declared my adherence to the cause, unreservedly joining the ranks of the workers who are to know no pause or rest while life and strength persist. The baptism was complete. Thereafter, it was my privilege to stand on many platforms by the side of Henry George; to share the intimacy of his home, and to use my tongue and pen in behalf of the new abolition."

In these and other ways the single taxers carried on such a vigorous, radical canvass in support of Cleveland[1] as to make the moderate Democrats murmur, "deliver us from our friends" and to cause the Democratic managers in New York to give out as a marching refrain in the party parade the lines

> "Don't, don't, don't be afraid,
> Tariff reform is not free trade."

Mr. George believed that this timid, defenceless position of the Democratic managers and lack of radical, aggressive tactics was the cause of Cleveland's defeat, just as a similar timidity had defeated Hancock in 1880. But looking beyond individual success or failure, he believed that the fight had brought the people face to face with the taxation question and helped to make way for their education on the single tax. As he had expected, Cowdrey and Wakefield, the United Labour Party's candidates for the presidency and vice-presidency had got an insignificant vote—in New York and Brooklyn, its strongest centres, less than eighteen hundred. It was charged that some of the managers had openly worked for the Republican candidate on election day. Perhaps the charge was made with reason, as one of the early acts of the new ad-

---

[1] Such was the enthusiasm among single taxers that Silas M. Burroughs crossed the Atlantic expressly to vote for Mr. Cleveland.

ministration was to appoint several of the leading managers of the United Labour Party to Federal office.

There had been a year of hard work for Henry George. His English friend, William Saunders, M.P., who was about to return to London after a short business visit in the United States, invited Mr. George to take a run with him across the sea for a change of scene. Mr. George accepted, and left soon after the election. But, as he wrote back to "The Standard": "When I heard the shouts from the approaching tender in Southampton and saw the placards of 'Welcome,' and still more when, at the Waterloo Station, the surging crowds of Mr. Saunders' constituents, who had been waiting from two o'clock in the afternoon till half past ten at night, pressed round us, I realised that I should not get much rest in England."

In the four years since he had last been there the truths he held so dear had made great progress towards the last of those three stages into which the progress of an idea has been divided, viz.: I—It is too ridiculous to be considered; II—It is against religion; III—We always knew it. One striking sign of this progress appeared in the form of a text-book on political economy. It was by Professor J. E. Symes of University College, Nottingham, England, and was written from the single tax point of view. Another unmistakable sign was that in starting a daily newspaper in London, "The Star," T. P. O'Connor, one of Mr. Parnell's most brilliant parliamentary supporters, announced in his salutatory the "taxation of ground values" (the term used in England for single tax) to be one of the basic principles of the paper. Still a third sign was the utterance of Lord Chief Justice Coleridge in an address to the Scottish Judicial Society the year before, in which, speaking with reference to the land laws of the United Kingdom, he was reported as saying: "These may be for the general advantage, and if they can be shown to be so, by all means they should be maintained; but if not, does any man with anything he is pleased to call his mind deny that a state of law under which mischief can exist, under which the country itself would exist not for its people but for a mere handful of them, ought to be instantly and absolutely set aside?" Yet a fourth sign was an interview with Count Leon Tolstoi which appeared in the "Pall Mall Gazette." In it the great Russian moralist said: "In thirty years private property in land will be as much a thing of the past as now is serfdom. England, America and Russia will be the first to solve the problem. . . . Henry George had formulated the next article in the programme of the progressist Liberals of the world."

But without these and many similar signs, the size, character and warmth of the assemblages before which Henry George spoke during his short stay in Great Britain must have been to the most casual observer an unmistakable indication of the set and strength of the tide of thought. He addressed a gathering of clergymen of the Established Church in Zion College under the auspices of the Guild of St. Matthew, of which Rev. Stewart D. Headlam was chief spirit; the congregation of Rev. Dr. Parker at the midweek service in the City Temple; a conference of Congregational ministers in Memorial Hall, on invitation of Albert Spicer; a meeting of the Knights of Labour at Smethwick, near Birmingham; a meeting of the Council of the Financial Reform Association at Liverpool, by whom he was presented with an engrossed address; a mixed audience in the City Hall, Glasgow; another at Lambeth Baths, London, and an assemblage of banqueting friends before leaving. It was at the Lambeth meeting that he uttered the pithy sentence which has since been much quoted: "Don't buy the landlords out, don't kick them out, but *tax* them out."

So strong seemed the effect of the two weeks' visit, that the friends in Great Britain—Saunders, Walker, Durant, Burroughs, McGhee and the others—pressed Mr. George to return very soon and make an extended speaking trip.[1] This he consented to do. His stay in the United States was therefore short. After some lecturing in the West; an address on taxation matters, in company with Tom L. Johnson and Thomas G. Shearman, before an investigating committee of the Ohio legislature; and attendence at a tariff reform conference in Chicago as a delegate from the New York Free Trade Club, Mr. George early in March (1889) returned to England, accompanied by his wife, his two daughters and Miss Cranford, daughter of John P. Cranford of Brooklyn.

Measuring his strength by his zeal, Mr. George laid out an immense amount of work for himself. In addition to lecturing almost nightly and meeting and talking with great numbers of people, he planned to write weekly letters to "The Standard." He spoke through the length and breadth of Great Britain and twice in Ireland. His audiences were no larger than on the former trips, but their character was different. He said at the reception given to him on his return home:

"The temper of the audience had changed. It was not this time to hear a strange thing that they gathered; it was to hear something of which they had more than an inkling. And the men who took part—who came for-

---

[1] At the New York welcome meeting to Mr. George on his return from Great Britain, Louis F. Post announced that an enthusiastic single taxer who had selected the name of Henry George for a new comer expected in his family, had found it necessary, on the development of events, to compromise on the name Henrietta Georgina.

ward to occupy the chairs—sat on the platform to move
the votes of thanks that are customary there on such
occasions—were men who formerly would not have
thought of being in such a place. They were, generally
speaking, the local notables, the file leaders, the active
workers, as we here would say, of the Radical wing of the
Liberal party. . . . Our ideas are in the air; men
get them without knowing where they come from; men
get them without thinking they are getting them, and
men get them who still look upon us as cranks and vi-
sionaries. Mr. Henry Labouchere, M.P., for instance,
recently declared in a speech to his constituents that he
was not such a visionary as Henry George. He did not
propose to take the land from the landlords and rent it
out again. What he was in favour of was putting a
tax upon land values!"

The first lecture was on the Eighth Commandment and
was delivered in a London Church—Camberwell Green
Chapel, Albert Spicer in the chair—and the last was on
the world-wide land question in the Dublin Rotunda,
Michael Davitt in the chair and making a straight-out
single tax speech in introduction. "Heckling" on this,
as on the former trips, was a distinct feature. We may
pause for a moment for a glimpse of a meeting showing
Mr. George's characteristics—a meeting of Welsh miners
at Rica. He opened in this way:

"Mr. Chairman, Ladies and Gentlemen: I shall gladly
answer any questions after my lecture, but 'turn about
is fair play.' Let me ask you a few questions first.
How much can a collier earn? (A voice: 'From 20s. to
25s.') For how long? ('All the year round.') How
much does that come to? ('Between £60 to £70.')
Well, for £60 to £70 a year a collier can get steady work
by risking his life and limb. It is not an easy occupation, I suppose? ('No.') And coal miners don't live

as long as Lord Chancellors? (Laughter. A voice: 'Not usually.') But men get used to anything. It is no wonder that people worship snakes, that human sacrifices are made, that women's feet are squeezed so that they cannot walk. I believe we could do all this if we were only educated to it. Look at the advent of the steam-engine, the railway, the telegraph, the sewing machine. Everywhere around us we see amazing things invented by the ingenuity of man to facilitate production, to lighten labour. All these things should have increased wages. But they cannot have increased wages if colliers can earn only £60 to £70 a year. Prof. Thorold Rogers of Oxford University told me last night that after making calculations of the purchasing value of money in the reign of Henry VIII. and that of to-day, he found that the labourers in those days had £145 a year. In those days when neither skill nor science had advanced to help mankind, they got as much and more than labourers get to-day."

Here is a passage from a lecture in the Town Hall at Aston-under-Lyne, England (Rev. Thomas Green, M.A., Chairman of the Liberal Association, presiding), that put the audience in roars of laughter.

"The man who owns the land, owns the air as well. (Laughter and applause.) . . . There has been only one attempt that I have ever heard of to make air separately property. . . . Near Strasburg, in Germany, about the 12th or 13th century, there was a convent of monks, who put up a windmill. One of the lords in that neighbourhood—they would be called robbers now (cheers)—finding he could not get any tribute from them, set up a claim to the ownership of the air, and when they put up their windmill said, 'All the wind in these parts belongs to me.' (Laughter.) The monks sent in hot haste to the bishop, and told him of this claim. The bishop 'got up on his hind legs'—(laughter) —and cursed in ecclesiastical language. (Renewed

laughter.) He said the baron was a son of Belial; that
he did not own the wind in that province; that all the
wind that blew over it belonged to Mother Church—
(laughter)—and that if the baron did not take back his
demand for rent, he would launch with bell, book and
candle the curse of Rome. (Laughter.) Mr. Baron
backed down. But if he had owned the land he would
not have needed to set up a claim to the wind. Men
cannot breathe the air unless they have land to stand
on."

In Richard McGhee's words, "Henry George made a
triumphant march through Scotland." The chief event
was in the City Hall, Glasgow, where on Sunday evening
April 28, Mr. George delivered a sermon on the subject
of "Thy Kingdom Come," under the auspices of the
Henry George Institute. Rev. J. M. Cruikshanks of St.
Rollox United Presbyterian church, assisted by two choirs,
conducted the services. Scarcely another person could
have squeezed into the large hall.[1]

Among the more notable events during Mr. George's
appearance in London were two debates—one in St.
James's hall with Henry M. Hyndman, the accomplished
socialist, and the other at the National Liberal Club with
Samuel Smith, M.P., the highly esteemed Liverpool benefactor, who defended established interests. Hyndman
reprobated the single tax for making no attempt to abolish industrial competition; Smith opposed it as immoral.
In each case time was so brief that Mr. George contented
himself merely with presenting the chief postulates of
the single tax doctrine.

A respite from the hard work came towards the end of

---

[1] This sermon, like many other of his Scottish addresses, was later
printed in tract form by the Scottish Land Restoration League, and scattered broadcast through Scotland.

the tour when, accompanied by his family and by a party of English, Scottish, Irish and American friends, Mr. George went to Paris to join in a land reform conference that Michael Flurscheim of Germany, an energetic land reformer, availing himself of the encouraging auspices held out by the management of the exposition then in progress in the French capital, had got up at short notice. The conference was in no sense a single tax gathering.[1] All shades of opinion were represented and half a dozen tongues. The latter fact put Mr. George at much disadvantage, since he could speak only his native language. Nevertheless he met Michael Flurscheim of Germany, Agathon de Potter of Belgium and Jan Stoffel of Holland; the Frenchmen G. Eug. Sîmon, author of "The Chinese City," M. A. Toubeau, Professor Charles Garnier and Charles Longuet of the Paris City Council, besides other men of continental thought and action, who were interesting both for their personalities and views. M. Toubeau especially invited attention by showing that land ownership in France was more concentrated than had been the case before the great revolution.

Mr. George had deep private anxieties at this time. Almost as soon as the family reached Paris the eldest daughter was taken down with a malignant form of scarlet fever and had a slow recovery. But the more lasting anxiety came from "The Standard" office in New York. For more than a year Mr. George's eldest son had been acting as managing editor of the paper. But the staff,

---

[1] "Progress and Poverty" had been translated into most of the European languages, and except in France, was getting attention, though as yet few advocates had appeared. The French translation, made by P. L. Le Monnier, had been published the year before, and the translation of "Protection or Free Trade?" by Louis Vossion, French Consul at Philadelphia, about the same time; but neither work sold widely.

composed of strong, masterful men with individual personalities and opinions, and brought together by Henry George himself, was not as a whole to be controlled by his son or by any one else. Discord soon began to brew in the chief's absence, and T. L. McCready and J. W. Sullivan, each of whom in his own way had done telling work in the columns of the paper, went outside and published in a weekly just started by Hugh O. Pentecost what Mr. George regarded as an attack upon the policy of "The Standard." Mr. McCready did not wait for Mr. George's return to withdraw from "The Standard," but Mr. Sullivan nominally remained and was dismissed. Two months and a half later he published in the Pentecost paper a long article entitled "A Collapse of Henry George's Pretensions," which began with abuse and ended with a charge that "Progress and Poverty" was based upon Patrick Edward Dove's "The Theory of Human Progression." Mr. George would have ignored the article as unworthy of attention had not the charge of plagiarism been extensively noticed in the press and elsewhere. He therefore reprinted the Sullivan article in "The Standard" (October 19, 1889), passed over the abuse, and answered the remainder by showing the absurdity of the charge on its face and by pointing out that if similarity of thought and priority of authorship on Dove's part had proved George a plagiarist, then the same reasoning would prove Dove to have copied from Herbert Spencer, who wrote similarly and earlier; it would likewise prove that Spencer stole from William Ogilvie, Professor of Humanities in Kings College, Aberdeen, from 1765 to 1819; that Ogilvie took from Thomas Spence of Newcastle-on Tyne, who wrote an essay on the subject in 1775; and so on. Then Mr. George made a direct denial in these words:

"When I first came to see what is the root of our social difficulties and how this fundamental wrong might be cured in the easiest way by concentrating taxes on land values, I had worked out the whole thing for myself without conscious aid that I can remember, unless it might have been the light I got from Bissett's 'Strength of Nations' as to the economic character of the feudal system. When I published 'Our Land and Land Policy,' I had not even heard of the Physiocrats and the *impot unique*. But I knew that if it was really a star I had seen, others must have seen it, too. And so with 'Progress and Poverty.' I said in that book that it would come to many to whom it would seem like the echo of their own thoughts. And beyond what I then knew, I was certain that there must have been others before me who saw the same essential truths. And as I have heard of such men one after the other, I have felt that they gave but additional evidences that we were indeed on the true track, and still more clearly showed that though against us were ignorance and power, yet behind us were hope and faith and the wisdom of the ages—the deepest and clearest perceptions of man."

This ended the controversy.

CHAPTER XI.

AUSTRALIA AND AROUND THE WORLD.

1890.   Age, 51.

WHILE in England in the fall of 1889, Mr. George had met Charles L. Garland, member of the New South Wales Parliament and President of the Sydney Single Tax Association. Mr. Garland travelled about with Mr. George for a short time and made some speeches from the same platforms. He brought urgent entreaties to Mr. George to arrange for a lecture tour through the Australian Colonies, such as had repeatedly been made through Great Britain. "Progress and Poverty" and the other books had been extensively circulated, discussion of economic subjects was on and all things seemed ripe for a big harvest. Letters bearing the same burden reached Mr. George after he had returned to New York, so that he concluded to go to Australia. He arranged to start in January of the new year.

Since his early boyhood, Australia had been a country of peculiar interest to him. At fifteen he had sailed to Melbourne, then famous for its gold discoveries. Since his manhood Australia obtained and held his admiration as a country of progressive thought and action; the home of the secret ballot system in advance of the rest of the world; the land where railroads and telegraphs are publicly owned and operated, where savings banks and a parcels express service are part of the postal system, and where many other things are done as a matter of course by the public which in many other countries would seem revolutionary.

Mr. George arranged to write letters for "The Standard" as frequently as lecturing and the mails would permit, but as a matter of fact, the campaign in Australia proved to be so extraordinarily exacting that he was able to write only irregularly and briefly.

The route lay by way of San Francisco. Mrs. George accompanied him on this trip to her native Australia, he playfully calling it their honeymoon. The truth was that he had grown so dependent upon her companionship that he would no longer consent to go far without her. On the other hand, his preoccupation needed her attention, for she wrote back from St. Louis to their children: "Your father this far on the journey has changed his own for other people's hats only five times!"

Mr. George spoke at Bradford, Pennsylvania; Denver, Colorado; and Los Angeles, California, on the way to the Golden Gate. In each city he had large, appreciative audiences. He also was induced during the few hours' lie over in St. Louis, where they stopped to see Sister Teresa, Mrs. George's sister, to accept a reception and six o'clock dinner at one of the large commercial clubs. It was a shining success, many of the representative men of the city being present, and as Mr. Keeler, one of the managers on the occasion, sententiously said, "twenty-five million dollars sitting down to table." All along the line of travel across country friends came trooping to the stations to greet the traveller, invariably bringing word of progress by personal propaganda.

One of these incidents had a touch of pathos. It was

in the Glorietta Mountains, in New Mexico, on the Santa
Fé road. The train stopped at nightfall for dinner at a
wretched little station in the barren country. As Mr.
and Mrs. George got off, a tall, thin man, with long,
ragged, grizzled beard approached and welcomed them.
But the stranger had to make some explanation before
Mr. George recognised him as a Methodist minister whom
he had met some years before farther East. "Yes," said
the clergyman, "I came West for my lungs, and now I
am going to die of heart disease in this thin atmosphere.
But while I am still here I propose to do all I can for the
cause. Go in to dinner, and when you come out your
disciples will be here to greet you." And when the travellers came from the repast they found the clergyman
waiting, and with him five other men, one of them a train
hand. There in that lonely place in the mountains they
were doing what they could to preach to whomsoever came
their way the doctrine of equal rights.

When Mr. George entered California all the papers of
the State talked of him in complimentary terms and of
the name he had won in the world; and they did not
leave off until he had sailed for Australia. A party of
San Franciscans went to Martinez and boarded the train,
and filled the car so full that the rest of the passengers
considerately withdrew to other cars. Henry George was
very happy sitting with his old comrades about him, listening and laughing over the stories they poured out.
Dr. Taylor with moistened eyes whispered to Mrs. George:
"Look at him. Not one bit spoiled by the world's homage; just the same light-hearted boy!"

The time was fully occupied from the moment they
arrived in San Francisco on Tuesday to the moment of
sailing out through the Golden Gate on Saturday. Mr.
George lectured twice in San Francisco and once in Oak-

land, made an address to a body of clergymen whom he met at the San Francisco Y. M. C. A., and was entertained at dinner at Delmonico's by his old-time friends.

The two San Francisco lectures, both in Metropolitan Hall (formerly called Temple) were on Tuesday and Friday nights, the first to a paid, general audience and the second to a free audience of working men. Both were successful in every respect. The building was packed each time. One of the daily papers said that "for fully five minutes after stepping to the front of the stage, Mr. George looked upon a scene of wild applause." When silence had come—a breathless silence—with a low trembling voice, that almost broke from emotion—the "Prophet of San Francisco"—the prophet who was being honoured by his former fellow-townsmen, said:

"As I rise on this stage, the past comes back to me. Twelve years ago—it seems so far and yet so near—twelve years ago; when I was halt of speech; when to face an audience, it seemed to me, required as much courage as it would to face a battery—I stood on this platform to speak my first word in the cause for which I stand now. I stood on this platform to see, instead of the audience that greets me to-night, a beggarly array of empty benches. It is a long time. Many times, in this country and in the dear old world, I have stood before far greater audiences than this. I have been greeted by thousands who never saw me before, as they would greet a friend long known and well loved. But I don't think it ever gave me such pleasure to stand before an audience as it does to stand here to-night. (Applause.) For years and years I have been promising myself to come back to San Francisco. I have crossed the Atlantic five times before I could fulfill that desire. I am here now to go in a few days to the Antipodes; perhaps I may never return—who knows? If I live I shall try to. But to San Francisco, though I never again can be a citizen of California—though my path in life seems away so far that California looks as but a ridge on the horizon—my heart has always turned, and always will turn, to the home of my youth, to the city in which I grew up, to the city in which I found so many warm friends—to the country in which I married and in which my children were born. Always it will seem to me home; and it is sweet to the man long absent to be welcomed home.

"Aye, and you men, old friends, tried and true—you men who rallied in the early times to our movement, when we could count each other almost as upon one's fingers—I come back to you to say that at last our triumph is but a matter of time (applause); to say that never in the history of thought has a movement come forward so fast and so well.

"Ten years ago, when I left, I was anything but hopeful. Ten years ago I should not have dared to say that in any time to which I might live, we should see the beginning of this great struggle. Nor have I cared. My part (and I think I can speak for every man who is enlisted in this movement)—my part has never been to predict results. Our feeling is the feeling of the great stoic emperor: 'That is the business of Jupiter; not ours.' 'Tis ours to do the work as we may; ours to plant the seed which is to give the results. But now, so well forward is this cause; so many strong advocates has it in every land; so far has it won its way, that now it makes no difference who lives or who dies, who goes forward or who holds back. Now the currents of the time are setting in our favour. At last—at last, we can say with certainty that it will be only a little while before all over the English speaking world, and then, not long after, over the rest of the civilised world, the great truth will be acknowledged that no human child comes into this world without coming into his equal right with all."

The lecture was a finished one. It told upon those who had not heard Henry George before, and with perhaps greater effect upon those who had known him at the beginning of his speaking career. Judge Coffey wrote East: "I was most gratified to find that Mr. George had developed such extraordinary capacity as a platform speaker." The "Examiner" said of the lecture to working men: "Hundreds unable to find seats stood in the aisles and along the walls. Woollen shirted men sat side by side with elegantly dressed women. The audience was thoroughly republican and cosmopolitan, and all the different elements that went to make up the crowd were equally enthusiastic, and the frequent applause shook the building."

All this demonstration over the returned San Franciscan was like honey-dew to the souls of his old comrades who clustered around him with every attention of affection. One of them tells how, while Mr. George stood on Market Street talking with acquaintances, one beggar after another came and asked him for money, which each one got. Some one observed to the philosopher that he was being imposed upon; that the men who were begging were lazy good-for-nothing fellows who would not work. "How can I tell about that?" he answered; "let the responsibility for their actions rest upon them."

Amid the sincerely warm wishes of a crowd of friends who came to the wharf to see them off, Mr. and Mrs. George sailed on February 8 on the steamship *Mariposa* for Sydney. The voyage to the Hawaiian Islands was pleasant but uneventful, and the vessel stopped a whole day at Honolulu, giving time for driving and sight-seeing. Mrs. George was sadly affected by a change for the worse in the general appearance of the city since her childhood's residence there. The familiar places showed the wreck of age, without the accompaniment of new buildings or improvements. But more significant than any-

thing else was the large number of Chinese, who seemed
to have pushed aside the Kanakas or effaced them by in-
termarriage. Mr. and Mrs. George were entertained at
dinner at Honolulu by a party of officers belonging to
the United States war vessels, *Nipsic* and *Mohegan,* most
of whom proclaimed themselves to be believers in the single
taxer.

Of still more importance was the stop at Auckland,
New Zealand. On setting foot ashore the Georges found
a party of friends at the wharf, who notified them that
the Anti-Poverty Society of Auckland had prepared an
illuminated address for presentation later in the day.
The travellers first drove to the residence of Sir George
Grey at Parnell and received a hearty welcome, for that
diplomatist and statesman had been one of the very first
among the eminent men of the world to read "Progress
and Poverty" and to hail its author. Mr. George wrote
to "The Standard" (February 28):

> "I was especially glad to meet him and to find his
> eightieth year sitting on him so lightly. It is worth
> going far to meet such a man, soldier, scholar, states-
> man and political leader—an aristocrat by birth, who
> when hardly thirty wielded the powers of a dictator;
> who has been four times governor of important colo-
> nies in the most important crises of their affairs, and
> then premier of the colony in which he made his home;
> who is yet an intense democrat, and who, unsoured by
> disappointments and undaunted by defeats, retains in
> the evening of life all the faith and hope that are com-
> monly associated with youth. . . . What struck
> me particularly in his conversation was not merely his
> wealth of information of European as well as colonial
> history and politics, but his earnest, religious tone, his
> calm, firm conviction that this life is but a part of the
> larger life beyond, and his deep interest in the well-
> being of those who are yet to come."

After luncheon Sir George drove his guests to one of the Auckland hotels, where the members of the Anti-Poverty Society had gathered. The complimentary address was presented to Mr. George, and Sir George Grey made a fine little speech, attesting his entire faith in the gospel of the single tax. He and Mr. George conversed until the very last moment of the stay, walking on the wharf together while the captain considerately held the ship something beyond her time. Mr. George promised to return to New Zealand and lecture on the single tax, if his Australian engagements would permit. But events were against his carrying out this plan, for two weeks after reaching Australia, he wrote back to New York: "I have spoken every night, Sundays included, and had I been able to cut myself up into half a dozen, would still have been unable fairly to meet and talk with those who have come to see me and who have had interesting things to say."

On the day of landing at Sydney, Mrs. George's native city, there was an official reception at the town hall by Mayor Sydney Burdekin, and a number of other city as well as colonial dignitaries, irrespective of political parties. Indeed, the Mayor himself was one of the largest land-owners of Sydney, so that his action bespoke a broad, generous mind. Mr. George had first to make a short speech from a carriage to a dense throng before the hall; and then when he entered and received the formal welcome of the Mayor, he made a long speech, of which this was a passage, as reported by the Sydney "Daily Telegraph":

" 'In 1883 I wrote an article in the "North American Review" proposing the introduction of the Australian system of voting in the United States, and I was warned to beware of the action I was taking. But when I left my country a month ago ten States had adopted it, and it is certain eventually to be carried in every one of the forty-two States and to become the American system. If you can teach us more, for God's sake teach it. Advance Australia!' A thunder of applause followed this declaration, which was delivered with an effect at once remarkable and indescribable."

Then began a whirl of meetings, receptions, interviews and handshakings, uninterrupted during the stay in Australia, except while sleeping and travelling. Every one showed the utmost kindness. Mrs. George wrote home: "These people make Americans blush when thinking of hospitality. . . . I am at this moment sitting in a bower of flowers."

The second night in Sydney the Single Tax League of New South Wales honoured its guest with a banquet in the town hall, with C. L. Garland, M.P., President of the League, as toastmaster. Again the "Telegraph" reports:

"Mr. George, who was received with enthusiastic and long-continued cheering, said: 'I do not like these banquets. To be stuffed first is not a good preparation for making a speech, and for a man to sit and listen to laudations such as the chairman has made is not pleasant. (Laughter.) If I am here this night, if I am here as an honoured guest; if I know this night that go where I may over the civilised world, I would find men who would gladly clasp hands with me—if it has been given to me to help forward a great movement—it is through no merit of mine; it is not from my energy; it is not from my learning; it is not from my ability—it is from the simple fact that, seeing a great truth, I swore to follow it. ("Hear, hear.") When I found the duty to do, I determined that with all the strength I could command, I would do it. ("Hear,

hear.") If I were to take to myself such flattering things as have been said to me to-night, my usefulness would soon be ended.' "

The first formal lecture took place on Saturday night, March 8, in Protestant Hall; a sermon followed next day in Pitt Street Congregational Church, the site of Mrs. George's childhood's home; and the next week was filled with lectures in Exhibition Hall and other places. The weather was unusually rainy, but the audiences were nevertheless very large. People flocked from far and near; and the newspapers, especially the "Telegraph," gave fine reports and extended editorials.

The single taxers who had long been labouring in the cold and with little to cheer them were now, as Mrs. George wrote home, "fairly delirious with delight" over the unexpected platform abilities Mr. George exhibited and the great public attention he awakened and held. "What is all the crowd about," John Farrell said he heard one man ask another outside the Pitt Street Church. "Oh, a novelty that's all," was the reply; "there's a man in there who is going to preach Christianity!" John Farrell and John Ramsey, two burning single taxers, were among the most brilliant writers in Australia. Another writer who had carried the fiery cross, Frank Cotton, editor of the Australian "Standard," wrote in his paper a fortnight or so after the lecturing had begun:

"Of the great reformer himself, all must admit that as a speaker and as a man he more than justifies all our preconceived admiration. His genial manner and outspoken democracy take the hearts of all true Australians by storm; and his infinite variety of illustration, his incisive logic, and at times passionate eloquence, stir his audience to laughter, to deep thought, or to tears almost at his will. . . . I have had the plea-

sure of hearing all his metropolitan utterances and almost every speech delivered in the country districts,
yet out of thirteen different orations, in no case was
there any repetition of words or phrases, although in
each the central truth was portrayed with the utmost
clearness."

What occurred in Sydney was repeated in all the lesser
towns of New South Wales in which Mr. George spoke,
and the experiences in the colony of New South Wales
were illustrations of what took place in the other colonies
of South Australia, Western Australia, Queensland and
Victoria. Few of the public officials appeared in Victoria; but in the majority of places in the other colonies,
the mayor and aldermen led the prominent men of the
respective localities to tender hospitalities, one accompaniment of which in a number of places was the presentation of handsome, illuminated addresses. At Newcastle, N. S. W., Mr. George was entertained at luncheon by
the mayor and aldermen, and the mayors of eight or nine
small neighbouring towns were said to have been at the
board. Lithgow, a New South Wales mining town,
varied things somewhat by turning out with a brass band
and a torchlight procession. Nor were the smaller places
to be ignored; for one morning the train on which the
Georges were travelling unexpectedly stopped at a way
station. The breakfast station lay beyond, and Mr.
George, who always was impatient for breakfast, put his
head out of the window and asked: "What in heaven's
name are we stopping here for?" "It is the Mayor and
Aldermen who have obtained permission from the Commissioners to stop the train for ten minutes to read an
address to Mr. Henry George," some one said. And the
hungry, informal man, who hated such ceremonies, had
to get out and be honoured.

In Queensland, Sir Samuel Griffith, formerly Premier
and soon again to hold that office, was among the first
to welcome the American. But South Australia, though
small, impressed Mr. George as being perhaps the most
advanced of the colonies. He told an English audience
on his way home that it "led the world in the single tax
policy." "There," said he, "they have a tax imposed on
land values, irrespective of improvements; and they have
at least shown the practicability of such a tax. The tax
imposed is only one half-penny in the pound on the capital
value, but the Government is proposing to increase it
upon a graduated scale to twopence in the pound."

Almost as soon as he set foot in South Australia, Mr.
George made the acquaintance of Chief Justice Way,
whose high standing, intellectually as well as officially,
in the colony made his attendance at every lecture and
speech Mr. George delivered in Adelaide a compliment that
the latter did not fail to appreciate. Another man who
strongly impressed him was Rev. Hugh Gilmore of Adelaide, who was preaching the single tax faith pure and
simple in the face of hot opposition and who on one occasion exclaimed: "By God's grace, so long as I have breath
in me, no man shall terrify me." Mr. George accounted
him to be a man of large personal powers and wide influence—a Dr. McGlynn of South Australia. Among the
younger single taxers in the colony at this time were
Louis H. Berens and Ignatius Singer, who together subsequently wrote "The Story of My Dictatorship"—a remarkable little work of fiction depicting political and social
conditions under an imagined regime of the single tax
and which came to be extensively read in Great Britain
and the United States.

But it was perhaps in Victoria that Mr. George achieved
his greatest success during the Australian tour—Victoria,

as strong in the faith of the protection principle as his own native State of Pennsylvania. It was said in Sydney that no matter how large his audiences might be in the other colonies, in Melbourne and throughout Victoria he must expect slender attention. But when the train on which the Georges travelled drew into the Melbourne station, there was a greater gathering than usually came to greet him, and a reception committee headed by Dr. Maloney, President of the Land Nationalisation Society. "Good heavens! another reception!" the philosopher exclaimed in dismay to Mrs. George, and explaining that he would meet her at the hotel, he bolted out of the door on the opposite side of the coach. When she recovered from her surprise, Mrs. George likewise tried to flee, but she was too late and was escorted by the committee with much politeness to a carriage in waiting. Presently Mr. George came, also, surrounded by an immense throng. He had been recognised and was compelled to endure the honours.

The first lecture (on the single tax) was delivered in the Town Hall to a fine audience in numbers and character. In this discourse the lecturer drew a picture of his coming to Melbourne thirty-five years before. The second lecture was to working men, on the subject of "Labour and the Tariff." Daniel Cottier, art connoisseur, of New York and London, with whom the Georges had become acquainted on the *Mariposa*, called upon Mrs. George before this second lecture, and though a strong free trader himself, earnestly advised her to influence her husband not to speak on that subject in Victoria. "The people will not stand it," he said. "They think protection brings them their bread and butter, and they will stone him if he denounces it." Mrs. George replied that Mr. George was not to be diverted from what he consid-

ered to be his duty, even if she wished to influence him
in another way, which she did not. Mr. Cottier admired
the courage, but deprecated the wisdom of such a policy.

The City Hall was crowded, with President Hancock of
the Trades and Labour Council in the chair. Mr. George
lost little time in going to the pith of his subject.

> "I am a free trader—a free trader absolutely. I
> should abolish all revenue tariffs. I should make trade
> absolutely free between Victoria and all other coun-
> tries. I should go further than that; I should abolish
> all taxes that fall upon labour and capital—all taxes
> that fall upon the products of human industry, or any
> of the modes of human industry. How then should I
> raise needed revenues? I should raise them by a tax
> upon land values, irrespective of improvements—a tax
> that would fall upon the holder of a vacant plot of land
> near the city as heavily as upon like land upon which
> a hundred cottages stood."

Thunders of applause that threatened to bring down
the gallery greeted this and the long series of audacious
free trade utterances of which this custom house abolisher
made up his address. It was as if Melbourne had waited
for but the radical word to bring forth an extraordinary
exhibition of clear and emphatic dissent from the policy
which hitherto had been only timidly opposed. Mr. Cottier sat in the audience beside Mrs. George, the embodi-
ment of astonishment and delight; and he was almost
past words when, after the lecture, three cheers were given
and hundreds of men in the audience lingered to hand in
their names for the formation of a free trade league—
some of them being prominent in Melbourne. All the
papers gave good reports and the Melbourne "Telegraph"
said:

"The lecturer very adroitly led up to his subject of land nationalisation and the single tax. Imperceptibly, almost, he landed his hearers in the midst of it, through a panegyric of Melbourne city, and regrets about poverty, and pleasant jokes and amusing anecdotes. Whether the lecture was carefully prepared in writing beforehand, or was absolutely extempore is not certain; but in either case the result was admirable. Mr. George must possess a marvellous memory; or equally wonderful powers of extemporaneous speech. Every sentence was carefully constructed and well rounded off; every word was in its proper place, and the most forcible and expressive word was used."

At a subsequent date, Mr. George debated the tariff question with Mr. W. Trenwith, M.P., who was put forward as representative of protectionist working men. The meeting occurred in Exhibition Hall before a crowded audience, "which," said Mr. George in "The Standard" (May 21), "though for the most part protectionist, gave me their heartiest applause and so laughed at Mr. Trenwith's alleged facts and preposterous assertions that I did not have to trouble myself to reply to them, but could occupy my time in pressing home the general principles, which, when once fairly considered, will destroy the protectionist superstition in the mind of any one who thinks at all."

Although he sailed for home from Adelaide, South Australia, and lectured there before embarking, the formal close of the Australian lecture campaign took place in Sydney a few days before. George H. Reid, M.P., President of the Free Trade Association and subsequently Premier of the colony, took Mr. and Mrs. George and a party of their friends on a steam yacht excursion over the famously beautiful bay. Mayor Burdekin at his residence gave a dinner in honour of Mr. George at which were present all the members of the New South Wales Ministry, except the Minister of Lands and the Premier, Sir Henry Parks, who was confined by an accident. Several ex-Ministers and other leading men of the community were also present. On the last day a reception was held in Temperance Hall, when Mrs. George was presented with a large album containing photographs of Australian friends. To her consternation and Mr. George's corresponding merriment, she was made the object of short but formal speeches, the gentlemen of the committee standing and addressing her directly. When she recovered from her first surprise, she looked towards her husband, sitting close beside her. He winked, and presently dropping his handkerchief to the floor said as he reached down, just loud enough for her to hear: "How do you like it?"

The farewell lecture was in Protestant Hall. The subject was "Protection a fallacy; real free trade a necessity." Mr. George was at his best and had the audience cheering throughout what the Sydney "Telegraph" called his "splendid deliverance." The men who called themselves free traders, but who had been afraid of what he called free trade, had come out at last, and President Reid of the Free Trade League was in the chair and paid him this high tribute on behalf of Australia:

"I don't think we should allow him to make this farewell address to us without the assurance that his name, famous in so many lands, has now become in Australia a household word. (Cheers.) The teachings of his wonderful books have already created a host of enthusiastic disciples to welcome him to these shores— (cheers)—and even I, who in some respects cannot call myself one of his disciples, can fully understand that enthusiasm. (Cheers.) He has thrice earned it. He has earned it as a thinker, he has earned it as a writer and he has earned it as an orator. (Cheers.) And I venture to say—and these are the concluding words in which, on behalf of this great meeting, I bid him farewell—that he may and probably will be regarded by posterity as one of those leaders of men who rise above the sordid level of things as they are, who seek to revive the spirit and the power of Christianity, who seek to enrich the human intellect with humane and generous ideas, who create in the minds of all noble ambition— new spheres of philanthropy and justice—quickening the world's great heart with the throbbings and gladness of the time to come, when the curse of toil shall cease from troubling, banished forever by the universal dignity and happiness of labour." (Prolonged cheering.)

There were mistakes—serious mistakes—in the management of the Australian campaign which caused Mr. George much round-about travelling and loss of time. This was due chiefly to unexpected demands from scores of places, which disarranged the plans. It is probably safe to say that no man speaking on social questions had ever before been so warmly and so generally greeted on the Island Continent. But it was three months and a half of hard work for Henry George, speaking every night that he was not travelling, save one Sunday, and frequently he spoke twice a day. Letters and cables came from Sir George Grey in New Zealand and from the Premier and Attorney-General of Tasmania warmly inviting him to each of these places but he was tired out and had to refuse.

Incidentally to his long exacting occupation he had seen much to interest and instruct him. At Melbourne he met and talked briefly with Henry Drummond; at the largest cities he was complimented with temporary membership in the clubs, and at Sydney he was greatly amused at the exploit of an enthusiastic single taxer, who, thinking that the American visitor ought to witness an Australian horse race, applied to a racing official to have Henry George made an honorary member. The official asked "Who is Henry George—has he any horses?" "Yes," said the single taxer; "'Progress' and 'Poverty'—and they are running with great success in the United States!"

The changes of sea and sky as they passed over the ocean's great expanse were the travellers' chief matters of observation from day to day as the steamship *Valetta* carried them north and eastward towards home. Then came India with its tropical scenes and the passage through the Red Sea. In traversing the Gulf of Suez they skirted the "barren shore of the peninsula of Sinai, its bare rugged mountains gleaming in the fierce sun, presenting in all probability precisely the same appearance that they did when Moses led the Israelites along their base." Passing into the Mediterranean, the Georges touched at the foot of Italy—Brindisi—where they disembarked and made a short, hurried tour through Naples, Pompeii and Herculaneum to Rome, which they reached in the worst possible time of year, all who could having fled from the heat and fear of fever. Writing to his art-loving friend. Dr. Taylor, afterwards, Mr. George said: "You would get sick of old masters. We had a good time in our own way, unknown and unknowing, and working our way by signs, largely." From Rome they proceeded to Venice and some other places, and thence through Switzerland and France to Great Britain, where Mr. George, during a few days' sojourn, made two speeches, one in the Glasgow City Hall and one under the auspices of the Radical Association of Walworth, London, in which he told of the great progress of the cause at the antipodes.

Accompanied by Rev. J. O. S. Huntington of New York, Mr. George during this short trip called upon Gen-

eral Booth of the Salvation Army, whom he had met in
London six years before. He now learned that Mrs.
Booth, who had large influence in the management and
spiritual guidance of the great army organisation, had
been for some time thinking of social questions, mainly
along single tax lines, and wished to initiate a policy
which should preach the salvation of the body as well as
of the soul—that should seek to better material conditions here, while holding out hope of a life hereafter.
Mr. George came away from this visit to the Booths with
sanguine feelings that the Salvation Army with its military organisation radiating from London all over the
globe would soon become a kind of world-wide Anti-
Poverty Society, that, with a religious enthusiasm, would
awaken thought and make way for the single tax idea.
But Mrs. Booth even then was stricken with an incurable
disease, and it soon after carried her away. With her
seemed to go the clearest head and the boldest heart in
that movement for a social reform policy, for only small
steps, and those along the lines of charity, were taken
by the army; and Mr. George reluctantly gave up hope
that the organisation would do anything towards the
single tax.

Mr. and Mrs. George arrived in New York harbour on
the steamship *Servia* on September 1, in time to take
part in the first national conference of single tax men,
which for two days met in the large hall of Cooper Union,
where the delegates exchanged glad tidings and discussed
measures for the propagation of the faith. It was an
exultant home-coming to him who since January had made
a circle of the globe, everywhere finding men and women
in twos or threes, in tens or scores, in hundreds or thousands, holding the same faith and glowing with the same
enthusiasm. On the second day of the conference, Sep-

tember 2, he was introduced as being "fifty-one years old to-day." He said:

"I have sat on this platform to-night with feelings of joy and pride. I have sat on this platform to-night with heartfelt thankfulness to God; and I believe that I only speak your voice, fellow single taxers of New York, when I say that the samples we have here to-night of the single tax men of the rest of the Union have nerved us and inspired us and given us more hope for the future than anything else could. (Applause.)

"Yes; it is my birthday to-day. (Voice: 'Long may you live.' Vociferous applause.) But not too long. Life, long life is not the best thing to wish for those you love. Not too long; but that in my day, whether it be long or short, I may do my duty, and do my best." (Applause.)

A consciousness of the uncertainty of life seemed ever present to Henry George, and suddenly death seemed to come close to him, for on December 5, on returning home from a little informal repast with some friends, he was stricken with aphasia. The long hard trip around the world, a lecturing trip into New England, then a longer one into the Southwest as far as Texas, and following on this, worry over the present and future of "The Standard," which, while not paying, was an embarrassment to plans he had for other work, had brought the climax.

Dr. James E. Kelly, the family physician, was next morning to sail to Europe on professional business, but he brought in Dr. Frederick Peterson, a young brain-specialist, and himself remained until within an hour of the ship's sailing. Dr. Peterson says of the case:

"Mr. George had a great pain on the left side of his head, in the neighbourhood of the motor speech centre in the brain. He talked quite clearly, but used wrong

words, and manufactured words at times. Shown a
watch and asked what it was, he said: 'That is a sep';
shown a pencil: 'That is a sep'; shown a thermometer
he said: 'That is a sep,' and seemed to think he had used
the correct words. He repeated words very well and
was very much interested in asking about his condition
and comprehended clearly the form of aphasia he was
suffering from and the nature of the lesion. He expressed great anxiety as to the prognosis. The trouble
was a slight hemorrhage in the particular part of the
brain which presides over articulate speech. He improved very rapidly; his mind was perfectly clear in
every way, aside from the difficulty in expressing himself. There was no paralysis of any kind. In three
days he was able to name objects correctly. By the
first of January the whole condition had been recovered from."

The friends showed loving attention, John Russell
Young personally calling at the house every day, and
August Lewis and Tom L. Johnson establishing a benevolent joint dictatorship and decreeing that as soon as he
should be strong enough, the sick man and Mrs. George
should go off to Bermuda to stay there beyond the reach
of all anxiety until he should have recuperated. Mr.
George fell in with the plans of his good friends. He
sailed early in the new year with Mrs. George, and accompanied by Mr. and Mrs. Simon Mendelson, parents of
Mrs. August Lewis. He was well enough to take out-
door exercise and to do a little simple writing before he
left, and among other things he made a brief entry on the
last page of his pocket diary for 1890—"A memorable
year. Much to be thankful for."

CHAPTER XII.

PERSONAL AND DOMESTIC MATTERS.

1891-1897.   AGE, 52-58.

"THE invalid is quite himself, eating and sleeping well, and constantly on the go," wrote Mrs. George from Bermuda. Mr. George took the exercise of a young man—walking, driving and rowing; and a young single taxer, William E. Hicks, came from New York with a bicycle expressly to teach him to ride. This came easily; nor was a boy ever more proud of a physical accomplishment than was Henry George of this achievement. Regardless of dusty and dishevelled appearance, he would come in from a "spin," his blue eyes shining and his face all aglow with pleasure. All his children learned to ride, and later became his frequent wheeling companions. His wife likewise made many attempts to learn, so as to be with him in this as in other things; but several accidents warned her to desist.

The wheel brought mental as well as physical good to Mr. George, for it proved to him that he had not lost his active powers; and up to a short time of his death he rode with keen enjoyment, getting much of the kind of exhilaration that in his younger manhood had come from horseback riding. It became at once a means of recreation and method of stirring his mind; and if the origin of some of the boldest conceptions and loftiest passages of his later writings could be traced, it might be found in these wheel rides.

This was Mr. George's second mechanical triumph, his first being over the type-writing machine, which he began to use in 1884 and continued to use until his death. With it he "blocked out" his work, and one of his sons or daughters, whoever at the time was doing amanuensis work for him, used another. The machine in 1884 was unknown in some parts of the world, and a correspondent in Paraguay, South America, inquired how he could afford to have his letters put in type and printed. Mr. George explained that he used a little mechanism having keys for the fingers to play on like a kind of piano.

For a while in 1891, Mr. George tried the phonograph, endeavouring to record dictations and have his amanuensis transcribe at leisure. But he could not habituate himself to talking into the inanimate machine and he succumbed to the disconcerting effects that almost invariably attack the user at the outset. The instrument was delivered at the Nineteenth Street residence one afternoon when Mr. George was at home writing and the other members of the family were absent. He sat down at once to do some dictating, but could not induce himself to take the instrument seriously. He could treat it only as a toy, and accordingly fell to playing with it. Into it he shouted a sailor song of his boyhood to the effect that

"Up jumped the shark with his crooked teeth,
Saying, 'I'll cook the duff, if you'll cook the beef';"

and then another song about a winsome bumboat damsel, who, saluted by the admiral of the fleet in terms she resented, answered

"Kind admiral, you be damned!"

This last line was roared into the machine in a hurricane voice that brought the wondering and dismayed domestics running up-stairs, only to find, when they peered into the room, that Mr. George was alone, seated before a little table and singing into a speaking tube.

During the stay in Bermuda Mr. Simon Mendelson noted some conversations in promise to his daughter, who had remained in New York. Among the notes is this:

" Monday, February 16, 1891.

"In the evening R. [Mrs. Mendelson] said to Mr. George: 'You put abrupt questions; may I ask you a similar one?'

"G. 'Certainly.'

"R. 'What is your conception of God?'

"G. 'Of this chair, or this bag, or the ship out there I can trace the genesis to man's mind. God is the Great Mind, the essence of all that is great and high.'

"R. 'And you consider Him a personal God?'

"G. 'Not necessarily, but I do like to believe Him such and do believe Him; but not in any positive shape or form.' "

Louis F. Post tells how one day, perhaps a year after the Bermuda trip, when out bicycling with Mr. George and riding a strange wheel, he spoke of the queer fact that one's own wheel comes to seem like part of one's own self. They had just previously conversed about the spirit: Mr. George had been giving reasons for belief in its existence. Upon his friend's remark, Mr. George asked if he saw nothing suggestive in that; if he could not discern an analogy between the relation of the wheel to his body and of his body to his spirit?

At another time while riding slowly along Fifth Ave-

nue, New York, with a son and a daughter, he observed
an undertaker's wagon stop before a residence, and two
men get down and carry up armfuls of black drapery.
"None of that when I am dead," he said to his children.
"Death is as natural as life; it means a passage into another life. If a man has lived well—if he has kept the
faith—it should be a time for rejoicing, not for repining,
that the struggle here is over."

Death was much in his thoughts from now forward.
"How much there is of joy and sorrow and tragedy in
the years that have rolled so noiselessly by since we first
knew each other!" he wrote to Judge Coffey of California; "and now we are what we then thought were old
men, and the years move all the faster." On another
occasion he wrote to Thomas F. Walker: "I have long
since ceased to have any dread of death, except for the
shock of parting." While on a western lecturing trip he
wrote to Mrs. George concerning the death of a fine St.
Bernard dog they had raised from a pup: "Poor old Thor!
I cannot help feeling so sorry for him, and I know that
you all must miss him very much. But we cannot tell.
Perhaps if not that, something worse might have happened. Even in a dog, though, we feel the mystery of
death. Let us love the closer, while life lasts."

Staunch as a rock was his belief in immortality, and
many of his friends loved to talk to him about it, even
those like Louis Prang of Boston who had little faith.
"Do you think we shall ever meet you in California
again?" asked Mrs. Francis M. Milne of San Francisco,
during the trip around the world. "I don't know," he
answered; "for there is much to do. But if not here,
then hereafter." Another friend, A. Van Dusen of New
York, questioned: "What do you regard as the strongest
evidence of the immortality of the soul?" The answer

was prompt, and to Mr. Van Dusen, conclusive: "The creation of human beings is purposeless if this is all." Over the body of William T. Croasdale, who died in the single tax faith in August, 1891, and was cremated, Mr. George in a funeral address said:

"Ceased to be? No; I do not believe it! Cease to be? No; only to our senses yet encompassed in the flesh that he has shed. For our hearts bear witness to our reason that that which stands for good does not cease to be. . . . The changing matter, the passing energy that gave to this body its form are even now on their way to other forms. In a few hours there will remain to our sight but a handful of ashes. But that which we instinctively feel as more than matter and more than energy; that which in thinking of our friend to-day we cherish as best and highest—that cannot be lost. If there be in the world order and purpose, that still lives."

When a young man, troubled in mind, raised the question of whether or not suicide was justifiable, Mr. George replied: "Many wise men among the ancients thought it was. But what do we know about life; and what do we know about death? We are here, conscious of things to do. We came here not of ourselves. We must be part of a plan. We have work to perform. If we refuse to go forward with the work here, how do we know but that it shall have to be performed elsewhere?"

August Lewis had on Mr. George's setting off for Bermuda given him a translation of Schopenhauer's "World as Will and Idea." Mr. George found it absorbingly interesting, but " 'From A to Izzard' like a red rag to a bull," for the German philosopher represented that hopelessness of things earthly and a negation of life hereafter which proved a direct antithesis to George's ever-strengthening hopefulness and faith. With all that, the brilliant mind of the great German exercised its fascination. Recognising in him a philosopher of rare originality and astonishing versatility, Mr. George became fond of consulting (or rather comparing) his views on the most varied topics. And he seemed to derive satisfaction from the fact that, in spite of its atheism, the underlying principle of Schopenhauer's philosophy was spiritual and not material.[1] Mr. George also seemed to take great delight in Schopenhauer's well known outspokenness against the professors, and indeed saw in the way that Schopenhauer had so long been ignored by them, a case analogous to his own. Perhaps many passages in Mr. George's later works bearing on this subject are somewhat to be ascribed to this influence.[2]

Mr. George's views of the essence of Christianity he set forth in his published writings. His beliefs relative to the person of Christ were, he said one day in the last year of his life to his son Henry, most nearly represented by a short sketch written by Thomas Jefferson, entitled "Syllabus of an estimate of the merits of the doctrines of Jesus,"[3] from which he quoted in "The Science of Political Economy."[4]

---

[1] See "A Perplexed Philosopher," Part III, Chapter iii, (Memorial Edition, pp. 125–128).

[2] While having only a grammar school education, Mr. Lewis' tastes and talents had always led him to spend his leisure hours in the study, and capacious and well filled book shelves in his home showed the choiceness and range of his reading. On questions of philosophy he was, at least in later years, the closest of Mr. George's friends ; and as to the Schopenhauer philosophy, they had frequent conversations subsequent to the Bermuda trip, in the studio of George Brush, to whom Mr. George, at Mr. Lewis' request, sat for a full-length portrait.

[3] "The Writings of Thomas Jefferson," collected and edited by Paul Leicester Ford, Putnam's Sons, Vol. VIII. p. 227.

[4] Book II., Chapter ii., p. 132.

To take another view of Henry George—here is a further excerpt from the Mendelson Bermuda notes:

"Sunday March 1, 1891.

"Read Henry IV. aloud. Mr. George thinks it highly superior in 'every way' to Coriolanus. He particularly enjoys the character of Falstaff. Finds no attraction whatever in the character of Coriolanus; considers him a bad, selfish man from beginning to end; and moreover cannot enjoy or approve of 'a piece of art without a high purpose.' Considers this business of war in Henry IV. as 'poor business.' 'The Chinese look down on soldiers. And is that valour? A big man ever so heavily armed like Douglas, the Scot, slashes the unarmed soldiers and kills and crushes them by his mere weight.' "

"Mr. George feels not the necessity of talking and of giving his thoughts to others, not even for the purpose of getting at their thoughts. In the latter case, he prefers asking direct questions abruptly. In his talk he seldom gets animated and seldom says things of a higher order. When he does, he looks very absorbed in his subject and quite handsome. . . .

"Though of deep feeling, he does not feel poetically. The poetry which he likes is not of the divine art, but the eloquence of feeling; that which finds its strong echo in his own heart. Of art *per se* he has no notion.

"His mind is of a beautiful caste—simple, direct and comprehensive."

The reading of Tennyson, Whittier, Swinburne, Browning, Longfellow, Macaulay, Buchanan and Arnold to himself or aloud in the family circle showed the poetic nature; and the frequent word of encouragement to such rising singers as Alice Werner of London, John Farrell of New South Wales and Frances M. Milne of California showed the listening ear. But like the Psalms to Crom-

well's Ironsides, the poetry that spoke most strongly to
him was that which moved with the intense purpose of
his soul. For verses solely of sentiment or reflection, no
matter how fine the language or picturing, his feeling was
set forth in a note to Dr. Taylor (June 1, 1892): "Thanks
for 'The Quiet Wood.' It is good, but—why, when the
great struggle is on, and history is being made, will you
go off into the woods and play the flute? I should rather
see you put your lips to the trumpet."

Perhaps it may be well to add some lines from a letter
Mr. George wrote subsequently (April 22, 1893) to his
actor friend, James A. Herne, who had just produced a
successful play, "Shore Acres":

"I left Boston with the spell of your genius upon me,
wishing very much to see you and sorry when I found
I could not.

"I cannot too much congratulate you upon your success. You have done what you have sought to do—
made a play pure and noble that people will come to
hear. You have taken the strength of realism and
added to it the strength that comes from the wider
truth that realism fails to see; and in the simple portrayal of homely life, touched a universal chord. . . .
In the solemnity of the wonderfully suggestive close,
the veil that separates us from heaven seems to grow
thin, and things not seen to be felt.

"But who save you can bring out the character you
have created—a character, which to others, as to me,
must have recalled the tender memory of some sweet
saint of God—for such loving and unselfish souls there
have been and are. I never before saw acting that impressed me so much as yours last night. I did not feel
like talking when I left the theatre; but I wanted to
grasp your hand. I did not want to see you in that
wonderful piece of acting of which they told me, where
you reduced man to the mere animal. I am glad to
have seen you in this, where the angel gleams forth."

In early life Richard III. and Hamlet of the Shake-
spearian plays most attracted Mr. George; but towards the
close of life the vaulting ambition pictured in Macbeth
made him think that in that the poet had reached his
supreme conception. He himself, who had come out of
obscurity and won intellectual triumphs such as no man
in his domain of thought had ever before so quickly won,
was keenly conscious of the dangers of ambition; and the
poet's impersonation stood forth as the very incarnation
of this tremendous human passion.

Reflecting upon the personality of Shakespeare and
history's brief account of him, Mr. George once in conversation with his elder son said: "No man can do great
writing without being conscious that it is great. But the
great man is a modest man, and may be careless of his
fame further than his achievements will speak for him.
England's greatest poet, like the great poet whose memory Scotland reveres to-day, Burns, was contented, after
doing his work, to live in retirement; feeling probably
that 'not marble, nor the gilded monuments of princes'
would outlive his 'powerful rhyme.'"

But always in comparing man with man, there entered
the relation of proportion. In answer to a question put
by one of his family he said: "Napoleon's mind at his
downfall was in no worse plight than that of the poor
devil who cannot make or borrow ten dollars is relatively
to the things that enter into his life." Edward McHugh
tells how, being out for a stroll with Mr. George at Fort
Hamilton, they dropped into the branch post office. There
they met a man who wished to send away some money,
but did not know how to fill out the official order. Mr.
George did it for him. "It is not every day that such a
man can have a philosopher to write for him," said Mr.
McHugh when the stroll was resumed. "A philosopher,"

was the reply, "is no better than a bootblack. Such terms
are only relative to our own small affairs."

As President Lincoln modestly said he would hold Mc-
Clellan's horse if that would help the general win the
country a battle, so Henry George always refrained from
assuming leadership. It was never "my principles," "my
movement," "my cause"; but always "our principles,"
"our movement," "our cause." To Dr. Taylor he wrote
(April 28, 1891) : "How persistent is the manner in which
the professors and those who esteem themselves the learned
class ignore and slur me; but I am not conscious of any
other feeling about it than that of a certain curiosity."
This was not assumed humility. He spoke in the simplicity of his nature—a simplicity that shone out in his
private life, as witness in a letter to Mrs. George, during
the summer of 1893 :

> "I slept at home last night. Post wanted me to go
> down with him, but I thought I should prefer to sleep
> here, I had unfortunately drank two glasses of iced tea
> at supper (which I took with Post and the Hibbards)
> and owing I suppose to that, I did not get to sleep till
> after two. But the house was delightfully cool, and I
> slept until after nine, then took a bath, and for fifteen
> cents got two cups of coffee and all I wanted to eat at
> the little bakery on Twentieth Street and Second Ave-
> nue. Then I came back to the house, where I have
> been waiting for the carpets to come, having sent yes-
> terday a notice that I should be here between 10 and
> 12 to-day."

As with many famous men, money matters gave Mr.
George much worry. Very little money would put him
at his ease, although to get it he was often put to borrowing. But unlike many celebrities, borrowed money with
him was always a sacred debt, and he never failed to re-

turn a loan punctually, if a time had been set; borrowing elsewhere, if he could meet the payment in no other way. One of his last acts before leaving New York in 1890 for the trip around the world was to send a check to John Russell Young in final settlement of loans that enabled the philosopher to leave California in 1880 and helped to sustain him until he got his start in New York.

Personal homage in every form Henry George treated with disfavour. "I do not like your over-praise," he wrote to Mrs. Milne, who sent him greetings on his return to New York from around the world. "If my words have spoken to your heart, it was because they came from my own; and though we may like to be praised for the little things, we do not for the big things." Once when an enthusiastic young chairman at a large meeting in Harlem, New York City, was making an earnest and sincere but very flattering speech in introducing Mr. George, the latter wriggled and writhed as though his character was being aspersed, instead of praised. Unable to bear it longer, he suddenly leaned forward and poked the chairman in the back with a walking-stick he had found beside him. The chairman, in a flood of bellowing eloquence, chopped off in the middle of a word, looked behind him, had a whispered conference with the philosopher, turned back to the audience, and said quietly: "Mr. George don't want me to get the rest of that off"; which tickled the assemblage into spasms of laughter.

The dislike of his younger manhood to social forms Mr. George never conquered. He could not endure the accompanying vapid, small talk. Moreover, he found the necessity of giving special attention to his raiment particularly irksome, a dress coat and its adjuncts amounting to an affliction; but he nevertheless tried to bear these ills with tranquillity, because as he reasoned, to conform to the small, polite usages tended to disarm antagonism to his crusade against giant wrongs in the vast body politic and body social. Yet a preoccupied mind often interfered with the carrying out of his good intentions, as for instance, he appeared at a reception at his home in Nineteenth Street with the studs of his shirt bosom wrong side out, the ladies of the family being busy with the guests. At a later period, when residing at suburban Fort Hamilton, he spent a whole day in the business portion of New York and the night at the somewhat formal Hotel Waldorf with Tom L. Johnson without discovering that he had been going about with very dusty boots. But he made amends by having them polished before starting back for Fort Hamilton.

This carelessness about dress led to many minor adventures, one of which was in a sleeping-car, of which Mr. George was the sole occupant. The colored porter, whose livelihood largely depended upon fees from passengers, lamented to him the "po'ness of business." He made out such a deplorable case that Mr. George was inspired to surprise him with a large tip, mentally resolving to give him all the change in his pocket. This proved to be much more than Mr. George expected and four or five times the customary fee, but he offered it nevertheless.

"Dat all fo' me?" exclaimed the man incredulously, looking from the money to Mr. George's not over-fastidious clothes, and then back to the money. And when Mr. George assured him that all the money was for him, the porter accepted it with a burst of thanks, adding: "I of'en heard it said, but I never would believe it; yo' never can tell about a frog until yo' see him jump!"

Forgetfulness from preoccupation brought many petty losses. Once on a lecturing trip, with mock gravity he upbraided his wife, who travelled some of the way with him, for forgetting her umbrella at one of the stops. "And what have you to report, sir?" she retorted. A smile swept his gravity aside. "Only that I left my night apparel in one place, my tooth brush at another and my overshoes with the Governor of Missouri." Half an hour later he might have added the loss of his watch, which he left in a hotel at the first stopping place, though this was speedily recovered. So common were losses of this kind with him that he was positively relieved when he found that other members of the family could lose things, too. Returning with one of his sons from a Western journey, he saluted Mrs. George on reaching home with: "I can see that your children grow more like you every day." "In what way?" asked Mrs. George. "Why, in losing things. Your son here lost our tickets from St. Louis back to New York." Neither Mrs. George nor the son saw much in the loss of two one-thousand-mile tickets to smile at, but to Mr. George the incident had something of humour, because, while the tickets were lost, he himself was not this time the culprit.

Abstraction not uncommonly carried him into a wrong street, took him to a wrong house and gave a wrong direction to a letter, but perhaps his most surprising experience was while travelling with one of his sons in a sleeping-car from Cincinnati to Cleveland, Ohio. They went to bed in opposite, lower berths. Unable to sleep part of the night, Mr. George arose, put on some of his clothes, went to the smoking section and enjoyed a cigar. Drowsiness at length creeping upon him, he returned to bed and slept until the breakfast call of the porter awoke him in the morning. Reaching across the passageway, he gave the curtains of the berth opposite a vigorous shake, calling out: "Do you hear the joyful cry?" But instead of his son's voice, a feminine voice replied: "I think you have made some mistake." Mr. George drew back in confusion. He looked about him to get his "bearings," only to find that on returning from his smoke during the night, he had taken the berth that some one else had apparently vacated, and so had finished his night's sleep in wrong quarters.

It has been said that Mr. George dreaded social occasions. Yet there were gatherings of a social nature which he really enjoyed attending. These were little private dinners that John Russell Young gave, sometimes at the Astor House in New York and sometimes at the Union League in Philadelphia. At one or the other of these dinners he met John Mackay, William Florence, Joseph Jefferson, General Sherman, Colonel Alexander McClure, Murat Halstead, Judge Roger A. Pryor, Chauncey M. Depew and Grover Cleveland. He had never before met the ex-President, and was much pleased with him, believing from what fell in conversation, that if renominated for the Presidency in 1892, Cleveland would make a radical fight.

John Russell Young, though he was always a strict party Republican, was at heart a radical—an absolute free trader and a good deal of a single taxer. But though he talked unreservedly in private, his public utterances were veiled, one of his signed newspaper articles drawing out this message from his downright friend, George:

> "I don't like your "Press" article. . . . I have some question whether the ordinary reader will know whether you are for Blaine or Harrison, and I fear that your delicate damnation of the tariff will in many cases be deemed by him an indorsement. The fine inferences by which skilled diplomatists may convey their meaning to one another will not be understood in a town meeting."

Henry George's judgment had to most of his friends a very singular quality. Of this Louis F. Post speaks, having many occasions, both public and private, for putting his impressions to the test:

"There was something unique about Mr. George's judgment. It was not intuitive, and yet it seemed at times to be infallibly so. I say it was not intuitive, because I never knew it to be of the slightest value, except when his intellect was aroused by a sense of responsibility; and then it was startling in its directness and accuracy. I have often said that if Henry George told me how best to go to Europe, and did so without a sense of responsibility in the matter, I should go the other way; but that if he acted under a sense of responsibility, I should follow his directions blindfold without a question or doubt."

An instance of the highly practical cast of Mr. George's mind when responsibility concentrated his faculties was given in 1893, when a general financial stringency was squeezing the banks of the country, and crippling and destroying strong and weak industrial enterprises. The large steel rail manufacturing company named after Tom L. Johnson, and located at Johnstown, Pa., was soon brought face to face with this problem. The president of the company, Arthur J. Moxham, had come into the single tax faith soon after Mr. Johnson's conversion in the middle eighties. His strength of character and high executive ability were attested by the people of Johnstown when the never-to-be-forgotten flood lay the centre of the city in ruins, killed thirty-six hundred persons, and sweeping away all established authority and order, gave place to horror, terror and frantic confusion. In that time of disaster Mr. Moxham was made dictator, with life and death powers; and for three days he held

that extraordinary office. Mr. George happened to visit
Johnstown and Mr. Moxham in 1893, at the moment when
the financial stringency had brought the affairs of the
Johnson Company to a crisis. He was told by Mr. Moxham that no course seemed to be left but to shut down,
for while he could get plenty of orders for rails, he could
get no money in payment. Whereupon Mr. George suggested that the bonds of the street railroad companies ordering rails should be taken in payment of their orders;
and that certificates to be used as money be issued against
them. Mr. Moxham took the idea and developed a plan,
calling a meeting of his employees, explained to them the
proposal to take steel railroad bonds, place them in the
hands of a trustee mutually acceptable to the company
and its men, and against these bonds to issue certificates
in small denominations with which to pay salaries and
wages by the Johnson Company. The employees gladly
accepted the proposal and appointed a committee to act
for them, and the plan was put into execution, one-third
of all salaries and wages being paid in currency and the
other two-thirds in these bond certificates. The store-
keepers and other townspeople accepted the certificates as
readily as money; and the company, with its several thousand employees, passed through the "tight" period without further trouble. Indeed, the earnings of the employees were greater at this time than at any other period
in the history of the company. Subsequently every one
of the certificates was drawn in and redeemed. Mr.
George regarded this as an illustration of what the United
States Government could do to clear up the currency
difficulties—issue from its own treasury a paper currency,
based upon its credit and interchangeable with its bonds.

Mr. George lived in the Nineteenth Street house, New
York, until the spring of 1895, when the family stored the

furniture and went to Merriewold Park—a little unpre-
tentious, woodland resort in the hills of Sullivan County,
New York State, where some single taxers had built a
few houses and had commenced to go each summer as
early as 1889. In the fall of 1895 the Georges came
down from Merriewold and occupied a house at Fort
Hamilton, Long Island, which had probably been standing there thirty or forty years when Henry George, as a
boy, had sailed out of the harbour past it on the ship
Hindoo, bound for Australia and India. It stood on the
bluffs at the "Narrows," between the inner and outer
bays. The house belonged to Tom L. Johnson, who, with
his father, had bought considerable land there with a
view to making themselves summer homes. "In the moving and arranging," Mr. George wrote to his friend, "I
have not been able to get fairly to work, but shall to-
morrow, and thanks to you, in the most comfortable quarters I have ever worked in since 'Progress and Poverty'
was written."

The first marriage among the children had occurred in
1888; the second son, Richard, having wedded Mary E.
Robinson of Brooklyn; and to this couple several children
had been born. Another marriage came in the spring
of 1895, Jennie, the third child and first daughter, being
united to William J. Atkinson of New York. The good
friend in the cause, Rev. James O. S. Huntington, had
performed the first marriage ceremony in a little Episcopal Church in Brooklyn. Dr. McGlynn, who had now
been restored to his priestly offices in the Catholic Church,
performed the second marriage at the George residence
on Nineteenth Street.

Up to the Doctor's reinstatement in December, 1892,
Edward McGlynn and Henry George had had no written
communication since their separation during the presi-

dential campaign of 1888 and had met only casually. The clergyman, while living the exemplary life of a priest, just as though exercising his full office, had meanwhile, with unabating persistence, preached the single tax faith at his Anti-Poverty meetings in New York and in lectures in many other cities. At length the wise men of the Church concluded that justice required a reconsideration of the case. Many have thought that the reply that Henry George made to the papal encyclical in 1891, of which we shall speak later, had influenced the broadminded Leo XIII. to review the case.[1] This may have been a contributing cause. When the Pope sent Archbishop Satolli to this country as his representative, Rev. Dr. Burtsell called upon him to suggest a reversal of the act of excommunication. Archbishop Satolli, evidently following instructions of the Pope, suggested that Dr. McGlynn should present to him a full explanation of his doctrine on the land question. Dr. Burtsell first presented an exposition of the doctrine, which Dr. McGlynn indorsed as clear and accurate. Later Dr. McGlynn presented his own statement of his teachings. It was direct and explicit, without extenuation, just as he had been teaching it from the beginning. These written statements were carefully considered by a committee of the professors of the Catholic University in Washington, who declared that they contained nothing contrary to the teachings of the Catholic Church. These professors were the Revs. Thomas Bouquillon, D.D. (Dean of the Theological Faculty), Thomas O'Gorman, D.D. (since appointed

---

[1] To Rev. Thomas Dawson, then of London, Mr. George wrote (December 23, 1892): "I have for some time believed Leo XIII. to be a very great man. . . . Whether he ever read my 'Open Letter' I cannot tell, but he has been acting as though he had not only read it, but had recognised its force."

Bishop of Sioux Falls, S. D.), Thomas J. Shahan, D.D., and Charles Grannan, D.D. Dr. McGlynn subsequently made a profession of his adhesion to the teachings of the Church and of the Apostolic See, and in general terms he recalled any word that may have escaped him not in conformity with the respect due to the Holy See. The papal representative suggested that, as Dr. McGlynn had not been able to join with the clergy in the regular annual retreat, he should go on retreat preparatory to reinstatement; but when he was made to realise that this was likely to be construed as a punishment, the ablegate refrained from urging it, and left the matter to Dr. McGlynn's judgment. The latter expressly stipulated that he should be free to continue to expound the single tax as long as he thought proper, to the Anti-Poverty Society or any gathering, at Cooper Union or elsewhere. With these things clearly understood, Dr. McGlynn gave his word to Archbishop Satolli to present himself to the Pope within three or four months to obtain his blessing. Then Archbishop Satolli in formal words, and in the name of the Pope, removed the ban of excommunication from Dr. McGlynn, and the first announcement of the Doctor's reinstatement was made by the papal representative from the Catholic University at Washington.

The next day, Christmas day, 1892, for the first time since 1887, Dr. McGlynn celebrated mass.[1]   In the evening he addressed the Anti-Poverty Society as usual. It

---

[1] By his own wish, Dr. McGlynn at the time of his restoration was not attached to any parish ; and it was not until December, 1894, two years later, that, on the advice of Archbishop Satolli, he applied for a parish to Archbishop Corrigan [of the Diocese of New York. The latter had, as Mr. George wrote to a friend, been " completely flabbergasted " by the restoration and the refusal of the Roman authorities longer to uphold the New York Archbishop in his declaration that the single tax doctrine was contrary to the teachings of the Church. But Archbishop Corrigan made

was a time with him for great rejoicing. He had made
the long fight and had triumphed. The odds had been
tremendous, but he had overcome them. Never again
could any man say that the teachings of the Catholic
Church were opposed to the single tax. And he celebrated mass with a thankfulness that he had been given
the strength to fight the great battle. He went to Rome
some months afterwards and was accorded an interview
by the Pope. The reference to the social question was of
the briefest description. "Do you teach against private
property?" asked his Holiness. "I do not; I am staunch
for private property," said the Doctor. "I thought so,"
said his Holiness, and he conferred his blessing.

When Henry George heard of Dr. McGlynn's restoration, his own rejoicing swept all other considerations
aside. He at once sent a telegram: "My wife and I send
heartfelt congratulations." Sentiments of warm feeling
were returned, and thus the relations of friendship, interrupted for four years, were re-established; and they lasted
until death.

---

the best of his utter defeat. He quietly assigned Dr. McGlynn to the
parish of St. Mary, in the little town of Newburgh, on the Hudson River,
close to Rondout, where Dr. Burtsell had been sent. Archbishop Corrigan at the same time engaged to give to him the first vacant parish in
New York City that would be suitable to Dr. McGlynn's talents.

CHAPTER XIII.

THE LAST BOOKS.

1891-1896.   Age, 52-57.

IT was in April, soon after the return from Bermuda, fully restored to health and vigour, that Mr. George wrote to Dr. Taylor: "During the last week I have got to work on the 'Political Economy' I have long contemplated, and if my health continues good I shall keep at it. I have thought that perhaps it would be useful if I could put the ideas embodied in 'Progress and Poverty' in the setting of a complete economic treatise and without controversy."

This was the "primer" that he had mentioned to Charles Nordhoff before leaving California in 1879. In answer to the pressing calls of Richard McGhee and other British friends, who believed they could get such a book into some of the schools there, he planned in the summer of 1889 to go straight at it and to publish by the fall. But other things crowded in to exclude this. Now, however, when he returned from Bermuda, August Lewis and Tom L. Johnson confirmed his judgment that he should withdraw altogether from "The Standard." And to this end they voluntarily, and "without suggestion or thought" from him, assured him that they would regard it as their best contribution to the cause to be allowed for a season to make him independent, so that he might, if he judged that to be best, devote himself to book-writing, such as only he was qualified to do. Subsequently dedicating "The Science of Political Economy" to his two friends, he made open acknowledgment of this in the inscription.

But almost at the outset of work on the proposed primer Mr. George realised the difficulty of making a simple statement of the principles of political economy—the real, everlasting political economy—while so much confusion existed as to the meaning of terms in the literature relating to the science. He therefore changed his plan, left the primer for an after labour and laid out at once a much larger work—one that should recast political economy and examine and explicate terminology as well as principles, and which, beginning at the beginning, should trace the rise and partial development of the science in the hands of its founders a century ago, and then show its gradual emasculation and at last abandonment by its professed teachers; accompanying this with an account of the extension of the science outside and independently of the schools in the philosophy of the natural order now spreading over the world under the name of the single tax.

"Progress and Poverty" was "an inquiry into the cause of industrial depressions and of increase of want with increase of wealth." This new book, as it broadened out, became far more ambitious in scope. It purposed to define the science that names the conditions in which civilised men shall get their living. No writer on political economy had ever before set himself so great a task; indeed, no writer ever before had assumed that he understood the full relations of the science, Adam Smith's immortal work being "An Inquiry into the Nature and Causes of the Wealth of Nations," and the most authoritative recent work, that of John Stuart Mill, being a treatise on the

"Principles of Political Economy." To Henry George's view, none of the economists, from Smith to Mill, realised the correlation of the laws of production or likewise those of distribution. But though he believed he himself saw clearly and felt that he could prove his reasoning, hé nevertheless hesitated to give his book the name its scope seemed to warrant until the writing was nearing its completion, a few months before his death. Then he definitely decided on the title which in his judgment the book should justly have—"The Science of Political Economy."

But scarcely had the enlarged plan of work begun to take shape in the spring of 1891 when a remarkable interruption occurred. No less a personage than Pope Leo XIII. entered the controversy on the land question, addressing an encyclical letter "to our venerable brethren, all patriarchs, primates, archbishops and bishops of the Catholic world." The encyclical was on "The Condition of Labour," and while there was a confusion of socialism and anarchism with the single tax, and neither Henry George nor the single tax proposition were specifically named, yet Archbishop Corrigan of New York hailed the papal letter as the highest sanction of his own opposition to the single tax doctrine as preached by Dr. McGlynn and Henry George. In London, Cardinal Manning told Mr. George's eldest son, who chanced to be there, that the Pope's letter aimed at the Henry George teachings; although he intimated that between the postulates and the deduction Henry George could drive a coach and four. Mr. George wrote to his son: "For my part, I regard the encyclical letter as aimed at us, and at us alone, almost.[1]

---

[1] On the other hand, a number of Mr. George's Catholic friends from the first contended that the Pope did not condemn the single tax doctrine, some like Rev. Dr. Burtsell holding that that was "free doctrine," to be adopted or rejected by individuals without justly incurring the dis-

And I feel very much encouraged by the honour." He later wrote (June 9) : "I think I ought to write something about it. Of course the Pope's letter itself is very weak; but to reply to him might give an opportunity of explaining our principles to many people who know little or nothing about them."

But this was not the trifling matter that Mr. George at first purposed to make of it; for the reply, which took the form of an open letter to the Pope, grew in his hands, as his writing usually did. It was not finished until September, and comprised twenty-five thousand words; twice as many as the encyclical, which he printed with it. He had intended also to publish Bishop Nulty's pastoral letter with it, but concluded that that would make the

---

pleasure or the rebuke of the Church through her officers. Mr. George himself, answering a correspondent in the columns of the "New York Sun," in January, 1893, said : "That the encyclical on the 'Condition of Labour' seemed to me to condemn the 'single tax' theory is true. But it made it clear that the Pope did not rightly understand that theory. It was for this reason that in the open letter to which your correspondent refers I asked permission to lay before the Pope the grounds of our belief and to show that 'our postulates are all stated or implied in your encyclical' and that 'they are the primary perceptions of human reason, the fundamental teachings of the Christian faith'; declaring that, so far from avoiding, 'we earnestly seek the judgment of religion, the tribunal of which your Holiness, as the head of the largest body of Christians, is the most august representative.' The answer has come. In the reinstatement of Dr. McGlynn on a correct presentation of 'single tax' doctrines, the highest authority of the Catholic Church has declared in the most emphatic manner that there is nothing in them inconsistent with the Catholic faith. From henceforth the encyclical on the 'Condition of Labour'— a most noble and noteworthy declaration that religion is concerned with the social evils of our time, and that chronic poverty *is not* to be regarded as a dispensation of Providence — is evidently to be understood not as disapproving the 'single tax,' but as disapproving of the grotesque misrepresentations of it that were evidently at first presented to the Pope."

volume too bulky. He wrote to his son (August 21):
"I think I have done a good piece of work and that it
will be useful and will attract attention. . . . What I
have really aimed at is to make a clear, brief explanation
of our principles; to show their religious character, and
to draw a line between us and the socialists. I have
written really for such men as Cardinal Manning, General
Booth and religious-minded men of all creeds."

The book was published simultaneously in New York
(United States Book Company) and London (Swan Son-
nenschein & Company) and at the same time an Italian
translation by Ludovico Eusebio was brought out in Turin
and Rome by the Unione Tipografico-Editrice, publishers
of the Italian translation of "Progress and Poverty,"
which Sr. Eusebio had made a year or two before. A
copy of the translation of the "Letter to the Pope," beautifully printed and handsomely bound, was presented to
Leo XIII. personally by Monsignor Caprini, Prefect of
the Vatican Library, though Mr. George never received,
directly or indirectly, aught in reply.

Mr. Walker of Birmingham voiced the feelings of the
multitude of friends everywhere who had been shocked
at the news of Mr. George's illness and had had linger-
ing fears of impaired powers. "The great charm of the
book to me," wrote Walker, "was that the work revealed
you in all your old intellectual vigour and showed in
every paragraph that you had recovered all your mental
powers, for which, most reverently I say, thank God!"

But the little book did not start the large immediate
discussion that its author expected, and he relapsed into
a feeling he had entertained before the papal encyclical
had appeared and which he had expressed in a letter (May
18) to a New Church friend, James E. Mills: "How sad
it is to see a church in all its branches offering men stones

instead of bread, and thistles instead of figs. From Protestant preachers to Pope, avowed teachers of Christianity are with few exceptions preaching almsgiving or socialism, and ignoring the simple remedy of justice." George at times had regrets that he had stopped work on his political economy to make reply to the Pope, but many of the friends thought the latter writing could ill have been spared on account of its brevity and exalted religious tone. After three editions had been exhausted in England, James C. Durant, of London, who had joined Mr. George in bringing out the sixpenny edition of "Progress and Poverty" in 1882, himself paid for a special edition of the "Open Letter to the Pope" for free circulation. Subsequently in the United States this little book became a favourite in propaganda work.

As has been pointed out many times, the essence of Henry George's economics is ethical—the natural order, justice. It carries with it a profound belief in an Allmaker; it pulses with the conviction of the fatherhood of God and the brotherhood of man. When, therefore, Herbert Spencer, goaded by a hot controversy raised in the British newspapers and periodicals over his early "Social Statics" (quoted by single taxers in support of single tax principles) made a recantation of his former sentiments on the land question and repudiated the principle he had put in such clear and unqualified terms that God had made the land for all the people equally, Mr. George was stirred to the depths. To his mind Spencer's offence was not merely that of a philosopher who attempted to explain away and shiftingly deny what before he had asserted to be a fundamental, obvious and everlasting truth, but that with his later philosophy, he had allowed materialism to take the place of God. Moreover, three magazine articles in denial of "natural rights," written in the materialistic vein, had appeared in 1890 from the pen of Professor Thomas H. Huxley, and the chief postulates of "Progress and Poverty" were probably to the eminent scientist's belief overthrown.[1]   George wrote to Taylor at the time (September 16, 1890): "I suppose you read Huxley's 'Nineteenth Century' articles. What do you think of him as a philosopher? I am itching to get at him, and will, as soon as I can get a little leisure." It was early in the new year (1892) that George again laid aside work on his political economy and took up Spencer. And he took the opportunity to include Huxley, picturing him in passing as "Professor Bullhead" in the allegorical chapter entitled "Principal Brown."

All of Mr. George's immediate friends who learned of his intention to write on Spencer were greatly pleased; and remembering his achievements in his "Letter to the Pope" and his preceding reply to the Duke of Argyll, they prepared themselves for an intellectual treat. But some of the friends were alarmed when told that he would incidentally touch on the synthetic philosophy. Dr. Taylor, whom Mr. George called "of old my representative of Spencerianism," thought that George ought to "leave any review of the Spencerian system of philosophy to those who are in that special field and who have had special training for such work." Continuing he said: "In your own particular field, I am satisfied you are invincible; but I should not feel so sure of you in metaphysics, philosophy or cosmogony. Remember that life is short, and the powers of the human mind limited, and that you have not yet produced (what you should produce) a monumental work on political economy."

---

[1] Professor Huxley republished these essays in a volume entitled "Method and Results."

George thanked Taylor for his frank counsel, which he took to be "the strongest proof of friendship." But there was no change of position. George wrote of the harshness of his tone towards Spencer and of his views on evolution in successive letters.

April 18, 1892.

"While I shall trim down or rather, alter in places my harsher references to Spencer, so as to bring them later—and had in fact already done so—I think they must appear somewhere. I do not regard this as controversy. It is rather exposure. In turning his back on all he has said before, Mr. Spencer has not argued, and no explanation is possible that does not impute motives.

"As for the philosophy, I think I take a truer view of it than you do. It is substantially the view I took in 'Progress and Poverty'; but it has been fortified by a closer examination. John Fiske does not truly represent Spencerianism, but has grafted his own ideas on it. So too, I think, with Professor LeConte—or rather that he holds what I should call the external of evolution, with which I do not quarrel; for though I do not see the weight of the evidence with which it is asserted, it seems to me most reasonable. What I do quarrel with is the essential materialism of the Spencerian ideas; and this seems to me to inhere in them in spite of all Spencer's denials."

April 29.

"I simply *don't see* evolution from the animal as the form in which man has come. I don't deny it, and as I said in a sentence I hardly think you noticed, I attach no importance to the question. All I contend for is something behind the form."

The book, bearing title of "A Perplexed Philosopher," was out in October (1892). But while it was widely and well read, it awakened no general demonstration in press or periodicals and the author had the same kind of misgivings that immediately followed in the wake of the "Letter to the Pope"—misgivings that he had misused his time in not keeping along with the political economy. Even while writing the Spencer book (in April, 1892) he wrote incidentally to Dr. Taylor: "Several times since beginning it, I have thought that perhaps it would have been better to have pushed ahead with other work." Spencer himself never directly or indirectly during George's life noticed the tremendous indictment, and "A Perplexed Philosopher" was the sole one of the George books that, for many years at any rate, was not translated into other languages. Whatever may have been the reason of the comparative non-success of this book, it could not have been that Henry George's name had lost its potency, for about this time occurred what must stand out as remarkable in the history of economic literature.

Tom L. Johnson of Cleveland, O., following the advice given by Mr. George at their first interview in 1885, had gone into politics, run for Congress as a free trade, single tax Democrat in 1888, had been defeated, had run again in 1890 in the same way and been elected. The Democrats were in power in the House of Representatives at Washington and brought forward a timid little tariff-reducing bill. Mr. Johnson conceived the idea of getting Henry George's "Protection or Free Trade?" into the "Congressional Record," the official report of the proceedings of Congress. "Protection or Free Trade?" had up to then had an extremely wide circulation, first in serial form in a number of newspapers, then in regular book form, and afterwards in cheap, popular form, through the efforts of educating groups known as "Hand to Hand Clubs," of which William J. Atkinson of New York and Logan Carlisle, son of John G. Carlisle, then United

States Senator from Kentucky, were the prime movers, and through whose efforts close to two hundred thousand copies had been put into circulation.

Tom L. Johnson now determined to exceed this. Under a "leave to print" rule, members of the House of Representatives had long been accustomed to publish speeches that limited time for debate prevented them from delivering, or to publish extensive supplementary printed matter to their delivered "remarks." But as the issue of the "Congressional Record" was necessarily limited, members invariably reprinted matter from the "Record" to send to their constituents or whoever else in the United States they chose. This printing they themselves had to pay for; but they had the privilege of sending out such matter free through the mails, under the "franking privilege." It was a time-honoured custom for members in this way to send a great quantity of reprinted "Congressional Record" matter into their districts, especially preceding congressional or presidential elections.

Acting upon this "leave to print" privilege, Mr. Johnson, with Mr. George's hearty approval, divided "Protection or Free Trade?" between himself and five other congressmen, namely, William J. Stone of Kentucky, Joseph E. Washington of Tennessee, John W. Fithian of Illinois, Thomas Bowman of Iowa and Jerry Simpson of Kansas. Each man on a separate day introduced his section of the book as a "part of his remarks" in the tariff debate. The Republican minority beheld this performance with astonishment. They wanted to expunge the work from the "Record" on the ground that an entire book had never before been so published. That it was not the "abuse" of the "leave to print" privilege, but that particular book which they opposed, became clear, when after having motions to expunge voted down, they endeavoured to offset

the effect of the Henry George book by themselves in-
serting in the "Record" a book by George Gunton defend-
ing monopolies, though there was not afterwards enough
call for the Gunton book to pay the cost of reprinting it
outside the "Record."

The Republicans then tried to make capital out of the
incident by charging the Democrats with going headlong
into the free trade heresy and making Henry George, with
his single tax doctrine, their political prophet. But the
Democrats, delighted to find something that made their
political adversaries cry out, and not over-particular as to
whether or not this book was consistent with their own
professed principles and policy, showed something resem-
bling enthusiasm in circulating the enormous edition of
the work that Mr. Johnson had printed. The Republican press all over the country took up and increased the
outcries of the Republican Congressmen, with the misrepresentation, perhaps unintentional, that the work was
being printed at public expense; while the Democratic
press defended the action of the Democratic Congressmen
and to some extent defended the book itself; so that the
entire country was for the time turned into debating clubs,
with "Protection or Free Trade?" for the subject matter.

Nothing could have better suited Mr. Johnson's purpose.
He had the book printed compactly in large quantities at
the rate of five-eighths of a cent a copy. The great advertising the Republican and Democratic papers had given
it made an immense demand for what was known collo-
quially in the House as "St. George," even stalwart Republicans from the State of Pennsylvania being pestered
for copies. Many congressmen sent large numbers of the
book into their districts, and Mr. Johnson himself sent
two hundred thousand copies into the State of Ohio. The
National Democratic Committee had seventy thousand

copies distributed in Indiana and the Reform Club of New York, which was active in anti-tariff educational work, placed one hundred and fifty thousand in the northwest. In all more than one million two hundred thousand copies of this edition of "St. George" were printed and distributed, and perhaps as much as two hundred thousand copies of a better, two-cent edition; so that of this single book by Henry George almost two million copies were printed within less than eight years after being written—something never approached by any other work in economic literature save by the incomparable "Progress and Poverty," which with its many translations may have exceeded that number of copies.

The expense of printing "St. George" was met partly by small popular contributions from free traders and single taxers scattered about the country; partly by larger sums from men like Thomas G. Shearman of New York, James E. Mills of California, Thomas F. Walker and Silas M. Burroughs of England; and partly by money from the National Democratic committee and the Reform Club of New York. But the chief expense was borne by Tom L. Johnson. Of course there was no thought of copyright in all this, Mr. George invariably sacrificing that when it would appreciably help the circulation of his writings. He looked to the propagation of the faith above everything else.

It was during this period, or more precisely, on the last day of August, 1892, that "The Standard" succumbed to the inevitable, and ceased publication. After William T. Croasdale's death, Louis F. Post had by general request taken editorial control. But the paper kept running behind and became too much of a financial burden longer to carry, as what Mr. George said in a signed statement in the last number had become more and more evident.

"The work that 'The Standard' was intended to do has been done, and in the larger field into which our movement has passed, there is no longer need for it. For the usefulness of a journal devoted to the propagation of an idea must diminish as its end is attained. Needed while it is the only means of presenting that idea to the public and keeping its friends in touch, that need ceases as the idea finds wider expression and journals of general circulation are open to it. . . . Its files . . . record an advance of the great cause to which it was devoted unprecedented in the history of such movements. Where in the beginning it stood alone, there are now scattered over the United States hundreds of local journals devoted to the same cause, while the columns of general newspapers of the largest circulation are freely opened to the advocacy of our views. They are, indeed, making their way through all avenues of thought—the pulpit, the stage and the novel, in legislatures, in Congress and on the political stump. The ignorance and prejudice which the earlier files of 'The Standard' showed that we then had to meet, have, in their cruder forms at least, almost disappeared, and among our most active friends are thousands of men who then believed our success would be the destruction of society. Within the last few months nearly a million copies of a single tax book have been distributed under the sanction of one of the great political parties; and the free trade sentiment to which we were the first to give practical and determined expression, has so grown that at the recent Democratic National Convention it was strong enough to break the slated programme and to force a free trade declaration into the platform.

"Let us say good-bye to it; not as those who mourn, but as those who rejoice. Times change, men pass, but that which is built on truth endures."

The hot and comparatively radical campaign, with most of the Democratic newspapers hammering on the tariff question, made up to some extent for the death of "The

Standard"; and then came Grover Cleveland's re-election to the presidency.

All seemed propitious for great events. Henry George wanted no office; he asked only that President Cleveland apply the chief principle involved in his election, and make war on the tariff. But Cleveland's first important official act brought a great disappointment, for he switched issues, by subordinating the tariff to the money question, in calling a special session of Congress to deal with the currency. While it worked directly into the hands of the protectionist faction in the Democratic party, it made the educational work of Johnson and George in circulating "Protection or Free Trade?" go for naught at that time, whatever might result in the future from so great a circulation of this book. And then, when the tariff question was up a year later, George wrote to Johnson (July 24, 1894): "The President's letter to Chairman Wilson of the Ways and Means Committee is very bad. Free raw material is taking the burden off the manufacturers and keeping it on the consumers."

Nevertheless, Mr. George sat in the gallery of the House of Representatives and listened with great happiness to Tom L. Johnson—a steel rail manufacturer—move to put steel rails on the free list and make a fervent free trade speech in support. The moderates in the Democratic party of course could not let such an incident pass. One of them, by voice and pointing finger, called attention of the House to the master in the gallery and the pupil on the floor; whereupon a lot of the more independent Democrats streamed upstairs to shake hands with the man who held no political office, who asked for no political patronage, who said bold things without counting consequences and who had a fascinating, indescribable influence over the thoughts of multitudes.

If Henry George was disappointed in Mr. Cleveland's first actions in this second term of the presidency, he was moved to great hostility to him over the matter of the Chicago railroad strike; when, setting aside State authority, indeed, in spite of the protests of Governor Altgeld, the President sent Federal troops to the scene. Not a New York newspaper opposed the Executive action. Yet ten thousand men, mostly working men, assembled at a mass meeting in and about Cooper Union. Rev. Thomas A. Ducey of St. Leo's Catholic Church, Charles Frederick Adams and James A. Herne the actor, were among the speakers, and spoke effectively and forcibly; while Henry George's speech seemed to hit the target's centre:

"I yield to nobody in my respect for law and order and my hatred of disorder; but there is something more important even than law and order, and that is the principle of liberty. I yield to nobody in my respect for the rights of property; yet I would rather see every locomotive in this land ditched, every car and every depot burned and every rail torn up, than to have them preserved by means of a Federal standing army. That is the order that reigned in Warsaw. (Long applause.) That is the order in the keeping of which every democratic republic before ours has fallen. I love the American Republic better than I love such order." (Long applause.)

And a little later Mr. George became freshly angered against the President for his special message to Congress that threatened war with Great Britain over the Venezuelan boundary dispute. Much as he hated war, George justified it when waged for natural rights—for liberty. But even talk of war between two great and enlightened nations like Great Britain and the United States, especially over what at bottom he believed to be a mere squabble of private parties as to mineral claims, raised the wrath within him, and he made an indignant speech against the President at a mass meeting at Cooper Union.

Henry George's estimation of the President had undergone a great change since he spoke and voted for him in 1892. He wrote in the New York "Journal" on the day before the Presidential election, 1896:

> "The philosophic historian, who, after our grandchildren have passed away, reviews our times, must write of him [Cleveland] as more dangerous to the Republic than any of his predecessors. The sequel has proved that it was the Whitneys and the Huntingtons who had really cause for rejoicing in his election; not men like me. For no Harrison, no McKinley; no chief of trusts and rings, such as Rockefeller or Morgan; no king's jester of monopoly, such as Chauncey M. Depew or Bob Ingersoll, could, if elected as a Republican, have used the place so to strike at the vitals of the Republic."

Despite this disappointment, cheer came from other points. Encouraging news of the progress of the single tax idea in political affairs was coming from Australia and New Zealand. Similar good news came from Great Britain. In the House of Commons in March, 1891, James Stuart's motion, that "in the opinion of this House, the freeholders and owners of ground values in the metropolis ought to contribute directly a substantial share of local taxation," had received 123 votes to 149 against; thus showing great strength for the idea. Since then it had been steadily creeping over the country and more and more becoming a leading question in the constituencies. The English Land Restoration League had been conducting, under the management of its able and untiring secretary, Frederick Verinder, a "Red Van" educational campaign—several

large vans that afforded two or three speakers living quarters, slowly travelling from village to village, for nightly
open-air meetings and the preaching of the faith. William Saunders, Thomas F. Walker, D'Arcy W. Reeve,
and S. M. Burroughs were among the contributors towards
this work; but the largest individual contribution came
from an Englishman in the United States who wished not
to be publicly known in the matter.

At home had occurred what must be a landmark in the
history of the single tax. Henry George wrote Richard
McGhee, of Glasgow (February 13, 1894):

> "Tom Johnson is doing great work in Congress, and
> James G. Maguire's single tax amendment to the in-
> come tax bill has brought our views for the first time
> into the Congressional arena. It got six votes: Those
> of James G. Maguire of California, Tom L. Johnson
> and Michael D. Harter of Ohio, Jerry Simpson of Kan-
> sas and John DeWitt Warner and Charles Tracy of
> New York—double what I had counted on, as there
> was no hope of carrying it and the measure was in a
> position in which we could not show our strength; but
> the sympathy is such among radical Democrats that
> the House cheered when the six men stood up. The
> direct line of our advance is however in State legisla-
> tion, and the single tax may in that way be brought
> into political issue at almost any time."

As Henry George surveyed the world from the quiet of
his workroom the hand of Providence seemed to show in
the rapid progress of the cause, and he set down, in rough
abbreviated form, these notes for a preface for "The Science of Political Economy," writing on the sheets the date
of March 7, 1894:

> "The years which have elapsed since the publication of
> 'Progress and Poverty' have been on my part devoted

to the propagation of the truths taught in 'Progress and Poverty' by books, pamphlets, magazine articles, newspaper work, lectures and speeches, and have been so greatly successful as not only far to exceed what fifteen years ago I could have dared to look forward to in this time, but to have given me reason to feel that of all the men of whom I have ever heard who have attempted anything like so great a work against anything like so great odds, I have been in the result of the endeavour to arouse thought most favoured. Not merely wherever the English tongue is spoken, but in all parts of the world, men are arising who will carry forward to final triumph the great movement which 'Progress and Poverty' began. The great work is not done, but it is commenced, and can never go back."

Mr. George's purpose was to allow nothing to interfere with the finishing of his "Political Economy," which he looked forward to bringing out in the fall of 1896 or spring of 1897; but the new alignment of national parties drew him from his retirement and once more into the current of politics.

The industrial depression and currency famine that reached its most acute stage in the summer of 1893, dragged along into 1896. Every field of industry in the country had suffered more or less during the protracted depression. Through the West and South the popular belief was that the cause of this lay mainly in an artificial shrinkage of the currency, and the demand now swelled to thundering tones for the remonitisation and free coinage of the silver dollar. In the East, at least among the working men, the tariff-protected trusts, the railroads and other monopolies were denounced as having much to do with the hard times. President Cleveland had no sympathy with any of this, and he added fuel to the fire of strong feeling, for he used his office against what Mr. George, among many others, conceived to be popular rights, and in support of property rights, by protecting and fostering the monopolies, and by making great concessions to the bank and bond powers. And when the election lines were eventually drawn and William McKinley, representing the House of Have, was nominated by the Republican party, and William J. Bryan, at the hands of the radical majority in the Democratic convention, and for the House of Want, became the champion of free silver, anti-monopoly and equal rights, Cleveland openly took the side of the House of Have and directly and indirectly worked for its success.

Since a young man, Henry George had advocated as the best possible money, paper issued by the general Government—paper based on the public credit. He regarded the silver coinage proposal as another form of the protective idea—to raise, artificially, the price of the silver commodity. But economically unsound as he held this principle to be, and expensive as he believed its adoption would prove to those least able to help themselves—the mass of the working population—he thought it greatly preferable to the principle of privilege which the monopolistic powers gathered around the gold, or so-called "sound money" candidate represented. He went to both the Republican and Democratic National Conventions and afterwards travelled over the middle West, writing signed articles to the New York "Journal" as to what he saw and thought. His sympathies were with Bryan in spite of the free silver doctrine; but at first he could see little hope of success. As he travelled, however, he became hopeful and at length confident that Bryan would win.

Tom L. Johnson, Louis F. Post and a great majority of the single taxers shared Mr. George's political views. But there were some who opposed Bryan on account of his free silver doctrine, which they raised above all other considerations. "To make the public understand" their position, they issued a kind of proclamation of their views, and noticeable among the signatures were those of Thomas G. Shearman, William Lloyd Garrison, Louis Prang and August Lewis, which proved the independent relations subsisting between Mr. George and his friends.

This surprised Mr. George. His attitude was characteristic. On the day before election he declared in the "Journal" his view of the issue to be, "Shall the Republic Live?"

"Of those friends of mine, the few single taxers who, deluded, as I think, by the confusion, purpose to separate from the majority of us on the vote, I should like to ask that they consider how they expected to know the great struggle to which we have all looked forward as inevitable, when it should come? Hardly by the true issue appearing at first as the prominent issue. For all the great struggles of history have begun on subsidiary, and sometimes on what seemed at the moment irrelevant issues. Would they not expect to see all the forces of ill-gotten wealth, with the control of the majority of the press, on one side, and on the other a reliance upon the common people—the working farmers and the artizan bread-winners? Is not that so to-day?

"Would they not expect to see the reliance of the aristocratic party to be upon an assumed legality and a narrow interpretation of the command, 'Thou shalt not steal'; based not upon God's law, but upon man's law? Is not this true in this case?

"Would they not expect to have every man who stood prominently for freedom denounced as an anarchist, a communist, a repudiator, a dishonest person, who wished to cut down just debts? Is not this so now? Would they not expect to hear predictions of the most dire calamity overwhelming the country if the power to rob the masses was lessened ever so little? Has it not been so in every struggle for greater freedom that they can remember or have ever read of?

"Let me ask them before they vote to consider the matter coolly, as if from a distance in time or space. . . . Gold and silver are merely the banners under which the rival contestants in this election have ranged themselves. The banks are not really concerned about their legitimate business under any currency. They are struggling for the power of profiting by the issuance of paper money, a function properly and constitutionally belonging to the nation. The railroads are not really concerned about the 'fifty-cent dollar,' either for themselves or their employees. They are concerned about their power of running the Government and making and administering the laws. The trusts and pools and rings are not really concerned about any reduction in the wages of their workmen, but for their own power of robbing the people. The larger business interests have frightened each other, as children do when one says, 'Ghost!' Let them frighten no thinking man."

But they did frighten thinking men. For though Bryan received nearly a million more votes than elected Cleveland in 1892, the fear of a commercial panic, of closed factories and reduced wages, with the factors of intimidation and corruption, piled up a still greater vote for McKinley. Mr. George had seen what he believed to be sure signs of Bryan strength and in the "Journal" articles had confidently predicted Bryan's election; so that when the returns on election night showed how he had miscalculated the strength of the opposing elements, he sustained a great shock. "Men will say that I am unreliable," he said with simple frankness to his eldest son as they went home together. And afterwards he said: "This result makes our fight the harder." But early next morning he went to the telegraph office and wired to Bryan a message of congratulation on his splendid fight and of cheer to keep his heart strong for the future.

CHAPTER XIV.

THE LAST CAMPAIGN.

1897.   Age, 58.

THOUGH now only in his fifty-eighth year, Mr. George felt further advanced in life than most men do at that age. While organically sound, the iron constitution with which he had started out was perceptibly weakening under the incessant toil since boyhood and the extraordinary strain of the last sixteen years in putting the breath of life into a world-wide movement and inspiring it with his own passionate enthusiasm. He became conscious as he travelled about during the recent presidential campaign that he had lost his old physical elasticity, and he found it required an effort to get back to the newspaper habits of his younger days. And when, instead of the victory he had expected, defeat came, he was more keenly disappointed than over any previous public event during his lifetime. It seemed to him, as he said afterwards, that the century was closing in darkness; that the principle of democracy, which had triumphed in 1800 with the acendancy of Thomas Jefferson to the presidency of the United States, might be conquered by the Hamiltonian principle of aristocracy and plutocracy in 1900. If he said little about these sombre thoughts at the time, he said less of the consciousness that he probably would not much longer be able physically to lead in the cause for equal rights. Yet that that must be done by younger men was clearly in his mind. But if he could not lead the army, he could define the law; and he quietly settled down again to "The Science of Political Economy"—the book that he hoped would prove the supreme effort of his life. And over and over he read in the family circle and softly repeated to himself, as was one of his habits, the lines of Browning's "Rabbi Ben Ezra," beginning:

"Grow old along with me!
    The best is yet to be,
The last of life, for which the first was made:
    Our times are in his hand
    Who saith, 'A whole I planned,
Youth shows but half; trust God: see all, nor
    be afraid!'"

Mr. George found some diversion in overseeing the building of a house adjoining the old house that the family occupied at Fort Hamilton. This was to be Mrs. George's home, and he took great interest in it. It was practically the only thing that took him away from his desk.

But while with an iron will he held himself to his work, he had not the old snap and vigour; and in March came what seemed like a severe bilious attack—nausea, dizziness, utter muscular weakness. Dr. Kelly gave warning that work must stop for a while. He proposed a sea voyage. Mr. George would not listen to going away. "I must finish the book before anything else," was the reply to all suggestions of cessation.

Yet the family made every effort to divert him. There was much reading aloud—a little of Conan Doyle, of Stevenson, of DeFoe for lighter things; of Tennyson,

Browning and Macaulay for poetry; of Thomas Jefferson's letters and Schopenhauer's works to engage reflection. The scriptures were a great solace. Again he listened to the old story of the image with head of gold and feet of clay; and to the story of the prophet at the king's feast reading the writing upon the wall: "Thou art weighed in the balances and art found wanting."

During all the early part of this year the second son, Richard, who had developed a talent for sculpture, was at work upon a bust of his father, doing the modelling in a chamber adjoining the writing room. At various times of day, suiting his own inclination, Mr. George came and posed; or rather reposed in an easy-chair, talking, reading or going to sleep, in any position, innocently supposing that he was doing all that the artist could ask. As with everything his children did, he took great interest in this piece of work, and he believed that under the patient, faithful fingers of his son, this piece of sculpture acquired essentials that former busts of him, one by Carl Rohl-Smith in 1888 and one by John Scott Hartley in 1894, did not possess. One day when both of his sons were present he said, after he had been for a while sitting for the sculptor and musing: "When I am dead, you boys will have this bust to carry in my funeral procession, as was the custom with the Romans."

This was not uttered in any spirit of morbidness, but in the calm contemplation of things touching death as well as life. For, one day, after he had quite recovered from the temporary illness and lay stretched on the couch in his work room, his wife in a chair beside him, and he talked of the progress of the cause, he sprang up and vigorously paced the room. "The great, the very great advancement of our ideas," said he, "may not show now, but it will. And it will show more after my death than

during my life. Men who now hold back will then acknowledge that I have been speaking the truth. Neither
of us can tell which of us will die first. But I shall be
greatly disappointed if you precede me, for I have set
my heart on having you hear what men will say of me
and our cause when I am gone."

And now came the lightning stroke out of the clear
sky. The married daughter, Jennie, with her seven
months' old baby boy, had come to visit the parents'
house, and after a few days' illness that seemed to be but
a form of influenza and neuralgia, suddenly died early in
the morning of May 2. As the light of dawn came into
his room, Henry George sat alone with his eldest son.
He said that he had for some time felt a disaster impending; that now it had come; that Herodotus, in his
own way and according to the imagery of the time, had
depicted a great truth in the story of Polycrates the
Tyrant of Samos and Amasis the King of Egypt; that
it was not in the order of things for men to have unbroken prosperity; that evil comes mixed with good; that
life is a strife; that there are defeats as well as victories
—disappointments as well as triumphs. Realising this,
he had felt that of late years he had had too much good
fortune; that success had crowded upon his efforts; that
even the seeming setbacks had turned into advancements.
Just within a few days a draft of several thousand dollars had come from England as the first part of a bequest
made by Silas M. Burroughs, the ardent single tax friend,
who had carried on a large drug business in Great Britain and her colonies. Mr. Burroughs, following William
Saunders in death, had bequeathed to Henry George a
one twenty-fourth interest in his estate. This filled the
cup of prosperity full to overflowing, so that Mr. George
had come to look for a reverse, a disaster—just as disas-

ters come to other men. He had apprehended that he might be incapacitated from further work in the cause. But the blow had come in another way.

Though this death was the first break in the family; though it came like a knife thrust in the heart, Henry George showed that outward cheer and courage and thought of others that seldom failed him. Even in so small a thing as sending messages to friends, he waited until the little telegraph station at Fort Hamilton should open, so as to help swell the business of the woman operator there, and to that extent increase her importance and help increase her pay.

As soon as they learned of the death, the intimate friends hurried to Fort Hamilton to pour out their hearts' deep but scarcely spoken sympathy. Mr. George, accompanied by one of his sons, went to Greenwood Cemetery, not far from Fort Hamilton, and selected a spot beside where Tom L. Johnson's father, Colonel A. W. Johnson, was buried—just over the crest of Ocean Hill, looking south and east toward the Atlantic. And there the dear daughter was laid on a radiant spring afternoon; Dr. McGlynn, who had married her two years before, now conducting the simple burial service.

To Thomas F. Walker, Mr. George wrote: "This is the bitter part of life that we had not tasted, but we have nothing but beautiful memories, and my wife and I have rallied for the duties that life still brings." Mr. Mendelson wrote and quoted the words of a German song—"wenn Menschen von einander gehn so sagen sie 'auf Wiedersehn' "—"When people take leave of each other, they say, 'To see you again.' " Mr. George replied: "The old German song you quote is very sweet. But it really goes back to the year 1. In one shape or another, that is the constant song of our race."

Among the first of these duties, was, they believed, that of preparing for the future, for the duration of life now seemed most uncertain. Both husband and wife drew wills, each making the other sole beneficiary, with their two sons as witnesses. Besides this there was the finishing of the house then being built to see to. But for Mr. George, the chief duty was to complete "The Political Economy" that had cost him so much more hard labour than any of his other books. So again he settled down quietly to writing.

Mr. George had divided "The Science of Political Economy" into five divisions or "books" and a general introduction, but, as with "Progress and Poverty," its final form followed many changes and rearrangements.[1]

Once or twice when conscious of physical weakness he had expressed to Mrs. George a doubt of being able to hold out to complete the work, and probably it was this feeling that impelled him to write Chapter VIII of

---

[1] The divisions settled upon were: "Book I—The Meaning of Political Economy"; "Book II—The Nature of Wealth"; "Book III—The Production of Wealth"; "Book IV—The Distribution of Wealth"; "Book V—Money: The Medium of Exchange and the Measure of Value." The last three books were largely written in the summer of 1897, but were not completed at the time of Mr. George's death; and when the work was published as it had been left by his hand, many critics spoke of the evidences of declining powers in the last three divisions and especially in the broken and even rough places in the part on money. The truth is that "The Science of Political Economy" as posthumously published is the best example that can be found of Henry George's method of work; for the last three divisions or "books" present much of his earlier drafting of the general work. The money division was written in 1894 and 1895, as dates on the rough-draft manuscript and in note-books indicate. The really last work he did was in smoothing and polishing the first two divisions, which Dr. Taylor assured him were equal in force, clearness and finish to his earlier high-water performance of "Progress and Poverty"; and in this opinion his own judgment concurred.

Book II, entitled, "Breakdown of Scholastic Political Economy—Showing the Reason, the Reception and Effect on Political Economy of 'Progress and Poverty.'" This chapter consists of nine and a half pages treating of the history of "Progress and Poverty" and of the standing of the new political economy it represents. No person save the second son, who was asked by the father to make a copy of this chapter, saw it until the author's decease, three months later, and there can be small doubt that feeling that death might claim him at any time, Henry George deemed it necessary to take this means of making clear to the world certain facts relating to the genesis of his writing and the progress and standing of his ideas.

This did not come from any petty sense of vanity, but from passionate pride in and zeal to press forward the cardinal cause with which the very fibres of his nature were interwoven. He had long thought of writing an autobiography, for he held that no one could have so exact a knowledge of essential facts as the subject himself. This he had looked to do at the close of his life. But the sudden death of his daughter and his own recurring weakness made him conscious that the end might be nearer than would be compatible with such a plan, so that without speaking of the matter, he now slipped these autobiographical notes into the manuscript of his big book, and he quietly put in order his more important papers, to many attaching notes and dates. He also more freely than ever before in his life talked of his personal history, and in the household and to immediate friends, in a casual way told of past scenes with a candour and unaffectedness that left lasting impressions on the listeners' ears. Later in the year, just after he had entered on his last campaign against the solemn warning of his medical friends, he was obviously more strongly impressed than ever with the necessity of making autobiographical notes, and he told Ralph Meeker, a newspaper friend, who had a stenographer present to take his words verbatim, something of the story of his life.

Henry George's final view of the effect of his teachings on the orthodox presentation of political economy he set forth in the "Progress and Poverty" chapter of his last work:

" 'Progress and Poverty' has been, in short, the most successful economic work ever published. Its reasoning has never been successfully assailed, and on three continents it has given birth to movements whose practical success is only a question of time. Yet though the scholastic political economy has been broken, it has not been, as I at the time anticipated, by some one of its professors taking up what I had pointed out; but a new and utterly incoherent political economy has taken its place in the schools.

"Among the adherents of the scholastic economy, who had been claiming it as a science, there had been from the time of Smith no attempt to determine what wealth was; no attempt to say what constituted property, and no attempt to make the laws of production or distribution correlate and agree, until there thus burst on them from a fresh man, without either the education or the sanction of the schools, on the remotest verge of civilisation, a reconstruction of the science, that began to make its way and command attention. What were their training and laborious study worth if it could be thus ignored, and if one who had never seen the inside of a college, except when he had attempted to teach professors the fundamentals of their science, whose education was of the mere common school branches, whose *alma mater* had been the forecastle and the printing office, should be admitted to prove the inconsistency of what they had been teaching as a science? It was not to be thought of. And so while a few of these professional economists, driven to say something about 'Progress and Poverty,' resorted to misrepresentation, the majority preferred to rely upon their official positions in which they were secure by the interests of the dominant class, and to treat as beneath contempt a book circulating by thousands in the three great English-speaking countries and translated into all the important modern languages. Thus the professors of political economy seemingly rejected the simple teachings of 'Progress and Poverty,' refrained from meeting with disproof or argument what it had laid down, and treated it with contemptuous silence.

"Had these teachers of the schools frankly admitted the changes called for by 'Progress and Poverty,' something of the structure on which they built might have been retained. But that was not in human nature. It would not have been merely to accept a new man without the training of the schools, but to admit that the true science was open to any one to pursue, and could be successfully continued only on the basis of equal rights and privileges. It would not merely have made useless so much of the knowledge that they had laboriously attained, and was their title to distinction and honour, but would have converted them and their science into opponents of the tremendous pecuniary interests that were vitally concerned in supporting the justification of the unjust arrangements which gave them power. The change in credence that this would have involved would have been the most revolutionary that had ever been made, involving a far-reaching change in all the adjustments of society such as had hardly before been thought of, and never before been accomplished at one stroke; for the abolition of chattel slavery was as nothing in its effect as compared with the far-reaching character of the abolition of private ownership of land. Thus the professors of political economy, having the sanction and support of the schools, preferred, and naturally preferred, to unite their differences, by giving what had before been insisted on as essential, and to teach what was an incomprehensible jargon to the ordinary man, under the assumption of teaching an occult science, which required a great study of what had been written by numerous learned professors all over the world and a knowledge of foreign languages. So the scholastic political economy, as it had been taught, utterly broke down, and, as taught in the schools, tended to protectionism and the German, and to the assumption that it was a recondite science on which no one not having the indorsement of the colleges was competent to speak, and on which only a man of great reading and learning could express an opinion. . . .

"Such inquiry as I have been able to make of the recently published works and writings of the authoritative professors of the science has convinced me that this change has been general among all the colleges, both of England and the United States. So general is this scholastic utterance that it may now be said that the science of political economy, as founded by Adam Smith and taught authoritatively in 1880, has now been utterly abandoned, its teachings being referred to as teachings of 'the classical school' of political economy, now obsolete."[1]

But to turn to external things. As early as June began the preliminary rumbling of fall politics. Various rumours were afloat that Henry George was to be asked to run as an independent candidate for the office of Mayor

---

[1] "The Science of Political Economy," pp. 203-208. It may also be said that Mr. George during the last months of his life had occasion to reset "Progress and Poverty" for new electrotype plates. Notwithstanding the very large controversial literature to which it had given birth, he had found no reason to change the book in any essential, though he did make some alterations respecting syntax and punctuation, cleared the phraseology of the plane illustration in the chapter on interest and the cause of interest, and made a distinction between patents and copyrights, condemning the former and justifying the latter—something he had not formerly done. With these minor exceptions, the book was reset identically as it had been set in San Francisco in 1879, notwithstanding the battery of criticism of eighteen years.

of the Greater New York which had just been formed by the absorption of Brooklyn and other adjoining municipalities, so that it now had become the second city in the world in respect to population. Though Mr. George discouraged the idea that he desired to run, and even told a number of his friends that the necessity of continuous work on the book and his physical condition would not permit him to run, yet only those closest about him understood his real condition and hundreds and thousands in the cause beyond were urgent for his candidacy. Mr. George's medical adviser, Dr. Kelly, hastened to warn him against the ordeal that such a campaign would certainly entail; and Dr. M. R. Leverson, a neighbour at Fort Hamilton, and a friend since the California days, set down some notes of a conversation with Mr. George touching the matter:

"One afternoon, after talking over the mayoralty subject, we went for a walk on Shore Road, just in front of his house. Mr. George was convalescent merely, indications showing to the physician the still existant condition. Continuing the conversation commenced in the house, Mr. George said to me:

"'Tell me: If I accept, what is the worst that can happen to me?'

"I answered: 'Since you ask, you have a right to be told. It will most probably prove fatal.'

"He said: 'You mean it may kill me?'

"'Most probably, yes.'

"'Dr. Kelly says the same thing, only more positively. But I have got to die. How can I die better than serving humanity? Besides, so dying will do more for the cause than anything I am likely to be able to do in the rest of my life.'"

To another medical friend, Dr. Walter Mendelson, brother-in-law to August Lewis, he wrote (September 30) in response to a letter of friendly warning: "I thank you very much for your friendly counsel. I shall take it, unless as I can see it duty calls. In that case I must obey. After all, how little we can see of the future. God keep you and yours."

And when some of the intimate friends came to Mrs. George to emphasize the danger and advise her to influence her husband to desist, she answered:

"When I was a much younger woman I made up my mind to do all in my power to help my husband in his work, and now after many years I may say that I have never once crossed him in what he has seen clearly to be his duty. Should he decide to enter this campaign I shall do nothing to prevent him; but shall, on the contrary, do all I can to strengthen and encourage him. He must live his life in his own way and at whatever sacrifice his sense of duty requires; and I shall give him all I can—devotion."

Some of the friends, anxious for his safety and seeing that he was not to be frightened off by the condition of his health, endeavoured to divert him in another way. They appealed to his sense of fitness, saying that while he was pre-eminent as a political economist and as a teacher of the principles of democratic government, he was unfitted by temperament and training for the laborious routine and multifarious harassments of such a position, and that he had not the experience such as made most appropriate the candidature, on an independent Republican ticket, of Seth Low, who had twice been Mayor of Brooklyn, and who had since held with distinction the great administrative office of the presidency of Columbia University, one of the largest and wealthiest educational institutions in the country, if not in the world. Mr. George's reply was that there might be many men fitted

to make better executives than he; but that sharing
Thomas Jefferson's view, that democratic government
called upon the people not to select men best qualified to
fill public office so much as to select men best qualified
to represent popular sentiment, if he ran for the mayoralty, it would not be because he thought he could make
a better executive than any other man, but that he would
represent certain principles that those who put him forward would wish to see promoted.

As time advanced it looked as though the Democratic
ring that ruled New York proposed to carry the election
with a high hand, putting up for its mayoralty candidate
Judge Robert Van Wyck, who was regarded as a mere
"machine" man, who would readily lend himself to the
kind of rotten politics that for generations had made the
name of New York Democracy a reproach to all the country. The call for George as an independent candidate
therefore became stronger than ever. The radical element in the Democratic party, moreover, appeared to be
ready to rally for a new fight against the plutocratic powers—the Jeffersonian forces once more lining up before
the Hamiltonian forces.

Following his custom, Mr. George called a meeting of
his more intimate friends early in October for consultation. The meeting took place in the New York office of
the Johnson Company. About thirty persons were present. It was a mixed company and much advice for and
against the fight was given, to all of which Mr. George
listened and said little, except to cut short every reference
to his health and strength, saying that the sole question
to consider was the one of duty; and to reply to allusions
relative to work on the book by saying that the essentials
were completed, the remainder indicating, should anything befall him, the direction of his thought.

As a result of this conference, Mr. George decided to make the fight, and the moment he came to that decision there was a remarkable change in his condition. A new vigour came to him. He had but one other person to consult with—his wife—and as he started for Fort Hamilton to talk with her, a new vivacity shone in his face, a spring was in his step, and he softly whistled to himself in the old, hopeful, boyish way; all unconscious as he passed down the steps from the Johnson Company office and out into the street that he almost brushed against Richard Croker, the political boss of New York, whose misrule he should denounce almost with his dying breath.

When he reached home, Mr. George told his wife of the conference with the friends and then said:

"Annie: Remember what you declared Michael Davitt should do at the time of the Phœnix Park murders in 1882—go to Dublin and be with his people, even though it should cost him his life. I told you then that I might some day ask you to remember those words. I ask you now. Will you fail to tell me to go into this campaign? The people want me; they say they have no one else upon whom they can unite. It is more than a question of good government. If I enter the field it will be a question of natural rights, even though as mayor I might not directly be able to do a great deal for natural rights. New York will become the theatre of the world and my success will plunge our cause into world politics."

Mrs. George answered: "You should do your duty at whatever cost." And so it was decided that he should run.

Mr. George's prediction as to the change his candidacy would make in the character of the campaign was verified at once. From the Tammany-Democracy point of view the issue was merely a "spoils-of-office" one, with a man for a figurehead who had for some years sat upon a judicial bench, but who outside of strictly local legal circles was scarcely known. The Republican party had set up a man of much wider name, General Benjamin F. Tracy, who stood high at the bar of the country and had held a portfolio in President Harrison's cabinet; but who scarcely less than the Tammany candidate stood for "spoils." Each was put forward by a "machine" and each was dominated by a "boss." Neither stood for any principle that from the outside country could claim other attention than distrust and regret. The candidacy of President Seth Low of Columbia College as an independent Republican in protest against corrupt politics awakened widespread interest—an interest which the entrance of Henry George at the head of a regenerated Democracy broadened and deepened.

But Henry George's appearance brought to the canvass more than a strengthening of the fight against "machine rule" and for "pure politics." Besides a political contest, it became a social struggle; for while, even if clothed with the mayoralty powers, there was no possibility of his doing much at once and directly to improve economic conditions, his victory would mean that social questions had found a strong lodgment in the body politic and must soon turn the larger, potent politics to its ends. Eleven years had passed over since he had stood for the mayoralty of the smaller New York—eleven years full of work with tongue and pen to spread broadcast through the world the hope of and faith in a natural order that would root out from the earth want and suffering, sin and crime. Those who had heard him speak had multiplied to scores upon scores of thousands and those who had read his written message had swelled to millions. Those who had aban-

doned old beliefs or awakened from dull despair and
claimed his optimistic faith and called him leader were
among all nations and spoke all tongues. Justice, Liberty,
Equality were the watchwords; where his banner waved,
there for them was the thick of the battle to make life for
mankind better and brighter. For that reason men travelled from distant parts of the country to participate in
this mayoralty campaign; and when news of the conflict
was brought, fervent words of God-speed went out from
responsive hearts across the wide seas in England and
Scotland and Ireland, in Germany, in Italy, in far-away
South Africa and the farther still antipodes; in the centres of knowledge and on the frontiers of civilisation;
even in those remote and isolated parts of the world
where communication is slow and intelligence of the candidacy did not reach until after death had intervened,
like starlight that for a time continues to shine on, though
the orb that gave it has ceased to be.

The canvass opened amid intense anxieties for those
nearest Mr. George. For when he arose in crowded
Cooper Union on the evening of October 5 to accept the
nominations of several political organisations, he was not
as he had been eleven years before—flushed with strength
and vigour—but with thin body and ashen face. He had
almost fainted on his way to the hall. But his words
had the old ring and courage:

"I have not sought this nomination directly or indirectly. It has been repugnant to me. My line lay in
a different path, and I hoped to tread it; but I hold
with Thomas Jefferson that while a citizen who can
afford to should not seek office, no man can ignore the
will of those with whom he stands when they have
asked him to come to the front and represent a principle.

"The office for which you name me gives me no power to carry out in full my views, but I can represent the men who think with me—men who think that all men are created equal; and whether it be success or failure matters nothing to me. (A shout: 'But it's something to us!') Aye, something to all of us; something to our friends and relatives in far off lands; something for the future, something for the world. (Cheers.) To make the fight is honour, whether it be for success or failure. To do the deed is its own reward. You know what I think and what I stand for. . . .

"A little while ago it looked to me at least that the defeat that the trusts, the rings and money power, grasping the vote of the people, had inflicted on William Jennings Bryan (applause) was the defeat of everything for which the fathers had stood, of everything that makes this country so loved by us, so hopeful for the future. It looked to me as though Hamilton had triumphed at last, and that we were fast verging upon a virtual aristocracy and despotism. You ask me to raise the standard again (applause); to stand for that great cause; to stand as Jefferson stood in the civil revolution in 1800. I accept. (Applause. Three cheers for Henry George were called for and given with cries of 'And you will be elected, too!')

"I believe I shall be elected. (Applause.) I believe, I have always believed, that last year many so-called Democrats fooled with the principles of the Chicago platform, but that there was a power, the power that Jefferson invoked in 1800, that would cast aside like chaff all that encumbered and held it down; that unto the common people, the honest democracy, the democracy that believes that all men are created equal, would come a power that would revivify, not merely this imperial city, not merely the State, not merely the country, but the world. (Vociferous applause.)

"No greater honour can be given to any man than to stand for all that. No greater service can he render to his day and generation than to lay at its feet whatever he has. I would not refuse if I died for it. (Applause.)

"What counts a few years? What can a man do better or nobler than something for his country, for his nation, for his age?

"Gentlemen, fellow Democrats, I accept your nomination (applause) without wavering or turning, whether those who stand with me be few or many. From henceforward I am your candidate for the Mayoralty of Greater New York."

Thus Henry George bravely spoke, but his words at times were low and slow, and only the few who crowded about him at the end and were with him until he left the hall realised the great physical effort he had made. They said little, but affection held them close about him like a bodyguard to save him every step, every effort, possible.

Thus commenced the campaign to be closed on November 2, a little over three weeks off. They were three weeks of happiness for Henry George. The breath of battle had entered into his nostrils, and when occasion called, roused to something like former strength his lion's soul. He had seriously agreed at the outset that he would make only three, four or five speeches during the whole canvass; but soon he had swept this aside as an idle resolve, until, by his own will, he was speaking at three, four and five meetings every night, more, probably than the other three candidates put together.

The new party called itself "The Party of Thomas Jefferson," a name suggested by Mr. George, as opposed to the name of "Democratic Party," which Tammany had degraded. It had headquarters in the Union Square Hotel, beside the old "Standard" office. The party had none of the machinery of organisation that professional

politicians believe essential, but it had the intense, almost
religious, enthusiasm that makes up for organisation.
Tom L. Johnson, August Lewis and John R. Waters made
liberal contributions towards what there was of a fund
for legitimate campaign expenses, and small sums were
collected at some of the meetings and came from other
minor sources. Against the wishes of his friends who
thought he should keep it all for his personal maintenance,
Mr. George turned over some of the money from the Burroughs bequest towards this purpose. But all told the
fund was ridiculously small in comparison with the other
party funds. It sufficed, however, as there were no campaign trappings and with but few exceptions, the host of
speakers paid their own expenses.

Willis J. Abbott, prominent in New York and Chicago
daily journalism and author of several popular histories,
was chairman of the campaign committee. Tom L. Johnson, being a citizen of another State, could not properly
be one of the committee. Nevertheless, he was too deeply
interested to be inactive, and he was consulted in everything, letting his own private affairs take care of themselves. And August Lewis, who at the outset had not the
remotest idea of taking a personal part in the fight,
quickly got into the very thick of it and became treasurer
of the committee. These were the two men to whom
Henry George had dedicated his yet unfinished book, and
love for the man and devotion to his cause and their cause
held them close beside him in this crisis.

The committee was composed of men schooled in the
art of politics, yet as one of them said to Arthur McEwen,
one of the intimate friends: "How it is I don't know,
but every move we have made in politics against George's
advice we have been wrong, and every time we have followed his advice we have come out right. We all think

we know more about the ins and outs of the game than
he does, but he has a sort of instinct that guides him
straight."

The friends shielded him from work as much as they
could. August Lewis lived in the neighbourhood. Every
day he took Mr. George off there to lunch, gently compelling him afterward to take a little rest. And it was in
intervals of relaxation that Mr. George on invitation sat
for his portrait in four different photograph galleries.[1]
There was not time for much correspondence, but one
letter that Mr. George found opportunity to write reveals
the man. Rev. R. Heber Newton, the boyhood friend,
had written words of God-speed, but said that in the peculiar circumstances he must vote for Low. Mr. George
answered (October 22):

"DEAR HEBER: Thanks for your advice and counsel.
We have been wiser than you at this time thought.
But this makes no matter. Vote for Low or vote for
me, as you may judge best. I shall in any event, be
true. What doth it profit a man to gain the whole
world and lose his own soul?"

Mr. George was confident of success, but showed only
flashes of enthusiasm, which Mrs. George noticed and
spoke of to him. "No," he answered; "little of the old-
time enthusiasm. Perhaps it is that with success, such
as has come to our cause, the mind advances to the contemplation of other things."

One night—a raw night, towards the end—after he
had come in from speaking, he left the hotel again with
Edward McHugh to look at one of the fruits of our one-
sided civilisation—a long line of decent-looking men
standing before a Broadway bakery, silently waiting for

---

[1] Schaidner's, Prince's, See & Eppler's, and Rockwood's.

a customary midnight dispensing of stale loaves of bread. Mr. George said little, but that little showed a full heart.

And then came the last night—Thursday, October 28 —five days before election. Five speeches had been planned, but the places were so far apart that the last had to be declared off, and as it was Mr. George did not get back to headquarters till near midnight.

Mrs. George, whom he now wanted near him at all times, had attended every meeting and was as usual with him this night, as also was his brother, John V. George. The first meeting was at Whitestone, Long Island, where he showed signs of weariness. But his sentences were clear, his words well chosen and his sentiments direct and strong.

"What I stand for and what my labour has been, I think you know. I have laboured many years to make the great truths known, and they are written down in the books. What I stand for is the principle of true Democracy, the truth that comes from the spirit of the plain people and was given to us and is embodied in the philosophy of Thomas Jefferson. The Democracy of Jefferson is simple and good, and sums up the majesty of human rights and the boundaries of government by the people. . . .

"Slowly but surely the Democracy of Jefferson has been strayed from, has been forgotten by the men who were, by its name, given office and power among the people. Error and wrong have been called by the name of the truth, and the harvest of wrong is upon this land. There are bosses and trusts and sumptuary laws. Labour-saving machinery has been turned like captured cannon, against the ranks of labour, until labour is pressed to earth under the burden!

"And must no one rise up in the land of liberty when labour must humbly seek, as a boon, the right to labour?"

In Turner Hall, College Point, Mr. George next spoke. There was a large audience, mostly of working men, and he was introduced as "the great friend of labour and Democracy." His first utterance was one of dissent:

"I have never claimed to be a special friend of labour. Let us have done with this call for special privileges for labour. Labour does not want special privileges. I have never advocated nor asked for special rights or special sympathy for working men!

"What I stand for is the equal rights of all men!"

Long and loud cheers showed that the speaker's sentiments found instant echo in the hearts of his hearers. The third speech was in the Town Hall at Flushing. Dan Beard, the artist, was in the chair. He relates this incident:

"I escorted Mr. George from the reception room to the stage and bowed to the audience, as the only way that the applause would permit me to introduce him. Mr. George took a few steps, faced the side of the stage, looked upward for a moment, and raising his right hand as if addressing some one overhead, said: 'Time and tide wait for no man.' His arm fell to his side, his head fell forward, the chin on the breast, and he stood as if lost in thought. Presently he roused, turned to the audience and said: 'I have only time to come, take a look at you and go away.'"

In this speech Mr. George said:

"Let me say a word about Mr. Low. On election day as between Mr. Low and myself, if you are yet undecided, you must vote for whom you please. I shall not attempt to dictate to you. I do entertain the hope, however, that you will rebuke the one-man power by not voting for the candidate of the bosses. I am not with Low. He is a Republican and is fighting the machine, which is all very good as far as it goes. But he is an aristocratic reformer; I am a democratic reformer. He would help the people; I would help the people to help themselves."

Many surged after Mr. George as he left the hall with his wife and his brother. Nearest of all to them was a poor, but neat, old woman, pale with emotion or ill health, who in low tones said and many times repeated: "God bless you! God bless you, Henry George! You are a good man." Presently Mr. George noticed the voice, and turning, said reverently: "And may God bless you, too; you must be a good woman to ask God to bless me." In a moment more there was a movement towards the carriage and the woman was lost in the throng.

On the way to the last meeting in the Central Opera House, New York proper, the candidate showed great weariness and climbed the stairs with evident labour. It was close to eleven o'clock when he arose to speak and a large part of the audience that had left the hall and got into the street to go home crowded back again. But while in the former speeches that evening, especially in the one at Flushing, he spoke with clearness and continuity, this last speech was disconnected and rambling. The contrast was marked to Mrs. George and the brother. But Mr. George spoke only briefly and then the party took carriage for the Union Square Hotel, where Mr. and Mrs. George were to sleep.

It was nearly midnight when the Georges and such of the friends who still lingered about the headquarters— ten in all—went to the hotel dining-room for a little supper. Mr. George had for several weeks been eating sparingly, breakfast being the largest meal. At half past five that evening, before starting on his speaking engagements,

he had taken a little soup and toast, and some weak tea.
At the midnight supper he had a few small oysters and a
glass of milk. Some of the friends spoke of the pallor
and extreme fatigue showing in Mr. George's face. Nevertheless, after the light supper he seemed to take comfort
from a cigar. Before retiring he complained to his wife
of a slight feeling of indigestion, and she waked in the
early morning hours to find that he had arisen from his
bed. She called and he answered that he was well, but
he did not return to bed. After a time she arose and
found him in an adjoining room of their suite. He was
standing, one hand on a chair, as if to support himself.
His face was white; his body rigid like a statue; his
shoulders thrown back, his head up, his eyes wide open
and penetrating, as if they saw something; and one word
came—"Yes"—many times repeated, at first with a quiet
emphasis, then with the vigour of his heart's force, sinking to softness as Mrs. George gently drew him back to
his couch. He moved mechanically and awkwardly, as
though his mind was intently engaged, and little conscious of things about him.

The elder son, the only other member of the family in
the hotel, was called, and then Dr. Kelly and Mr. Lewis
and Mr. Johnson, who lived close at hand. Mr. George
was entirely unconscious when Dr. Kelly arrived. A
stroke of apoplexy had fallen. The great heart had worn
out the physical body, and a thread in the brain had
snapped. The physician's sympathy went out to the wife,
and then in utter helplessness he cast himself face down-
ward upon the floor. For at that moment Henry George's
spirit was answering the call of the All-Father.

With tears and fierce resolution his party companions
vowed to push on with the contest. They put forward

the dead man's oldest son and namesake to carry the campaign banner; but the son drew only the votes that his unknown and untried personality could command.

Beyond party lines, Henry George's fellow-men gave him the acknowledgment he had said would come when he was dead. He had made his fight the theatre of the world, and messages poured in not merely from neighbouring cities and all parts of the nation, but from Great Britain, France, Germany and Denmark, from Africa, Australia, Japan and China to lay garlands of tribute on his bier. To the watching world he had fought the greatest of battles and won the supremest of victories: he had risked and met death to proclaim justice. "To-day," they said, "the earth loses an honest man." The press far and wide rang with encomiums. "He was a tribune of the people," said a city paper not of his camp—"poor for their sake when he might have been rich by mere compromising; without official position for their sake when he might have had high offices by merely yielding a part of his convictions to expediency. All his life long he spoke, and wrote, and thought, and prayed, and dreamed of one thing only—the cause of the plain people against corruption and despotism. And he died with his armour on, with his sword flashing, in the front of the battle, scaling the breastworks of intrenched corruption and despotism. He died as he lived. He died a hero's death. He died as he would have wished to die—on the battle-field, spending his last strength in a blow at the enemies of the people. Fearless, honest, unsullied, uncompromising Henry George!" Said a paper of another faction: "Stricken down in the moment of supremest confidence, Henry George, the idol of his people, is dead. He was more than a candidate for office, more than a politician, more than a statesman. He was a thinker whose work

belongs to the world's literature. His death has carried
mourning into every civilised country on the globe. As
a thinker, a philosopher, a writer, he was great; but he
was greatest as an apostle of the truth as he saw it—an
evangelist, carrying the doctrines of justice and brotherhood to the remotest corners of the earth."

While the press of the world hailed this man's name,
the pulpit, trade union meetings, gatherings of the unlet-
tered, councils of the learned, in many nations and many
tongues, sounded praises of his purity of heart and the
greatness of his purpose; while in his own city came
the unknown and forlorn and wretched to gaze wistfully
into the casket and burst into tears at this last glimpse
of him whom they instinctively felt to be their champion.

All day Sunday the body lay in state in the Grand
Central Palace, with the bronze bust executed by the son
Richard looking down upon the bier. From early morning old and young, poor and rich, passed to take a silent
farewell. "Never for statesman or soldier," said one of
the press, "was there so remarkable a demonstration of
popular feeling. At least one hundred thousand persons
passed before his bier and another hundred thousand were
prevented from doing so only by the impossibility of getting near it. Unconsciously they vindicated over his dead
body the truth of the great idea to which his life was
devoted, the brotherhood of man."

And in the afternoon, with doors closed and the great
hall thronged to the last possible inmate, occurred the simple but majestic public services, as catholic as his own broad
religion. Voices from Plymouth's Congregational choir
sang the solemn hymns; Dr. Heber Newton read from the
beautiful ritual that as boys he and the dead man had
listened to each Sunday in old St. Paul's in Philadelphia;
Dr. Lyman Abbott recounted the peerless courage, Rabbi

Gottheil the ancient wisdom, Dr. McGlynn the pulsing sympathy and John S. Crosby the civic virtue of the great heart lying silent in their centre, till strong feeling rent the funeral hush and cheers burst from smothering bosoms.

As night descended the long funeral procession moved. In advance a volunteer band alternated the requiem throb of Chopin's "Funeral March" with the Marseillaise' exultant "March on to Victory!" Then followed the mortal remains, mounted high upon a draped and garlanded funeral car, drawn by a double line of led horses. Behind came the vast, winding column of those, riding and walking, rich and poor, high and low, distinguished and unknown, who wished to pay homage to the dead man's worth and high-born principles—moving along without pomp or demonstration, save only the fluttering of occasional trade union banners. Chief in the multitude were such as had personally known and talked with Henry George, who had accepted his teachings and were counted among the faithful. Now in the closing drama they followed their friend and leader, so eloquent in death that all the world seemed to reverence—gathering each present shifting scene, each past look and word, to leave as a priceless heritage to their furthermost posterity.

Night deepened and the great city's lights shone out as the funeral concourse moved on through the people-lined avenues, heads uncovering and eyes glistening as the funeral car rolled by. There was a halt for a silent moment before the hushed and darkened City Hall, where perhaps had he lived Henry George may have sat as chief magistrate; thence the procession crossed the bridge to the Brooklyn City Hall, where the cortege was disbanded and the casket given to the relatives. "The world yesterday paid the highest tribute, perhaps, it has ever paid to the quality of sincerity," were the words of an opposing party paper.

Next morning—Monday, November 1, 1897—with the light streaming in on the home at Fort Hamilton, two Episcopal divines—George Latimer, the cousin, and John W. Kramer, the friend—read the service of their Church, after which Dr. McGlynn testified to their dear one's inspiring faith in immortality. Then the relatives and intimates bore the body to Greenwood and lowered it at the chosen spot on the hill-crest, beside the beloved daughter. All was enveloped in the soft grey light of an autumn day, and beyond to the south lay the shimmering Atlantic.

On the stone that his fellow-citizens soon raised there are fixed in metal letters these words from Henry George's first great book—words to which, after long years of labour, he bore final testimony with his life:

> *"The truth that I have tried to make clear will not find easy acceptance. If that could be, it would have been accepted long ago. If that could be, it would never have been obscured. But it will find friends—those who will toil for it; suffer for it; if need be, die for it. This is the power of Truth."*

INDEX

613

HENRY GEORGE, JR. (1862-1916) devoted his life to carrying on his father's work. He served as secretary to his father and later as editor of his newspaper, The Standard, continuing to advocate his father's principles during his tenure in the U.S. House of Representatives (1911-16). In addition to his father's biography, George wrote numerous newspaper and magazine articles and published two books, The Menace of Privilege and The Romance of John Bainbridge.

Professor of History at the University of Virginia, PAUL M. GASTON was born and reared in Fairhope, Alabama, a Henry George single-tax colony founded by his grandfather in 1894. He is presently writing a history of the community. His first book, The New South Creed: A Study in Southern Mythmaking, won the Lillian Smith Award for distinguished writing about the South.